MW01067370

Bluejackets and Contrabands

To
Eugenie,
I hope you enjoy
the book. My
grandfather USNA class of 1902
got me started on naval
history. Barbara

BLUEJACKETS AND CONTRABANDS

AFRICAN AMERICANS AND THE UNION NAVY

BARBARA BROOKS TOMBLIN

THE UNIVERSITY PRESS OF KENTUCKY

Copyright © 2009 by The University Press of Kentucky

Scholarly publisher for the Commonwealth,
serving Bellarmine University, Berea College, Centre College of Kentucky, Eastern
Kentucky University, The Filson Historical Society, Georgetown College, Kentucky
Historical Society, Kentucky State University,
Morehead State University, Murray State University, Northern Kentucky University,
Transylvania University, University of Kentucky, University of Louisville, and Western
Kentucky University.
All rights reserved.

Editorial and Sales Offices: The University Press of Kentucky
663 South Limestone Street, Lexington, Kentucky 40508-4008
www.kentuckypress.com

Maps by Eric Truesdell, Brit Frasure, and Dick Gilbreath
at the University of Kentucky Cartography Lab.

13 12 11 10 09   5 4 3 2 1

Library of Congress Cataloging-in-Publication Data

Tomblin, Barbara.
   Bluejackets and contrabands : African Americans and the Union Navy / Barbara
Brooks Tomblin.
      p. cm.
   Includes bibliographical references and index.
   ISBN 978-0-8131-2554-1 (hardcover : acid-free paper)
   1. United States. Navy—African Americans—History—19th century. 2. United
States. Navy—History—Civil War, 1861–1865. 3. United States—History—Civil War,
1861–1865—Participation, African American. 4. United States—History—Civil War,
1861–1865—Naval operations. 5. United States—History—Civil War, 1861–1865—
Blockades. 6. African American sailors—History—19th century. 7. Fugitive slaves—
United States—History—19th century. I. Title.
   E591.T66 2009
   973.7'415—dc22   2009019200

This book is printed on acid-free recycled paper meeting the requirements of the
American National Standard for Permanence in Paper for Printed Library Materials.

♾ ⊛

Manufactured in the United States of America.

 Member of the Association of
American University Presses

CONTENTS

Photo insert follows page 184

MAPS

ACKNOWLEDGMENTS

This study of African Americans and the Union Navy would not have been possible without the assistance and encouragement of many persons. Over the past fifteen years I was fortunate to have access to the resources and advice of librarians at the Alexander Library at Rutgers University, the Firestone Library at Princeton University, the Pennsylvania Historical Society, and the University of North Carolina at Chapel Hill. Following my relocation from New Jersey to California, I enjoyed the resources of the Huntington Library in San Marino, the Honnold Mudd Library of the Claremont Colleges, the E. P. Foster Library of Ventura, and Thousand Oaks Library.

The thoughtful criticism and valuable suggestions made by Craig Symonds and Joseph P. Reidy, who read the manuscript several times, contributed immeasurably to this study. I am deeply grateful to my daughter Brooke Tomblin for assisting me in research at the Library of Congress; to Montgomery Wolf for research at Duke University; to Brie Davidge for research in Charleston, South Carolina; and to Kevin Leonard at the Naval Historical Center and National Archives.

My gratitude also goes to the editorial staff of the University Press of Kentucky, especially to Steve Wrinn and Anne Dean Watkins.

I owe special appreciation to my sister Liz Day and her husband Ray for their support and the use of their Palm Desert home, where I spent many hours writing and rewriting this book, and to Rose-el Richardson, Gloria Brooks, and Vandra Lloyd at Caribella in Anguilla. During the years of working on this study I have been blessed, and I sincerely thank my son-in-law James Marca for his computer expertise and my daughter Page and her husband Dan Wilson, who continue to indulge my love of history and to offer encouragement, computer advice, and moral support. As always, my husband Fred was patient and ever ready to assist with myriad technical details.

Finally, I hope that someday this book will help my grandchildren,

Grace and Emma Tomblin Marca and Theo and Miles Wilson, to understand the contribution of African Americans to the Union cause and to the cause of freedom.

INTRODUCTION

When the Civil War began in 1861, the population of the United States included nearly 4 million African Americans, most of them residing in the Confederate states. Of these, only 182,000 in the southern states claimed to be free blacks; the rest were slaves. Almost all these persons of color were affected in some way by the outbreak of war. In the southern states, the new Confederate government put many able-bodied black males to work as laborers building fortifications, working in plants that produced armaments and other war-related products, and in shipyards constructing warships. Other African American males followed their white masters into military service as body servants or served on ships running the Union blockade. Those who remained at home on plantations or farms soon felt the pinch of food shortages and a lack of basic necessities caused by the war and eventually by the Union blockade. When southern men went off to war, leaving their wives, children, and the elderly behind to manage plantations, farms, and small businesses, African Americans found themselves even more valuable on the home front. Many remained loyal or feigned loyalty to their masters and mistresses, but others sought freedom by crossing Union lines or fleeing in small boats, canoes, dugouts, and other small craft to Union warships lying in the tidal estuaries, rivers, and sounds along the southern coast.[1]

Although more research is needed in this area, a growing body of scholarly evidence suggests that during the Civil War, runaway slaves and other refugees sought freedom using long-established pathways and depending on sympathetic persons and an informal network of escape routes that had been assisting African Americans to freedom for decades before the outbreak of hostilities between North and South in 1861. In his persuasive study of African American watermen in maritime North Carolina, David Cecelski argues that "slaves used waterways to escape not only in North Carolina but throughout the South." Historians debate whether these escape routes can be termed an "underground railroad."

Some maintain that such a network existed prior to the Civil War and that it provided signals, safe houses, transportation, and other assistance to slaves fleeing the South to seek freedom in the North. This network was locally organized and, according to one source, "existed rather openly in the North and often just beneath the surface of daily life in the upper south and certain Southern cities." Larry Gara and others argue, however, that the underground railroad was more legend than fact. What is not the subject of controversy is that many fugitives took advantage of the country's numerous rivers and creeks to make their escape, preferring waterways to well-traveled roads because they afforded concealment and made it more difficult for dogs to sniff out a fugitive's trail.[2]

Although many of the routes of the so-called underground railroad ran inland into Canada, other routes taken by African Americans were by sea, on sailing vessels departing from ports such as Charleston, Norfolk, Savannah, and Wilmington. Advertisements frequently cautioned boatmen against aiding runaway slaves, leading some historians to argue that many slaves did in fact go north via waterways, stowing away amid ships' cargoes or bargaining with the captains or crewmen for passage north. Other fugitives signed on as hands on northbound ships and jumped ship once they arrived in port. Their appearance on board ships may not have been a cause for concern or suspicion, for during the antebellum period, African Americans composed between 10 and 20 percent of all American merchant seamen.

Southern towns located on rivers with access to the coast, towns such as New Bern, Edenton, Beaufort, and Plymouth, North Carolina, also played an important role in assisting slaves to freedom. Black watermen from these towns served as vital links to plantations and communities of blacks living far inland up southern rivers. Black watermen in Beaufort were particularly active in assisting runaways to safety. "No pattern emerges more forcefully than that of black watermen serving as key agents of antislavery thought and militant resistance to slavery," Cecelski argues. He also points out that the maritime city of Beaufort was home to many black abolitionists.[3]

The majority of slaves who attempted to escape to freedom in the North probably did so on their own initiative, perhaps assisted informally by other blacks, including black watermen. They followed well-known paths, taking refuge in swamps and other isolated areas and remaining for weeks or even years in port cities until passage could be found. The Great Dismal Swamp in North Carolina, for example, was known as a refuge and a route to freedom for hundreds of fugitives. At many other maritime locations, some of which are still unidentified, people continued to assist escaping slaves to Union gunboats and other vessels lying offshore when the blockade made regular coastal travel more difficult. Notable among these sites is the route associated with the Pasquotank River, which flows past Elizabeth City, North Carolina, to Albemarle Sound, where Union naval vessels repeatedly picked up fugitive slaves during the war. Edenton, North Carolina, with its wharves and waterfront, was another departure point for many fugitives. In many other cases, however, black men, women, and children simply slipped away from plantations and followed well-known routes to the coastal areas where they had gone seasonally for years, or even generations, to fish or gather oysters.[4]

Although the exigencies of war forced many individuals associated with the informal escape network to move away or otherwise disrupted its operations, vestiges of the network probably remained to assist fugitives across Union lines or out to Union Navy ships. Based on the number of African Americans as well as Confederate deserters and white refugees approaching Union vessels and asking for sanctuary during the war, it is clear that the locations of these vessels patrolling along the coast and in southern inlets, sounds, and rivers were well known. Although southern whites tried to keep their slaves ignorant of war news, slaves learned about recent events from what historian Leon Litwack calls the "grapevine telegraph," or they gathered to exchange information, including the presence of Union gunboats. "The roads were patrolled and every effort was made to keep the slaves on the plantations at night," Allen Parker recalled, "and it was very hard to get a pass to leave home at all; but nevertheless we did manage to get away quite often and many conferences were held, in which the doings of the 'Yankees' were talked over, and ideas in relation to freedom exchanged by the slaves." Furthermore, in the antebellum period a number of church denominations—black, Quaker, and Baptist—had assisted runaways and continued to do so after the beginning of hostilities. Undoubtedly, many of those involved in this informal network were black, both free and slave, but one historian credits "the lowly watermen, slave stevedores, piney woods squatters, reclusive swampers, and sometimes even slaveholders' wives and children" with defying the law to sustain "tenuous pathways by which fugitives might pass from land to sea."[5]

The establishment of the Union blockade during the Civil War may have shortened the route to freedom for many slaves, but it did not eliminate the risks entailed in the escape. Fleeing slaves still faced danger from white citizen patrols, bloodhounds, Confederate pickets, river patrols, and even nervous Union pickets who shot first and asked

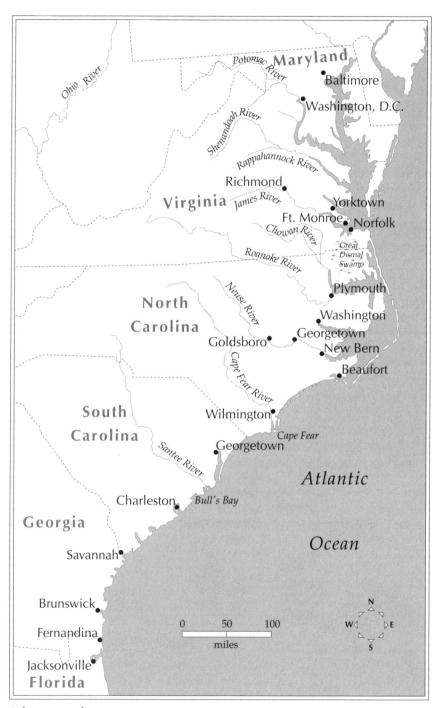

Atlantic coastline

questions later. Fugitives often endured bad weather and a lack of food, and in an effort to avoid pickets and patrols, they took routes through marshes, swamps, and creeks; they swam across rivers or took to the water in dugouts, canoes, and rowboats that could overturn or ground on sandbars. Those slaves caught escaping faced certain and often severe punishment.

According to the provisions of the Fugitive Slave Law of 1850, runaway slaves were to be returned to their masters. However, in 1861, as the number of blacks seeking asylum increased, Union Army commanders began to ignore the law and employ the runaways in army camps and on army fortifications. Using international law as his justification, on May 23, 1861, General Benjamin F. Butler declared slaves the property of the enemy and subject to confiscation. By defining slaves as "contraband of war," Butler was able to argue that refusing to return them to their owners would deprive the enemy of valuable labor. Secretary of War Simon Cameron upheld Butler's definition of contraband in a letter written on May 30, 1861, and gave Butler the authority to employ slaves in government service and pay them for their labor. The newly freed people thus became known as "contrabands." During the course of the war, the Union Army pressed thousands of black fugitives into service as servants, laborers, cooks, laundresses, and informants.[6]

To the surprise of Union Navy officers on ships blockading the southern coast, African Americans also began to seek freedom and sanctuary on board federal vessels lying in rivers, creeks, inlets, and sounds. When the Navy Department created the Atlantic Blockading Squadron in 1861 under the command of Louis M. Goldsborough, neither he nor any of his commanding officers anticipated this development. These men, women, and children came from plantations or villages near the coast, from cities such as Savannah and Charleston, and from as far as 200 miles inland, following paths on their own initiative or assisted by persons or organizations that had probably been aiding African American slaves for decades.

Union Navy commanders occasionally returned these fugitives to the masters who came to claim them, but in most instances they refused to send them back into slavery. After March 1862 they were forbidden by law to do so. The navy sent a large number of these contrabands to southern ports such as Port Royal or gathered them in contraband camps along the coast, but they also shipped some contrabands north. Always short on manpower, the Union Navy encouraged the able-bodied males to enlist. As crewmen of navy ships and gunboats, these black sailors served alongside their white shipmates on blockade duty, on expeditions up rivers and creeks, or in naval landing parties; some of them were injured or killed.

Although historians of the Civil War occasionally mention the contribution of free blacks and fugitive slaves to the North and South Atlantic Blockading Squadrons' war effort, there has been no full-length treatment of the relationship between the Union Navy and African Americans, especially contrabands. This study describes the often mutually beneficial relationship between the officers and men of both blockading squadrons and the men and women they assisted to freedom or gathered into contraband colonies and from whom they obtained vital information and services as sailors, river pilots, stevedores, guides, skilled mechanics, purveyors of fresh meat and produce, cooks, laundresses, spies, and boat crews.

Because most African American slaves and many free blacks were not permitted by law to learn to read and write, they left behind few letters and journals describing their journeys to freedom and their wartime experiences. To uncover their contributions to the Potomac Flotilla and to the North and South Atlantic Blockading Squadrons during the war, historians and scholars must rely on official Union Navy and Union Army reports and the letters and diaries of white Americans who lived during that period. A few African Americans, such as contraband-turned-sailor William B. Gould, kept diaries or wrote memoirs of the war, but most of what is known about contrabands and free blacks comes from senior naval commanders, naval officers, sailors, and soldiers, as well as whites who traveled to the South as missionaries, teachers, or plantation superintendents or found themselves living in southern states during the war. From these sources, however, a wealth of information emerges about the vital contribution of African Americans to the operation and success of the Union Navy's Potomac Flotilla and the North and South Atlantic Blockading Squadrons during the Civil War.[7]

CHAPTER 1
UNION NAVY POLICY TOWARD CONTRABANDS

The slaves must be with us or against us in this war.

—*Gideon Welles*

On a warm July day in 1861, Flag Officer Silas H. Stringham, commanding officer of the Union Navy's Atlantic Blockading Squadron, received an unusual communication from the captain of the screw steamer *Mt. Vernon.* Unlike most reports from officers on blockade duty, this one from Commander Oliver S. Glisson was hardly routine. Glisson reported that on the morning of July 15, 1861, one of *Mt. Vernon*'s lookouts had observed a small boat adrift near Stingray Lighthouse, a hexagonal screwpile built in 1858 in the Chesapeake Bay, east of the entrance to the Rappahannock River. Glisson sent an officer with a boat crew out to the lighthouse to investigate. To the bluejackets' surprise, they discovered six black slaves occupying the lighthouse. The men had deserted from shore and taken shelter there during the night, leaving their boat adrift to avoid detection.

Glisson told Stringham the six escaped slaves "appear to be very much frightened and state that people on shore are about arming the negroes, with the intention of placing them in the front of the battle." According to Glisson, the threat of being used in the rebellion had caused "much excitement" among the black population. They "are deserting in every direction," he told Stringham. In addition to the six fugitives at Stingray Light, two other boats filled with runaways had put out from shore the previous night, hoping to be picked up by a friendly vessel. In the absence of specific orders for such situations, Glisson informed Stringham that he had taken the six black deserters on board the *Mt. Vernon*.

He listed the men's names: John Hunter, Samuel Hunter, Miles Hunter, Peter Hunter, Alexander Franklin, and David Harris. "I have rationed these negroes on board of this vessel, until I receive orders from you as to their disposal," he said.[1]

On board his flagship, the frigate USS *Minnesota*, sixty-three-year-old Stringham pondered Glisson's report. A career naval officer who had entered the U.S. Navy in 1809 as a midshipman, Stringham was no stranger to war. He had served on the schooner *Spark* during the Algerine war in the early 1800s and on the *Cyane* off the coast of Africa and had participated in the bombardment of Veracruz during the Mexican War in 1847. A competent manager who had been commandant of the New York, Boston, and Norfolk Navy Yards, Stringham had taken command of the Union blockading squadron in 1861. Stringham knew his officers and had confidence in Glisson, an Indiana native who had entered the U.S. Navy as a midshipman in 1826, served during the Mexican War on the sloop *Reefer*, and accompanied Commodore Matthew C. Perry on his Japanese expedition in the mid-1850s before being appointed commanding officer of the *Mt. Vernon* in 1861. Although Stringham did not doubt Glisson's report, he knew of no existing naval regulations that covered this situation. Furthermore, a second report from Glisson dated July 17, 1861, quickly dispelled any hope that this incident might be an isolated one. According to Glisson, "three more negroes, Lewis Ransom, Robert Brookes, and Albert Hutchings, belonging to a John Dunlavey of Mathews County, Virginia," had asked for refuge on the *Mt. Vernon*. Faced with what appeared to be an influx of runaway slaves, Glisson asked Stringham, "Will you please inform me how I shall dispose of these men and how I shall act in future when they come on board?" He concluded his report on a note of urgency, writing that the deserters "say if they should be returned they would be murdered."[2]

The following day Stringham sent a copy of Glisson's reports to his superior, Navy Secretary Gideon Welles, with a cover letter in which Stringham argued, "If we are to receive the reports of these negroes at all, I can not see how we can divide their statements, accepting only that which may appear useful to us and rejecting the balance." Stringham clearly felt that the Navy Department should take the testimony of the six men at face value, noting that they had reported the Confederates' murder of a Union man and given Glisson information about the disposition of traitors in Mathews County. If this information was indeed true, Welles argued, "I can not see how we can escape receiving the other portion of their statements, that the rebels propose using them in their armies, etc., and that if they are forced to return (they will not voluntarily) they fear being murdered."[3]

The reports of slaves, including women and children, fleeing their white masters and seeking aid and protection from Union naval vessels came as no surprise to Welles. From the earliest days of the Union blockade off the southern coast, navy ships stationed on rivers and inlets had occasionally encountered free blacks and fugitive slaves. Their response to these individuals varied. On June 8, 1861, Captain W. R. Palmer, a topographical engineer and assistant with the U.S. Coast Survey, reported to his superior, Professor A. D. Bache, that he had completed a reconnaissance in the small steamer *Resolute* off Lower Cedar Point, Maryland, and then Mathias Point and White House Point, Virginia. Enclosing sketches of the area, Palmer felt confident that the rebels had not erected batteries at either of these points along the Potomac River. He then told Bache, "The negro slaves expressed a strong desire that I should take them with me; this I declined doing."[4]

At first, Commander Stephen C. Rowan took a similar view toward blacks seeking refuge on federal vessels. In a report on blockading operations in the Potomac sent to Welles on June 12, 1861, Rowan wrote: "A colored man came off this morning in a small boat, stating that he belonged to a Mr. Healy, and asked my protection. Having little faith in the loyalty of the people residing on the Maryland bank of this river, I declined to receive him. He left the ship and continued down the river."[5]

On this occasion Rowan chose not to accept the black man on board his vessel, but he did not always dismiss local African Americans who came to his ship. Less than one week later, in an effort to obtain information about the provisions stowed in a fish house by a man he suspected of trading with the enemy, Rowan questioned local blacks. "The most of my information is derived from colored people, who answer questions without reserve when opportunity offers," he told Welles. Convinced of the man's guilt by his suspicious activities, including a recent two-week stay in Virginia, Rowan ordered the hogsheads and barrels in the fish house seized and loaded onto a wood schooner that happened to be loading there. He then directed Lieutenant Mygatt of the tug *Reliance* to tow the schooner to the navy yard at Washington and deliver the provisions to the commandant of the yard, Commander John A. Dahlgren.[6]

During a reconnaissance of Mathias Point on June 25, 1861, Rowan once again encountered a black man wishing to come on board his vessel, the USS *Pawnee*. Rowan told Welles, "A negro man, who was standing by a boat on the beach that I sent Lieutenant Chaplin to bring off or destroy, came off and gave us information that 200 troops are kept on the beach constantly, and the remainder in camps aforesaid." The information provided by this black man may have proved useful, but he presented Rowan with an unusual and awkward situation. According to the provisions of the Fugitive Slave Law, which still remained in effect, slaves were to be returned to their rightful owners. If the man on the beach was a runaway slave and his owner appeared to claim him, Rowan would be faced with a difficult choice. Rowan took a cautious tone in writing to Welles: "I regret that the negro was brought off, but being on board I don't know what to do with him. I send him in the *Guy* to the navy yard to be disposed of as you may direct."[7]

Incidents involving runaway slaves such as those reported by Rowan did not demand a response from the Navy Department, but the two reports of fugitive slaves sent by Glisson to Stringham in July 1861 did. In his reply to Stringham's July 18 letter, Welles set the tone for the navy's initial response to runaway slaves, explaining that the government's policy was not to invite or encourage this class of desertion. However, Welles argued, "under the circumstances no other course than that pursued by Commander Glisson could be adopted without violating every principle of humanity." The secretary observed that to return the fugitive slaves to their owners or to southern authorities would be "impolitic as well as cruel" and suggested that Stringham pursue his idea of using the black fugitives as crew on Union store ships.[8]

Thus, the Navy Department initially pursued a tentative policy toward these fugitives, one based on humanitarian grounds and on the department's suspicions that the Confederacy had been employing blacks in its war effort against the Union. General Benjamin F. Butler had used a similar argument to justify his refusal to return three fugitive slaves to a Virginia militia officer after his forces had occupied the Hampton area in May 1861.[9]

The Confederacy's use of black slaves as labor troops gave Union officials ample reason to confiscate them as property. Offering newly freed slaves compensation for their labor, however, demanded approval from federal authorities. Fortunately, early in the conflict Stringham had observed that fugitive slaves seeking refuge on Union naval vessels often arrived without proper clothing. In a bit of clever bureaucratic maneuvering, Stringham used that as a pretext for offering contrabands compensation in the form of a clothing allotment for their Union service. "Have I permission to distribute some clothing as well as their food rations?" he asked Welles on August 7, 1861. The secretary replied, "If employed, they are entitled to compensation, and articles of clothing could be furnished them in payment."[10]

Throughout the summer of 1861 Union naval officers continued to raise concerns about the growing number of blacks seeking refuge on Union vessels or in areas controlled by Union forces. On July 23, 1861, Rowan, now senior officer in the Potomac, wrote to Welles: "Early on Saturday morning last while off Point Lookout three negroes came to the ship in a canoe from the Virginia shore. They say they were free, but have no free papers, and assign as a reason for running away that they were required to fight." In addition to these new refugees, Rowan had two slaves on board, "taken from the Virginia shore by the late Commander J. H. Ward; they say they belong to Mrs. Stewart, a widow, residing near Mathias Point. I respectfully request instructions in relation to all these people." Three days later Welles sent Rowan the following instructions concerning certain free blacks and slaves now on board the *Pawnee:* "It has not been the policy of the Government to encourage the emigration of this class of persons, whether bond or free; but where you have them, as in this case, on board, you can, as I understand verbally you do, employ the slaves, and those who are free need not be returned."[11]

Welles's instructions to Rowan make it clear that the U.S. government did not encourage slaves to escape their masters or free blacks to seek refuge on Union vessels or behind Union lines, and Navy Department policy did not strictly forbid officers to return slaves to their owners. Many naval officers refused to give the fugitives back to their masters, but others continued to turn them over to persons claiming to be the rightful owners. It remains unclear whether the latter's sympathies lay with the slaves' southern masters or whether, as naval officers, they felt duty bound to comply with federal laws, including the Fugitive Slave Act of 1850. Technically, failing to return a slave to its rightful owner represented a violation of that law, but abolitionists and many antislavery northerners rejected the act. Earlier in 1861, before Abraham Lincoln took office as president and Welles became secretary of the navy, sixty-eight U.S. Navy officers had resigned their commissions and returned to the South, many to serve in the Confederate Navy, leaving northerners to make up the majority of officers in the Union Navy. When Welles took the helm of the department, he appointed then-Captain Silas Stringham to a newly created bureau with the task of "reviewing all of the navy's remaining officers and vouching for their loyalty." More resignations followed the outbreak of war, and eventually, Welles reported, 322 officers had "traitorously abandoned the flag." Hoping to eliminate disloyal officers at the Norfolk Navy Yard before they could destroy navy ships, ordnance, and property or turn them over to the rebels, Welles dismissed seventeen more officers. Presumably, these dismissals and resignations left the Union Navy with a substantial number of officers loyal to the Union and possessed of antislavery sentiments or sympathy for slaves seeking sanctuary on their vessels. Most of these officers, however, probably shared the northern public's mixed feelings about the emancipation of slaves and equal rights for blacks.[12]

Naval officers' views on slavery and its abolition varied. When the war began in April 1861, many probably agreed with the vast majority of white Union soldiers who found the institution of slavery abominable but believed the government had no authority to interfere with it. Emancipation of the slaves would require amending the Constitution, many claimed, for Congress did not have the authority to legislate an end to slavery. By the end of 1861, however, many Union soldiers had come to the conclusion that slavery had caused the war, and only the destruction of slavery could end it. Freeing the slaves was one thing, but for many northerners and military personnel, granting them full citizenship was another. Although some navy men may have been antislavery, they, like most northerners, expressed racist views about persons of color and were reluctant to grant African Americans equal rights.[13]

For many naval officers, service on board vessels blockading the South altered their perceptions of the institution of slavery and their attitude toward abolition. Writing to his wife, Anna, in late March 1862, William Keeler, a paymaster serving on board the USS *Monitor*, assured her, "You need have no fear of my becoming tainted with pro-Slavery doctrines. The more I see of the hideous deformity the more I hate it." Keeler admitted, however, that some of his fellow officers might harbor pro-slavery sentiments. But, he told his wife, "If any of our naval men are of that way of thinking they have the good sense to keep it to themselves. They are enough of gentlemen not to intrude sentiments they know are distasteful & odious to companions they associate with."[14]

In candid letters to his wife, Sophie, the commander of the South Atlantic Blockading Squadron, Flag Officer Samuel F. Du Pont, explained how his wartime experiences had changed his attitude about slavery. Noting that his gunboats daily overlooked "the estates of the Pinckneys, Rhetts, Seabrooks, Hutchinsons, Marches, etc, etc.—the descendants of good people who were all friends of my parents," Du Pont wrote on the next to last day of 1861, "My ideas have undergone great changes as to the condition of the slaves since I came here and have been on plantations." Reminding Sophie that he had been, and remained, a "sturdy conservative" on the question of slavery and had defended it "all the world over, as patriarchal in the U.S. compared with the condition of the race in Africa," Du Pont confessed, "God forgive me—I have seen nothing that has disgusted me more than the wretched physical wants of these poor people, who earn all the gold spent by their masters at Sarasota and in Europe. No wonder they stand shooting down rather than go back with their owners."[15]

Du Pont's antislavery views were shared by many Union Navy officers and men as well as Union Army soldiers and southern civilians, but he differed with others on the issue of upholding the Fugitive Slave Law and returning slaves to their masters. Writing again to his wife in April 1862, Du Pont defended the Union Navy's policy of not returning slaves to their rightful owners. He specifically criticized the stand of Delaware senators Willard Saulsbury and James A. Bayard, who had opposed emancipation in their district. The two senators, Du Pont wrote, "don't wish these men gradually freed, they must return to a pound of meal, one suit of clothes, rarely meat, to whips with knots, to nails driven through the soft parts of their ears, and the bloodhounds; for we have ascertained there is a man in Florida whose trade is to keep them and hire them out to chase the runaway Negroes—but besides this they let the dogs on them for punishment." Du Pont asserted, "I have not been able to ascertain that [a] single officer of this squadron *voted for Lincoln,* but there is not a proslavery man among them."[16]

Throughout April 1862, Sophie Du Pont and her husband continued their discussion of the slavery question. "You will have seen by some of my previous letters that I do not concur in all your opinions about slavery. I know it to be a great wrong and a great curse. But I do not think that justifies us in *doing wrong* to hasten the abolition of it," Sophie wrote. Sharing a view held by many northerners, Sophie continued, "If we are fighting for the Constitution, we are bound to regard it. We have no *right,* as I understand it, to deprive a loyal Southern man of his slaves; nor a rebel, who is willing to submit, and return to allegiance and does not use his slaves against the government." Du Pont's response to his wife's position on slavery succinctly captures the profound effect the war had on his opinions about slavery and abolition, which many naval offices had come to share. "I agree with you entirely, in law, and what is more important in morals and religion and truth and right of all kind, but I meant to say that they violated the Constitution, a pact, an agreement, a partnership for a certain purpose, and we are absolved from it as a political agreement." Then Du Pont confessed, "I was ready for twenty years to help to return the fugitive to his master—but the later has run away and broken his part of the agreement; do you think I am going to give him back his slave any more? He may keep him and take him even as we stand yet—but he must not expect me to help him—that's all."[17]

Discussions of the slavery question also found their way into the letters of Samuel Gilbert Webber, a naval surgeon serving on the monitor USS *Nahant*. In May 1863 Webber expressed his view on slavery to his wife in reference to sermons preached by a Mr. Wells. "I find I can agree with him in regard to most that he says about slavery," he wrote. "I feel that this war will settle that question finally or else—there will be another war by & by will settle it. I mean, by destroying the system. It has a strong grasp on the country as is shown by the violence of this struggle." Many Union soldiers in 1863, weary of war and scarred by the horrors of the battlefield, agreed with Webber's view that the institution of slavery had to be destroyed. The "perpetuation of slavery" had caused the war, they argued, and slavery was a serious threat to the virtue required if the United States was to remain a republican government. After so much bloodshed, a significant number of Union troops rejected fighting for the old Union. "We now want a new one, that knows nothing of slavery," Private Thomas Covert wrote.[18]

However, on the issue of equal rights for African Americans, Webber expressed a different view: "Though I do not believe the negro equal to the white or that the african race will approach the caucasian in intelligence until after many years of training; yet I do believe them entitled to freedom. It may be that after many generations the degradation of slavery, its debasing & lowering influence will be overcome & they will rise higher than most expect; but if this ever happens it must be after a long training first." Webber hoped that the "convulsion" of the war would not destroy the nation and concluded, "it seems to me as tho' God were intending for greater service, but must first purify us from this enormous sin & prepare us to serve him." According to historian Chandra Manning, the majority of Union soldiers had anticipated Webber's conclusion. As one Illinois soldier put it, "Any country that allows the curse of slavery and amalgamation as this has done, should be cursed, and I believe in my soul that God allowed this war for the very purpose of clearing out the evil and punishing us as a nation for allowing it."[19]

The Lincoln administration, too, struggled to define its policy toward slavery and emancipation. Months after the fall of Fort Sumter, neither Lincoln nor his cabinet had come to any agreement on the issue of the emancipation of slaves. The Republicans had endorsed opposition to the extension of slavery as a central plank in the party platform for the 1860 election, but in his inaugural address President Lincoln had promised not to interfere with slavery in the states where it already existed.

Lincoln, one recent biographer wrote, "made no attempt to disguise his antislavery feelings," telling a group of border state representatives that he thought slavery "was wrong and should continue to think so." Nevertheless, confronted with the secession of the southern states, the new president expressed reluctance to raise the issue of emancipation. Lincoln distanced himself from his pro-slavery predecessors but remained wary of taking a strong stand against slavery that could alienate the border states of Kentucky, Missouri, and Maryland. Furthermore, Lincoln initially referred to the conflict between the United States government and the Confederate States of America as a rebellion, not a war. This meant that all federal laws remained in effect, including the Fugitive Slave Law. The issue of arming blacks and the emancipation of slaves divided Lincoln's own cabinet as well. Secretary of the Treasury Salmon P. Chase, a strong antislavery man and advocate of equal rights for African Americans, nonetheless favored the "separation of the races" and backed a plan to colonize slaves. This plan had the support of Lincoln's postmaster general, Montgomery Blair; his father, Francis Preston Blair Sr.; and the influential Blair family, including Elizabeth Blair Lee, wife of Captain Samuel Phillips Lee, who in 1862 would assume command of the North Atlantic Blockading Squadron.[20]

While the Lincoln administration struggled to define its policy toward slavery and fugitive slaves, Congress took action and on August 6, 1861, passed the First Confiscation Act, which helped clarify the Union position on fugitive slaves. According to the provisions of this act, owners who used slaves to construct fortifications or entrenchments; to work in navy yards, in armories, or on ships; or to provide any military or naval service to aid the Confederacy's war effort forfeited any claim to said slaves. The provisions of the First Confiscation Act did not protect slaves in states loyal to the Union or in the border states, nor did it define the status of slaves abandoned by their owners after the Union occupation of Port Royal and other Sea Islands. Although it advanced the cause of emancipation, the act did not technically "free" the slaves, prompting many abolitionists to label it halfhearted. Congress's passage of this new legislation clearly reflected Lincoln's concern that more radical measures to free slaves would alienate Union supporters in the border states where slavery remained legal.[21]

The First Confiscation Act naturally caught the attention of Secretary Welles at the Navy Department, who had been receiving reports of African Americans approaching Union Navy vessels not only from states in rebellion but also from border states such as Maryland. Numerous contrabands had, in fact, been seeking refuge on federal vessels in the Rappahannock River. On October 27, 1861, for example, Lieutenant James C. Chaplin of the USS *Valley City* informed Flag Officer Louis M. Goldsborough that forty-four black men and one black woman from Northumberland and Lancaster counties had been taken aboard his vessel. Three days later Commander William Parker reported that vessels employed in the blockade of the river had picked up and given refuge to several contrabands. Parker did not indicate that any of his vessels had turned these refugees away or returned them to their owners. Clearly, Parker and other naval officers on duty in the Rappahannock preferred to take the fugitive slaves on board and offer them protection. The difficulties inherent in disproving a slave's status as a Confederate laborer had, perhaps, convinced Union Navy officers to err on the side of protecting any slaves seeking safety on board Union ships.[22]

Most naval officers, in fact, allowed black fugitives to remain on board temporarily, using the able-bodied males on the ship and sending the others, often women and children, to navy yards or army posts or putting them ashore to form colonies under Union Navy protection. Beginning in the summer of 1861, commanders of ships of the North Atlantic Blockading Squadron began sending contrabands to Fortress Monroe in the Department of Virginia. The very day that Congress passed the First Confiscation Act, Butler, then the commander at Fortress Monroe, issued a special order stating, "If the *Wilson Small,* or the other vessels are found conveying away negroes for the purposes of aiding or comforting the rebellion, such negroes, if they desire, will be permitted to come to Fortress Monroe, where they will be employed or cared for."[23]

These boatloads of refugees seeking food and protection on Union vessels quickly became a mixed blessing for the squadron. On the one hand, they could rapidly diminish a ship's supply of water and rations; on the other hand, these runaways provided valuable information about Confederate defenses and activities. Often short of crew, Union Navy officers quickly realized that the able-bodied males among these refugees could be a source of manpower to fill out the ship's complement. Responding to this new and unexpected windfall, Welles expanded his earlier policy of allowing Stringham to employ able-bodied black males on Union Navy store ships. Welles authorized navy commanders to "ship" or enlist contrabands with a rating of "boy," pay them $10 a month, and issue them one ration a day, compensation equivalent to that of army privates. Explaining the new regulation to Goldsborough in September 1861, Welles wrote, "The Department finds it necessary to adopt a regulation with respect to the large and increasing number of persons of color, commonly known as contraband, now subsisted at the navy yard and on board ships of war." Welles justified the enlistment of contrabands and their allotment by noting that these runaways were a burden to blockading vessels, consuming water and rations, and as newly freed people they could not "be expelled from the service to which they have resorted, nor can they be maintained unemployed, and it is not proper that they should be compelled to render necessary and regular services without a stated compensation." Welles authorized his officers to enlist them "under the same forms and regulations as apply to other enlistments."[24]

Prior to Welles's authorization to enlist African American contrabands, free blacks or foreign nationals of color had been allowed to enlist in the navy and had served with the same pay, privileges, and opportunities for promotion as white sailors. Evidence from one naval critic in the 1830s suggests that in the antebellum period the U.S. Navy had even allowed a few slaves to enlist on men-of-war such as the USS *Java* or to be employed in southern navy yards. From all available accounts, in the years before the outbreak of hostilities between North and South, the U.S. Navy treated black sailors far better than their army counterparts, although existing naval logs and court-martial records fail to indicate whether black sailors were punished more often or more severely than white sailors. The antebellum navy did, however, often assign black sailors as mess boys, stewards, and wardroom attendants, menial jobs the navy considered more appropriate for persons of color. Clearly, racial prejudice existed in the U.S. Navy. Historians have uncovered numerous examples of racist attitudes and racist testimony by naval officers during the antebellum period, attitudes that continued well into the Civil War years. Furthermore, before the war the navy instituted a policy limiting black enlistments to a quota of 5 percent per week or per month. This may have allowed Welles to enlist more than 900 black men in the navy in 1861 without attracting attention, but the Navy Department's policy of equal treatment of blacks ended abruptly in September 1861 when Welles authorized the enlistment of contrabands as "boys" but limited their advancement to that rating. By December 18, 1862, however, Welles had changed this policy, issuing a circular amending and expanding the navy's policy toward contraband sailors. "Persons known as contrabands will not be shipped or enlisted in the naval service with any higher rating than that of landsman," the circular read, "but if found qualified after being shipped, may be advanced by the commanding officer of the vessel in which they serve to the ratings of seaman, ordinary seaman, fireman, or coal heaver." The circular further stipulated that the contrabands could not be transferred to another vessel with a rating higher than landsman, but if they were being discharged or serving in a vessel going out of commission, they might keep their present rating.[25]

Thus, by the end of the first year of the Civil War, the Navy Department had established a policy of welcoming fugitive blacks, both slave and free, on board Union blockading ships; offering them protection from claims by disloyal southern masters; and providing them with food and shelter. Union Navy commanders had the option of keeping the able-bodied male contrabands as crewmen on their vessels or sending the refugees to navy yards, Fortress Monroe, or other Union-occupied areas. As the war progressed, the Union Navy transported contrabands north to navy yards at Philadelphia, New York, and Boston. The exact number of African Americans sent north during the Civil War is still unknown, but testimony to the American Freedman's Inquiry Commission by General Rufus Saxton suggests that most did not go north voluntarily. "There is no disposition in these people to go North," the report stated, despite Saxton's offer to provide papers for that purpose. "They are equally averse to the idea of immigrating to Africa. These feelings are universal among them," he wrote. The preliminary report of the American Freedman's Inquiry Commission explained that black refugees held strong local attachments and preferred the mild southern climate to that of the North, with "its winters of snow and ice."[26]

In the first months of the Civil War, the Navy Department discouraged officers from returning fugitive slaves to their owners but did not expressly forbid it; however, Welles's opinions on the matter and his antislavery sympathies were likely well known to most officers. Prodded by Radical Republicans, in March 1862 Congress took a more definitive step by enacting an article of war prohibiting military officers from returning fugitive slaves to their owners. Furthermore, returning slaves to their owners became a military crime punishable by dishonorable discharge. Commander Percival Drayton, himself a southerner with a brother in the Confederate Army, welcomed the new legislation. In a letter to Du Pont from Fernandina, Florida, in April 1862, Drayton cited the authority of the recent article of war and stated, "I could not allow a slave, even voluntarily, to return to his master."[27]

In contrast to Drayton's staunch antislavery views, some commanders, perhaps with southern sympathies, continued to honor claims by slave masters and to turn over contrabands, forcing the Navy Department to call them into account. One of the most flagrant violators of the ruling was Captain Thomas T. Craven, commanding the screw sloop USS *Brooklyn* in Flag Officer David G. Farragut's Western Gulf Blockading Squadron. Craven's pro-slavery views must have been well known among the officers corps, for on July 19, 1862, Commander Christopher R. P. Rodgers wrote to Du Pont, "I hear that Craven has been recalled. I suspect that he has been giving up Negroes, etc." Two days later, Elizabeth Blair Lee wrote to her husband, Samuel Phillips Lee, "F. said that Craven had been summoned back to Washington for returning slaves back to some plantation owned & governed by 'a Lady rather than woman' who had them stript & lashed in sight of his ship—when they had been in service of the Govt—he is recalled here to make explanations." Lieutenant Selim Woodworth had, in fact, complained to David Dixon Porter, commander of the Mortar Flotilla, that Craven had taken unauthorized custody of some forty contrabands given refuge by Woodworth. Thus Elizabeth Lee commented to her husband that Craven had been suspended by a court of inquiry "as to the Negro matter."[28]

That the fifty-four-year-old Craven, a Washington, D.C., native and career naval officer who had served in the African Squadron and as commander of the Potomac Flotilla, shared the racial prejudices of his day and held to racial stereotypes is evident from his correspondence with his wife, Emily Henderson Craven. On June 3, 1862, Craven wrote to her from the USS *Brooklyn*, describing a trip up the Mississippi River: "It was interesting and sometimes exciting, as we steamed along inshore to witness the dense crowds of spectators. In front of the large sugar plantations their white occupants were collected in groups, gazing askance at us, the ladies often turning their backs upon us showing by their manner that they would give worlds, if they had them, to be able to crush us from the face of the earth." The reaction of African Americans watching the federal ship steam by was quite different. "Then as we passed the groups of darkies, particularly if they were hidden from their masters' view by intervening trees or houses, such demonstrations of joy, such jumping and bowing, and such antics and grins could only be imagined by those who are familiar with the monkey traits of the negro character," Craven wrote. Captain Craven expressed little sympathy for white rebel planters but seemed to have admiration and empathy for the white pro-Union families caught in the South during the war. Observing the white inhabitants along the Mississippi shoreline, Craven noticed a "brave lady" standing on a levee in front of a "magnificent mansion, alone under the shade of a live oak, her servants grouped together about fifty yards further up the levee." As the *Brooklyn* neared, she "unrolled a large flag and handed it to them and made them spread it out and wave it over their heads, she, poor lady, waving her kerchief and wiping the tears from her eyes at the same time." It was the flag of the United States. "God bless that brave woman," Craven told his wife Emily. "I felt at the time as if I could jump to the shore and kiss her, as if she had been one of my nearest and dearest kin."[29]

Craven's admiration for this woman and the plight of pro-Unionists in the South may have influenced his decision three weeks later with regard to contrabands who had taken sanctuary on an island in the river and on board some of Porter's Mortar Flotilla vessels. In a message to Porter, Craven explained that he had been informed by a Midshipman McFarland that there were "a number of runaway negroes on board some of the mortar boats—and others on the island which have been landed there by some of the vessels comprising the Mortar Flotilla." He ordered Porter to direct "that no slaves are to be received on board any vessel of the 'Flotilla' or taken from the custody of their lawful owners." Craven then pointedly told Porter to "deliver up any of the slaves on board the mortar boats to their owners." When Porter received Craven's written instructions, he replied quickly, reiterating his position with regard to the runaway slaves that he claimed had been taken away by an officer without his knowledge. He insisted, "The only slaves that have come into the flotilla have sought refuge there, and have in no case been taken from the custody of their masters." Porter told Craven, "I must decline returning any slaves to the custody of those claiming to be their masters." He offered to send any future refugees who came to his vessels to Craven and, in an accompanying letter, further explained his reasons for not returning them to their masters. The four slaves alluded to in Craven's communication had come on board Porter's vessels that night or the previous night, and since Porter had "no way of judging whether they have been employed on Confederate works, except by their own word, I send them to you to dispose of them as you think fit."[30]

The day following this incident, Craven wrote to his superior David Farragut, commander of the Western Gulf Blockading Squadron, attempting to justify his actions. "Yesterday morning I was visited by a lady and gentleman from the right bank of the river (Mrs. Grove and Dr. White) who informed me that their slaves had run away, and that they had reliable information that they have been received on board of some of our vessels." When Craven ascertained that fugitive slaves had indeed gathered on Porter's mortar vessels and on an island in the Mississippi, he directed Midshipman McFarland to take Dr. White and Mrs. Grove to the island and to any vessel "where negroes were likely to be found" and, if they could identify their servants, to request the officers in charge to "deliver them up to their legal owners." McFarland returned an hour later and reported that all but one of Mrs. Grove's servants had been discovered on the island and five of Dr. White's on board mortar boat No. 4. But McFarland told Craven that he had received "an impertinent reply from Lieut. Woodworth with his flat refusal to give up the negroes." In the end, despite Woodworth's protestations, the slaves went back to Dr. White and Mrs. Grove. As Craven explained to Farragut, "after nearly the entire day had been consumed in a very unnecessary correspondence between Commander D. D. Porter and myself the negroes were restored to their owners." If Craven imagined that this would end the incident, he was sadly mistaken, for Lieutenant Woodworth made a formal complaint, which may account for the rumors that Craven had been recalled to Washington to explain his actions in violation of the act of Congress passed in March. In fact, Craven asked to be relieved of command following another dispute with Farragut. On July 2, 1862, the disgruntled Craven left the *Brooklyn* with "all hands cheering," and his replacement, Commander H. H. Bell, assumed command. The incident involved the bombardment of Vicksburg and a letter of censure from Farragut to Craven and was apparently not connected to the contraband issue.[31]

Craven's court of inquiry took place in mid-July 1862, about the same time Lincoln initiated conversations with members of his cabinet about the government's policy toward slavery. During a carriage ride with Lincoln and Secretary William Seward to the funeral of Edwin Stanton's infant son on Sunday, July 13, 1862, Welles recalled that the president "first mentioned to Mr. Seward and myself the subject of emancipating the slaves by proclamation in case the Rebels did not cease to persist in their war on the Government and the Union, of which he saw no evidence." Lincoln told both men that he had given the subject a good deal of thought and, Welles noted, had concluded that "it was a military necessity absolutely essential for the salvation of the Union, that we must free the slaves or be ourselves subdued, etc. etc." The president asked Seward and Welles for their opinion on the delicate subject of emancipation and begged them to give the measure serious deliberation. In his diary Welles admitted that he did not know what to make of Lincoln's request, for during previous interviews on the subject of emancipation, Lincoln had "been prompt and emphatic in denouncing any interference by the General Government with the subject." According to Welles, members of the cabinet had once shared Lincoln's opinion about emancipation. However, according to Welles, "reverses before Richmond" and the continuing rebellion had changed their minds. "The slaves, if not armed and disciplined, were in the service of those who were, not only as field laborers, and producers, but thousands of them were in attendance upon the armies in the field, employed as waiters and teamsters, and the fortifications and entrenchments were constructed by them."[32]

On July 22, 1862, Lincoln showed his hand by submitting a draft for a preliminary emancipation proclamation to his cabinet. By then, almost a year after passage of the First Confiscation Act, Congress had approved a Second Confiscation Act that stated, among other provisions, that slaves of civilian and military Confederate officials "shall be forever free." The Second Confiscation Act, passed over Lincoln's objections, applied only to slaves belonging to disloyal owners in states rebelling against the Union. Pro-Union masters in slave states could keep their slaves. Furthermore, the act could be enforced only in areas of the South occupied and controlled by the Union Army or on Union Navy vessels. By failing to free slaves in loyal states and border states, the Second Confiscation Act greatly disappointed abolitionists and others sympathetic to the cause of emancipation. It also left the Fugitive Slave Law in place and meant that runaway slaves in the free states and the District of Columbia could be returned to their owners. However, together with Congress's passage of the act forbidding military officers to return fugitive slaves, the Second Confiscation Act probably encouraged naval officers to harbor runaways and enlist able-bodied males without fear of having to account for Confederate property in the future.

Lincoln chose not to announce the Emancipation Proclamation publicly, preferring to wait for a Union victory. However, word that the president had given his cabinet a preliminary emancipation proclamation spread quickly to Washington insiders, among them the influential Blair family. "Mr. Holt was out here yesterday he is full of the emancipation project," Elizabeth Blair Lee wrote to her husband that same day, July 22, 1862.[33]

After Union forces won a decisive battle at Antietam on September 22, 1862, Lincoln called a special cabinet meeting to discuss the emancipation of the slaves in the states still in rebellion. "For several weeks the subject had been suspended, but the President never lost sight of it," Welles noted in his diary. Lincoln had, Welles insisted, ascertained the views of everyone in his cabinet but "formed his own conclusions and made his own decisions." During the "long and earnest" discussion of the issue, Lincoln remarked "that he had made a vow, a covenant, that if God gave us victory in the approaching battle, he would consider it an indication of Divine will, and that it was his duty to move forward in the cause of emancipation." The president, Welles wrote, felt that "God had decided this question in favor of the slaves." Lincoln then read the document of emancipation, Seward made "one or two unimportant amendments," and the secretary of state took the document in order to publish it the following day. Of the Emancipation Proclamation, Welles wrote, "It is momentous both in its immediate and remote results, and an exercise of extraordinary power which cannot be justified on mere humanitarian principles, and would never have been attempted but to preserve the national existence. The slaves must be with us or against us in this war."[34]

Many Union soldiers and navy officers and enlisted men welcomed the news of the Emancipation Proclamation. Writing from Port Royal, South Carolina, on October 3, 1862, James Himrod, a corporal with the Forty-eighth New York Volunteers, referred to the "late proclamation of Abraham" as a "glorious Christian act" and "the only salvation of our Country." William Keeler, a paymaster on the ironclad *Monitor,* wrote to his wife, Anna, from Newport News on September 24, 1862: "Something has turned up at last, the very greatest event which any combination of circumstances could possibly have turned up in our Country's revolving wheel of fortune—the President's proclamation freeing all slaves in rebellious states after the first of Jan'y. Now isn't this enough to satisfy the most radical abolitionist—if not, what more could they ask." Keeler's views about the inevitability of emancipation were shared by many soldiers. One soldier wrote, "if the President's proclamation had been proclaimed one year sooner than it was I think the war would have been just so much nearer the end." The news did not surprise Keeler, who wrote, "I am not at all surprised. I knew it must come, but did not expect it quite so soon. I felt satisfied from the nature of events that it must come about & have so expressed myself to you adding that I felt satisfied to wait patiently the time."[35]

In a lengthy letter to Du Pont written just before Christmas 1862, Drayton confided his expectations for the Emancipation Proclamation. "It is generally supposed that New Year will see the President's proclamation for freeing the slaves," he wrote, "as I for one do not believe that there will ever be a peace worth having on this continent so long as slavery is permitted on it. I hope it will sweep the institution clean away, as standing directly in front of the settlement our difficulties and as being a disgrace to the civilization of the nineteenth century." Drayton's hopes for the future of the country were less sanguine. "I don't say that such a measure will bring about a reconstruction of the Union, but am quite satisfied that nothing else will."[36]

Naval surgeon Webber's opinion of the Emancipation Proclamation grew over the final years of the war. "Others spoke of the presidents proclamation, rejoicing over it. I feel relieved now that it has come out. From

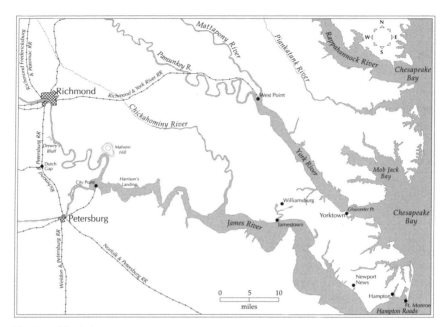

Eastern Virginia

the beginning or very near it I have felt that we should have something of the kind before we finished the war. I have felt during our defeats that God might be bringing us to a point when such a proclamation would be legal, necessary. . . . I have wished all along that it might be possible legally to get rid of slavery." Reminding his wife that, as a naval officer, he had sworn to uphold the Constitution, Webber added, "If it can be constitutional & legal to release the slave I rejoice." In January 1865 he wrote again to his wife of the Emancipation Proclamation: "All our great success have occurred since Jan.1, 1863 when Abe Lincoln issued his emancipation proclamation. I know that causes can be found in the nature of the contest for this. We may say that the South has become exhausted by the prolonged war & has since Jan.1, 1863 been less able to meet the North, which had such vast supplies, on an equality. But when we remember that the battle is not always to the strong & that God watches over nations as well as over individuals it is not unreasonable to imagine that our national conduct has an influence with him. It is not unreasonable that the release of the slaves (abolition of slavery) will be followed finally by peace & reunion."[37]

By the spring of 1862, assisting runaway slaves and enlisting able-bodied male contrabands into naval service had become accepted practices in both the North and South Atlantic Blockading Squadrons;

however, arming former slaves or even free blacks for military service remained a controversial issue. Fortunately for Welles and the Navy Department, Lincoln had looked the other way on the issue of enlisting contrabands in the navy, but as the Union entered the second year of the war, neither the Lincoln administration nor Congress seemed to favor arming African Americans or allowing them to enlist in the Union Army. The administration's qualms did not bother the new commander of the Department of the South, General David Hunter, whose commitment to the abolition of slavery and his determination to arm former slaves in his department brought both issues into the spotlight.

In April and May 1862 Hunter began recruiting former slaves for a regiment of black troops. Hunter followed his recruitment drive with General Order No. 11, declaring the slaves in his department—South Carolina, Georgia, and Florida—free. The general's announcement caught most if not all Union commanders by surprise. Referring to General Order No. 11, Du Pont told Sophie in a letter dated May 11, 1862, "No one knew of it, no word whispered to *me*." Du Pont's imme- diate reaction, he told Sophie, was to question whether a commanding general, "sixty hours in time from Washington, not even operating in the field, could do such a thing." Du Pont's suspicion that the Lincoln administration would not welcome Hunter's emancipation proclamation proved accurate. On May 19, 1862, Lincoln declared Hunter's proclama- tion void and asserted that the president alone, not commanders in the field, had the authority to declare slaves free.[38]

Hunter's brash initiative to arm blacks raised a furor in Congress, especially among congressmen from the border states. When one Ken- tucky representative asked whether a regiment of former slaves had indeed been raised in the Department of the South, Secretary Stanton shrewdly instructed Hunter to reply. He then forwarded Hunter's let- ter to Congress. Hunter argued that he had based his authorization to recruit black soldiers on former secretary of war Simon Cameron's order to "employ all loyal persons offering their services in the defense of the Union." Cleverly citing a loophole in Cameron's order, the general noted that Cameron had not specified the "color or character" of such per- sons, nor whether they were to be employed in civil or military service. Hunter's black regiment remained controversial, however, and the War Department refused to fund it.[39]

Following passage of the Second Confiscation Act in July 1862, the Lincoln administration's attitude toward the arming of blacks became more favorable. In August the Reverend Mansfield French, who had gone to Port Royal in 1861 to assist the freed people, and Robert Smalls, a black pilot who had commandeered the Confederate steamer *Planter* and escaped to freedom, met with Stanton and Chase in Washington. After Smalls recounted his "thrilling story" of escape from slavery, the Reverend French presented a plan, proposed by General Rufus Saxton and endorsed by Hunter and Du Pont, that black troops be recruited to provide security for the many contrabands living and working on the Sea Island plantations. Stanton then gave Saxton permission to "arm, equip, and receive into service of the United States such volunteers of African descent as you may deem expedient, not exceeding five thousand." Saxton had already been given authority to recruit black volunteer laborers and to pay them $5 a month for common (unskilled) labor and $8 for skilled labor.[40]

Passage of the Second Confiscation Act clarified questions about the return of fugitive slaves, and the Militia Act passed by Congress gave Lincoln authority to draft soldiers from state militias into federal service for three years. The new legislation, which included the enlistment of African Americans "for any military or naval service for which they be found competent," was a boon for the Union Navy, strapped as it was for manpower. Although the Second Confiscation Act cleared up the issue of accepting fugitive slaves, Du Pont found it necessary to remind one of his officers of the new law. "You are aware of the law of Congress in reference to contrabands, to return none by whomever claimed, but make a proper entry in the log book of the name of the fugitive and owner or claimant," he inquired of Commander Charles Steedman. Despite these gentle reminders and other issued instructions, Union Navy commanders continued to express confusion about the procedures for enlisting or "shipping" contrabands. "Let me know whether I am to discharge my men as fast as their times expire. They are certainly entitled then to be discharged," Lieutenant Commander C. W. Flusser asked of Commander Henry Davenport in mid-September 1862. Flusser also inquired, "Are contrabands to sign the shipping articles?" In October Flusser again queried Davenport, "I have lately shipped several contrabands. Shall contrabands sign the articles or not? I think it is better not to make them sign, they can then be sent ashore, within our lines, whenever they become worthless or dissatisfied."[41]

Union naval commanders' concerns about the status of contrabands persisted well into 1863. On March 24, 1863, for example, Captain Charles Boggs, senior officer off Wilmington, North Carolina, asked Lee for instructions with regard to persons taken off vessels seized as prizes for violating the blockade. "I also request instructions as to what dispositions shall be made of the contrabands that may escape to the fleet,"

Boggs wrote. "Some have come off and many more may be expected, both women and children. Are we obliged by any law or regulation to receive all contrabands that may ask asylum? I am aware that law imposes a penalty on any officer who shall return or give up any contrabands."[42]

In response to this query, Lee sent Welles a copy of proposed instructions for dealing with fugitives—white, free, and slave—from the insurrectionary region and black crewmen from captured vessels. Lee felt that such instructions would supply blockading officers with definitive information on these matters, "of which they stand greatly in need and for which they frequently ask." The enclosed instructions stated "that all white and free colored persons from the insurrectionary region, taking refuge on board any of the blockading vessels, will as soon after being so received as practicable, be landed again at any safe point along the coast, in order to avoid the possibility of making our blockading vessels convenient vehicles to assist in conveying such persons to places where they can operate as rebel agents or spies or as pilots, or otherwise aid in attempts to violate the blockade." With regard to contrabands, Lee wrote, "all such as may ask asylum will be received according to law, and taken as soon as practicable to Beaufort, where they will be put in charge of the military authorities."[43]

In 1863, as enlistments expired, the Union Navy was hard-pressed to find new enlistees and was anxious to deprive southern slave owners of their labor force. Thus, the navy began to actively encourage Union sympathizers and African Americans to desert. Hoping, perhaps, to retain some of the contrabands on the vessels in his squadron, Du Pont wrote to Welles on June 15, 1863, "These persons are very useful, particularly as there is difficulty in obtaining men in the Northern ports. Many of them have been enlisted for a year, and as their times have expired, request their discharge, and to be sent on shore at Port Royal." Du Pont requested instructions about discharging them, and Welles replied, "They are entitled to their discharge on the expiration of their terms."[44]

A month later Welles informed Du Pont's replacement, John A. Dahlgren, that he was sending him 200 men on the *Aries* and 60 on the *Bermuda* from Philadelphia. Welles directed Dahlgren, "You must use the contraband element, as far as it can be with advantage to the service, in supplying deficiencies in the squadron." Four days later Welles told Dahlgren the *Aries* would bring him 200 men and, upon its return to New York, 200 more. Then he cautioned, "The Department desires you to enlist for service in the squadron as many able-bodied contrabands as you can especially for firemen and coal heavers. There is great demand at present from all quarters for seamen, and the contraband element must be used where it can with advantage."[45]

Fortunately for the Union war effort, as conditions in the Confederacy deteriorated, more and more refuges—white as well as black—sought safety on Union naval vessels or requested to be rescued. The increasing number of fugitives presented Union Navy commanders with excellent recruiting opportunities, and Dahlgren took specific steps to promote this policy. On November 19, 1863, he ordered Lieutenant Commander Samuel L. Breese to sail the *Ottawa* to St. John's, Florida, and take charge of the blockade there. "Be vigorous and vigilant in sustaining and encouraging the friends of the Union, and in suppressing those who are clearly inimical to it," Dahlgren instructed Breese. He told Breese to send him "accurate information of the condition of things: 1. Is there Union sentiment prevailing that can be turned to good account? 2. Are the refugees sincere in their offer to take up arms against the enemy, if I give them the opportunity by sending a suitable force? 3. What is the strengthened position of the enemy?" Dahlgren closed his orders to Breese by telling him, "You will offer every possible encouragement to deserters, refugees, and contrabands."[46]

The Union Navy's policy toward African American fugitives, tentative at the beginning of the Civil War, now not only welcomed black runaways but also actively encouraged them to desert their masters and seek Union protection. In 1861 the navy had struggled to fashion a policy toward these unexpected fugitives, a policy that reflected the restrictions placed on commanding officers by the Fugitive Slave Act and a prewar limitation on enlistees of color. During the first months of the war the arrival of runaway slaves seeking protection on Union Navy vessels had caught the Navy Department and senior commanders by surprise, yet many commanding officers welcomed these fugitives and refused to return them to their southern owners. In the absence of a formal policy toward these contrabands, officers often kept refugees aboard their vessels, putting the able-bodied men to work and sometimes employing the women and children as cooks and laundresses. Confronted with rapid wartime expansion of the navy and the need to fill out crews, commanders quickly realized the value of enlisting not only free blacks but also former slaves or contrabands. In July 1861 the Navy Department seized on the opportunity to employ the numerous contrabands making their way to Union vessels by authorizing Flag Officer Stringham to enlist able-bodied male contrabands on store ships. Two months later Welles expanded the policy by allowing commanders to enlist contrabands with the rating of "boy," and before the end of the first year of the war he extended the opportunity for black sailors to achieve higher ratings. Continuing manpower needs motivated the Navy Department and senior commanders not only to welcome and protect black runaways but also to encourage slaves to flee their southern masters. By January 1, 1863, when Lincoln's Emancipation Proclamation took effect, the Union Navy had finally settled on a clear, consistent policy toward African American refugees. Furthermore, after two years of war with the Confederacy, contraband sailors had proved themselves by their willingness to serve, their courage under fire, and their ability as seamen. Although many still served aboard Union vessels as cooks and stewards, others had been given higher ratings as seamen and ordinary seamen, and some had served under fire in gun crews, boat parties, and landing parties.

CHAPTER 2
GOING TO FREEDOM

My mother say, "Son, data in't t'under, dat Yankee come to gib your freedom."

—Sam Mitchel

Within weeks of Fort Sumter's fall, African Americans began seeking sanctuary on Union Navy vessels. The regular appearance of federal vessels along the coast or patrolling southern rivers and creeks offered slaves, Confederate deserters, and even free blacks golden opportunities to make their way to freedom. Many of the earliest wartime escapes to Union Navy vessels occurred on the wide Potomac River, which connected the nation's capital to the Chesapeake Bay but also divided the border state of Maryland from the Confederate state of Virginia. The Potomac's numerous creeks and bays offered pro-southern smugglers myriad possibilities for transporting contraband goods from the Maryland shore to Virginia and gave Confederate blockade runners access to the open ocean. Furthermore, Maryland's southern tobacco counties and the eastern shore of the Chesapeake Bay were pro-Confederate or secessionist.

In the early days of the war the Navy Department expressed serious concerns about blockade running in the river and the need to secure the Potomac as a major commercial waterway from the Atlantic to the nation's capital at Washington. In late April 1861 these concerns prompted Navy Secretary Gideon Welles to order *Pocahontas, Pawnee, Anacostia, Mt. Vernon,* and *Keystone State* to the Potomac to escort troop transports, patrol the river in search of suspicious movements by vessels or persons on shore, and reconnoiter for enemy batteries or fortifications along the riverbanks. Union commanders soon recognized the difficulty of patrolling the Potomac River and Chesapeake Bay with just five vessels, so on April 27, 1861, Welles decided to create a small naval force, or "flying flotilla," to patrol the river. To command this new flotilla he chose Commander James H. Ward, a career naval officer and veteran of the Mexican War who had planned the relief of Fort Sumter. Ward selected the side-wheeler *Thomas Freeborn* and the small screw steamers *Resolute* and *Reliance* for duty in the Potomac and Chesapeake, and by mid-May his "Potomac Flotilla" had assembled at the New York Navy Yard. Within days these vessels departed New York for the Chesapeake, where they began aggressively searching for signs of rebel activity or small craft carrying contraband goods. Ward quickly learned from local citizens that most inhabitants on the Maryland side held strong pro-Union sentiments, but disaffected Marylanders had taken to crossing the Potomac from a point below Port Tobacco, Maryland, to Mathias Point, Virginia, with the intention of joining rebel forces there or transporting supplies to the Confederates. Alerted to this fact, Ward ordered Union Navy vessels operating in the Potomac to search suspicious vessels for contraband. Commander John P. Gillis's flagship *Pocahontas* and the side-wheel steam frigate *Powhatan* under Lieutenant J. Glendy Sproston had already begun probing up the Rappahannock and Piantank rivers, where Sproston assured nervous inhabitants on the riverbanks that the navy intended to attack only those who had taken up arms against the United States or actively assisted the rebels.[1]

Enforcing the blockade and keeping the Potomac open for traffic to and from Washington kept the Potomac Flotilla busy, stopping or intercepting suspicious vessels and carefully watching for any signs of enemy activity on the shore. Their presence also began to attract runaways—slaves, free blacks, and white deserters. The reaction of Union Navy commanders to these runaways varied, in some cases depending on whether the runaways were white or black. Take, for example, two incidents involving the USS *Pawnee*. On June 12, 1861, the *Pawnee*'s commanding officer, Commander Stephen C. Rowan, reported: "A colored man came off this morning in a small boat, stating that he belonged to a Mr. Healy, and asked for my protection." Rowan refused to receive the black man, who continued downstream, but he did not hesitate to send a boat to rescue a white man seen swimming toward the *Pawnee* from the Maryland shore nine days later. The man identified himself as John Dowling, a carpenter by trade, and stated that he had joined the Confederate States Sentinels in May to avoid being arrested as an abolitionist but had deserted. Unable to escape the South, Dowling had joined the Confederate Navy and reported to Aquia Creek. "On the evening of the 20th I went to bathe," Dowling told Rowan, "and started from the end of the burned wharf for the *Pawnee.*" After about half a mile the rebels opened fire on Dowling, but the tide swept him down to the shore near Maryland Point. His escape clearly impressed Rowan, who wrote, "This escape showed coolness and nerve, as well as great physical endurance." In contrast, Rowan expressed little admiration for the black refugee who had asked for protection earlier, and he offered only a brief explanation for his refusal to take the man on board. "Having little faith in the loyalty of the people residing on the Maryland bank of this river, I declined to receive him," the commander told Welles.[2]

Whether by swimming, sailing, or rowing in small boats, refugees both white and black continued to make their way out to Union gunboats throughout the first summer of the war. When three slaves—James Minor, George Washington, and Samuel Bunn—made it from the Virginia shore to the USS *Union* in a small boat on September 9, 1861, Acting Lieutenant P. G. Watmough sent them to the *Release.* Mindful of the provisions of the First Confiscation Act passed that summer, the *Release's* skipper, Thomas Pattison, informed the Potomac Flotilla commander, Captain Thomas T. Craven, that the slaves belonged to Phelan Lewis of Virginia, "who is at present acting with the rebels." When another slave named James Lawson arrived at the *Union* the next day, Watmough also sent him to the *Release,* and Pattison received him, probably because the refugee claimed that his master was a colonel in the rebel army.[3]

Initially, many of the slaves rescued by navy landing parties or making their way out to Union vessels were men or boys. However, a few early reports mention women being picked up and taken on board blockading ships. In September 1861 a boat from the steam sloop *Seminole* discovered a party of contrabands, four men and one woman, making their way out from the Virginia shore in an old scow. They claimed to belong to T. B. Robinson of Ohio Farm, Virginia. In his report, Lieutenant C. S. Norton noted, "As the presence of a woman, from want of accommodation, is rather embarrassing, I respectfully request, at your convenience, instructions as to their disposition." Captain Craven duly dispatched the five contrabands to the Washington Navy Yard, along with a rebel deserter.[4]

The number of families or groups of women and children making their way to freedom across Union lines or out to Union vessels along the coast increased as the war progressed. In late August 1863 George Adams Bright, a naval surgeon serving on the *South Carolina,* wrote to his wife, "Horrid monotony. To vary it a family of six darkies floated down the river to us the other day. Father mother and children." The appearance of this family of black refugees briefly relieved the boredom of blockade duty for Bright and the crew of the *South Carolina,* which had been left on blockade duty while other federal ships participated in Rear Admiral John A. Dahlgren's August bombardment of Forts Sumter and Wagner.[5]

On occasion, mention of these escapes made their way into the letters of correspondents from the *New York Herald.* Their reports offer rare glimpses of black runaways and their journeys to freedom. Writing from a blockade ship off Charleston on June 3, 1863, the *Herald's* naval correspondent wrote, "A few nights ago seven more contrabands made their escape in some 'dug-outs' from the vicinity of Charleston, and reached the fleet. Two of them are women. They have all been sent to Port Royal." The same correspondent also gave a lengthy description of another boatload of escapees:

> On the 17th ins't., just after daylight, one of the gunboats picked up, near the North Channel, a dug-out boat containing four men and two women, with a large quantity of baggage, etc. They stated that they had come down one of the back inlets in their frail boat, during the night, passed the sentinels unobserved, and passed out an Inlet in safety. The boat was loaded to within four inches of the water, and the oars were pieces of board 4 feet long. The men are young and good looking negroes and belonged to one of the first families in Charleston. One of the women is almost white, has straight black hair and is quite handsome. They have been sent to Port Royal.[6]

Not all the refugees rescued by Union vessels during the summer of 1861 were Confederate deserters or runaway slaves. Free blacks began making their way out of the South as well. Most of the approximately 250,000 free blacks in the United States in 1861 lived in the South, where they enjoyed the right to marry, accumulate property, and control their own labor. Yet the southern states denied free blacks the right to travel freely, testify in court, bear arms, and, in some cases, hold property. Free blacks dissatisfied with life in the South and yearning for true freedom saw the approach of Union forces and Yankee gunboats as an opportunity to flee, and many seized the moment. When two black men arrived at Acting Master's Mate James L. Gray's schooner *Bailey* on the evening of July 10, 1861, he wrote: "One, William Jenkins, says he is free; the other, Sam, says he is a slave, belonging to Colonel T. R. Shackelford, of Warsaw, Va., who is now at Mathias Point with the rebel troops." Gray told Craven, his superior, that he had retained the

two black men on board his vessel. There is no correspondence from
Craven about these two men, but on August 11, 1861, he sent Welles a
detailed report concerning the capture of ten other African Americans
and enclosed a report from William Budd of the *Resolute.* In a raid on a
depot at Herring Creek, near the mouth of the Machodoc Creek in Virginia, Budd had taken ten contrabands belonging to a Colonel Brown,
who, Budd claimed, had been receiving and forwarding supplies and
recruits for the Confederates. Budd then sent the contrabands off in the
schooner *Dana.* Budd wrote, "The foreman of the contrabands, who is
a remarkably intelligent negro, informs me that an expedition is organized in Machodoc to capture any of the schooners that are anchored or
becalmed in that vicinity."[7]

The vast majority of slaves making their way to Union vessels along
the southern coast were not, in the parlance of the day, "intelligent," a
term frequently used by Union commanders to denote educated or lit-
erate African Americans. Unable to read or write, these runaway slaves
could not record their journeys for posterity. A few educated slaves
or free blacks, however, wrote letters or kept diaries describing their
escapes. Others told their story to interviewers after the war. William
Summerson, a twenty-three-year-old slave picked up in June 1862 by
federal gunboats in the Stono River, told readers of the *National Anti-
Slavery Standard:* "My mother was of mixed blood. My father was Robert Summerson, a white man, from the North. He left two children when
he went North, my brother and myself." When their owner sold Summerson's mother, seven-year-old William remained with his aunt. When
he grew older, Summerson hired himself out, working "on a steamer
between Charleston and the head of the St. John's River, Florida. I got
along as well as I could in a state of slavery," he recalled, "until the death
of my owner." After the Civil War began, Summerson left his job, "lest I
should be obliged to do something against the Federal forces," he said.
After working in Charleston at an arsenal and then as a waiter at the
Charleston Hotel, Summerson married in March 1862. "The May following, my wife was to be carried back into the country, and I might
never see her again; so I hid her from the last of April until we escaped.
. . . She was hidden with some of my friends, and as the slaves escaped
so constantly to the blockade, no one searched for her."

In its December 1862 issue the *National Anti-Slavery Standard* fea-
tured the story of Summerson's daring escape from Charleston with his
wife and another man. This is one of the few detailed descriptions of
how slaves made their way to freedom on federal vessels during the Civil
War. On June 13, 1862, Summerson's mistress sent him to her brother, a

lawyer named Porter, on Broad Street. Porter asked Summerson "if he would rather go into the country with our mistress or be sold?" When Summerson replied that he would prefer to go with his mistress, Porter informed him that he could not follow her and must be sold. No one would buy him, Summerson wrote, so "I lifted my heart to the Almighty, and besought him to make a way for me to escape." That night he prayed and said that God "put a plan in my head which carried me safely to freedom."

Summerson planned to escape from the city with the aid of a slave friend who went into Charleston from Sanandros Parish three times a week to sell vegetables. "I thought after he had disposed of his load, I would get him to put me in a rice barrel and take me back in his wagon. . . . He had a pass for the wagon." At noon on Saturday, Summerson met his friend at a piazza and got into the barrel. Then, he wrote, "he headed me up, and I was put into the waggon, and he drove way." They went over the Ashley River bridge past fifty Confederate sentries who allowed the wagon to pass. Following a four-and-a-half-hour ride in the rice barrel, he arrived at the plantation at 10 P.M. The driver then returned to Charleston to pick up Summerson's wife and take her out of the city in the same barrel. Unfortunately, the mule pulling the wagon had grown tired, "so they had to stop and rest," making the journey take twice as long, "so she was eight hours and a half therein." Summerson continued: "On the road one of the rebels got into the wagon and sat on the barrel she was in, and rode half a mile in that way, and only the power of the Almighty kept that barrel from breaking and bringing her to light. After she got there, she could not move and was drenched with perspiration." They fanned her, and she recovered.

On Wednesday, Summerson and his wife walked three miles through a swamp in water up to their knees and crossed a railroad bridge. Beyond the bridge they were met by the driver of the vegetable wagon, who had a boat. A rebel gunboat and a fort guarded the fifteen-mile water route to the federal blockader. "I meant to wait till the tide fell, so that the gunboat would go back in the Cut where she lay at low water, but I did not see her till I got close upon her, and heard the men talking, and looked up and saw them on deck." Keeping close to the marsh, Summerson managed to get the boat around the point and pass the fort. When day broke, he recalled, "I looked back and could not see the fort, and I knew I was out of their reach." About two and a half hours later they reached the federal gunboats in the Stono River. "When I got in sight of the Union boats, I raised a white flag, and when I came near, they cheered me, and pointed to the flagship *Pawnee*. There I had the pleasure of a breakfast of hot coffee, ham, nice butter, and all under the American flag.—all strange things in Charleston." On board the *Pawnee,* Summerson told "the Captain about Charleston harbor, and how the vessels run the blockade, and the next day but one they took two vessels from the information I gave them. Then we were put on board a transport vessel for Port Royal and reached there in safety." The *Pawnee's* skipper, Commander Percival Drayton, confirmed that on June 19, 1862, two contrabands had boarded the ship from Charleston. As he told Flag Officer Samuel F. Du Pont, they "represented the harbor as completely blocked up, the ordinary channel stopped, and vessels obliged to come over the middle ground (probably at high tide) and close to the palmetto fort erected there recently."[8]

William Summerson escaped from the city of Charleston, but many other slaves, most of them field hands or servants, fled from rice or cotton plantations. Often located near rivers and creeks, these plantations gave runaways access to small boats or other watercraft with which to make their way to freedom. Not surprisingly, some of these plantation slaves made a living as watermen or pilots and willingly assisted other slaves out to Union Navy vessels. An excellent example of such an escape is the story of five contrabands who left Blake's plantation near Cape Romain, South Carolina, and fled to the bark *Gem of the Sea* on the morning of June 5, 1862. One of the five fugitive slaves belonged to a Mr. A. Blake and claimed to have been a pilot in rebel service on the Confederate steamer *Chesterfield* for nine months "in and about Charleston." He referred to himself as "Captain" Blake and told Acting Volunteer Lieutenant I. B. Baxter, *Gem of the Sea's* commanding officer, that he had left Charleston on May 12, 1862, and arrived at his master's plantation three days later. The five contrabands were "Captain," Robert, and three boys—Prince, John, and Michael. According to Baxter, an Englishman named Blake owned the plantation but had departed for England a week after the fall of Fort Sumter. Before leaving, Blake had owned between 600 and 700 slaves, according to Baxter's report, "but a great many had died from neglect and want of medicines, nearly one-half." One hundred fifty slaves remained, but an equal number had been taken back to a pine woods called Hammond's Hall. The escape of these two men and three boys probably encouraged others to make their way to freedom, for in late June 1862, *Gem of the Sea* rescued a large number of slaves who then became the nucleus of a contraband colony on North Island.[9]

Confederate authorities in Virginia did not sit idly by while Blake and other slaves commandeered small boats and ran off from plantations, leaving their masters short of field hands and servants. In May 1861 the

Virginia State Convention passed ordinances designed to punish Union officers who aided and abetted slave revolts and escapes. These offenses, deemed felonies, carried fines of as much as $10,000 and sentences of up to twenty years in prison. In October of that year the General Assembly of Virginia passed an additional law requiring Union officers to pay double the value of the runaway slaves plus 6 percent interest, and it later imposed a $50-a-day penalty for Yankees employing former slaves. To reduce the number of escapes made via small boats from the Tidewater area, the General Assembly enacted stiff penalties for persons transporting slaves by boat without the slave owner's permission and instituted measures to allow unattended boats to be confiscated.[10]

In addition to these stern measures in Virginia, southern slave owners advertised for runaway slaves, offering rewards and recapturing some of them. During the summer of 1862 disgruntled planters in Georgia wrote to the Confederate commander in the area, General Hugh W. Mercer, arguing for stiffer penalties for runaway slaves. Noting that roughly 20,000 slaves had fled coastal Georgia counties, the planters urged the general to treat the fugitives as traitors and execute those who were captured. In their letter to the general, the planters wrote, "We allude to the escape of our Slaves across the border lies landward, and out to vessels of the enemy Seaward & to their being also enticed off by those who having made their escape, return for that purpose, and not unfrequently, attended by the enemy." Their argument that runaway slaves should be treated as traitors rested in part on the fact that "they go over to the enemy & afford him aid & comfort, by revealing the condition of the districts and cities from which they come, & aiding him in erecting fortifications & raising provisions for his support . . . and by enlisting under his banners increasing his resources in men, for our annoyance & destruction."[11]

Former slaves serving as enlisted men on navy ships, employed as servants to Union Army officers, or living in Union-occupied areas vulnerable to Confederate attack faced possible capture, re-enslavement, and punishment for running away. When rebel raiding parties ambushed navy landing parties or captured Union vessels, any contraband sailors unfortunate enough to be on board fell prisoner to the Confederates. As naval personnel, black sailors should have been treated as prisoners of war and sent to Confederate prisons, but the Confederacy did not recognize their right to be treated as prisoners of war, and in a few cases, the Confederates simply hanged black sailors. Contrabands employed by Union Army officers as servants, cooks, or grooms could technically be deemed civilians and liable to re-enslavement. This possibility haunted some Union officers such as George Harlan, a surgeon who resigned his navy commission in August 1861 to join a cavalry unit. As a cavalry officer, Harlan found himself in the front lines and was often called to ride on forays into enemy territory, both of which posed the risk of capture. On May 24, 1862, he wrote to his wife, Margaret, from Suffolk, Virginia, to inform her that, rumor aside, he had not been captured by the enemy. Fearing for the safety of his horse and his black servant boy in the event of capture, he predicted, "My poor darkey would not have seen Yankee-land soon again." Harlan then reassured her, "These two are always my first thoughts when things begin to look doubtful and I ordered them to the rear twice during the fighting at Carsville." Harlan told Margaret that the boy had plenty of pluck and never budged. "I am always sure of finding him where [he] was left holding on tight to the reins."[12]

In rare instances, southern slave owners willingly abandoned their black slaves to Union forces. For example, during a reconnaissance in the Wilmington Narrows and Turner's Creek in late March 1862, Commander John P. Gillis reported that rebel scouting parties had compelled all the white residents of Wilmington and Withers Island to leave. The soldiers had even forcibly removed some of them, "afterward wantonly destroying property to a great amount and carrying away the negroes." In his report, Gillis recounted that one white resident of Withers Island had requested that the soldiers leave the blacks, "as he would be unable to provide for them in Savannah, so it was better for them to fall into Northern hands."[13]

The great majority of African Americans escaping to Union vessels did so in secret and on their own initiative, but in at least one case, slaves fled at the suggestion of their owner. On August 3, 1861, Commander Benjamin M. Dove of the second-class sloop USS *Pocahontas* reported that while cruising in the lower Potomac River he had picked up "two colored men" off Maryland Point. The men told Dove that they belonged to Daingerfield Lewis of Marmion and that the governor had ordered Lewis to send his people to the mouth of the Rappahannock to assist in building a fort. According to the refugees, their master "did not like it, and told them to get off if they could, and that they followed his advice and escaped." In his report to Captain John Dahlgren, commander of the Washington Navy Yard, Dove explained that the two slaves had fled in an old, leaky boat caulked with strips of guano bags, "one of the men bailing her constantly, the other rowing." They brought with them two bags of clothes and a bag each of cornmeal and peaches. "There was a heavy fog on the river all morning, to which they owed their safety, as the shores seemed to be well guarded," Dove noted. In a report of this incident to Flag Officer Silas Stringham, commanding the Atlantic Blockading Squadron, Welles provided additional information about the two slaves and their master. The slaves were part of a quota furnished by Lewis, a wealthy farmer in Virginia, who had been ordered by the governor to send a draft of 500 slaves from Fredericksburg to erect fortifications on Mosquito Point, on the left bank near the mouth of the Rappahannock River.[14]

Encouraged by their master to escape, these two slaves managed to gain freedom, but thousands of others found themselves forced by the Confederate Army to build or reinforce gun batteries, fortifications, and other defenses. The mere threat of being used to construct rebel fortifications or assist the Confederate Army prompted many slaves to risk the flight to freedom. Not long after the *Pocahontas* rescued the two slaves in the lower Potomac, lookouts on the wooden screw steamer *Reliance* sighted a boat acting in a suspicious manner. When they hailed the boat, it pulled alongside the *Reliance,* anchored at the time off Piney Point. The crew, composed "of four negroes," told Acting Lieutenant J. P. Mygatt that they belonged to a Colonel Forbes, who lived on the Machodoc River, Virginia. As Mygatt explained to Craven, "They stated that they had run away from their master because he intended to use them for military purposes, or, to use their own words, 'because he wanted to send them to the wars.'" Mygatt detained the four back men and, on orders from Craven, sent them to Washington on the *Resolute.*[15]

Although many African Americans, pro-Union in sentiment, found working on coastal Confederate defenses objectionable, most had little choice. Black laborers working on Confederate entrenchments and gun batteries on points of land near rivers and creeks, however, quickly discovered that these locations afforded them opportunities to escape to Union vessels lying offshore. Describing one of these escapes to Welles on August 30, 1861, Craven wrote: "This morning as we were passing Upper Cedar Point there came on board four colored men, one, named James Scott, states that he belongs to a Mr. Benjamin Weaver of King George Court-House, Va., and that he and Henry Young have been employed to build batteries at Mathias Point." The foursome had left Virginia in a small skiff the previous evening. Young and the two others, William Henderson and Grandison Piper, both of whom belonged to Virginians, told Craven that the batteries at Mathias Point expected to receive their heavy guns sometime that week. Craven sent the men to the Washington Navy Yard. Several days later, Lieutenant Foxhall Parker at the navy yard sent Craven a report obtained from Young. According to Young, the rebels had hidden a keg of powder and a sack of musket balls in a barn on Captain Cox's plantation three miles from Chapel Point, Maryland. "Young further says that Captain Cox's colored overseer told him he could show him a place where many arms were concealed." Young's provision of valuable information was not an unusual occurrence, for black refugees often offered reports of Confederate activity and other bits of useful information. The role of contrabands as informants and spies is discussed in later chapters.[16]

African Americans, both free blacks and slaves, risked fleeing the South for various reasons, including conscription, harsh wartime conditions, threats of being sold or sent into the interior by their owners, and to avoid being put to work on Confederate fortifications and other defenses. Foremost, of course, was the deep desire of thousands of black men, women, and children to be free from bondage. From almost the beginning of hostilities between the Union and the Confederate States of America, many slaves assumed that if they could avoid Union pickets and cross safely into Union lines, they would be free from their masters. Although the Lincoln administration initially refused to acknowledge the conflict as more than a rebellion, and certainly not a war about slavery, the majority of slaves believed otherwise. "We gwine to freedom," many cried. Union Navy commanders did not always share the slaves' concept of "freedom," however. In his diary entry for April 25, 1863, Dr. Samuel Boyer of the bark *Fernandina* wrote, "Today 4 intelligent contrabands made their appearance in a dugout, having come all the way from the vicinity of Savannah having traveled ever since Sunday last, and doing without anything to eat since last Tuesday. They were dressed in rags. All appear to have one idea, and that is to be 'free' . . . to do nothing and have plenty to eat and drink."[17]

Threats of being sold prompted many slaves to flee their masters or mistresses. In a letter to his wife, Sophie, Du Pont described the arrival of a contraband from Savannah: "This contraband and another who got away with him belonged to a widow woman; they had determined to remain with her as she had been kind and take their chance, hoping the North would be successful, but they found themselves sold to traders one morning—this one for $1,500, the other for $2,000. They then determined to run even if caught and shot, rather than go 'back' with the traders, and succeeded by way of Wassaw Inlet."[18]

Although many slaves made their way to freedom during the Civil War in small boats or canoes, William Summerson's account (described earlier) is one of only a few detailed, personal stories of these wartime escapes to Union gunboats. Another is the tale of Harry Jarvis, a slave born in Virginia who was interviewed in Hampton, Virginia, in 1872. Jarvis worked for "de meanest man on all de Easte'n Sho'," where "dey don't think so much ob deir niggers as dey do ob deir dogs. D' rather whip one dan eat any day." Jarvis told an interviewer he had escaped during the first year of the war. "It war bad enough before, but arter de war come, it war wus nor eber." After being shot at by his employer, he decided to run away. "I tuk to der woods. I lay out dere for three weeks." His master sent dogs out to find Jarvis, but they lost the scent. Slaves sent out to search along the shore would have turned him in, he told the interviewer, "but I had frien's who kep me informed how t'ings war gwine one, an' brought me food." When the master hosted a big birthday party, Jarvis saw his chance to flee, "so I tuk de opportunity to slip down to de sho; in de night, got a canoe an' a sail, 'n started for fort Monroe." He stole the canoe from a white man and the sail from another black and went "thirty five miles across de bay, 'n when I got out o' shelter ob de sho', I struck a norther dat like to tuk away my sail. Didn't pear as ef I'd eber get to lan." Jarvis recalled that he had not been afraid. "You see it war dearth behind me, an' I didn't know what war ahead, so I jes' asked de Lord to take care ob me, an' by-am-by de win' went down to a good stiddy breeze straight fur Ol' P'int, an' I jes made fas de sheet 'n druv ahead, 'n nex' mornin' I got safe to de Fort." Jarvis asked General Benjamin F. Butler if he could enlist, but Butler told him, "it warn't a black man's war. I tol' him it would be a black man's war 'fore dey got thru." Butler gave Jarvis work, but he subsequently hired onto a ship going to Cuba and eventually enlisted in the Fifty-fifth Massachusetts Regiment.[19]

Harry Jarvis escaped alone by stealing a canoe, but other slaves escaping to Union vessels along the southern coast made their way to freedom in cooperative group efforts. On May 25, 1863, Captain John J. Almy, commanding the USS *South Carolina,* described one such escape: "Yesterday (Sunday), observing a party upon Bull's Island Beach resembling negroes, at the distance which we were, 1½ miles, men women and children with a piece of white cloth flying, I directed two boats to be manned and armed and sent them in under command of the executive officer, Acting Master Magune, with orders to approach with caution and reconnoiter." When Magune approached the beach, he ascertained that the party on shore was in fact a group of runaway slaves, who were taken in the boats and brought on board the steamer. "They comprised thirteen all told, men, women, and children, and represent themselves from different plantations in Christ Church Parish in this vicinity." That these thirteen slaves had run away from a number of plantations and then assembled to attract the attention of the *South Carolina* suggests that at least some escapes from slavery were organized, coordinated affairs.

Almy wrote, "In thus rescuing these persons from slavery and bringing them on board of a United States Federal vessel is, I consider, carrying out the spirit of the President's proclamation of January 1, 1863, and I trust that it will meet with the approbation of the admiral." Five of the contrabands, he said, could be made useful on board the steamer, which was short of men. The others he put on board the *Lodona*. Reporting the incident to Du Pont, Commodore Thomas Turner wrote, "I have allowed him to retain five of the men, who are not connected by any ties of relationship to the remainder of the party. The remaining 8, consisting of 2 men, 3 women, and 3 children, I send down to Port Royal."[20]

In his published recollections, former slave Allen Parker described how he and some fellow slaves planned and carried out an escape to a Union gunboat. "During the month of August 1862 slaves living on the adjoining plantation together with myself began to form plans of in some way getting to the 'yankees,'" he recalled. They talked often but "for a time did nothing." Learning that lots of slaves had run away from a neighboring plantation, they decided to take their chances and flee, according to Parker, "as soon as we could get away." When they heard a gun early one morning and saw a "United States gunboat out in the river," Parker and his three friends, Joe, Arden, and Dick, "all slaves belonging to one Robert Felton," decided to escape that night. "We waited till everything was quiet for it happened there were no 'partie rollers' out that night; and then stole our way down to the river bank, where we knew there was a boat." Managing to break the chain that fastened the boat to a tree, Parker and his friends pushed off from shore and "bid goodbye to the old plantation and slave life forever." When they rowed out to the Union vessel, an officer hailed them. Parker recalled, "My friends said that they were from Rob. Felton's plantation, and I told them that I belonged to Miss Annie Parker. They then inquired if our owners were Union people or not, and we replied that they were not." The four slaves asked to be allowed to stay on board, and the officer went to ask permission of the vessel's commander. He returned with an invitation for them to remain on the ship. "We immediately accepted his invitation, and being very tired, were soon fast asleep on the deck of the vessel."

In the morning, when those on shore realized the slaves had escaped, a number of men "armed with guns and accompanied by dogs" came to the riverbank, but Parker and his friends were not alarmed, as a stretch of water separated them from the rebels. "The captain watched them for a while, then ordered a gun loaded with a shell to be fired in their direction. The shell burst in the air, but our friends did not stay to see another fired." The following night, Parker recalled, the sailors took Joe as a pilot, went to the Felton plantation, and took some chickens, ducks, and geese. They subsequently returned, surrounded the house, took Robert Felton prisoner, and brought him back on board. When Felton's wife came to visit him, she was astounded to see Joe, their former slave. "It happened that Joe was the son of Mr. Felton, and his mother was one of Col. Felton's slaves. But the tables had turned, Joe remained on the vessel a free man, and Felton was a prisoner of war," Parker added. Days later, Allen Parker enlisted in the Union Navy and "was placed on board a vessel that had been captured from the rebels where he served for [a] year."[21]

During the Civil War, Union Navy vessels encountered many individuals or small parties of runaway slaves, but the vast majority of slaves liberated along the southern coast were freed as a result of Union military operations and expeditions. One of the earliest and most dramatic instances came in November 1861, when Union forces commanded by Du Pont and General Thomas W. Sherman captured Hilton Head Island and Port Royal Sound. For African American inhabitants of this area and the Georgia Sea Islands, the Union victory was a momentous and, in many cases, a life-changing event. Sam Mitchel, age eighty-seven when he told his story to an interviewer in the 1930s, remembered the day: "Dat wednesday in November w'en gun fust shoot at Bay Pin [Point] I t'ought it been t'udner rolling, but day ain't no cloud. My mother say, 'son, data in't no t'under, dat Yankee come to gib you freedom.' I been so glad, I jump up and down." Mitchel said his father was splitting rails when the master came back from Beaufort in his carriage yelling for a driver. He "told he driver to git his eight oar boat named Tarrify and carry him to Charleston. My father he run to his house and tell my mother what Maussa say. My mother say 'You ain't gonna row no boat to Charleston, you go out dat back door and keep agoing.' So my father he did so."[22]

The Union occupation of Hilton Head and Port Royal also left Confederate positions on the numerous Sea Islands north of Savannah untenable, compelling many plantation owners to flee their homes and property in the city of Beaufort and other coastal areas. The inhabitants of the Port Royal area had been warned of the impending attack by newspaper articles predicting a Union invasion at some point along the coast. Although they did not know the exact location of the operation, some planters guessed that Port Royal Sound, with its sheltered waters, would make a fine anchorage for the Union Navy's blockading squadron. When the federal ships arrived off Hilton Head, Brigadier General Roswell Ripley advised those at Port Royal to evacuate. In the words of Dr. Joseph Walker, rector of St. Helena's Episcopal Church, "all over town, trunks were packed, carts and horses were drawn up, and household servants began busily loading family possessions. For some slaves it was the last act they were to perform for their masters." Walker's niece Emily recalled that her mother sent for a trusted slave named "Daddy Jimmy," who brought the longboat and six slaves who rowed Emily, her father, her cousin Sarah Stuart, and two infants across the Coosaw River to the mainland that night. On nearby St. Helena Island, planters gathered on Dr. Jenkins's veranda to watch the Union operation in Port Royal Sound. When a Union victory seemed assured, many of them rode off to warn other white inhabitants to evacuate. Some of the white planters tried to take their slaves with them, but many refused to leave. Captain Jon Fripp fled but told his slaves to stay on his plantation and plant crops to feed themselves. According to Union soldier Alexander Campbell, serving with the Seventy-ninth New York Regiment, "I was out on Port royal Island a few days ago and the negroes told me that the white people stripted the Negroes of any of them that [had] good cloth[e]s. . . . They Left here in suc[h] a hurry that they had not time to [take their] cloth[e]s." As soon as white South Carolinians and plantation owners headed inland from coastal areas near Beaufort, African Americans began arriving on Hilton Head from the Georgia Sea Islands. A Union soldier stationed on Hilton Head recounted that "negro slaves came flocking into our camp by the hundreds, escaping from their masters when they knew of the landing of 'Linkum sojers,' as they called us . . . many of them with no other clothing than gunny sacks."[23]

In a letter to a northern newspaper, a correspondent named "Vagabond" told readers, "At a place called Seabrook, the blacks flock in, men, women, and children from all the surrounding counties, the main and islands. Between three and four hundred are now within our lines, at work, digging entrenchments, rowing boats, and landing stores." He said they all told one story. "They have been expecting our advent; they disbelieve the stories of the rebels, that we intend to harm them; they are willing to work, but they want to be free. No blacks that can get away will remain with their masters; none will follow them in their flight before your army." This correspondent confirmed that in several instances masters had fired on their slaves when they refused to flee. He explained that Union officials had not invited the blacks into Union lines, nor were they being repulsed. "No enticements are to be held out to them, but they evidently need none," he wrote.[24]

At first, Union officials did not realize that whites had fled the Port Royal area in great numbers. Shortly after occupying Hilton Head, Lieutenant Daniel Ammen took several Union ships into Port Royal Sound and up to the city of Beaufort. Sherman and Du Pont accompanied Ammen in the screw gunboat *Seneca*. A correspondent who accompanied this expedition up Port Royal Sound filed a report to the *New York Herald* from Hilton Head Island on November 9, 1861: "I hasten to say that this morning the gunboats *Pembina* and *Seneca* started up for Beaufort, and, much to their surprise, did not meet with any resistance." Ammen's vessels proceeded on their way, he wrote, "unmolested and reached the town, which is some twelve miles distant from here, and contains about five thousand inhabitants." In his memoirs, Ammen recalled arriving in Beaufort and finding the city deserted of its white inhabitants. What he did see were "hundreds of negroes on the wharf and on the streets; all the scows were in requisition and were being loaded with furniture and personal effects of all kinds, provisions, and lumber to erect sheds elsewhere; on the part of the negroes it was an exhibition of wild confusion and great joy; they imagined they were setting out on a picnic for life." Former slaves who remained in Beaufort told Ammen that the whites had left the island, and "many slaves had been shot by their masters while making an attempt to escape while being driven to the Port Royal ferry to be taken to the mainland."[25]

The Union Navy's delay in occupying Beaufort had, in fact, given plantation slaves the opportunity to come to the city and ransack it. A white plantation owner who returned to his Beaufort home on November 8, 1861, discovered one of his slaves, a woman named Chloe, "seated at Phoebe's piano playing away like the very devil and two damsels, upstairs dancing away famously." Other eyewitness accounts, including those of the slaves themselves, verified reports that plantation hands had participated in the looting. Although Du Pont had given Ammen specific orders to protect the homes of peaceable private citizens, by the time the gunboat arrived, much of the looting had already taken place. Entering Beaufort, Du Pont found that "the stores were all rifled and (Beaufort) looked like a sacked town." He later wrote to this wife, "On my asking an old blacky of Mr. Nat Hawards', as he is called, why the remainder of his furniture in his handsome mansion was not carried off, he replied, 'Massa, because Yankee tell 'em they shoot 'em.'" In a letter to his wife, Jane, Alexander Campbell wrote, "I was out on another island on a scouting expedition and every house is deserted. Nothing but negroes. All white has runn & left there houses & everry thing that's in them. They told the negroes to runn for we would Kill them. They are coming in to the fort everyday. We will soon have a rigement of them."[26]

Alarming reports of slave owners coercing or even shooting slaves who would not join them in their flight from the Union invasion accompanied these unfortunate incidents of plundering and disorder in Beaufort prior to the Union occupation. Black informants gave convincing testimony to Union officials and naval officers that slaves had been shot to death resisting removal, and others had been burned to death in their cotton houses. Although some of these stories of mistreatment and coercion may have been exaggerations or even erroneous, as historian Willie Lee Rose has written, "the sheer weight of the evidence leads to the belief that many white men were willing to go to extreme lengths to retrieve their human property."[27] Furthermore, it is likely that these stories of mistreatment by white owners prompted Union naval officers to respond with alarm to rumors or reports of slave owners returning to the Sea Islands to recover or shoot former slaves.

Federal ships arriving in the waters near Hilton Head and Beaufort in November 1861 quickly attracted the attention of local African Americans, whose presence allowed Union Navy officers and sailors to gain information and provisions. On November 8, 1861, a correspondent wrote to a northern newspaper describing the scene as his ship lay at anchor: "On one side of us a dozen or more contrabands gazing upon us in open-mouthed wonder we sent off toward them an armed boat, to pick up information, and endeavor to purchase some fresh provisions. Up towards a cornfield ran the darkies, all but one who lingered, hat in hand, a bundle of traps under his arm. He waded out to meet the boat, evidently expecting to be brought off."[28]

Going ashore, Union naval officers encountered other slaves confidently expecting to be offered freedom. On November 30, 1861, Commander Drayton wrote to a friend named Hoyt describing a recent trip up the Ashepoo River: "I visited Hutchinson island and found everything in pretty good order, I suppose considerably over a hundred slaves as usual doing nothing as the overseer had gone off." The slaves, Drayton told Hoyt, "seemed delighted to see us, and asked me when we were going to free them, and offered to lead me to the nearest picket of confederates, about two miles off, when we heard heaving firing in the direction of the *Pawnee* which I had left at the entrance of the river." Drayton hurried off to investigate the source of the gunfire, which proved to be a false alarm. He did not mention in this letter the fate of the slaves left on Hutchinson Island.[29]

After the fall of Hilton Head Island and the Port Royal area, Du Pont's gunboats conducted reconnaissance patrols up nearby rivers and creeks, where they found more deserted plantations. The sudden abandonment of so many plantations and cotton crops by the white residents of the Beaufort area puzzled Du Pont and other Union officials. Admitting that he was unable to account satisfactorily for this situation, Du Pont surmised "that the owners connected our success with an immediate servile insurrection, for they are afraid of their slaves, unarmed as they are. And I no longer wonder at it. I have seen the institution 'de pres,' and may God forgive me for the words I have ever uttered in its defense as intertwined in our Constitution."[30]

In November federal troops from Hilton Head went to occupy St. Helena Island. In a letter to the *Christian Recorder*, a Lutheran chaplain assigned to the Seventy-ninth Regiment's New York Highlanders described his visit to St. Helena. The chaplain had been rowed "up and back [to the island] by negroes," he wrote, "who amused me exceedingly by their songs. All their singing was tinged with religion, even when the subject was comical." A large crowd of blacks greeted him when he landed at Dr. John J. Jenkins's plantation, and he preached to them in the moonlight in the backyard. "They seem to have perfect confidence in our soldiers, and render all required services with great pleasure. I have heard no profanity, and witnessed no drunkenness among them." He also told readers, "The negroes tell us that great was the consternation of all, and loud were the lamentations of the fair ones, when they ascertained that the Yankee fleet had effected a landing on the sacred soil of South Carolina. They left a vast amount of valuable property behind." He predicted, quite accurately as it turned out, "I have not the least doubt that the negro population would on the first opportunity array themselves on the side of the Union army."[31]

In addition to thousands of slaves left behind by their white owners, Union naval officers discovered acres of cotton fields and unginned cotton on the Sea Islands. In Beaufort, Du Pont and his commanders freely took what he termed all the "public" property, but obviously they had not anticipated the discovery of so much valuable cotton. Although the Treasury Department, headed by antislavery advocate Salmon P. Chase, was responsible for confiscated property, in the first weeks following the capture of Port Royal, the government failed to adopt a policy with regard to the unginned cotton and the unharvested cotton crop. In the absence of a government policy, Du Pont and his commanders struggled with what he termed "the cotton problem." Meanwhile, Drayton took a practical approach. "Drayton went up today in one of the tugs and got some of last year['s cotton] in bales to put round and protect the machinery of the *Pawnee*," Du Pont told his wife. When one of Du Pont's armed tugs came back in late November from an expedition up Johnson's Creek and the crew reported finding new plantations and much cotton, Du

Pont did not hesitate. "I am going to take it for the government to hold, not as a prize to us—I have well matured this and think it right."[32]

While Du Pont and Sherman grappled with the problems generated by thousands of former slaves (now contrabands) and valuable cotton crops, back in Washington, D.C., the Lincoln administration made only feeble efforts to define the status of the African Americans in the newly occupied areas of the South. In her book on the Port Royal experiment, Rose quoted one Washington observer who thought that Lincoln "was frightened with the success of South Carolina, as his opinion of this success will complicate the question of slavery." In his message to Congress on December 3, 1862, Lincoln tried to shift the responsibility to Congress and again brought up the concept of colonizing liberated blacks. However, in early December, Chase took matters in hand and met with Lieutenant Colonel William H. Reynolds of the First Rhode Island Artillery, an experienced cotton trader. Within the month, Chase had sent Reynolds to Port Royal as a government agent to collect the cotton.

Dealing with the situation of thousands of newly freed people at Port Royal was another matter. In many cases, their former owners had abandoned them before doling out the year-end allotments of food and clothing. Unfortunately, the army had also taken food from plantation storehouses, leaving the freed people to go hungry. In late December, concerned that if the blacks did not plant a new cotton crop they would have to be sustained by government charity, Chase sent Edward L. Pierce, a Boston attorney and close personal friend, to Port Royal to investigate the contraband problem. The secretary had confidence in Pierce, who had been stationed at Fortress Monroe and supervised the contrabands crossing Union lines in that area. Because Pierce did not leave for South Carolina until January 13, 1862, responsibility for the contrabands remained the purview of Du Pont and Sherman.[33]

Following the successful operation to seize and occupy Port Royal Sound, the Atlantic Blockading Squadron conducted a joint expedition with the Union Army to attack Roanoke Island, North Carolina, in early 1862. As Roanoke Island guarded the entrance of two major sounds off the southern coast, Union strategists considered it a valuable target. The arrival of large numbers of federal warships off the coast of North Carolina created additional opportunities for interaction between naval personnel and African Americans. Only twelve miles long and about three miles wide, this low, swampy island had been fortified by the Confederates on its western side with three sand forts and some smaller batteries to the east. The Navy Department assigned the mission of conveying

Major General Ambrose Burnside's force of 13,000 troops to Flag Officer Louis M. Goldsborough's flotilla of sixty-seven ships.

On January 12, 1862, the Burnside expedition sailed for Hatteras Inlet, but a winter storm scattered many of the army transports and wrecked three, forcing Goldsborough's vessels to remain at the inlet until the expedition had reassembled. It was there that many Union soldiers and sailors encountered escaped black slaves or contrabands for the first time. John C. Abbot wrote, "Quite a number of contrabands, some fifty in all, had now made their appearance on shore at the camps. Through a thousand hair breath escapes they had made their way to the Union flag. They were all intensely loyal, and were kindly received." Abbot described one particularly harrowing escape: "Five or six came down the Sound in an open boat. Their clothing was in rags, their bodies emaciate with hunger, and they had suffered all but death from the exposure on the land [and] on the sea." The refugees had escaped from one of the northern counties in North Carolina. "For weeks they struggled through the woods, traveling mostly by night, and living upon roots and herbs," Abbot wrote. "Reaching Albemarle Sound, they seized a boat which they found upon shore, and paddled down the eastern side of Roanoke Island to the fleet. They were fired on frequently by the rebel sentries, but ran the gauntlet in safety."[34]

Goldsborough's ships went on to support the army's attack on Roanoke Island and remained offshore, attracting more African Americans bent on escaping to freedom. Lookouts on navy blockade ships had to be on constant alert for rebel blockade runners, and their vigilance proved advantageous for refugees trying to escape in small boats. Abbot offered one example: "On the morning of February 4th," he wrote, "a small sailboat was seen far away in the horizon, and a gun-boat was sent in pursuit of it. Nineteen patriotic negroes were found in the boat, who had escaped from the enemy, and were seeking refuge on board the Union fleet."[35]

Although some of the refugees told Union authorities they had found and commandeered small boats or watercraft, others admitted they had stolen the boats. In a diary entry dated January 31, 1862, D. L. Day noted the arrival of a small schooner: "A boat went out and met her, she contained seven darkies who said they stole the schooner and left in her from Roanoke Island. They were put aboard the steamer *S. R. Spaulding*, and the little schooner hitched astern. They can probably give some valuable information in regard to affairs on the island."[36]

Encouraged by the capture of Roanoke Island, Union commanders decided to exploit this victory by seizing and occupying Fernandina, Florida, and other points along the southern coast. These Union operations during the first half of 1862 caused considerable disruption for local blacks, but it gave hundreds more an opportunity to flee to freedom. Union troops in effect "liberated" many slaves when they arrived to occupy towns or camped near plantations and villages. All these joint army-navy operations involved support from Union Navy vessels, which convoyed army transports to their objectives, bombarded rebel batteries, provided gunfire support while the troops landed, and continued to support them once ashore. The presence of the Union Navy during joint operations afforded contrabands access to gunboats and other vessels lying in rivers or near the shore, and many seized the opportunity to escape from bondage. When Union gunboats crossed the bar into the St. John's River in March 1862, for example, "the sight of the stars and bars fluttering from the stern was signal of hope for families of enslaved and free blacks," writes historian Daniel L. Schafer.[37]

By the end of March 1862, Union forces had occupied Fernandina and St. Augustine, Florida; Brunswick, Georgia; Hilton Head, Port Royal, and Beaufort, South Carolina; Roanoke Island and Hampton Roads, Virginia; and the strategic port and rail hub at New Bern, North Carolina. As they had in other Confederate towns, the African American population of New Bern greeted the arriving Union troops warmly. Commander Stephen C. Rowan's fourteen Union vessels convoyed 11,000 federal troops, including marines, to New Bern on March 12, 1862. As they approached the town, D. L. Day could see that it was on fire, and "the terror-stricken inhabitants [were] fleeing in every direction. The negroes were holding a grand jubilee, some of them praying and in their rude way thanking God for their deliverance; others, in their wild delight, were dancing and singing, while others, with an eye to the main chance, were pillaging the store and dwellings." After securing the forts guarding the town, Rowan landed the Union troops, and a quick-thinking Lieutenant Charles Flusser organized some local citizens, black and white, and doused the flames.[38]

Troops occupying New Bern quickly encountered other local African Americans. One correspondent wrote from New Bern, "Friday night, or rather afternoon, some seventy contrabands arrived at the wharf, near our house, coming up in a boat from near the place of the fight last Sunday night. Such another set of mortals I never saw—all sexes and all ages, dressed up in all sort of clothing. Some women decked with coats and hats for want of female clothing, and nearly all the women toting a baby." Writing to the *Boston Evening Press*, this correspondent described an encounter with one little five-year-old boy who said he had run away from his master. "I asked him what he ran away for, not thinking the little fellow could realize anything, when he answered, promptly, 'Kase, I didn't want to be a slave—I'se want to be free.'" The slaves understood affairs pretty well, the correspondent told readers. "The people have told the slaves most horrible stories about the Yankees, but the negroes say, 'Oh Lor, massa, dunna' bleve word day say—we knowed dey lied—wee's been praying to de Lord dat Yankees might come.'"[39]

The advance of General George B. McClellan's army during the Peninsular Campaign in Virginia in May and June 1862 also created a tide of refugees. "Numerous refugees and contrabands are coming in daily, who report that the main body of the rebel army have fallen back to Richmond," a reporter informed the *Christian Recorder* on April 19, 1862, when Union forces occupied the north bank of the Rappahannock River. "As soon as the Yankee got here," wrote Joseph Lawson, a freedman living in Fredericksburg, "the slaves began to run away from their mistresses and masters by hundreds. . . . Fifteen miles from here they got to the Potomac, and the Yankee gunboats would take them right to Washington." In a letter to his brother, one soldier described the arrival of hundreds of contrabands who crossed the Rappahannock River daily to reach the Union encampment near Fredericksburg, "where they feel safe, even though Secessionists had spread rumors that the Union soldiers would sell African Americans to Cuba to pay the expenses of the war." As they advanced up the peninsula, soldiers of McClellan's Army of the Potomac passed many homes abandoned by their inhabitants, except for "very bitter" women and slaves. One signal corpsman wrote that the slaves "are in miserable condition & the huts they live in would not be considered up north for animals."[40]

Union naval vessels conducting operations in the James and York rivers in support of McClellan's campaign attracted runaways as well. Their presence near plantations and villages along the riverbanks allowed numerous groups of contrabands to make their way out to federal vessels. In letters to his wife, George Geer, a fireman on the USS *Monitor,* often mentioned the arrival of black runaways. Writing from off City Point on May 20, 1862, Geer told her, "The Counterbands come of [f] to us every night but we send them back in most cases, as we have no room for them." Although the *Monitor*'s commanding officer, Lieutenant William N. Jeffers, could not offer the contrabands more than temporary shelter, the crew did their best to welcome and assist the fugitives. According to Geer, "While I am writing you we have two men and two Woman, all of them young, not over twenty two or three, in the Engine Room, drying their Cloaths as it Rains very hard. They came from a Plantation some five miles up the River."[41]

William Keeler, the *Monitor*'s paymaster, also wrote of black run-aways coming to the ship. "This time a boat full of men, women, & children that had been driven out of City Point, when it was shelled by our vessels & had taken refuge with a good many others on the opposite side of the river . . . they were driven off by the overseer of the plantation." In this letter to his wife, Anna, Keeler expressed a deep compassion for the refugees. "They were in a most miserable plight, having no shelter from the pouring rain of last night & today. What few clothes they had was soaked through & muddy. No homes, no friends, nothing to eat, no where to go, their few earthly possession were tied up in bundles & appeared to be nothing but a few ragged clothes." Jeffers sent them aboard the *Stepping Stones* to spend the night, Keeler wrote, "and to get something to eat." Explaining that the *Monitor*'s cramped conditions prevented Jeffers from taking on these refugees, Keeler continued, "We see a good many such sights which although they excite our sympathy & compassion we cannot to any extent relieve. Most of the contrabands appear bright & intelligent & many of them seem to be well posted in the events of the war in this vicinity." As they had in New Bern and elsewhere, southern slave owners living along the banks of the James River had tried to discourage their slaves from fleeing by spreading rumors that the Yankees would send the slaves to Cuba. One of the contrabands picked up by the *Monitor*, Keeler wrote, "said Massa Carter had told all his slaves that they might go with the Yankees if they wanted to, they would be taken off to Cuba & sold, & advised them to stay on the plantation where there was land enough for them, & raise their children."[42]

Following the Army of the Potomac's retreat from Malvern Hill on July 1, 1862, more blacks sought safety within Union lines near Harrison's Landing. They gathered in a camp near the James River, hoping that the federal gunboats in the river would protect them along with the thousands of Union soldiers recuperating from the heavy fighting of the Seven Days' Battle. For six long weeks, sweltering in the ninety-degree heat of the Virginia summer, plagued by mosquitoes and flies, McClellan's troops remained encamped at Harrison's Landing, protected by the ironclads and gunboats of the James River Flotilla. Then, on July 31, 1862, Confederate artillery opened fire on Harrison's Landing, smashing into the steamers and vessels at anchor and into the camp of the Third Pennsylvania Cavalry. According to Private Robert Sneden, "The contraband camp caught it also, and Negro women, children, and darkies ran in all directions for the woods, stampeding the horses and mules with their yells of affright." Hearing the gunfire, the *Wachusetts* and *Cimarron* steamed back to Harrison's Landing and in twenty minutes drove off the enemy and silenced the guns. The following day, Sneden wrote, "During the attack last night ten men and thirteen horses were killed, besides fifteen more wounded, some mortally. Several contrabands were also killed and wounded."[43]

On August 3, 1862, President Lincoln ordered McClellan to withdraw and join forces with General Pope's army preparing to move on Richmond from northern Virginia. A disappointed McClellan delayed the withdrawal as long as he could, but on August 14, 1862, the first troops marched off to Yorktown. At Harrison's Landing the numerous contrabands who had gathered there under Union protection watched the army break camp and feared for their future. However, according to Sneden, federal vessels took many of them off. Describing the departure of the Army of the Potomac, he wrote: "All the vessels and steamers weighed anchor and got under weigh about 8 P.M. . . . All the sick had been got aboard safely. Then came vessels and steamers of all kinds and sizes carrying horses, forage, stores, ammunition, tents and all the baggage of the army. Several hundred contrabands, with women and children, were also on the vessels, and by 10 P.M. the landing was deserted. The fleet moved slowly down river." The following day, William Keeler awoke on board the USS *Monitor* to find the river all but empty of schooners and steamers. "Contrabands, wagons, & artillery all were gone & nothing left to mark the spot till now occupied by McClelland's large army with its immense amount of material, but a smooth, extensive plain of yellow dust," he wrote.[44]

On August 19, 1862, Commander Maxwell Woodhull wrote to James River Flotilla commander Charles Wilkes, informing him that the army had passed the river and that the Confederates occupied McClellan's old camp at Harrison's Landing. All appeared to be well, he noted, except that "there are now on James Island upward of 100 contrabands, men, women, and children. They are in a great state of alarm, fearful that they are to be abandoned." Then Woodhull asked, "Shall I send them to Fortress Monroe in the empty coal schooner?" Although Wilkes's reply is not in the official records, on August 28, 1862, Woodhull reported that the *Yankee* had left him in charge of a small pleasure sloop, the *Day Book*, which had nine or ten contrabands on board. Woodhull retained the sloop but sent the contrabands to Jamestown Island for the evening. The next morning he received a note from Colonel Totten explaining that he had lent the *Day Book* to a contraband named Monroe to take the contrabands to Fortress Monroe. So Woodhull sent Monroe off downriver with his cargo of former slaves.[45]

The promise of freedom lured enterprising and courageous slaves out to Union ships of the South Atlantic Blockading Squadron as well. Commanders dutifully noted their arrival in official reports and occasionally included the contrabands' names and bits of information about their escape. When six contrabands in a rickety canoe arrived at the pilot boat *Blunt* on June 5, 1862, for example, Commander John B. Marchand, the senior officer present, told Du Pont: "Their names are Alexander, Robert, Samuel Quamer, Tony Duhar, Monday, and Thomas Hamilton. Some of them represent that they have been hiding in the woods for a period of sixteen and nineteen months. Their owners reside at Charleston, but they are field hands." Seeing soldiers on Bull's Island, the refugees had left their hiding place that morning, Marchand explained, because friends had told them "that bloodhounds would be sent after them." He now had the contrabands on board his ship and informed Du Pont that he intended to enlist those who could be useful and send the others to Port Royal.[46]

In some instances, Union naval officers offered slaves "liberated" in raids or expeditions a choice about accompanying them. *Commodore Morris*'s paymaster, Calvin Hutchinson, described one instance. In June 1863 *Commodore Morris, Commodore Jones, Winnimissimet,* and the army gunboat *Smith Briggs* went up the Mattapony River to Walkerton with infantry troops to find and destroy a rebel foundry. In the process, the expedition liberated almost 200 slaves, who then waited for transportation downriver. As Hutchinson sat on the grass eating hardtack, "A little colored boy . . . naked save for a fringed belt of rags about his waist laid there on his belly playing with the Colonel's beautiful sword which he had unbuckled and cast off." A great number of men, women, and children began hurrying to the boats in the river. Hutchinson asked the boy, "'Do you want to go on board the gunboat?' 'Yes Massa!' he answered. 'Why?' I said. 'Kase I want to git free?' was his answer." Next, Hutchinson asked the little boy why he wished to be free. "The child said, 'Massa John Toliver sends me after soft crabs and when I don't get the soft crabs he beats me.' A perfectly good reason from a child who was bad sometimes." After dark Hutchinson went back to his gunboat, where he found a large number of blacks of both sexes and all ages. "Next morning I found among them this little boy who had exchanged his rags for a new suit of tow cloth shirt and trousers and followed me off to the river and boat. I had to leave him at Greelyville near Yorktown with the rest of his people."[47]

Slaves continued to flee from plantations along the coast, but some also came from as far as 200 miles inland. When asked by the American Freedman's Inquiry Commission about contrabands in his area, Captain C. B. Wilder, the superintendent of contrabands at Fortress Monroe, testified, "They come here from all about, from Richmond and 200 miles off in North Carolina." According to Wilder, contrabands at Fortress Monroe managed to communicate with others still in slavery, and some newly freed slaves went back to rescue others still in bondage. He told the commission, "we have men here who have gone back 200 miles." Wilder's testimony offered some interesting observations about the slaves' reasons for escaping. "When I got the feelings of these people," he told the commission, "I found they were not afraid of slaveholders. They said there was nobody on the plantations but women and they were not afraid of them." Hundreds had left their wives and families behind, and he asked them why. They told him "they had heard these stories and wanted to come and see how it was. 'I am going back again after my wife,' some of them have said, 'when I have earned a little money.'" When Wilder asked them if they were afraid of returning, they answered, "No, I know the way." As he explained to the commission, "Colored men will help colored men and they will work along the paths and get through." Before the war, he argued, many slaves were afraid to risk escaping, but now "the white people have nearly all gone, the blood hounds are not there now to hunt them and they are not afraid." Some told Wilder, "We are not afraid of being carried back, if we are, we can get away again."[48]

In addition to simply wishing to escape from bondage, to free their wives and families, or to avoid the increasingly harsh conditions in the South, slaves sought sanctuary on Union vessels or in Union-occupied areas to avoid being used by the Confederacy—either as servants for their owners, who had joined the military, or as laborers to build fortifications and other defenses. From the beginning of the war, the Confederacy pressed slaves into duty as laborers, and in February 1864 President Jefferson Davis signed an act authorizing the employment of up to 20,000 slaves in noncombat duties with the rebel armies. The Confederacy persistently refused, however, to allow blacks to serve as soldiers until March 1865.

In early 1864, Rear Admiral John A. Dahlgren's blockade vessels in Florida welcomed numerous contrabands and other refugees, including whites, fleeing from conscription. When the *Oleander* arrived at Port Royal from the South carrying more than a hundred refugees, some fifty of them white men, women, and children from the upper part of the St. John's River, the commanding officer at Port Royal informed Dahlgren that these white refugees had fled to avoid conscription. "The rest are contrabands from various places, many of them old men, women,

and children, also one white woman, sent up by *Braziliera* as a dangerous person." Lacking a place for them, the commander at Port Royal
asked the authorities at Hilton Head to receive them but added, "A hundred more are reported at the St. John's, awaiting an opportunity for this
place." The admiral then asked Secretary Welles for instructions on what
to do with them, noting, "My general practice now is to turn them over
to the military authorities."[49]

As he had in the past, Welles instructed Dahlgren to turn over refugees and rebel deserters to Union military authorities. Although he did
not specify where to send the contrabands, common practice dictated
that they be sent to Beaufort or to Port Royal, the South Atlantic Blockading Squadron's logistical and repair facility and a popular liberty port
for Union Navy crews. Contrabands taken from federal blockaders to
Port Royal joined other contrabands, 500 of whom were working to produce cotton on area plantations owned by Bostonians.[50]

The threat of conscription prompted many southerners to flee, but as
the Union blockade tightened and wartime shortages of food and clothing became increasingly burdensome, growing numbers of both whites
and blacks sought to escape the harsh conditions in the South. In fact,
on rare occasions, white refugees sought safety on Union vessels and
brought their slaves with them. One of the first escaped slaves seen by
Dr. Samuel Boyer when the *Fernandina* arrived in St. Simon's Sound
came out with her mistress, the wife of a rebel soldier. "A poor forlorn
being in the shape of a female with female child and two slaves (now
free) escaped from Secesh and came to our fleet," he wrote in his diary
on January 14, 1863. The woman told Boyer she could not bear the hard
times in the Confederacy any longer. According to Boyer, *Fernandina's*
officers took up a purse for her and "also supplied her with food and rai-
ment. As soon as 'Jack Tar' heard it, they (the boys) also made up a purse,
not wishing to be outdone by no one as regards charity."

Conditions in Savannah, Georgia, and along the southern coast continued to deteriorate. When another group of contrabands arrived on
board the *Fernandina* in late April, Boyer wrote, "Starvation stares the
Rebels in the face." Hunger and forced labor had caused one of the
men, whom he described as the "smartest one of the party," to run away
from rebel pickets once before. "The first time he was caught and for
his trouble was favoured with 70 lashes on his bare back, after which he
was hired out by his mistress at $15 per month to a man to cut rails, who
compelled him to split 1,000 rails a week." Unhappy with being a rail
splitter and being given nothing to eat but cornbread, the man ran away
again. "He says that his mistress told him that as soon as he came to the

Yankees, so soon would they put a harness, prepared for that purpose on him and compel him to drag cannons and wagons about like horses, and whenever they found that they could not work them (the slaves) any longer, why, then they would sell them and send them to Cuba." But the contraband told the men on the *Fernandina* that he "knew better all the time and that she was only trying to fool him so that he would not run away." Boyer wrote, "He as well as his companions are 'bressing de Lord' for helping them to escape—and 'Tank God, we are free!' etc. etc." Because the *Fernandina* had no room for these refugees, the commander sent them to St. Simon's and then to the *Keystone State.* "From there I suppose they will be shipped North, where they can earn their daily bread and live like human beings and be treated like their free colored brethren of the North are," Boyer noted.[51]

This almost continuous stream of refugees and contrabands did not abate as the Civil War entered its fourth year. Just three weeks into 1864, two men arrived at the USS *Morse* off Yorktown with a permit from General Butler to go to Mathews County to get their families. Butler had requested that a gunboat be sent along on the expedition "for protection," so the *Morse,* carrying 100 soldiers of the U.S. Sixth Infantry Regiment at Yorktown, got under way the next morning, accompanied by the *Crusader* and the *Samuel Rotan.* They went upriver and anchored in Mobjack Bay at 9 A.M. They then lowered all their boats and disembarked the troops. All the officers in charge of boats had orders not to allow their crews to land. Lieutenant Commander Babcock reported, "Received on board three families of refugees and 9 contrabands, in all 25 persons." The next day they returned to Yorktown with their passengers, including the nine blacks. Although Babcock did not specify, the nine contrabands were probably slaves or servants belonging to the Union families.[52]

Not all fugitive slaves who risked escaping to freedom on Union vessels succeeded. Examples of failed escape attempts are few and far between in the official records, but on February 2, 1864, the senior officer present off Wilmington, Commander James Madison Frailey, reported one such incident to Admiral Lee. "Last evening, as the steamer *Governor Buckingham* was going toward her station," he wrote, "a small boat was descried making toward her, containing a number of male and female contrabands." When *Governor Buckingham's* skipper, Acting Volunteer Lieutenant W. G. Saltonstall, saw a boat off the starboard bow signaling to attract attention, he stopped the engine, threw the contrabands a line, and hauled them alongside the ship. "The sea was rough from southward and eastward," he wrote, "and the boat striking against the ship's side, and being very rotten, immediately swamped and sank." Saltonstall dropped an anchor, lowered his boats, and picked up "4 men, 2 women, and 3 children, named as follows: Peter Smith, Forten Kirby, Philip Smith, Joe Holden, Theresa Hewitt, Phillis Holan, and three children. One of the latter was dead when brought on board." Sadly, *Governor Buckingham's* boat crews could not rescue all the fugitives. "I regret that 1 female and 3 children were unfortunately drowned," Frailey told Lee. The contrabands informed Saltonstall that they had escaped on Sunday evening from Shallotte Inlet and that another boat had started out at the same time but had probably been captured. The lieutenant intended to send the contrabands north by the supply ship *New Berne*. In his report to Lee, Commander Frailey expressed the opinion that one or two of the men were "very intelligent" and could provide information on the rebel coast guard.[53]

Another attempt to rescue contraband families that ended in tragedy took place in September 1864. African American government employees from Fort Monroe and hospitals in the Hampton, Virginia, area appealed to General Edward Wild to be allowed leaves of absence to go to Smithfield and rescue their families from bondage. The general had no boats but offered to send a captain and fifteen dismounted cavalry troops to assist them. After gathering sailboats for the trip up Smithfield Creek, the contrabands landed at Smithfield at night and attempted to bring off the women and children. When more refugees than expected showed up, the men packed them in extra boats they picked up there and towed them along, but three miles downstream a force of about 100 irregular rebel troops with dogs, rifles, and shotguns attacked the contrabands, killing one man and one woman and wounding another woman. The contrabands rowed over to the bank and scattered into the marshes. When the rear boats came up bearing Captain Whiteman's soldiers, they landed but discovered they were outnumbered and barely escaped with their lives. General Wild did not know how many more of the contrabands had been wounded in the attack, noting that three of the soldiers were missing in the woods and marshes.[54]

In the fall of 1864 a new wave of black refugees began making their way east, following the army of General William Tecumseh Sherman as it advanced from Atlanta toward Savannah in what may be the largest voluntary exodus of African American slaves during the war. In mid-December, after Union forces laid siege to Savannah, Confederate defenders withdrew, and on December 21, 1864, Sherman's men entered the city. According to Charles P. Ware, the thousands of African Americans who had trailed Sherman through Georgia to Savannah followed the army northward, many of them heading for the Port Royal area. "They are said to be an excellent set of people, more intelligent than most here," he wrote, "and are eager for work. They will get distributed onto the plantations before a great while." Referring to them as "the Georgia refugees," Harriet Ware wrote on January 6, 1865: "Miss Towne gave us quite an interesting account of the Georgia refugees that have been sent to the Village. The hardships they underwent to march with the army are fearful, and the children often gave out and were left by their mothers exhausted and dying by the roadside and in the fields." One couple had twelve children. Each parent carried one child and tied the rest, she wrote, "all together by the hands and brought them all off safely, a march of hundreds of miles." Harriet Ware also noted that "the men have all been put to work in the quartermaster's department or have gone into the army, and the families are being distributed where they can find places for them."[55]

In February 1865, Sherman sent 7,000 contrabands to Beaufort. "Many of them are from far up Georgia, and a long, weary and sorrowful tramp they have had. Many of them, with little children, have not brought a thing with them, and have most miserable covering. Bales of clothing can be disposed of among them," Sherman told General Rufus Saxton. In turn, Saxton noted, "They were utterly destitute of blankets, stockings, or shoes; and among the 7000 there were not fifty articles in the shape of pots or kettles, or other utensils for cooking, no axes, very few coverings for many heads, and children wrapped in the only article not worn in some form by the parents."[56]

The thousands of African American men, women, and children who followed Sherman's army to Savannah added to the already large number residing in special camps established for contrabands, as well as those working or living on plantations abandoned by white owners. Other contrabands had gathered in or near Union-occupied towns such as New Bern, Port Royal, Beaufort, and Fernandina. In a report made on August 1, 1865, to Rufus Saxton, Freedmen's Bureau agent H. G. Judd noted that since January 1 of that year, 17,000 freedmen had arrived at Beaufort, although many had gone elsewhere by August. Judd also wrote, "Many of those who followed Genl. Sherman from Georgia, suffering from the toilsome march, exposure and insufficient clothing & food died soon after reaching Port Royal, leaving friendless and unprotected orphans, of this class a large number subsist we hardly know how, mainly in Beaufort." In addition, by October 1864 the District of Columbia had absorbed, by one account, 40,000 emancipated slaves. "Most of them are refugees from Virginia. Every new success of Grant, and every fresh advance of Sheridan, adds to their number," J. M. M'Kim wrote to the secretary of the Edinburgh Ladies Emancipation Society. "This city is filled with them."[57]

These new refugees had been liberated by Sherman's army, but the many African Americans, slave and free, who made their way to Union Navy vessels during the Civil War did so on their own initiative or in coordinated group efforts by traveling hundreds of miles, in some cases, from the interior. They escaped along trails that may have been known for decades, assisted along the way by other blacks or even sympathetic whites, often hiding in swamps and other isolated areas or in towns before finding or stealing small watercraft to row or sail out to Union vessels offshore. As the war progressed, more freed slaves risked recapture to go back to rescue their families. Others made it to the shoreline and either signaled to Union ships or were sighted by ships' lookouts and rescued. The presence of Union Navy blockade ships near shore or on patrol in southern rivers and creeks gave African Americans in the South an unprecedented opportunity to flee their masters. From naval officers and enlisted men's reports and correspondence, it appears that many slaves expected to be welcomed and taken on board Union vessels. They sought freedom for various reasons—to avoid being sold or conscripted as laborers for the Confederate war effort, to escape brutal masters and punishment or harsh wartime conditions, or to locate friends and relatives who had already escaped—but most simply wanted to be free. Many slaves discounted their owners' threats that if they fled to Union lines the Yankees would send them to Cuba. Although these journeys to freedom could be arduous and dangerous, and some ended in failure, many blacks yearning for freedom obviously considered seeking refuge on Union vessels simpler, less dangerous, and therefore more appealing than prewar escape routes. Furthermore, many may have decided that, given the war with the Confederacy, Yankee sailors might be more willing to take them in and offer them refuge.[58]

Initially, however, many Union Navy commanders looked on these runaways with suspicion. They doubted the escaped slaves' loyalty to the Union and, required to adhere to the First Confiscation Act, had to ascertain whether the slaves had run away from disloyal, rebel masters or masters who were still loyal to the Union. Naval officers, especially those serving in Florida, walked a fine line when determining whether to return slaves to so-called loyal pro-Union owners. Commanders' attitudes toward black or white runaways varied, sometimes according to race, but more often because refugees threatened to consume the ships' limited supplies of food and water and added to shipboard crowding.

Clearly, this influx of runaways caught the Union Navy by surprise. Tasked with establishing and then maintaining a blockade of the southern coast, Union Navy officers and enlisted men expected to devote their time and energy to watching for and intercepting rebel blockade runners going into and out of Confederate ports. The sudden appearance of runaway blacks clamoring for protection compelled commanding officers to expand their mission. In making decisions about accepting these refugees, feeding and providing for them, enlisting some as crewmen, and sending others ashore, Union commanders and their crews found themselves playing an important role in what one historian called "a unique experiment in social equality."[59]

Although often moved by the refugees' plight, commanding officers were not always eager or prepared to participate in the effort to rescue, shelter, feed, and protect so many refugees, including women and children, and some sought to send the contrabands to other vessels or ashore. Sailors' letters and diaries suggest that many sympathetic Union sailors welcomed the contrabands and tried to accommodate them, temporarily, on board their vessels. Though not, for the most part, abolitionists or vehement antislavery men, these Union bluejackets admired the contrabands for their persistence and courage and were shocked and appalled by their stories of slavery. Many sailors, born in northern states and largely unfamiliar with African Americans, adjusted quickly to their new role as "liberators," befriending the contrabands, teaching them to read, and offering the new arrivals clothing and food. The navy often enlisted the able-bodied males and sent the others to Fernandina, Port Royal, Beaufort, or Hampton Roads or shipped them north to New York, Boston, or Philadelphia. Once on board Union gunboats, the contrabands were technically "free," but once these newly freed people were put ashore in Union-occupied areas or sent north, most if not all of them were dependent on the U.S. government for sustenance, employment, and protection.

CHAPTER 3
CONTRABAND CAMPS

*I am much interested in the contrabands within our lines. They tell
me there are from eight to ten thousand. They are daily increasing at
Edisto, and I have induced the general to send a regiment to Edisto.*
—Samuel F. Du Pont

For thousands of contrabands, many of them former plantation slaves,
freedom meant the sudden loss of regular sustenance from their white
masters. Some possessed valuable skills as carpenters, mechanics, barbers, boatmen, and the like, but the majority of slaves had spent their
lives as household servants or field hands dependent on their masters for
food, provisions, and clothing. Slaves often tended their own small garden plots, fished or collected oysters for their own use, or earned money
by trading items or hiring themselves out. When they fled to safety on
Union warships, however, most arrived with few provisions or household items and had to be fed, clothed, and protected. Although Union
naval officers welcomed runaways on their vessels, they worried that if
kept on board for any length of time, these fugitive slaves might exhaust
the ships' supplies. Commanding officers preferred to retain the able-
bodied male contrabands as crew members and put the others ashore.

Union operations along the southern coast in 1861 created opportunities for hundreds of slaves to seek freedom either on Union ships
or in areas occupied by Union forces. When General T. W. Sherman's
men occupied Port Royal, South Carolina, in November 1861, Hilton
Head Island and Beaufort became refuges for hundreds of contrabands,
who joined the thousands of slaves abandoned at Port Royal and the
nearby Sea Islands by their white owners. Now, in effect, free, these
former slaves soon became the responsibility of the government. This
timely arrival of so many fugitive slaves at Port Royal proved a god-

send to Sherman, however, who willingly employed them as laborers to unload supplies and provisions at Port Royal, where the lack of adequate wharfage forced his troops to unload ships through the surf across the beaches. Sherman's quartermasters also needed laborers to build roads, erect warehouses and other buildings, and construct defenses. To shelter and provide for these former slaves, Sherman ordered temporary "contraband camps" set up at Beaufort and on Hilton Head for those now employed as laborers for the Union, and he assigned responsibility for them to the chief quartermaster, Captain Rufus Saxton.[1]

In addition to the hundreds of slaves who had fled their masters, an estimated 8,000 blacks remained on plantations in areas now occupied by Union forces. As "de facto freed people" no longer dependent on their old masters, most were willing to work for their former drivers, but others were not averse to helping themselves to provisions in pantries and storehouses. Furthermore, having been abandoned by their former owners, hundreds of these newly freed slaves now faced a winter without adequate food and clothing. The superintendent of the contraband camp on Hilton Head Island, Barnard K. Lee Jr., confirmed this fact. Testifying in 1863 before the American Freedman's Inquiry Commission, Lee recalled, "I commenced with 60 or 70 at my camp, male and female. They were very destitute and were mainly slaves from Hilton Head & St. Helena islands. They came in rapidly in parties of 10, 20, 50, and 100."[2]

In February 1862 Edward L. Pierce reported to Treasury Secretary Salmon P. Chase that 600 contrabands resided at the Hilton Head camp, 279 of them from the mainland, 77 from Hilton Head Island, 62 from nearby Pinckney Island, 38 from St. Helena Island, 8 from Port Royal, 7 from Spring, and 1 from Danfuskie. An estimated 600 more freed people had gathered at Beaufort. Shortly after the occupation of Port Royal, Lee was instructed to assure those contrabands hired as laborers that they would be paid "a reasonable sum" for their work. The government issued the contrabands blankets and clothing captured from the rebels, fed the women and children without charge, and built what Pierce's report called "commodious barracks" for them, with a guard to protect their quarters. Guards had become necessary in the wake of reports that Union soldiers on foraging expeditions had taken food and livestock from the newly freed slaves, sometimes looting and pillaging their possessions and terrifying many. In his report, Pierce expressed concern about the soldiers and sailors mingling with the newly freed people, explaining that he had met with Flag Officer Samuel F. Du Pont about the situation. Du Pont had issued an order that "no boats from any of the ships of the squadron can be permitted to land anywhere but at Bay Point and Hilton Head, without a pass from the fleet Captain." Du Pont had also instructed his commanders, Pierce explained, to "give special attention to all intercourse between the men under their command and the various plantations in their vicinity."[3]

Not all the former slaves on the South Carolina Sea Islands managed to reach the newly established contraband camps on Hilton Head and St. Helena, and some, eager to find a new life, sought assistance from Union Navy gunboats. The first instance came less than a month after the Union occupation of Port Royal. In early December 1861 Sherman informed Du Pont that he had decided to occupy Otter Island, Tybee Island, and St. Helena Sound but had been unable to determine the exact location of a Confederate battery or the number of rebels on the islands. He asked Du Pont to send several gunboats for a reconnaissance. Agreeing with Sherman that the occupation of St. Helena Sound would be a valuable move, Du Pont ordered Commander Percival Drayton to take four vessels to St. Helena Sound to assist the army in taking Otter Island. Drayton, in the USS *Pawnee,* promptly set sail with his little flotilla and anchored off Otter Island, an isle of dunes, forest, and marsh in St. Helena Sound across from Edisto beach at the tip of Edisto Island, about forty-five miles south of Charleston. Soon after the *Pawnee*'s arrival, several blacks came out to the ship and informed Drayton that they had seen Confederate troops up the Ashepoo River near Mosquito Creek. Twice the commander took the *Vixen, Unadilla,* and *Isaac Smith* up the Ashepoo, which runs between Hutchinson's Island and Otter Island, in search of the reported rebels. The second time, Drayton landed on Hutchinson's Island and discovered that the rebels had burned all the slaves' houses, overseers' homes, and outbuildings. The rebels had tried to drive the blacks off, even shooting at some of them. They had also picked the cotton. "The scene was one of complete desolation," Drayton wrote to Du Pont. "The smoking ruins and cowering figures . . . of those negroes who still instinctively clung to their hearthstones, although there was no longer shelter for them, presented a most melancholy sight, the impression of which made even stronger by the piteous wailing of the poor creatures, a large portion of whom consisted of the old and decrepit." Drayton then took his little flotilla on to explore the Coosaw River. With just the shallow-draft *Vixen,* he went up to the entrance of Beaufort Creek and anchored off a plantation. Going ashore, Drayton learned that the cotton house had been burned and many of the slaves taken away. On the beach, however, he found numerous black refugees from Hutchinson's Island lined up with all their household effects. "Some of them begging to go to Otter Island, saying that they had neither shelter nor food," he wrote. Drayton felt compassion for the homeless former slaves and took them with him, depositing 140 of them on Otter Island—in effect, establishing a colony of contrabands. When the *Pawnee* steamed back to Port Royal, Drayton left his fledgling contraband colony in the hands of Lieutenant James W. A. Nicholson, who remained in St. Helena Sound with the *Dale* and *Isaac Smith*.[4]

Later, in January 1862, Drayton defended his actions toward the fugitive slaves in a letter to his brother Heyward. "You seem to think I am not sound on the nigger, [but] . . . if you will look at the reports of the secretary of the navy, you will find that we are directed to take charge of and protect refugees from the insurgents without regard to color, and this is all I have ever done." Drayton went on to say, "The fact is that when the poor creatures come in to me, frightened to death from having been hunted down and shot at and I know if I send them away it will be merely to expose them to a continuation of the same treatment, I cannot enter cooly into discussion of the legal points of the question, and am obliged when in sight of a mother wailing over the loss of her child to look upon them as persons not things."[5]

And so, although it never set out to establish a colony of former slaves on Otter Island, in December 1861 the Union Navy found itself quite unexpectedly responsible for the care and protection of more than 100 contrabands. The task of supervising them fell to Nicholson, who immediately set out to find provisions for the new colony. On December 10, 1861, Nicholson took forty men and some marines in the *Dale*'s boats, followed by twenty contrabands in boats, up the river to reconnoiter and to obtain a supply of potatoes. The expedition also yielded some corn, a corn mill, two horses, and one cart, he wrote, "to make the contrabands more comfortable." The following day Nicholson went ashore with Lieutenant W. T. Truxtun and several officers from each vessel and formally turned the fort (which he had named Fort Drayton in honor of Percival Drayton), the contrabands, and Otter Island over to Union Army garrison troops under the command of a Colonel Welsh. The navy's responsibility for the protection of Otter Island did not end with the transfer of command ashore, however. Two days later Nicholson again went up the Ashepoo River in the *Isaac Smith*, taking the *Dale*'s marines with him. After the marines landed to make a reconnaissance of Fenwick Island, Nicholson traveled upriver as far as Mosquito Creek. Spotting several mounted men at a house previously ascertained to be rebel headquarters, he ordered a seven-inch shell fired from the *Smith*, which dispersed the rebels. Nicholson then landed the marines, who burned the rebel headquarters.[6]

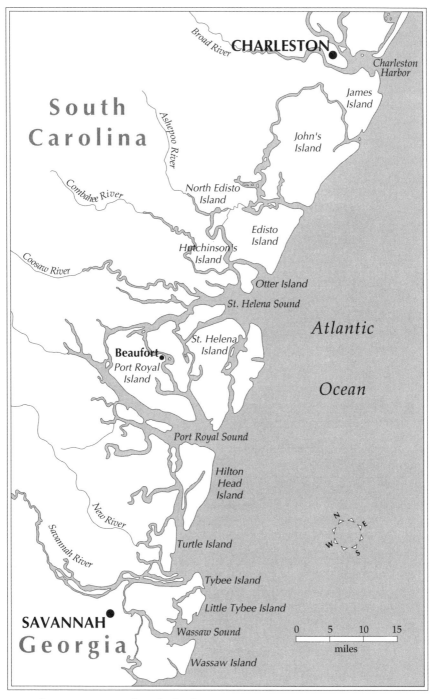

Coast between Savannah and Charleston

Nicholson's aggressive patrolling allowed the Otter Island contraband colony to remain relatively free of rebel harassment. Nevertheless, Union officials were concerned that Confederate troops might be camped in the area and might try to harm the contrabands. In mid-December Du Pont ordered Drayton to make a reconnaissance up the Edisto River with the *Pawnee*, *Vixen*, and *Seneca*. When they crossed the bar into the river, Drayton reported that he could "plainly perceive fortifications ahead, on Edisto Island, distant a mile and a half." He had been told that enemy troops occupied the fortifications, but when the *Pawnee* and *Seneca* fired at the works, they received no reply. "On landing I found the fort, which was entirely deserted, to consist of two redoubts with five guns each," he told Du Pont. "The guns, as the negroes had informed me, had been removed toward Charleston some weeks back."[7]

Meanwhile, Lieutenant Daniel Ammen had taken the *Seneca* up the river; this alerted the rebels, who began burning cotton houses and outbuildings. When Drayton learned from local African Americans that some 500 rebels had encamped at Rockville, between Adams Creek and Bohicket Creek on Wadmalaw Island, he put a force of marines ashore near Rockville the next morning. By the time the landing party reached the camp, however, the enemy had fled. Ammen recalled that the Confederate colonel had "abandoned his tents and some other stores at their encampment a mile back at Rockville." In his report, Drayton noted that the first thing he saw were "negroes pillaging a building in which was a large quantity of commissariat stores, consisting of rice, sugar, bacon, corn, etc." They were grabbing up whatever they could find in the rebel camp, which Drayton thought had been there for many months. His men collected about forty Sibley tents and anything else worth removing and took the items back to the boats. The rebels' hasty evacuation had caused great consternation among the black population, and when Drayton returned to the *Pawnee*, he discovered that nearly 150 blacks, "all in a great state of alarm," had collected on board the different vessels seeking refuge. Drayton instructed Lieutenant Thomas A. Budd, commanding the USS *Penguin*, to land them on the point of Edisto Island and assist them if necessary. According to Ammen, the fugitive slaves finally located themselves on a belt of woods along the seacoast of North Edisto Island, where a broad marsh "afforded them fair protection against a raid from the Confederates." Drayton departed, leaving Budd in command in the river. When Budd informed Drayton that the blacks had reported that rebel troops might reoccupy their old camp at Rockville, Drayton returned to his anchorage.[8]

The *Seneca* and *Penguin* remained in the North Edisto area until year's end. On December 29, 1861, Ammen reported that he had run up the North Edisto and found "that the blacks under [the *Penguin's*] charge on Botany Bay Island [on the Atlantic side of Edisto Island] were constantly increasing in number and amounting at this time to between 700 and 900." In his memoirs, Ammen wrote, "They had a number of scows, and local knowledge of where sweet potatoes had been buried for winter use, and where cattle were to be found, and had ample time to help themselves to all that could be picked up. There was an abundance of raccoon oysters, fish, and the heart of palmetto, which makes a very good substitute for cabbage." Although the contrabands had made shelters of palmetto leaves and appeared content, Ammen feared that "their supplies of corn will soon fall short, owing to their improvidence and the limited extent of country over which they range." Ammen worried about the contrabands' safety as well. He told Du Pont that gangs of rebels had been found on the islands of Wadmalaw, John's, and some parts of North Edisto, and he observed that the rebels' "principal, if not sole, object is to drive the negroes into the interior." Expressing concern about a large rebel camp near Rockville, Ammen informed Du Pont that the *Seneca* had shelled a rebel headquarters and a woods on White Point where some rebel cavalry had taken refuge. "They left in haste," he wrote.[9]

As Ammen had predicted, contraband colonies were not always self-sustaining. From the beginning of 1862, Union naval commanders found themselves responsible for securing provisions for their contraband colonies as well as defending them against rebel attack. The continuing threat to the contrabands from Confederate raiding parties also prompted the Union Navy to undertake raids and joint army-navy expeditions to intimidate rebel forces. On January 4, 1862, for example, Lieutenant T. A. Budd took a raiding party in the USS *Penguin* up the North Edisto River to Bear's Bluff, hoping to find a quantity of corn rumored to be kept there by the rebels. After firing a few shots, Budd sent a party of sailors under the command of Acting Master's Mate Anderson ashore in a flatboat armed with a rifle howitzer. When rebel troops ashore began firing on the sailors, the *Penguin* and its boats quickly dispersed them with small arms, grapeshot, and shell fire. Anderson's men came ashore and hoisted the flag on a house, "allowing the contrabands who followed the vessel up the river to fill their boats with corn." Anderson then "set fire to the buildings and their contents, thus depriving the enemy of this place of shelter and subsistence."[10]

The Bear's Bluff expedition provided the Edisto contraband colony, which now numbered about 1,000 persons, with 100 bushels of corn, satisfying the colony's need for food but not for security. As senior naval officer in St. Helena Sound, Ammen recommended to Du Pont that two vessels be stationed there. If the army did not intend to occupy "this important point," he stated, then all the blacks who desired to leave should be given the opportunity to do so. This would, Ammen felt, "avoid in some measure the exertions which will otherwise be made sooner or later to capture them."[11]

From his station at Port Royal, Ammen continued to oversee affairs in the area and to be concerned about sustaining and protecting the local contrabands. "I have endeavored to impress upon the negroes the necessity of obtaining supplies," he wrote on January 21, 1862, "and for that purpose they have visited the plantation of John Townsend, which lies with[in] range of an XI-inch gun, from the usual anchorage at North Edisto." According to Ammen, two blacks had gone out early in the morning in a heavy fog and had narrowly escaped being injured or captured by a party of about twenty rebels. "One of the negroes was shot through his clothing," Ammen wrote in his report. As soon as the fog cleared, he took the *Seneca* to a position from which he could observe any rebel activity, but seeing no signs of life, Ammen did not order the crew to open fire. Although obviously willing to use his gunboat to protect contrabands foraging for food and supplies, Ammen doubted the contrabands' ability to sustain themselves. If Union forces did not occupy Edisto Island, he wrote to Du Pont, "I fear the colony, now numbering about 1,200, will be in want of food, perhaps within a fortnight. As every party going after maize will have to be accompanied by armed boat crews and a howitzer, I fear collecting food over the country will fall below or hardly exceed the consumption." Noting that there were small quantities of unginned cotton hidden in various localities on nearly all the Edisto Island plantations, Ammen asked if the contrabands should be encouraged to bring in the unginned cotton and offered compensation for it. In this same letter, Ammen offered an additional observation about the contraband community: "It is worthy of note, as indicating the change in the blacks, that now they express themselves most anxious to obtain arms." The colony's black superintendent wanted to land his forces in Rockville and drive the soldiers back, Ammen said, and expressed "the utmost confidence that with about twenty old muskets that they had picked up, many of them with flint locks, he would be able to effect his object."[12]

Fears of a Confederate raid on the Edisto Island colony proved to be well-founded. In fact, on the day after Ammen made his report, a large Confederate raiding party commanded by Colonel E. P. Stevens of Holcome Legion attacked contrabands gathered at Point of Pines. With a force of 120 infantry and 65 cavalry, Stevens crossed the Dawho early on January 22, 1862, and marched to Edisto. At William Whaley's place, Stevens found four blacks and questioned them. One of the men, named Joe, said he had heard of an attack by blacks the previous Saturday and could lead them to the rendezvous of the attacking party. With old Joe as a guide, the colonel took some of his men to Miss Mary Seabrook's place, but, he wrote, "no trace of the negroes could be discovered." After spending the night at Whaley's place, the Confederates set out down the main road, rounding up blacks as they went. A black man named Paul led them toward Point of Pines, across the river from Seabrook Island, where he claimed that "a number of negroes were assembled." When Stevens arrived at Edward Whaley's home, he found that many blacks had gathered there, apparently fleeing from danger. "While securing them several others were taken in the adjoining roads and field, some in buggies, some on horseback, and some in carts." However, Stevens noted, "By this time the alarm had been given and the negroes were on the move for the lower part of the island, the number captured was therefore less than it would have otherwise been." In the meantime, Major Palmer had been scouring the plantations for blacks, whom he either captured or pursued.[13]

At this point, Colonel Stevens observed a Union gunboat approaching Seabrook's place. Although he did not know the gunboat's name, it was probably the USS *Seneca*. Leaving a picket at Seabrook's, Stevens assembled his scattered command and moved back to Edward Whaley's, where he left the contrabands under guard and then rapidly returned to Seabrook's with his infantry to resist what he supposed was an imminent Union landing. Unbeknownst to Stevens, the federals had no intention of landing. The *Crusader,* with Lieutenant Alexander Rhind commanding, had just arrived off the Edisto Bar the previous day to replace the *Seneca* on blockade duty. Ammen took Rhind on board his vessel for a reconnaissance, and they found "a body of horsemen, fifty or a hundred strong, and expended three XI-inch shells in getting them in motion." The cavalrymen sighted by Rhind and Ammen were, of course, Stevens's men. In his report, the colonel acknowledged the *Seneca*'s gunfire: "On the march two shells were thrown at the Seabrook house, but by the time my party came up the boat had retired." Stevens expressed regret that at the Legare and Seabrook places, "3 negroes were either shot or drowned and a fourth wounded, 2 women, and 1 man ran into the water, and refusing or failing to come out, were fired upon and disappeared beneath the water." Confederate General Nathan Evans claimed that the expedition had captured about fifty blacks.[14]

The Confederate raid on Edisto Island sent scores of African Americans scurrying for safety. In his report, Rhind took pains to account for the increased number of contrabands in the colony. On January 23, 1862, Rhind explained to Du Pont that when he learned of Confederate troops landing on Edisto Island and "moving off and shooting blacks," he had gotten the *Crusader* under way and gone upriver, where he had found 100 to 150 blacks collected at Point of Pines wharf. After sending boats from the colony to collect the refugees, Rhind had ordered the *Crusader* to steam upriver to shell houses reported to be occupied by rebel troops. When he had completed that mission, he turned back to Point of Pines wharf, only to discover that more blacks had come in. "Since that time they have been constantly coming in small parties," he reported. Many of these newly freed people settled on one of Edisto Island's barrier islands, Botany Bay Island.[15]

Although clearly concerned about the condition and safety of the contrabands on Botany Bay Island, Du Pont told Rhind on February 5, 1862, that he could not send another vessel to North Edisto immediately but would do so as soon as possible. He then instructed Rhind to keep a close watch on all enemy movements and inform him of the condition of the contrabands at Botany Bay. Du Pont considered the Union possession of North Edisto of great importance and told Rhind that the commanding general would soon send a regiment there for future joint operations.[16]

Two days later, as instructed, Rhind reported to Du Pont on the status of the contrabands at Botany Bay. "Since the departure of the *Seneca* there has been a larger addition to the colony of negroes on Botany Bay Island," he wrote, "and taking the number estimated by Lieutenant Ammen at that time at 1,000 to 1,100, there must be at present at least 1,400 collected there." To feed his growing contraband colony, Rhind took his gunboat upriver, hoping the contrabands might collect corn from plantations on Steamboat Creek. Instead, they began to plunder the houses. "I have endeavored to check their propensity to plunder, but with only partial success," he lamented. Rhind expressed his concern that "the negroes on Botany Bay Island are in such numbers and leading such an idle and improvident life here that I fear, unless they are speedily removed, disease and want will appear among them." Although they had sufficient supplies, Rhind had learned from experience that the contrabands tended to destroy or trade away many of their provisions. "If I go anywhere to enable them to collect corn or potatoes they begin to plunder the houses of furniture and other articles entirely useless to them," he wrote. In a lengthy report dated February 3, 1862, Treasury Agent Edward L. Pierce expressed similar concerns about the new arrivals at the Botany Bay contraband colony. "The number has within a few days . . . increased to 2,300. Among these great destitution is said to prevail." Pierce expected weekly additions to this number but hoped that the entire island could be farmed as soon as troops could be spared to occupy it.[17]

On a more positive note, Du Pont affirmed Rhind's energetic supervision of the colony and informed him that a regiment of soldiers would depart immediately to occupy the island. Du Pont also wasted no time contacting General Sherman about the contrabands' situation. On February 15, 1862, he told Welles that Sherman had sent a small regiment of soldiers to North Edisto, which he felt would help protect the contraband colony on Edisto Island.[18]

Du Pont's concern for the plight of these former slaves is clearly revealed in his correspondence with the Navy Department. Writing from his flagship *Wabash* at Port Royal on February 10, 1862, Du Pont penned a private, confidential letter to Assistant Navy Secretary Gustavus Fox, explaining, "I am much interested in the contrabands within our lines. They tell me there are from eight to ten thousand. They are daily increasing at Edisto, and I have induced the general to send a regiment to Edisto." Candid about what he called "the contraband question," he explained to Fox the intricacies of establishing a policy toward these contrabands—"who to employ them, who is to control, what positions are they to have, what authority to be given to those who work them? The various so-called agents who come down here—more or less accredited—the collectors of cotton, the collectors of negro statistics, the people of God, the best of the party who want to establish schools, do not all agree." The one thing everyone involved in the contraband situation did agree on, Du Pont told Fox, was their "degraded condition." Then he added, "Do not mistake from my using the word 'contraband' the relatively few who happen to be employed by the Government and the negro population on the plantations who are without work."[19]

According to Sergeant John M. Head of the Third New Hampshire Regiment, the troops promised for Edisto Island left Hilton Head on February 19, 1862. In his diary, Head wrote: "N.Y. 47th started for Edisto Island." Colonel Henry Moore, commanding the Forty-seventh New York Infantry, reported that he had indeed gone ahead to Edisto and, after reconnoitering the island, located his post at Point of Pines. "The enemy are all around us," he told Lorenzo Thomas, the adjutant general. Moore hoped "by the aid of the light-draught gunboats, which I am expecting daily from Port Royal, to keep them at bay, if troops sufficient, say at most 10,000, could be forwarded here, in less than three days we could be in Charleston." Moore considered Edisto Island "a great key to Charleston."[20]

While Du Pont's commanders were rescuing contrabands and establishing and protecting colonies of the former slaves along the South Atlantic coast, to the north the officers and men of Flag Officer Louis M. Goldsborough's North Atlantic Blockading Squadron were also encountering refugees. In early February 1862 Goldsborough's flotilla successfully landed Major General Ambrose Burnside's federal troops at Roanoke Island off North Carolina, and in short order they wrested control of the island from its Confederate defenders. Soon after the Union occupation of Roanoke Island, fugitive slaves began seeking sanctuary at Union headquarters there and on Union vessels offshore. According to Henry Van Brunt, the flotilla flag secretary, twenty contrabands had "come in" on Wednesday, February 12, 1862. Hundreds of African Americans from nearby parts of North Carolina flocked to Roanoke Island as well. Slaves, both men and women, used their maritime skills and every raft, dugout, or flatboat they could find to organize a boat lift to rescue slaves and bring them to freedom on the island. "How they succeeded is a wonder to all," remarked one Union soldier. In addition, black watermen employed their small vessels to bring slaves downriver to Union gunboats from as far inland as Washington, North Carolina. One enterprising slave pilot even commandeered his master's vessel at Columbia on the Scuppernong River and sailed twenty-four slaves to Roanoke Island. Many of these black refugees settled near Union headquarters on the island, possibly using the camp of the Twenty-first and Twenty-third Massachusetts Regiments to form the nucleus of a freedmen's colony. General Burnside declared these persons "contraband" of war and freed people, and he ordered his officers to support them and put the able-bodied men to work.[21]

Soon after the battle Vincent Colyer came to Roanoke Island to work with these freed people. "A party of Fifteen or twenty of these loyal blacks, men, women, and children, arrived on a 'Dingy' in front of the General's headquarters, where my tent was located," Colyer wrote. "They came from up the Chowan River, and as they were passing they had been shot at by their rebel masters from the banks of the river, but escaped." The refugees seemed to be a happy party, he wrote, "rejoicing at their escape from slavery and danger." The officers and men of the New England regiments gave them a hearty welcome. With unbounded joy, Colyer recalled, the fugitive slaves came within Union lines to freedom. "Many of the officers, notwithstanding the rain, gathered around the tent to hear them sign the hymn, 'The precious Lamb, Christ Jesus, was crucified for me.'"[22]

By the close of 1862 this contraband colony on Roanoke Island had grown to 1,000 persons, and by the end of 1863 to 3,000. Although many had come from the mainland and were strangers to one another, they formed a community, establishing schools and several churches. "From one to two hundred arrive every few days," Elizabeth James, one of the missionaries assigned to Roanoke Island, wrote in December 1863. "They land at headquarters about three miles south of the camps, and walk up, bringing their children and parents, (the aged are not forgotten,) and goods and effects, when they have been so fortunate as to bring any thing with them." Many, however, had escaped "with the skin of their teeth" and needed "friendly eyes to look after them and friendly hands to aid." Finding shelter for so many new arrivals taxed the authorities on the twelve-mile island, but according to Miss James, they laid out "avenues" and marked off one-acre lots on which men with families could build homes and cultivate the land.

To recruit more black troops for his North Carolina regiment, General Edward A. Wild decided in the summer of 1863 to dedicate the freedmen's settlement on Roanoke Island to the families of black soldiers and to establish a colony that differed from the regimental villages that had grown up around Union Army posts in North Carolina and elsewhere in the South. Wild knew that if he wanted to attract black recruits, he would have to assure them that their families would have government support and security from rebel attacks. Many black enlistees had escaped slavery only to leave their families behind in bondage. Furthermore, black soldiers had discovered that if they were seriously wounded, killed, or captured, their loved ones could not count on the emotional or financial support of the local community or of state or federal agencies. Roanoke Island offered Wild the opportunity to provide a secure settlement for his troops' families. Roanoke Island's superintendent, Horace James, hoped the colony would be a model community for blacks where, in the words of historian Richard Reid, they could "achieve a free and independent social unit imbued with middle class values."[23]

In January 1865 Lucy Chase, a Quaker woman from Worcester, Massachusetts, went to Roanoke Island to teach the contrabands. In a letter to her sister Sarah, she described her first tour of the island: "In whatever direction we walk upon this Isd we see negro cabins with their acre and a half (or more). The school house is on a broad magnificent avenue." Lucy Chase also noticed that "white refugees are scattered amongst the colored people." Some of these refugees had fled from Plymouth, North Carolina.[24]

In the spring of 1862 Union forces also seized St. Simon's Island,

Jehossee Island, Fernandina, and the town of St. Mary's in Florida, giving them control of the coast and inland waters south of St. Simon's. Federal gunboats pushed up the St. John's River to Jacksonville as well. Union occupation of these coastal points gave many slaves a long-awaited opportunity to flee. "Contrabands continue to come to us. I sent a number by the *Potomska* to Fernandina, and also several by the *Connecticut*," Commander Sylvanus Godon wrote on March 30, 1862, in a lengthy report to Du Pont. The presence of Godon's gunboat *Mohican* seemed to attract black families seeking refuge, and on a reconnaissance upriver to Brunswick, he took on board another twenty-seven contrabands. Godon reported, "it now became necessary to obtain food for these people, as by now they mustered over forty men, women, and children, and both my provisions and these of the *Pocahontas* were getting low." In his report, Godon failed to mention his crew's reaction to the arrival of so many contraband families. Nor did he report whether the African American sailors on board, among them thirty-two-year-old John Brown from New London, Connecticut, extended a special welcome to these refugees. To supply this growing group of contrabands, Godon stopped at Colonel's Island, where he discovered 150 bushels of corn, a quantity of peas, and sweet potatoes. Learning that the rebels had as many as 150 soldiers on Colonel's Island, Godon proceeded to St. Simon's Island, about four miles off the Georgia coast, east of Brunswick. He landed the contrabands there, along with their corn and tools, thus establishing yet another contraband colony along the southern coast. Godon set the contrabands to work planting potatoes and working the ground for corn. In his report he told Du Pont that St. Simon's was a "fine, rich island, about ten miles long," and he believed that a gunboat at either end and a marine battalion might be sufficient to secure the island from rebel attack. The commander thought a colony of as many as 1,000 blacks could be usefully employed and made self-supporting, but he did not know Du Pont's intentions toward the contrabands and requested instructions.[25]

The possibility of a rebel attack on the colony at St. Simon's concerned Godon, however. Other naval officers shared his fears about Confederate harassment of contrabands. Having established these contraband colonies, the Union Navy now found itself responsible for aiding the army in defending them. Federal garrison troops assigned to the Sea Islands were always in danger of sudden enemy attack and depended on the navy for support in the form of transports to bring in reinforcements, gunboats to provide naval gunfire, and boats, howitzers, and sailors to man landing parties in case of attack.

In addition to Edisto Island, by June 1862 the Union Navy had assumed responsibility for provisioning and defending several coastal colonies of contrabands, as well as the Union troops on the islands. This represented an expansion of the navy's original mission to blockade the southern coast. Many navy officers welcomed the new mission, citing compassion as a rationale for rescuing and protecting former slaves, but also embracing the opportunity to strike a blow against the Confederacy by depriving plantation owners of their slaves. In late May 1862, for example, Commander George A. Prentiss, senior officer on the blockade in Winyah Bay, the entrance to Georgetown, South Carolina, seized an opportunity to deprive one of the rice plantations in that area of its slaves. Prentiss took the *Albatross* and *Norwich* up from Winyah Bay, passing Georgetown, and sailed up the Waccamaw River for about ten miles. Noting the "beautiful country," Prentiss reported that he stopped "at a public mill, seized a lighter of rice, several boats, and about eighty contrabands" who, he said, "claimed my protection." He then returned to his anchorage near the lighthouse and founded a colony of contrabands that was, he wrote, "rapidly increasing." Prentiss's expedition up the Waccamaw had frightened the rebels, causing them to leave "their plantations in every direction, driving their slaves before them to the pine woods." The fruitfulness of the area and the large quantities of rice stowed along the banks for the Confederate armies at Charleston and Savannah greatly impressed Prentiss, and he longed to capture and transport the rice.[26]

Although anxious to take a more aggressive approach to the rebels in the area, Prentiss had but one vessel in the bay. "I have been confined in my movements to the security of North and South islands," he told Du Pont, "and the safety of my little colony of contrabands, numbering about 120 now, but which I can increase indefinitely if it is the policy (of) the Government to deprive the rebels of their slaves." Prentiss asked Du Pont for general instructions with regard to the contrabands—should he detain them or send them to Port Royal? He queried Du Pont as well about pursuing some of the prominent inhabitants of the region and about the disposition of their property, including their slaves. He asked, "Shall I capture or destroy the rice, turpentine, mills, etc. of known rebels?" In response to Prentiss's questions and concerns, Du Pont ordered the *Hale* and *Henry Andrew* to Georgetown, accompanied by some marines from the ships off Charleston, and he instructed Prentiss to receive and protect all contrabands that came in and to send them, if convenient, to Port Royal. The admiral authorized the destruction of rebel property, such as cotton and rice, but he advised Prentiss not to destroy buildings or houses unless they were used by rebels for stationing pickets or other military purposes "which might be annoying." Du Pont did, however, approve of Prentiss's idea of destroying a railroad bridge, writing, "If you can destroy that bridge, it will be a very handsome thing." As this incident clearly demonstrates, by June 1862 Du Pont had adopted a clearer policy toward the destruction of Confederate property, the confiscation of slaves, and the seizure of rebel commodities such as rice, turpentine, and cotton.[27]

The contraband colony founded by George Prentiss, now one of several along the southern coast, had to be sustained and protected by the Union Navy from harassment and even raids by rebel troops. African Americans living on or near abandoned plantations on the Georgia Sea Islands required protection as well, for Union officials feared for their safety. As the experience of Commander John Marchand illustrates, their fears were not unfounded. When Marchand took the *Unadilla, Pembina,* and *Ottawa* up the Stono River on a reconnaissance mission in mid-May 1862, he hardly expected to become a witness to a Confederate attack on helpless slaves living on John's Island. The forts at the mouth of the river offered no resistance, so the federal vessels went up the Stono to the junction of the Stono and Kiawah rivers and anchored. Marchand then sent Commander Collins and Coast Survey Assistant Charles O. Boutelle ashore to the abandoned village of Legareville to conduct a search. There they encountered contrabands, who told them about a nearby plantation owned by a Union sympathizer named Paul Grimball. Collins and Boutelle rowed to a small wharf, where they met an elderly gentleman about seventy-five years of age. "He begged us protection as he was a good Union man and represented that the rebel cavalry infesting the country on the south side of the Stono River . . . had repeatedly urged him to leave and take away his slaves," Marchand noted in his diary entry for May 21, 1862. The previous evening the rebels had come back, telling the man that "the Yankees in the gunboats would bayonet him in his bed and do the same to all his slaves." Afraid for their lives, Grimball and his slaves had spent the night hiding in some pine trees a mile away. "His gratitude extended to tears that we would not molest but protect him from our own men. Several old Negro women, bowed down and thanked the officers that they did not come to bayonet them," Marchand recorded in his journal.[28]

The *Unadilla* continued up the Stono to within four miles of Fort Pemberton, a Confederate battery, then the *Unadilla* and *Ottawa* dropped downriver to the mouth of the Kiawah River and anchored. "About four o'clock in the afternoon we heard the most terrific screams ashore," Marchand wrote in his diary, "the lookouts at the mastheads having previously reported a stampede of slaves on the cotton and corn-fields to the south of the river. A company of cavalry was seen to emerge from the pines . . . charging at full speed among the flying slaves." At first Marchand assumed that the soldiers were Union troops on their way from North Edisto to Charleston, but "the cavalry fired their pistol on all sides amongst the negroes and then I knew it was not part of our army but the rebel force so I directed the gunboats to open fire upon the mounted men." A half dozen shells drove the rebels from the fields and "from amongst the pines where they thought themselves safe." Lieutenant Bankhead then pulled off in his gig to rescue slaves gathered at the water's edge. The seventy-one rescued contrabands were mostly women and small children, as their owners had sent most of the able-bodied men into the interior. The number of contrabands seeking the protection of the Union gunboats quickly grew. To Du Pont, Marchand confided, "The 400 contrabands are quite an annoyance, as the only place they can be landed within protection of our guns is approachable by the enemy."[29]

These 400 contrabands were indeed fortunate, for if the incident described by Marchand is the same one referred to in Confederate Brigadier General Nathan G. "Shanks" Evans's report of a rebel raid on Union soldiers camped on John's Island, they barely escaped being enslaved again. On May 22, 1862, Confederate units crossed the Stono onto John's Island, intending to drive the Yankees from it. Much to their surprise, they found neither Union soldiers nor plantation owners, but a number of slaves. "[The] negroes were immediately ordered to be removed, and the troops had collected about 200 before I left," Evans wrote in his report. "I have directed them to be sent to workhouse to be fed and taken care of by owners. I was compelled to issue rations to them till provisions could be secured."[30]

By the time Marchand left to return to his blockade duties off Charleston, his attitude toward the contrabands had changed. On his way back to Charleston aboard the *James Adger,* Marchand visited the colony of contrabands he had founded on Cole's Island at Stono Inlet, which now numbered "about 400 souls." Although disappointed to be leaving the Stono, Marchand departed on an optimistic note concerning the contrabands. "They were a happy set of darkies enjoying themselves in doing nothing."[31]

The new contraband colony on Cole's Island remained viable only because Union vessels supplied it with provisions and protected the inhabitants from harassment by rebel troops. Although more established, the colony at St. Simon's Island, Georgia, also depended on the Union Navy for protection. Fortunately for the contrabands, Du Pont took a personal interest in their welfare. In a letter to his wife, Du Pont described a visit to St. Simon's Island on the USS *Uncas,* where Louis Goldsborough told him, "Commodore, God put into your mind to send the *Uncas* down just when you did." Half an hour after the *Uncas* arrived, Goldsborough explained, boats with rebel soldiers had appeared, and they would have killed everyone if the *Uncas* had not opened fire. When Du Pont returned to St. Simon's for a visit in late May, he and Commander Godon had breakfast together before going ashore. They rode about the island in a carriage, and although it was not a warm day, Du Pont told Sophie, "I enjoyed the ride." He saw corn being planted, and as they rode through T. Butler King's plantation, Du Pont observed women washing and ironing clothes for the officers. With some pride, Godon showed Du Pont the corn mill he had captured.[32]

Du Pont wholeheartedly supported contraband colonies such as St. Simon's, but other Union Navy officers had varying responses to the mission of protecting these colonies on the Georgia Sea Islands. The plight of the fugitive slaves deeply moved some naval officers, but others viewed contrabands with suspicion and felt frustrated by the need to protect and provision them. Those who were sympathetic to the blacks cited their lack of proper clothing, their poor diet, and the destitute condition in which many slaves found themselves after being abandoned by their white owners. The condition of the black slaves on the Sea Islands shocked Du Pont, who was, by his own admission, a conservative on the question of slavery. Du Pont wrote, "Oh my! What a delusion—there are no swine in Massachusetts not better cared for. The Dahomeys and Congos are better off—these cotton lords who have been boasting of their wealth and power, will you believe it, have never spent a dollar in ameliorating the condition of these people physically." When Du Pont complained to a fellow officer about the lack of even common decencies for slaves on a plantation he had visited, the officer replied, "Why sir, those slaves are living in luxury compared to the general run!"[33]

At least one commander in the South Atlantic Blockading Squadron took a genuine, if paternalistic, interest in the contrabands. After attending religious services aboard his vessel on August 11, 1862, Acting Volunteer Lieutenant H. St. C. Eytinge of the sailing ship USS *Shepherd Knapp* went ashore, "among my dependent contrabands on Otter island," he wrote to Du Pont, "and read them the morning service of the Episcopal church. I never saw poor humanity more pleased with the consolations of the divine promises, and when they thanked me after service I could not repress a tear of joy in having been instrumental even in limited good."[34]

When George Prentiss's gunboats the *Hale, Western World,* and *Henry Andrew* steamed up the Santee River in late June 1862, they attracted hundreds of contrabands who came under Union protection. Short turns in the river forced Prentiss to order his vessels back downriver, and after passing Blake's plantation, rebel artillery, riflemen, and cavalry opened fire on them. Prentiss then landed a party of marines and seamen, who burned the mill and other dwellings, "together with about 100,000 bushels of rice." A brief firefight ensued when the landing party's skirmishers ran into rebel troops as they cautiously advanced into the woods. After this firefight, about 400 slaves came down to Prentiss's vessels and were taken aboard. The commander wrote, "This plantation has long been the headquarters of a regiment stationed there to protect vessels running the blockade through South Santee and Alligator Creek." Leaving the South Santee on June 28, Prentiss took the contrabands to North Island and put them ashore, adding to the colony he had founded in late May. He then ran up the Waccamaw some thirty-five miles and returned with "five lighters of rice for support of the contrabands."[35]

Feeding and protecting the North Island contraband colony continued to absorb the attention of Prentiss and then Lieutenant I. B. Baxter, who was left in charge to maintain the blockade and protect the contrabands, who now numbered more than 600. On July 15, 1862, Baxter reported that a refugee from Georgetown had informed him that 500 rebel troops located near that city planned to cross over in boats to Pawley's Island and from there to the north end of North Island, "with the intention of destroying the contrabands which we have on the south end of North Island, which number about 700 men, women, and children." Concerned about this threat to the colony, Baxter took the *Gem of the Sea* into Winyah Bay and assured Du Pont that he had enough force to protect the contrabands. But, he wrote, "The contrabands are very destitute of clothing and food, and if it is possible to have them removed to a place of greater safety I should think it advisable." Clearly, Baxter judged the rice collected by Prentiss in late June insufficient to provide a proper, balanced diet for the hundreds of contrabands on North Island.[36]

As the Civil War progressed, and the appearance of fugitive blacks became more common, Union Navy commanders had to devise creative means of providing for these often unwelcome "guests." Take, for example, the crew of the USS *Dale,* whose inventive scrounging attracted the attention of T. Edwin Ruggles of the cotton planting agency. When Ruggles wrote to Du Pont complaining that the *Dale*'s men had been taking sheep from Otter Island, Du Pont wrote to Edward L. Pierce, reminding him, "It must be borne in mind also that the contrabands on Otter Island were first gathered there, protected, and fed by the naval forces long before any agencies were established on any of the islands in St. Helena Sound or any military force sent there—and in order to do this, supplies were in part obtained from the surrounding plantations from which many of them have been driven."[37]

In June 1862, pressed to feed the contrabands on St. Simon's Island, Commander Godon ordered the USS *Madgie,* with Acting Master Meriam commanding, to Barrett's Island near Darien, Georgia, rumored to house a large supply of rice. On board were thirty "selected" contrabands to serve as stevedores to load the bags of rice. Godon also directed the *Wamsutta* to accompany the *Madgie* and assist in gathering the rice. The ships returned the following day with 630 bushels of rice, but Meriam reported that a large quantity still remained on the island. Not one to waste an opportunity, Godon sent Meriam and the *Madgie* back to Barrett's Island two days later with a twelve-pound howitzer to reinforce the battery of two rifled guns. The extra firepower proved useful when Meriam learned from the contrabands that a rebel schooner lay hidden in a creek near the island. "With much promptness," Godon wrote, "he pushed his vessel on and took possession of the schooner, which proved to be the *Southern Belle,* of Brunswick, towed her to the rice depot, and brought her in to St. Simon's, [along with] 3,000 bushels of rice, which I have now stored in suitable houses." This successful expedition secured an ample supply of food for the fledgling contraband colony on St. Simon's and motivated Godon to report: "The colony improves, the crops grow finely, and the people are contented. Their large supplies on hand now by the addition of the rice leaves them nothing to fear on that head."[38] Godon's rice expedition is just one example of how the need to supply and protect these contraband colonies afforded naval officers a perfect excuse to aggressively patrol the southern sounds and rivers and, in some cases, take rebel ships as prizes.

Before Godon took the *Mohican* north to Philadelphia for some badly needed repairs, he sent a final report to Du Pont that included notes on the contraband colony at St. Simon's Island. This enclosure provides a glimpse into the organization and administration of that particular colony, which may or may not reflect the conditions at other contraband camps run by the Union Navy during the war. In these notes, which were actually suggestions to his relief, Commander John R. Goldsborough, Godon discussed at length the provision of food for the contrabands. He explained to Goldsborough that once a week the contrabands killed two head of beef on Jekyll Island, and he issued weekly rations of four quarts of corn or two of hulled rice. "If bread is given to them I reduce the amount of corn, if beans with rice, give no corn. The beef is extra. The green beans now on the vine might be picked from the vine twice a week and served out." About clothing he wrote, "I leave some domestic goods for clothes for the men (most in need of it); the women are well supplied." The commander suggested that work be found for those contrabands who were carpenters, as they did not work in the fields; that new houses be built; and that the blacks be removed from Butler King's plantation. He also sent Goldsborough a list of persons to be taken from St. Simon's to Fernandina, saying, "They will be of little use on the island."[39]

That Godon ran a tight ship on St. Simon's is evident from these notes. "Where work is neglected my rule has been to stop off the ration of beef or something else; and I have placed men in irons for punishment. The rule works pretty well," Godon wrote. When he first arrived on St. Simon's, Godon had insisted that the contrabands "become of use to themselves," planting cotton and other crops. At first the former slaves resented being made to labor in the fields, forcing the commander to employ a black foreman to supervise them. Even the foreman needed "pushing," Godon noted, to keep the men at their work. He had set Saturday aside as a cleaning day in all the houses and grounds and suggested to Goldsborough that an appropriate person be appointed to supervise the task, but he cautioned, "You will find that you will have to look to things very much yourself." Godon raised concerns about theft and recommended that when the crop began to ripen, guards be placed over the corn and melons and that they be held responsible for any theft. In addition to growing crops, the contrabands on the island had been cutting wood for use on the steamer *Darlington,* and Godon recommended that they be paid at a certain rate for doing so. As an additional means of income, whether for the contrabands or, more likely, for the government, Godon informed Goldsborough that the MacArthur cotton gin was in working order, "and all the cotton can be ginned and sent north."[40]

Theft was not Godon's only concern. In view of the fact that rebels had landed on the island in the past, he had made it a rule to send out groups of twenty or thirty men to visit various locations and look over the island, "of course with proper officers and under strict military rules," he wrote. Although he told Du Pont that he had taken most of his supplies from Pierce Butler's plantation, Godon carefully noted that he had "discouraged the sale of chickens, eggs, etc. even to the officers, in order to keep up a supply." Before departing for the North, Godon also suggested that Goldsborough might need to harvest a field of corn growing on Sapelo Island, which could be easily and safely reached by boats and would increase their corn supply. He assured his replacement and Du Pont that any contrabands visiting Jekyll Island were required to obtain permission to do so, night or day. Concluding his notes to Goldsborough, Godon wrote, "I would also remark that idleness, improvidence, theft, and a disposition to vagrancy are the besetting sins of the contraband race on the island. There are some marked exceptions, however. Our utmost efforts will be required to counteract the evil effects of the above vices in the colony."[41]

In general, Du Pont supported the Union experiment of settling former slaves on abandoned plantations and continued to take a genuine personal interest in the contraband colonies. When he sent Goldsborough to relieve Godon on St. Simon's Sound, Du Pont instructed him to watch for "possible attempts at running the blockade, as well as [to provide for] the humane protection of the contrabands." Though concerned for the contrabands' welfare, Du Pont was not averse to using them in the Union cause. Take, for example, his request to Godon on June 11, 1862: "Select, if you can do so, thirty stout contrabands for work on boats, and bring them with you to Port Royal. They should be single men, of course." Du Pont's concerns about breaking up contraband families reflects the former slaves' newfound ability to reconstitute their family units, which had often been separated by the institution of slavery. Contrabands living in camps also had opportunities to go to school, earn wages outside the camp, organize prayer meetings or start congregations, and find blacks with healing skills to care for those who suffered injuries or fell ill. However, some unscrupulous traders took advantage of the contrabands on St. Simon's Island. "I have to report Captain Godfrey, of the *Darlington,* for trading and speculating with the contrabands of this island, charging the most extravagant prices for all manner of articles, such as hoops, calicoes, trinkets, etc., for women," Goldsborough reported, "realizing, or, at least, reaching in many instances over 200 per cent of the real value." Godfrey, the commander noted, "has been in this kind of business along this coast for many years."[42]

On July 17, 1862, Charles Steedman, commanding the USS *Paul Jones,* visited John Goldsborough on St. Simon's. "It is really amazing to see John G with his colony of darkies," Steedman wrote to his wife. "Godon, who commanded the colony, and was the original governor, can tell you what a fine place it is. We are anchored abreast of a Mr. Tom Butler King's plantation and his dwelling is now occupied partly by a dozen respectable contrabands who wash our clothes." Steedman appreciated such amenities and observed, "We have been able to have our clothes washed cheaply and very well, and besides have been able to procure vegetables and fruit. The figs are very fine and I have a fine mess every day for breakfast."[43]

While Godon, Goldsborough, and other Union naval commanders enforced the blockade off the Georgia Sea Islands and along the coast of South Carolina, to the north, General George B. McClellan's Army of the Potomac engaged the Confederates in a series of battles in Virginia. Even before McClellan began his campaign, contraband colonies felt the pinch of troop withdrawals from the Department of the South to reinforce McClellan's army. Federal troop withdrawals left the Georgia Sea Islands even more vulnerable to enemy harassment and attack, and the Union troops' departure from Jacksonville, Florida, had a similar effect on blacks living in that area.

On June 14, 1862, Lieutenant J. W. A. Nicholson took the *Isaac Smith* up the St. John's River and anchored fifteen miles above Jacksonville. "Shortly after dark the contrabands commenced coming in, and when I started on my return, Monday morning, I had 43 on board, 12 of whom were children, besides 4 blacks," he wrote to Captain Rodgers. In his report, Nicholson noted that he had taken aboard so many contrabands as well as other passengers that he had to send the *Uncas* to Fernandina because he could not accommodate them all. The blacks had fled because there were no troops left in Jacksonville, he told Du Pont, "the regiment that was stationed there having been sent to Tennessee." Nicholson could see the positive aspects of the situation, however, and wrote to Rodgers, "the banks of the river as far as one can see is planted with corn. They say enough corn in Florida for all of the Southern rebel states. If we carry off their darkies they cannot gather it; one consolation." Ten days later Nicholson sent another report about a visit to Jacksonville: "Numbers of contrabands continue to come in. I house and feed them on shore, allowing their owners, on application, if they satisfy me that they are not disloyal, to go on shore and get them off if they can, as no assistance is given them." But according to Nicholson, only two people had been given this privilege provided for in the Fugitive Slave Act of 1850, which technically remained in force in the United States until mid-1864. "Attempts (by Confederates) have been made," Nicholson said, "to run the free blacks into the interior, [and] several have come to me for protection." He had sent four white and eleven black refugees to Fernandina but asked Du Pont for instructions "on this contraband question." These contrabands sent to Fernandina undoubtedly joined the colony already established there.[44]

The withdrawal of so many Union troops from the Georgia Sea Islands put the Union Navy in a difficult position as well. "I have written you how shamefully the poor contrabands are abandoned on these islands, after remaining or rushing to our protection," Du Pont confided to his wife in mid-June. "Truxtun sent another load today since the descent on Hutchinson's Island—but the truth is we have not a military force to hold what the Navy has taken in a proper way—making a show of at least protecting loyal people."[45]

Rebel raiding parties continued to harass the Sea Islands. In July, Truxtun reported that rebel marauding parties had increased, fifty men "calling themselves rangers" visiting Hutchinson's Island on July 8, 1862, to carry off chickens and hogs. Du Pont sent him the *Hale,* but General David Hunter finally ordered the withdrawal of the remainder of the garrison on Edisto Island. According to the island's commander, General Horatio G. Wright, most of the soldiers on Edisto had been removed in early June, and the only troops left on the island were men of the Fifty-fifth Regiment, Pennsylvania Volunteer Infantry; one squadron of Massachusetts troops; and two pieces of field artillery with detachments of the Third Rhode Island Regiment to serve them.[46]

On July 11, 1862, Hunter ordered Wright to remove the rest of his troops whenever transportation could be arranged and advised him to consult with a Mr. DeLa Croix "as to the best means of collecting all the negroes within our lines and on adjacent islands, and forwarding them to these headquarters." Thus, with much regret about abandoning such rich farmland and crops, the superintendent of the contrabands on Edisto Island gathered up about 1,600 former slaves, together with their pigs, chickens, and personal effects, and had them ferried across to St. Helena village, where they spent the remainder of the war. One of the refugees, Maria Middleton, recalled that they were taken off in large flatboats camouflaged with tree branches to conceal them from the Confederates.[47]

Union officials lamented the evacuation of Edisto Island. In a letter to his wife, Steedman wrote, "The withdrawal of the greater part of General Hunter's command has obliged him to evacuate Edisto Island, bringing away all the contrabands and . . . leaving one thousand acres of fine cotton and corn *to go to grass.* I don't think the enemy will attempt to take possession of the island, yet [it] is likely that marauding parties will cross in the night and commit depredations. If our gun boats are increased the Navy can easily manage to hold everything in status quo until the army can be increased and offensive operations resumed." Du Pont shared Steedman's concerns and had more of his own. As he wrote to his wife, Sophie, on July 10, 1862, "The worst of this Richmond affair is that this transport has come for all the troops in the Department, and I would not be surprised if Beaufort were not burnt in a week, the plantations will be invaded, the negroes driven, etc." This increased Du Pont's labors and anxieties, but, he wrote, "I shall tell General Hunter plainly what I can do and what I cannot do. I will do all in my power, but I have no responsibility in the safety of anything which they abandoned." When Edward Pierce protested to Salmon P. Chase about the abandonment of beautiful Edisto Island and the Lincoln administration's lack of support for his experiment in black labor at Port Royal, Chase blamed "McClellan's infatuation" and the president's very conservative opinions on the role of blacks in the war effort. The evacuation also proved fatal for Edisto's superintendent, Francis E. Barnard, who had been assigned to the island shortly after Union troops occupied it. He died suddenly on October 18, 1862, on St. Helena Island. "The evacuation of Edisto in June, the heat, and the labor involved in bringing away and settling his people at the village on St. Helena Island, . . . were too much for him. His excessive exertions brought on malarious fever."[48]

Confederate pressure on the Sea Islands continued throughout the summer. On the night of July 20, 1862, a white refugee from Georgetown arrived on board Lieutenant Baxter's vessel in Winyah Bay and informed him that rebels were planning to attack the contrabands on North Island. The refugee, a man named Wingate, claimed to be a member of Ward's artillery stationed at Georgetown. "He informs me that a portion of that company were to leave for Polly's [Pawley's] Island, where Ward has his salt works," Baxter reported, "and that it was the intention of a portion of the troops to cross over on North Island to massacre the contrabands, who are under our protection." After consulting with Sam Gregory of the *Western World,* Baxter went up the coast to Murray's Inlet, which separates Pawley's Island from the mainland. On the mainland they found and destroyed an extensive Confederate salt-works "capable of making from 30 to 40 bushels of salt per day."[49]

The threat to the North Island contraband colony so concerned Du Pont that he ordered Lieutenant George Balch in the *Pocahontas* down to Georgetown, South Carolina, to assume command of the blockade. Du Pont had confidence in Balch, whom he described as "a fellow with pluck, energy, and skill in handling guns." He wanted Balch to provide increased protection to the contrabands on North Island until Hunter could dispatch a steamer to transport them to Port Royal. Informing Balch that there were 700 contrabands, including women and children, on North Island, Du Pont ordered him to select 100 of the best contrabands who were "fit for general service" and send them to him at Port Royal.[50]

Balch went to the island on July 22, 1862, accompanied by Baxter of the *Gem of the Sea* and the *Pocahontas*'s medical officer, Dr. Rhoades. The latter, he told Du Pont, "selected some ninety" contrabands who were fit for service, "who will be sent by the *Western World,* which I shall dispatch to-morrow afternoon." Balch also had twenty-one hogsheads of rice transferred from the *Western World* to the *Ben De Ford* for use in provisioning the contrabands. The following day Balch reported that he had retained "a few contrabands, some of whom have been sick and some few others to look out for matters on shore as also to do picket duty on North Island." He did not expect an attack because, according to Baxter, "the lesson they [the Confederates] received at Ward's salt works a few days since will keep them quiet." As a precaution, however, Balch intended to go up Winyah Bay to destroy some fortifications from which riflemen were in the habit of firing at escaping contrabands. He informed Du Pont that Acting Master Gregory had furnished fifteen or twenty "very destitute" refugees on the island with clothing and bedding from the *Western World* and that Baxter had given them some clothes, but he needed instructions as to their subsistence. *Gem of the Sea*'s role in protecting the contraband colony at North Island must have pleased the newly enlisted contrabands in its crew, among them Jacob, Michael, Prince, and Robert Blake and Dick Blake, who had joined *Gem of the Sea* in mid-June. From their common last name, one can surmise that Robert and Dick were kinfolk, or perhaps they had taken their last name from the Blake plantation located near Georgetown, South Carolina.[51]

The War Department fulfilled its promise to send a steamer to North Island to evacuate the contrabands, for in his report, Balch praised both Captain Baxter and Captain Gregory for their zeal and energy, noting, "they have been indefatigable in aiding in every way the embarkation of nearly 1700 contrabands." Although authorities evacuated most of the contrabands on North Island in July, fugitive blacks and occasional white refugees continued to seek protection on the island. Some of them arrived alone or in small groups on their own initiative, but in August 1862 a Union expedition up the Black River in search of the rebel steamer the *Nina* liberated a large number of contrabands. Led by Balch, the attempt to capture the *Nina* not only originated from intelligence reports by contrabands and others but also profited from information provided along the way by friendly blacks. Learning from "a number of negroes" that the rebels had placed batteries on the banks of the Black River, Balch had volunteers from *Gem of the Sea* sheath the tug *Treaty* with two-inch pine planks and place hammocks inside them to protect the crew from rifle fire. On August 14 the *Pocahontas* and *Treaty* proceeded upriver some twenty miles and shelled the batteries, which did not return fire. The rebels had fled. With the awnings furled during the bombardment, the heat on the decks became intense, so at 10:15 A.M. Balch "piped down" so the awnings could be unfurled for shade and the men could rest. "Numerous contrabands were in attendance, some of whom wished to come to us, all of whom were taken on board," he reported. From these contrabands Balch heard that the rebels were congregating in the woods, preparing to open fire on the two federal vessels when they steamed back downriver. Balch ordered dinner to proceed as usual, but suddenly, without warning, enemy soldiers hiding in the woods attacked. Both vessels returned fire with their guns and small arms, but the *Pocahontas* dragged its anchor in the narrow stream, and the ship's stern went aground hard and fast. "I called the men to the forecastle," Balch wrote, "when the enemy opened on us again, but strange to say, hit no one of the crowd collected there." When the *Pocahontas* finally floated free, the vessels steamed up the Black River for several miles, then turned around and headed back as enemy riflemen fired down on them from the bluffs above the river. The third assistant engineer, John A. Hill, was wounded, but Balch estimated that they had inflicted serious losses on the rebels. Although he heard various reports about rebel casualties, Balch noted, "The contrabands state that the whites studiously avoid letting them know the details." Balch brought the contrabands back to North Island and told Du Pont, "They are in good health, but are useless here and are consuming rations which we can not well spare."[52]

In late September Baxter reported that he now had 124 contrabands and 18 white refugees under his protection. "They are all in a destitute condition for the want of food and clothing," he told Du Pont, but then reassured the admiral that he was feeding them half rations from his ship, *Gem of the Sea*, and from his supplies of captured rice. The enterprising Baxter took seriously his responsibility for protecting the island from rebel attack. He had assigned twelve contrabands to picket duty, ordering them to take turns reconnoitering North Inlet twice a day to look for any signs of an enemy landing. He explained to Du Pont, "to make sure that those pickets do their duty I have placed pickets at the north end of the island, that they may bring me one back on their return to report."[53]

Rebel activity near the Georgia Sea Islands continued to challenge the Union Navy, and by the summer of 1862 the future of the remaining contraband colonies off the coast was problematic. On July 16, 1862, Captain John R. Goldsborough, senior officer in St. Simon's Sound, informed Du Pont that the colony on St. Simon's had increased "so largely (over thirty have been added since my arrival and more coming) that I have every reason to believe it is beginning to excite the serious attention of the rebel authorities of the State." According to Goldsborough, the rebels had increased their seacoast guards and multiplied their pickets on the mainland. With his own blockading vessels "far out of sight of each other," Goldsborough suggested that the military take possession of the island immediately to ensure proper security and to prevent a night landing by the rebels.[54]

In mid-August Goldsborough's fears came true. Writing from the USS *Florida* in St. Simon's Sound, he admitted to Du Pont, recently promoted to admiral, that despite their utmost zeal and perseverance, his men had been unable to capture a group of rebels who had landed on St. Simon's. The Union forces had destroyed all the boats on the island, thus cutting off the rebels' means of escape, yet these fifteen to twenty men continued to evade capture and resorted to what Goldsborough called "guerilla warfare." Although no recent casualties had been suffered by his forces, Goldsborough reported that "one of the colored picket guard is still missing." These rebels probably came from a small force of only thirty-eight men of the First South Carolina Regiment guarding Butler's Point. In addition to Goldsborough's men on the northeast side of St. Simon's, he had armed all the contrabands and landed an additional force from the *Florida* every night for the better protection of the colony. However, he told Du Pont, "I do not think the feeble military force now stationed on the island of St. Simon's at all adequate to its protection, and General Saxton agrees with me in these views." Du Pont expressed his approval of Goldsborough's handling of the situation, but because he anticipated a rebel attempt to run the blockade off Georgia, the admiral needed every available vessel to guard the various entrance points. "If the colony on St. Simon's should require more protection, it will have to be given by the army," Du Pont insisted.[55]

The Union Army was stretched thin in the Department of the South, however, as Du Pont well knew. On August 18, 1862, he wrote to Lieutenant Eytinge, commander of the USS *Shepherd Knapp* in St. Helena Sound, acknowledging the importance of his position but advising the lieutenant that "it is impossible for the Navy alone to hold the islands bordering the waters of St. Helena Sound and as the Army has withdrawn their forces from the fort on Otter Island, I do not propose to occupy it with sailors." Du Pont did, however, promise to send Eytinge a light-draft steamer when one became available. "I approve entirely of your conduct towards the contrabands and advise they be directed to go to St. Helena to the plantation where agents are placed," Du Pont told Eytinge. "If I can get any seeds for your garden they shall be sent."[56]

In the wake of McClellan's failed James River campaign and the army's retreat to the banks of the Potomac, the War Department ordered even more troop withdrawals from the South in August and September 1862. These withdrawals forced Hunter to abandon the contraband colony on St. Simon's Island and send to Port Royal some 4,000 contrabands who had settled and planted crops on the island—a tragic development for the contrabands, who could not plant new crops at Port Royal so late in the season. Those former slaves who remained on the Sea Islands now had to assume responsibility for their own protection. As General Rufus Saxton pointed out to Secretary of War Stanton in a letter dated August 4, 1862, "I very much regret the necessity which caused the evacuation or prevented occupation of all these islands, by our troops, and I most earnestly, and respectfully call your attention to the importance of reoccupation as soon as the existence of the service will permit." Not willing to wait for that eventuality, Saxton told Stanton that he had sent twenty to thirty muskets to each plantation under his command to be kept in the armory under the superintendent's supervision, "ready for service in case of attack." If the army could no longer protect his contraband colonies, and the navy would not send marines or sailors ashore to defend them, Saxton decided to take 400 to 500 muskets to St. Simon's Island, arm the blacks, and let them defend themselves.[57]

On August 16, 1862, Saxton wrote again to Stanton, requesting permission to enroll a force not exceeding 5,000 able-bodied men from among the contrabands in the Quartermaster Department. "The men are to be uniformed, armed, and officered by men detailed from the Army," he wrote. To justify his request to arm the contrabands, Saxton cited the blacks' fear of attack by rebel masters and reminded Stanton of the devastating effects of the recent removal of 1,500 people from Edisto Island after the withdrawal of Union troops. "Six hundred and ninety-seven acres of cotton, 835 acres of corn, and 30 acres of potatoes, the product of many months of labor, were abandoned, and unless destroyed or gathered by our forces may fall into the hands of the rebels." If, the general explained, he could arm contrabands as additional security against recapture, "the rebellion would be very greatly weakened by the escape of thousands of slaves with their families from active rebel masters." The people could then return in safety to these islands, Saxton argued, and the navy could protect them. "Guarded by these men [the armed contrabands], as well as assisted in the field work by them, the people could secure all those crops, a good harvest of figs and oranges, as well as comfortable homes for their suffering families." To bolster his argument, Saxton also cited the recent rebel attack on St. Simon's, a beautiful island "with a colony of 400 very interesting refugees, gathered and protected by the Navy alone, and thus far sustained, without any expense to the Government." According to Saxton, rebel soldiers had landed on St. Simon's with the intention "of slaughtering every man, woman, and child on the island." Black pickets, who had been guarding the island for some time, vigorously attacked the rebels and forced them to flee, but not before two of the pickets had been killed and one wounded. Saxton feared that the rebels would return. Reminding Stanton that contrabands had been employed and given rations in several places but had not received pay for their labors, the general urged the War Department to allow him to organize, discipline, and employ contrabands to provide the necessary security to protect these islands against further enemy attacks.[58]

Not long after sending his request to the War Department, Saxton sent Mansfield French and Robert Smalls to the capital to plead his case to Stanton and Chase. In this endeavor, Saxton had the full support of Du Pont and Hunter, whose own attempts to recruit, arm, and employ blacks in the war effort had come to an end when the War Department would not authorize paying them. With the added bonus of Smalls's dramatic story of his own flight to freedom, French succeeded in convincing Stanton and Chase of Saxton's argument. On August 26, 1862, Stanton gave Saxton the authority to arm and equip up to 5,000 black recruits, a bold change in the government's established policy of not allowing African Americans to bear arms and enlist in the Union Army. The War Department also authorized him to detail officers to command the black recruits and instruct them in military drill, discipline, and duty. In this same letter, Stanton instructed Saxton to reoccupy, if possible, all lands and plantations previously occupied by the government and to secure and harvest crops and cultivate and improve plantations. Furthermore, Secretary Stanton gave Saxton permission to pursue his idea of conducting operations up southern rivers and creeks into the interior to induce slaves to flee their masters and join the Union cause. He authorized Saxton to use every means in his power to "withdraw from the enemy their laboring force and population, and to spare no effort consistent with civilized warfare to weaken, harass, and annoy them, and to establish the authority of the Government of the United States within your department." To do so, Saxton would have to work closely with Du Pont and the vessels of the South Atlantic Blockading Squadron. Fortunately,

Stanton gave Saxton permission to turn over to the navy any number of "colored volunteers that may be required for the naval service" and reminded both Saxton and Du Pont that, by a recent act of Congress, "all men and boys received into the service of the United States who may have been slaves of rebel masters are, with their wives, mothers and children, declared to be forever free."[59]

In the coming months, Du Pont carefully issued instructions regarding contrabands to his commanders. For example, in late October he ordered Commander Charles Steedman to proceed with the *Paul Jones* and assume command of the blockade in St. Simon's Sound, Georgia, and instructed him, "All friendly contrabands asking protection you will receive and ration, if need be, until sent for by General Saxton." The admiral informed Steedman that Saxton wanted the *Darlington* to be sent up the Altamaha River to procure more rice for the contrabands. "Please give her such protection as maybe desirable which will not interfere with your blockading duties," Du Pont told the commander.[60]

By September 1862, however, the War Department had replaced Hunter as commander of the Department of the South with General Ormsby Mitchel. Shortly after assuming command, Mitchel expressed concerns about the condition of the freed people living in camps or temporary shelters on Hilton Head, prompting a local newspaper to report on October 4, 1862: "Some wholesome changes are contemplated by the new regime (not the least of which is the removal of the Negro quarters beyond the stockade . . . where they can at once have more comfort and freedom for improvement)." The article explained that a spot had been selected near the Drayton plantation for a "Negro village. They are able to build their own houses, and will probably be encouraged to establish their own police. . . . A teacher, Ashbell Landon, has been appointed." The village became known as Mitchelville and by 1865 had grown to accommodate 1,500 people.[61]

By the fall of 1862 abolitionists, philanthropists, and Quaker missionaries had established about thirty schools on St. Helena Island as part of what became known as the "Port Royal experiment." Numerous philanthropic groups collected funds and supplies for the contrabands, which they shipped to camps at Point Lookout, Fortress Monroe, Craney Island, Washington, D.C., and other locations. In early 1863 Dr. O. Brown acknowledged the shipment of goods to Craney Island and noted, "It has saved the people upon the Island an immense amount of suffering, and has saved us the misfortune of witnessing such suffering, without the means of relieving it."[62]

In 1863 and 1864 newly freed people continued to go to Port Royal and to other contraband camps along the coast that were under Union Navy protection against Confederate raids. In some cases Du Pont made reference to specific measures taken to secure these Union posts and colonies. On April 1, 1863, for example, Du Pont informed Steedman that military authorities had asked him to protect Hilton Head Island and the surrounding waters. The admiral told Steedman to send the *Wabash* and *Vermont* over to the Hilton Head side of the harbor and keep the *Madgie* in Station Creek. He also sent the *Marblehead* up to Port Royal and ordered Commander J. C. Beaumont to take the *Sebago* to Calibogue Sound to cover the approaches to the west end of Hilton Head Island, prevent attacks by rebels in boats, and signal the picket stations on shore. In other cases Du Pont could not guarantee protection for contraband colonies and had to make difficult decisions about their safety. One such case took place in late March 1863 when Du Pont decided to remove the colony on North Island. He ordered Beaumont to take the *Sebago* back to Port Royal with the contrabands from the North Island colony. The admiral apologized for being unable to provide a transport to take the people off but assured Beaumont that "your passage will be brief and you must make the best arrangements you can."[63]

Unhappily, in one notorious case, the presence of federal gunboats failed to protect the contrabands on St. Helena from the rampages of federal troops—the very men responsible for protecting them from rebel raids and harassment. For three days in mid-February 1863, soldiers from the Ninth New Jersey, 100th New York, and Twenty-fourth Massachusetts Regiments "went bezerk and terrorized" St. Helena Island. According to Laura Towne and Superintendent Hammond, the gangs of soldiers killed and stole livestock, took money from blacks on the island, beat some, and burned all the cabins on the David Jenkins plantation. In a letter dated February 19, 1863, Harriet Ware wrote, "Besides the actual loss to the people—and in many cases it has been their all—the loss of confidence in Yankees is an incalculable injury. . . . The scenes some of the superintendents have had to go through with are beyond description." Ware stated that Sumner "had a pistol put at his breast for trying to stop the soldiers and protect the negroes, and Mr. Hammond when he went with General Saxton to tell Hunter of what had been done under his very eyes on his own plantations burst into tears." That soldiers from her home state of Massachusetts played a role in the affair distressed Ware, who wrote, "It is disgusting that any Massachusetts regiment should be mixed up with such savage treatment and [that] the Twenty-fourth should be is shameful in the extreme."[64]

Union Navy officers continued to seek ways to support the contrabands already located in camps or villages along the coast. In May 1863 Acting Master J. C. Dutch, commanding the bark *Kingfisher* in St. Helena Sound, discovered large quantities of corn on several estates on Edisto Island. "It being much needed by blacks, and also by horses on St. Helena Island, I invited the superintendents to send their boats and take it away," Dutch reported. On the morning of May 13 he sent a launch with twelve riflemen, accompanied by seventeen boats, from St. Helena to Edisto. Five days later they returned loaded with 800 bushels of "very good corn." He told Du Pont, "My object in doing this was, first, to prevent its falling into rebel hands, and, second, to supply the people in this vicinity. Hope you will justify the course I have pursued." Less than a week later Dutch took a boat party up the South Edisto River to Aiken's Landing on Jehossee Island, explaining to Du Pont that he had learned from contrabands "that a large schooner was lying at a place the contrabands call Grimball's, on the Paw-Paw River, near the junction of the South Edisto and Dawho rivers." Dutch's landing party came ashore but found no sign of the enemy or any contrabands on the island, so they crossed over to the Aiken residence and went down to the landing. Not seeing any schooner, they returned to their boats, but on the way, Dutch and his party entered the Aiken residence through a side window. Although they saw "a large amount of rich and valuable furniture, and a very expensive library," Dutch did not allow the men to take anything. Du Pont commended Dutch, writing, "Your course in having the corn removed from Edisto Island for the purpose of feeding the blacks is approved, as well as your prudent conduct in preventing any plundering of Mr. Aiken's residence. No good can result from any wanton destruction of rebel property. It does no benefit to us and is contrary to my general instructions relating to the destruction of private property."[65]

By the end of 1863 Union Navy vessels of both the North and South Atlantic Blockading Squadrons had not only enforced the Union blockade but also managed to give hundreds of fugitive slaves avenues to freedom, settled them in contraband colonies along the coast, provided for them, and, with some exceptions, kept them relatively safe from rebel harassment. Many other contrabands had been shipped north to navy yards at Boston, Philadelphia, and New York or sent to contraband camps in Washington, D.C., and Alexandria, Virginia. Other refugees had collected at Fortress Monroe, Hilton Head, Hampton, Craney Island, and Fort Norfolk and in towns such as Yorktown, Portsmouth, and Suffolk, Virginia, and New Bern, North Carolina. According to one source, "Some of them were conducted from these camps into York, Columbia, Harrisburg, Pittsburg, and Philadelphia, and by water to New York and

Boston, from which they went to various parts seeking labor." Numerous contrabands settled at Five Points, New York, in a camp at Duff Green's Row on Capitol Hill, or at Freedman's Village on Arlington Heights. One estimate claimed that by 1864, 40,000 blacks from plantations in the South had come to Washington, D.C. In 1864 Levi Coffin testified that 41,150 contrabands were "in military services as soldiers, laundresses, cooks, officers' servants and laborers in the various staff departments."[66]

Neither the Union armed services nor the Lincoln administration seems to have anticipated this influx of former slaves into Union-occupied areas of the South and to border cities such as Alexandria and Washington. Focused in the early months of the war on bringing rebellious states back into the Union and on raising troops and organizing to prosecute the war, the Lincoln administration avoided references to abolishing slavery and was reluctant to make the war about slavery. Although Secretary of the Navy Gideon Welles was a self-proclaimed antislavery man, he served the president and carefully avoided antagonizing Lincoln and his cabinet on the issue of abolition. Consumed by the demands of establishing and maintaining a blockade of the southern coast, Welles and his squadron commanders did not initially see themselves as liberators of slaves or protectors of free black runaways. Only when Union Navy vessels stationed along the coast or patrolling rivers and creeks began to attract these refugees did the navy have to confront the issue of accepting or rejecting these people. Most runaway blacks saw federal gunboats and other vessels as potential havens or sanctuaries, hoping or perhaps even assuming that if they could reach the ships they would be welcomed and would be "free." Although some blacks believed their masters' admonitions that the Yankees would make them fight or send them to Cuba, evidence suggests that most recognized these threats for what they were—attempts to keep slaves in bondage—and fled their masters when the opportunity arose.

Once on board Union vessels, these refugees had to be fed and sometimes clothed, and to prevent them from consuming the ships' limited supplies of food and water, they had to be sent ashore. Early in the war, the arrival of black refugees forced commanding officers to make difficult decisions about taking them on board, sending them back, or returning them to their rightful owners. Although not advocating that commanders intentionally seek out and liberate slaves, by the fall of 1861 Navy Secretary Welles had set a policy authorizing them to accept refugees but, in a timely manner, to put women, children, and elderly men on shore and to enlist able-bodied males. Many of these refugees went to Fortress Monroe or Hilton Head, where former slaves had gathered under federal protection or the government had established contraband camps. In other cases, commanders of vessels burdened with refugees sought the most practical, expedient solution—simply putting them ashore on islands or at convenient coastal locations. In certain instances, slaves presented themselves to Union vessels and begged to be taken to safety in specific locations, such as Otter Island.

Sympathetic to their plight, naval officers often felt responsible for the contrabands' welfare once they were sent ashore to improvised camps, such as the ones on North Island and Otter Island. Naval officers attempted to find food for the newly freed people in these camps, to protect them from rebel harassment and raids, and, at least on St. Simon's Island, to administer these camps with rules and regulations. According to one account, some of the contrabands refused to move from their homes in vulnerable areas to more secure camps on Edisto or St. Helena because they trusted the navy gunboats to protect them. Commanding officers, with the express approval of senior squadron commanders, deployed their vessels to patrol the vicinity of these contraband camps and even conducted raids to intimidate rebel soldiers who might threaten them. Although few reports on the organization and daily operation of these navy contraband camps survived the war, they may have been better supervised than army- or government-run camps for contrabands. Certainly, Du Pont encouraged his commanders to care for and protect contrabands, and he agreed with Truxtun that the government was bound by "every principle of justice and policy" to shield them from attack. Confederate forces did in fact raid contraband colonies, sometimes capturing blacks or causing injury or even death to these innocent civilians. These incursions incensed and puzzled Union naval officers, who could not account for what one officer termed the "extreme barbarity" against the blacks who had been living peacefully on plantations.[67]

Protecting and providing for these freed people taxed naval commanders' patience and ingenuity, however. The vulnerability of contraband camps to rebel attack prompted blockade squadron commanders, especially Du Pont, to urge the Navy Department to convince the army to send federal troops to garrison some of the colonies. Union soldiers were sent to Edisto, St. Simon's, and St. Helena not only to protect the contrabands but also to prevent the rebels from reoccupying these Sea Islands. In turn, the Union garrisons on these islands were dependent on navy gunboats and other vessels to protect and support them, but the navy did not always have the resources necessary to accomplish that mission. Furthermore, in the summer of 1862, after the withdrawal of troops from these islands, the navy reluctantly had to evacuate the contraband colonies on Edisto and St. Simon's. Despite northerners' opposition to the migration of freed people to their states, the navy eventually shipped hundreds of contrabands to navy yards in New York, Boston, and Philadelphia. Although many of them found employment in these navy yards, the fate of the others is unknown. Presumably they remained in the North for the remainder of the war, finding work as servants, laundresses, cooks, waiters, or laborers and possibly reuniting with relatives who had escaped earlier from slavery and settled in the North. When the war ended, some probably went south to locate family and resettle in familiar places, but others, preferring not to return to the place of their bondage, may have stayed near the navy yards in these northern cities. Many of the former slaves who did return to the South could not locate relatives who had been sold by their masters or mistresses and scattered by the war.[68]

The Union Navy's role in assisting hundreds of these former slaves to freedom, sending them north, or settling them in contraband colonies along the southern coast has been little studied and never fully appreciated.

CHAPTER 4
INFORMANTS

One of the contrabands gave information that nightly six steamers were expected from Nassau and England and one (the South Carolina) *and two sailing vessels [were soon] to go out. This information caused me to alter the positions of the blockading vessels.*

—John Marchand

Whether liberated in Union raids and expeditions into the interior, captured on rebel blockade runners, or picked up in rowboats, canoes, or sailboats, most black refugees possessed valuable intelligence about Confederate morale, illicit trade, troop deployments and defenses, Confederate blockade runners, and ironclads under construction or in commission. Within weeks of the fall of Fort Sumter, African American refugees seeking sanctuary on Union naval vessels offered valuable information to the ships' commanding officers. Commander Stephen Rowan's June 1861 rescue of a black man who told him about rebel troops patrolling at Mathias Point was just one of many such instances as the summer wore on. At this early stage of the war, few naval officers were familiar with the white inhabitants of the areas their ships patrolled, but they soon discovered that African Americans, though not always educated, could be observant and willing sources of useful information about the enemy. Union Navy officers patrolling in the Potomac and Rappahannock rivers, for example, quickly came to rely on local blacks for information about illicit trade. Owing to their southern sympathies, many white Marylanders were reluctant to share information about Confederate activities and looked the other way when smugglers carried on an active trade between the Maryland and Virginia shorelines. Commander Thomas Tingey Craven reported, "From all I can see and learn of the people of Maryland I am convinced that along the shores of the Potomac there is not one in twenty who is true to the Union." He speculated that many hundreds of them were "thoroughly organized into companies, perhaps regiments, and prepared to act against the Government at any moment."[1]

As the commander responsible for enforcing the Union blockade in the Potomac, Craven needed reliable information to identify persons who supported the rebellion and actively engaged in what he termed "traitorous acts." Fortunately, Craven had an African American steward with him on board the side-wheel tug USS *Yankee* off Piney Point. In his August 11, 1861, report to Welles, Craven explained, "This evening at sunset a negro came on board and intimated to my steward that he could give me some important information." When Craven questioned the man, the informant told him about an Irishman named Maddox who had been active at Herring Creek in procuring volunteers for the Confederate Army, as well as munitions of war and clothing for the rebels, which he sent by boat across the river to Virginia. Maddox carried out his activities in cooperation with a Dr. Combe, the black informant told Craven. They employed their "negroes, horses, and wagons in transporting recruits to the various landings, at night, watching their opportunity when our cruisers are out of sight." The black informant identified other individuals engaged in illicit trade and a home used as a depot for rebel recruits. "This statement, although made by a negro, has every appearance of being truthful," Craven wrote, "and from hints which have come to me from the proprietor of the hotel there, I am convinced that these persons are active participators in the rebellion and are constantly engaged in traitorous acts."[2]

On the basis of this story, Craven ordered a landing party of eight men under Acting Master's Mate Street to seize the two boats at Herring Creek. On the following morning, August 12, a vindicated Craven informed Welles that Street had "returned with three fine boats as prizes." Earlier, Lieutenant William Budd, commanding the *Resolute,* had led another successful action to break up a depot used by the rebels to receive recruits and supplies from Herring Creek. Although greeted by musket fire from shore, Budd and his men landed, destroyed the premises, and captured a large boat from Maryland. They then liberated ten contrabands belonging to a Colonel Brown, the owner of the premises, who proved extremely useful as sources of intelligence about enemy intentions.[3]

Street's and Budd's successful raids against illicit trade contributed to the Potomac Flotilla's mission. However, Craven lamented that he had too few vessels to intercept the unusual amount of traffic between the rebels on either side of the river, and those he did have were "half equipped and manned." Nonetheless, Potomac Flotilla vessels continued to scour the banks for enemy boats and suspected rebel smugglers, and naval officers eagerly sought information from local African Americans. They soon learned, however, that they could not always count on blacks for reliable information, even those who appeared to be sympathetic to the Union cause. When Washington Navy Yard commandant John A. Dahlgren sent a 150-man detachment of the Seventy-first Regiment to Port Tobacco in June 1861 to seize a cache of arms rumored to be stored there, he regrettably had to report: "The expedition has returned from Port Tobacco without finding any arms. It was conducted with secrecy and expeditiousness, but it is probably that the negroes were afraid to give information as to the place of concealment."[4]

An incident involving the ex–U.S. Coast Survey schooner *Dana* confirmed Dahlgren's suspicion that fear, rather than loyalty to the Confederacy, was the reason for the reluctance of some African Americans to provide information about rebel activities. On August 14, 1861, a white man named Smith came alongside the *Dana* requesting protection for himself and other pro-Union inhabitants of St. George's Island who had been threatened by Captain Edward Code and several parties residing on the Maryland shore who were engaged in contraband trade. *Dana* and the schooner *Bailey* went to St. George's Island, but the *Bailey's* skipper, Master's Mate James L. Gray, believed he was not authorized to search Code's home for illicit goods without an order from his superior. He and Acting Master's Mate Robert Ely, commanding the *Dana*, thus concocted an elaborate ruse. Pretending to be the good "secessionist" captain of the schooner *John Grant,* Ely went to Code's house and engaged the captain in genial conversation. After enjoying wine and cigars, Ely departed with the information he had been seeking. "I was led to believe that there were organized companies of armed men ready to cooperate with any forces which might land from Virginia in an attack upon the Government," he explained. While Ely was visiting Captain Code, a runaway negro owned by Colonel Code (the captain's father) and his son-in-law, Dr. Coombs, had sought refuge on the *Bailey.* "The negro says that his master threatened to shoot him for reporting certain boats to you as having been engaged in contraband trade and that he ran for his life," Ely told Craven. Both Coombs and Colonel Code came to Piney Point demanding that the black man be returned to them, but Gray refused to give him up.[5]

Determining the loyalty of Maryland residents as well as the crew and passengers on vessels plying the Potomac was an ongoing problem for Union Navy commanders. Blockade vessels regularly pursued and intercepted suspicious vessels in the river, but ascertaining whether the passengers had valid "passes" or the vessels carried contraband cargo could be a difficult task. Interrogating crew members and passengers about the ship's cargo and itinerary might yield false information if those questioned had pro-Confederate sympathies. Navy commanders needed the testimony of reliable, trustworthy crewmen to resolve discrepancies, and they quickly discovered that most African American crewmen were loyal to the Union.

As an example, when the side-wheel tug USS *Yankee* overhauled the schooner *Remittance* off Lower Cedar Point in late August 1861, the testimony of black crewman William Posey proved invaluable in revealing the schooner's clandestine activity. One of the passengers, John P. Richards, claimed that his trunk had been "passed" by boarding officials at Baltimore and contained nothing more than a few articles of clothing, but Posey, who had been sailing with the *Remittance* for several years, told Craven that the trunk had not been inspected in Baltimore. In fact, as Craven reported to Welles, Posey stated "that it was tightly packed with some heavy articles which he believes to have been contraband and that they have been conveyed over into Virginia." Tipped off by Posey, the *Yankee's* officers discovered that the trunk had a false lining "which was stuck to the true lining by wafers, affording a space between the two where letters, etc. could have been concealed." Craven considered the trunk's owner a suspicious character, and when Richards could not account for this false lining, Craven sent him to Washington for further questioning. Information provided by the black sailor also enabled Craven to identify the *Remittance's* master, James H. M. Burroughs, as a "rank secessionist" who used his vessel to transport contraband goods from Baltimore and his boats to convey goods, men, and horses across the river to Virginia. Posey also implicated Burroughs and his brother Thomas in an incident in March when rebels set afire a light boat off Cedar Point. Posey suggested that one of the light-boat keepers might be able to identify the men. Given this information, Craven detained the *Remittance* and sent both Burroughs brothers to Washington, along with the witness Posey. When Welles received Craven's report, he ordered the schooner sent as a prize to the Washington Navy Yard. In turn, Craven had the schooner towed up the Potomac with the passengers and remaining crew, "John Bradley (white) and Henry Lockett (colored)."[6]

Sympathetic, intelligent black crewmen like William Posey gave Union commanders a distinct advantage in determining the true identity of individuals engaged in illicit trade with the Confederacy, but in some instances, commanders expressed reluctance to trust these friendly blacks. Take, for example, Lieutenant Budd's suspicious reaction to a black man caught attempting to cross the river into Virginia on the night of August 21, 1861. Budd questioned the man, who claimed he had been sent by two men from Maryland to assist in the construction of a battery between Possum Nose and Cockpit Point. According to the informant, a man named Renner had a schooner engaged in the wood trade that, on return trips, brought ammunition bundled in small parcels stowed under the cabin floor. However, as Budd told Craven, "The negro's conduct, the circumstances of his capture, etc., are calculated to excite suspicion. He says he belongs to a Mr. Griffin in Virginia, was sent across three weeks ago for safe-keeping. I am of the opinion he is a spy or trap of some kind." Despite these occasional misgivings, Craven and his commanders continued to rely on African Americans for information about illicit activities and Confederate attempts to erect batteries at various locations along the Potomac River. On August 30, 1861, while passing Upper Cedar Point in the USS *Yankee,* Craven came upon four black men, two of whom, James Scott and Henry Young, had been employed building rebel batteries at Mathias Point. Young told the captain the rebels planned to mount three heavy guns at the battery "sometime during the present week." The other two men, William Henderson and Grandison Piper, had left Virginia in a small skiff. Craven sent the men to the navy yard at Washington, where at least one of the black refugees gave Union authorities more information about suspicious rebel activities.[7]

As commander of the Potomac Flotilla, responsible for enforcing the blockade of that vital waterway, Craven responded to reports of Confederate batteries being erected at Mathias Point with alarm. "The more I witness the operations of the rebels, the more I am satisfied that if some prompt and efficient step is not taken to prevent it, the navigation of the Potomac River will be entirely cut off," Craven warned Welles. He feared that if Union forces did not construct batteries opposite Mathias Point and send federal troops to occupy White House and the Maryland shore, his vessels might be "threatened with some serious disaster." Unfortunately, Welles took no immediate action, merely passing Craven's concerns on to Secretary of War Simon Cameron.[8]

Less than two weeks later Craven obtained further intelligence when four contrabands—James Minor, George Washington, Samuel Bunn, and James Lawson—escaped from Virginia to the USS *Yankee.* Lawson, a house servant belonging to John Tayloe, a colonel in the rebel army, told Craven that the rebels intended to bring seven guns for their new battery from Fredericksburg to Hop Yard Wharf on the Rappahannock and then across to Mathias Point. According to the contraband, the rebels also had 700 militia encamped five miles back from Mathias Point on Machodoc Creek and another 2,000 men on Potomac Creek. "The statement of this man is similar to that I have received from other sources," Craven told Assistant Navy Secretary Gustavus Fox. Concerned that rebel forces might close the Potomac at certain points, Craven vainly sought reassurance from Welles, who merely urged him to obtain sufficient supplies and provisions to allow his vessels to maintain their position if the rebels gained control of the river. Clearly displeased, Craven wrote to Welles again, urging that troops be sent to occupy Mathias Point to prevent the Confederates from crossing the Potomac.[9]

In lieu of army support, Craven ordered his vessels to keep a close eye on Mathias Point and Pope's Creek for signs of rebel activity. To no one's surprise, when the steamer *Rescue* went back to Pope's Creek on September 21, 1861, to tow a suspicious schooner, a force of 200 cavalry peppered the *Rescue* with musketry. The ship returned fire, which sent the rebels scurrying for safety. Two days later the sloop *Seminole* picked up a party of four black men and one black woman, who informed Lieutenant C. S. Norton of a rebel battery being erected at Freestone Point. When *Seminole* and *Jacob Bell* steamed down to Freestone Point to confirm the contrabands' report, they found men excavating the ground, preparing a site for a gun battery. *Jacob Bell* fired six shells, which dispersed the workers, but when *Seminole* also opened fire, the rebels replied with rifled shots, initiating a half-hour duel between the rebel battery and the two Union vessels.[10]

Two weeks later a ten-gun rebel battery at Evansport, on the right bank below Quantico Creek, fired on the *Pocahontas* and *Seminole*. "So long as the battery stands at Shipping Point and Evansport the navigation of the Potomac will be effectually closed," Craven warned Welles. When Craven refused to attempt to reduce the battery with the vessels at his command, Welles called on the commander of the Department of the Potomac, Major General George B. McClellan, for assistance, arguing that the erection of extensive batteries and the stationing of troops in their vicinity "imperatively requires action of the Army, unless communication by the river is to be abandoned, which on many account would be unfortunate and almost disastrous." To Craven's disappointment, McClellan did little to assist the navy in securing the Potomac River.[11]

Vessels in the Potomac Flotilla continued to harass the rebels at Mathias Point, and commanders continued to rely on contrabands for information about rebel activity. By November the *Island Belle* had picked up twenty-three black men, women, and children, making a total of forty contrabands in Lieutenant A. D. Harrell's vessels. Although

Mathias Point seemed quiet, Harrell told Craven, "The talk among the negroes, however, is that a battery will be opened there soon as they can get soldiers." Sparked by this new information, Captain Harris of the *Island Belle* and Samuel Magaw of the *Freeborn* put together an expedition with 400 soldiers from Colonel Charles K. Graham's Fifth Regiment, Excelsior Brigade, to land at Mathias Point and determine whether the rebels had erected a battery there. When the *Freeborn* was unable to participate, the schooner *Dana* took its place. They landed at Mathias Point on November 10, 1861, made a thorough inspection of the area, seized "a large amount of rebel property," and skirmished with enemy pickets. In the process, they also determined that the rebels had only three unfinished entrenchments and, according to the *Dana*'s skipper, Master William Street, these had not been worked on or occupied "for some time."[12]

By then, the existence of Confederate batteries on the Virginia shore had temporarily halted commercial traffic up the Potomac River. On October 31, 1861, Craven informed Welles that he deemed it "an impossibility" for any vessel drawing more than eight feet to pass up or down the river. This turn of events proved the last straw for Thomas Craven. On November 20, 1861, he asked to be relieved of command of the Potomac Flotilla, citing health concerns and the "utter uselessness" of the flotilla in protecting the river. After weeks of urging the Union Army to take action against the rebels along the Potomac, John Dahlgren sent Craven the welcome news that General Joseph Hooker was on his way with a division of 8,000 men and eighteen guns to "cooperate" with him. Nonetheless, the Potomac River remained closed to commercial navigation until the Confederates voluntarily abandoned their batteries in March 1862.[13]

African Americans continued to seek refuge on federal vessels throughout the fall and winter of 1861 and into 1862, bringing reports of Confederate morale, blockade runners, defenses, and troop movements. Furthermore, Union operations in November 1861 had created a new and valuable source of African American informants for officers of the South Atlantic Blockading Squadron and for Union Army commanders. When the federal fleet attacked Hilton Head Island and seized strategically important Port Royal Sound, plantation owners and other whites fled into the interior, taking some of their slaves with them, but abandoning thousands of others in Beaufort, on Hilton Head, and on other Sea Islands. Union troops and navy gunboats at Port Royal attracted slaves and free blacks from areas such as Savannah as well, some of whom brought information about Confederate activities and defenses. In a letter written shortly after the fall of Port Royal, Flag Officer Samuel F. Du Pont told his wife, Sophie: "We get various rumors from contrabands, of course what they say must be sifted well. In one thing, however, the burden of their story is the same—the great terror produced by the blow."[14]

In January 1862 Du Pont began receiving additional reports of conditions in the city of Savannah. The day after New Year's, Commander John P. Gillis sent him a report containing information received from a contraband who had approached the *Seminole* in an old canoe. The man, whom Gillis described as a mulatto, claimed the rebels had 15,000 troops in and around Savannah but stated, "They are short of ammunition [and] much disheartened on account of an apology by Lord Lyons, [as the rebels] had hoped for a war between us and England; that they will fight to the last about Savannah and burn the city down rather than give it up." According to this contraband informant, provisions in the city were "scarce and dear," and all who could had left Savannah following the Union attack. The contraband described the Confederate gun batteries at Skiddaway, Thunderbolt, and Green Island and claimed that the rebels had supplied Fort Pulaski well with provisions. Gillis told Du Pont that according to the contraband, "Commodore Tattnall's fleet is complained of, and he [is] pronounced too old." Although Gillis did not place much confidence in this story, Du Pont trusted the information sufficiently to repeat much of it to his wife in a letter written the following day. He included a more recent report that Tattnall had resigned "from infirmities of age." Josiah Tattnall had not, in fact, resigned, but reports of poor morale in the Confederacy continued to reach Du Pont's flagship. In February 1862 Du Pont wrote to Charles Du Pont, "from all we can infer from what runaway contrabands and deserters tell us, the demoralization has commenced—150 soldiers deserted in one day from Savannah, saying it was a rich man's war and not theirs, that the former were going into the interior of the state with their gold and their Negroes and leaving them to do the fighting."[15]

Despite reports of poor Confederate morale in Savannah, Union officials chose Fernandina, Florida, as the target for their next major operation, which would be a joint attack by the South Atlantic Blockading Squadron escorting transports bearing army troops and a marine battalion under the overall command of General Thomas W. Sherman. In 1861 the Strategy Board had included Fernandina's sheltered harbor, lying just 430 miles from Nassau in the Bahamas and a favorite destination for Confederate blockade runners, as one of several deep-water ports along the coastline needed to enforce the blockade.[16]

The town and harbor of Fernandina could be approached from the northeast via Cumberland Sound and a channel guarded by Fort Clinch. General Sherman proposed to use this approach, but Du Pont expressed reluctance to expose his ships to fire from the fort in the narrow channel. Du Pont then convinced Sherman to take the western or inland approach behind Cumberland Sound, while the remainder of the fleet bombarded and silenced the batteries on Amelia Island so the transports could enter the Amelia River and land troops to occupy the town of Fernandina.[17]

After weather-related delays, the Union expedition steamed to St. Andrews Sound and anchored on the morning of March 2, 1862. That evening, as the expedition prepared to pass from St. Andrews through Cumberland Sound, Du Pont received some startling information from a contraband that contributed substantially to his decisions about the operation. As Du Pont later explained to Welles, he had "learned from a contraband who had been picked up at sea by Commander Lanier, and from neighboring residents on Cumberland Island, that the rebels had abandoned in haste" and were retreating. In a letter to his wife, Du Pont elaborated: "Captain Lanier discovered a canoe with one man in it, of course a darky, and now comes a story." The runaway, who had been in one of the forts, "got permission to go up to Fernandina, and then slipped out over the bar, not knowing the fleet was on the coast but hoping to meet one of the blockading ships and saying he had made up his mind to take his chance of drowning or escape." The contraband, named Louis Napoleon, reported that the forts had been dismantled, the guns removed to St. John's Bluff on the St. John's River, and that the Georgia troops manning forts on Cumberland Island had all left for Savannah. "They had more forts than we thought," Du Pont wrote, "and Clinch was armed, and when I asked Louis Napoleon how he accounted for the stampede he said they were ordered to give up by the general—the people wanted to fight." Du Pont was "exultant" when he heard that the Confederates had abandoned their defenses, John Marchand noted, "though many of the junior officers were disappointed." The news, in Du Pont's words, evoked "long faces at lost laurels." Until the timely arrival of this black runaway, neither Sherman nor Du Pont knew that after the Union capture of Forts Henry and Donelson in Tennessee in mid-February 1862, the Confederates had withdrawn from all their fortifications along the Florida coast.[18]

Acting on this contraband's report, which was confirmed by a white pro-Union lighthouse keeper, Du Pont immediately instructed Captain James L. Lardner, commanding the *Susquehanna,* to cut off any attempted rebel retreat by sea and "to endeavor to ascertain . . . if the defenses of Fernandina have been abandoned." Lardner proceeded toward Fernandina at high tide to gather information and draw the fire of the forts, but he was unable to get in. Rather than wait until the morning tide, Du Pont ordered Commander Percival Drayton to take the *Pawnee* and all the ships with a draft of less than eleven feet and proceed "in haste with the evening tide, through Cumberland sound into Fernandina harbor," and take possession "of all public and private property, and to secure prisoners and munitions of war."[19]

The next day Drayton sent armed launches, cutters, and companies from the *Wabash* into Fernandina and ordered Lieutenant White of the *Ottawa* to hoist the flag on Fort Clinch, "the first of the national forts on which the ensign of the Union has resumed its proper place since the first proclamation of the President of the United States was issued." The fleeing rebels fired a few musket shots before boarding a train, which Drayton and his men chased for two miles, firing several shells at the locomotive. General Horatio Wright's brigade subsequently moved into Fernandina, allowing the Union Navy to turn over responsibility for the town and harbor to the army.[20]

Information from contrabands played a vital role in the Union Navy's subsequent operations along the Georgia and Florida coasts during the spring of 1862. When Du Pont learned that the Confederates had abandoned Brunswick, Georgia, presenting him with an opportunity to secure even more of the Georgia coastline, he ordered Commander S. W. Godon to take the *Mohican* and *Pocahontas* up the coast to St. Simon's Sound. Finding the forts below Brunswick deserted, Godon sent Lieutenant George Balch with an armed landing party to take possession of St. Simon's Island, "hoisting the American flag on one of the batteries thrown up by the rebels." Balch and another landing party subsequently took possession of Brunswick, which he found "entirely deserted of its inhabitants." After securing Brunswick and Jekyll Island, Godon took the *Potomska* and *Pocahontas* through the inland passage to the Altamaha River toward Darien, where he had heard two rebel steamers might be located. Although contrabands had reported that the river was staked entirely across, Godon cleared a roughly forty-foot passage and pressed on, but another obstruction dashed his hope of reaching Darien during the night. To his further disappointment, the two rebel steamers could be seen moving off from the wharf at full speed up the Altamaha River. Hampered by the *Potomska*'s broken shaft bearing, Godon chose to return to his anchorage at Brunswick, stopping to visit a number of plantations on St. Simon's Island along the way. From contrabands

Godon learned that Darien was deserted, "a company of horsemen only remaining in the town, with the intention of firing the place should the steamers approach it."[21]

Although he had not actually landed there, Commander Godon accepted the contrabands' reports that the rebels had indeed abandoned Darien, giving the Union Navy possession of the entire southern Georgia and northern Florida coasts. Furthermore, on March 27, 1862, Du Pont sent Welles the welcome news that Gillis had come on board the flagship and informed him that the rebels had evacuated batteries on Skiddaway and Green islands, giving the Union complete control of Wassaw and Ossabaw sounds and the mouths of the Vernon and Wilmington rivers, which were important approaches to Savannah. He enclosed a memorandum of information obtained by Gillis from a contraband picked up by the *Norwich*. The man claimed to have left Savannah on March 22, 1862, and stated, "Folks are going and coming, some who had left are returning, and they are sending negroes and cotton inland and are moving all the cash money to Macon, and threaten to burn the city if they should be unable to hold it, and are in daily expectation of our attack." Despite this Confederate expectation, Du Pont had no plans to attack the city of Savannah at that time.[22]

Refugees and contrabands proved to be sources of intelligence for North Atlantic Blockading Squadron commanders as well, who used the information to organize and conduct numerous Union Navy expeditions up southern rivers and creeks, some of which were extremely successful in capturing Confederate supplies, destroying schooners and small craft laden with rebel supplies, and liberating African Americans. The arrival of two black men on board the bark *Restless* on the morning of February 11, 1862, for example, led to an armed boat expedition that destroyed a sloop and two schooners. That morning, lookouts on the *Restless* sighted a sailboat coming out of Bull's Bay and making for their ship. The small yawl contained two contrabands, Harry Reed and William Maxwell, who had been hired by Captain Francis Roberts of the schooner *Theodore Stoney*, which was headed from Santee to Charleston with a cargo of 2,500 bushels of rice. From these two contrabands, who seemed "quite intelligent," Acting Volunteer Lieutenant Edward Conroy, skipper of the *Restless*, learned of twenty-five schooners and sloops taking supplies to the rebels at Charleston. According to Reed and Maxwell, shallow vessels such as the *Thomas Stoney* were able to navigate the inland route from Charleston to the Santee and Georgetown. Frustrated by watching three or four vessels a day pass and repass his station off Bull's Bay, and unable to get closer than four or five miles, Conroy suggested to his superior, Commander Enoch G. Parrott, that a small, light-draft steam tug be sent to "cut off this source of supplies."[23]

Conroy did not wait for Parrott to send him a tug. When he discovered a vessel on a shoal in Bull's Bay, Conroy sent two armed boats after it. "Upon boarding they found her to be [a] very old and worthless craft, without a cargo, and only four negroes on board," Conroy reported. While on board, however, Conroy's disappointed men sighted three more vessels lying at anchor inside the shoals. These vessels had evidently come from the Santee River and were headed for Charleston laden with rice for the city, making them potentially lucrative prizes for the *Restless*'s officers and men. After receiving this exciting news, at 1:30 A.M. Conroy sent another armed boat with orders to cut these vessels out or destroy them. The lack of wind, the shoals, and the presence of a rebel battery prevented the boat party from sailing the three vessels out as prizes, so Conroy ordered them sunk and the *Theodore Stoney,* with its 2,500 bushels of rice, burned. Although a great disappointment to the *Restless*'s officers and crew, this loss of prize money had positive consequences for the Union war effort. In his report, Commander Parrott claimed that the destruction of these three vessels, made possible in part by the contraband informants Harry Reed and William Maxwell, had dealt a serious blow to rebel inland navigation in the neighborhood of Bull's Bay.[24]

As the experience of the *Restless* clearly shows, intelligence gleaned from contrabands could make valuable contributions to the Union war effort. These African Americans often possessed intimate knowledge of coastal navigation and had the ability to get close to Confederate posts, camps, and other places from which to observe potential blockade runners or other suspicious activities. Obtaining recent and reliable information about rebel blockade runners and their possible routes to and from southern ports gave Union commanders a decided advantage in intercepting them, thus increasing their chances to tighten the Union blockade and possibly gain prize money. Although by law half of any prize money went to the government and 5 percent to the squadron commander, ordinary seamen could receive hundreds if not thousands of dollars from such prizes.

Consider, for example, the January 5, 1862, report of the *Monticello*'s commanding officer, Lieutenant Daniel L. Braine. According to Braine, on December 30, 1861, two contrabands had provided fresh information about the state of affairs at New Inlet, the upper of two approaches to the Cape Fear River leading to Wilmington, North Carolina. They described the fortifications at New Inlet and reported that the rebels

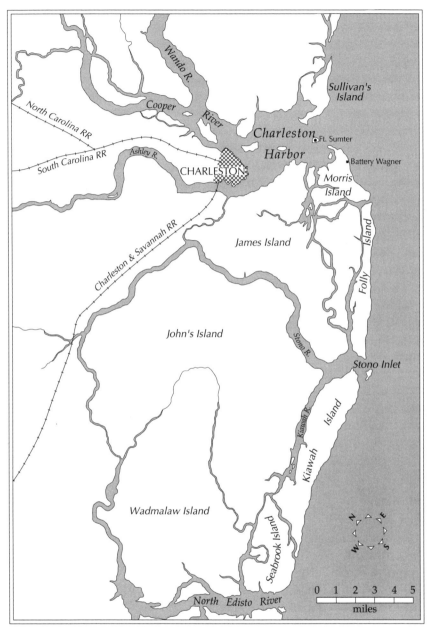

Charleston Harbor and vicinity

had about 1,400 men and four fieldpiece artillery units stationed there. Braine explained that one of the contrabands, Kent Newton, had worked for several years on the ferryboats that crossed the river at Wilmington and had described the recent arrival of the steamer *Gordon* or *Theodora* from Cuba with a cargo of coffee and fruit. Newton confirmed Braine's suspicions about a steamer he had observed over a period of three weeks that had changed its usual route, no longer passing east of Zeek's Island or in the outer channel, as it had during the month of November. Newton explained the steamer's change of course by describing four heavy wooden cribs sunk by the rebels near Zeek's Island, effectively blocking the channel. "This fact has been the subject of comment among the officers," Braine wrote to Commander Oliver Glisson, the senior officer of the Wilmington blockade, "and now that we are aware of the fact that these cribs have been sunk in the channel at Zeek's Island, I know that it is an impossibility for her to pass, or any other vessel drawing 9 feet of water." By escaping to the *Monticello*, Kent Newton and his contraband companion not only earned their freedom but also gave Braine extremely valuable information to share with Glisson and the officers charged with enforcing the blockade of the important southern port of Wilmington. Railroads connected Wilmington to New Bern, allowing the fast shipment of goods brought in by blockade runners and rice from nearby plantations. Before the outbreak of the Civil War, sometimes thirty ships a day docked at Wilmington's wharves, and even in 1862 and 1863 the port continued to see blockade runners going in and out of the river.[25]

By the spring of 1862 the Navy Department and the Lincoln administration had begun exerting tremendous pressure on Du Pont and his squadron to effectively enforce the blockade. Their concerns about the blockade stemmed in part from a number of reports about steamers running the Charleston blockade, reports that had sparked controversy about the blockade's effectiveness. On April 7, 1862, a statement in the British House of Commons that armed vessels passed freely into and out of the city cast the legality of the blockade into question. All these reports prompted the chairman of the Senate Committee on Naval Affairs, John P. Hale, to begin a federal investigation into the effectiveness of the blockade of Charleston. Happily for Du Pont, in late April 1862 Commander Ridgley of the *Santiago de Cuba* captured one of the most elusive Confederate blockade runners, the *Isabel* (*Ella Warley*), heading from Havana, Cuba, to Charleston, and brought it into Port Royal Harbor.[26]

At about this time, a boat carrying fifteen contrabands came alongside the USS *Bienville*, which had departed the blockading station off

Charleston. Commander John Marchand, the senior officer off Charleston, had the "most intelligent" contrabands taken on board his ship, the *James Adger,* for questioning. "I learned that the Steamer *Cecil* from Nassau ran the blockade and entered Charleston before daylight in the morning of last Friday or Saturday," Marchand wrote in his journal entry for April 28, 1862. From these refugees he received a description of the route out of Charleston taken by blockade runners and learned that the rebels had two wooden gunboats under construction but had not laid keels for any ironclads. Of more importance, Marchand wrote in his journal, "One of the contrabands gave information that nightly six steamers were expected from Nassau and England and one (the *South Carolina*) and two sailing vessels [were soon] to go out. This information caused me to alter the positions of the blockading vessels . . . [to] more thoroughly protect [the] blockade."[27]

Alerted by this new information, squadron commanders spent the night, Marchand wrote, "brightly on the lookout" for the *South Carolina.* Neither that ship nor the two sailing vessels, *John Randolph* and *Mackinaw,* appeared, but the *Unadilla* arrived with orders for Marchand to turn command over to Parrott and return to Port Royal for repairs and supplies. After taking on board the fifteen contrabands from the *Bienville,* the *James Adger* headed back to Port Royal, where Marchand promptly called on Du Pont. He wrote in his journal that Du Pont "was much surprised and pleased with the information obtained from the contrabands in relation to affairs about Charleston."[28]

This information about Charleston undoubtedly encouraged Du Pont to solicit and value even more highly any bits of intelligence gathered from black or white refugees. Although information from contrabands about the locations and intentions of rebel blockade runners could warn commanders about steamers preparing to run the blockade, advance notice did not always result in successful pursuits. Naval surgeon George Adams Bright, who kept a journal while serving off Charleston on the *South Carolina,* recorded one such incident. On November 15, 1862, he wrote: "The Flagship telegraphed us this P.M. that two vessels were to run out or run in tonight. Probably the news arrived this morning from the *Mercedita,* at any rate we were all ready for the secesh, only they didn't come but sent a heavy sea instead, to shake us up." Two days later he noted that news of the rebel vessel had come "from some contrabands from shore getting off to the *Memphis.*" The senior officer present, Captain William R. Taylor, confirmed that four contrabands had escaped from Charleston on the night of November 14. William King, Adam Hewbank, Kento Barton, and Henry Dakan had left the railroad

wharf in a boat and reached the *Memphis* at about 4 A.M. Dakan claimed
to be a fireman, and the other three were wheelmen employed as pilots
on the St. John's River. These four contrabands stated that three Eng-
lish ships, the *Herald, Hero,* and *Leopard,* were "all inside, loaded with
cotton and waiting for a chance to run out." Bright's journal entry about
heavy seas to the contrary, another steamer ran out of Charleston on
November 15, with the *G. W. Blunt* giving a spirited chase. One shell from
the *Blunt* struck the steamer, which ran aground briefly on a shoal off
Dewess Inlet but still managed to escape.[29]

Despite information provided by contrabands about these blockade
runners, Union ships had been unable to capture the fast, elusive rebel
steamers. However, when the schooner *Annie Dee* tried to slip past federal blockaders on November 20, the gunboat *Seneca* nabbed it. "Last
evening at 8 o'clock (very dark and rainy) an attempt was made by a
schooner, the *Annie Dee,* to escape from Charleston by Maffit's Channel," Captain S. W. Godon reported. The *Seneca's* commander fired three
shots at the schooner and took it as a prize. The *Annie Dee* carried a
cargo of 140 barrels of turpentine, a quantity of resin, a crew of four
men, and three passengers. An hour after the schooner ran out, the *Housatonic* thought it spotted another blockade runner, chased it for fifty
miles, but could not find the ship. Godon admitted that it might have
been a false alarm but told Du Pont, "The night, however, was so dark
that a vessel may have passed out."[30]

During the first half of 1863, forty-five rebel steamers ran the blockade in and out of Charleston. Hoping to reduce the number of suspicious vessels trying to run the blockade and to be rewarded with prize
money, Union Navy commanders naturally welcomed any information
about potential blockade runners. Furthermore, officers commanding
federal vessels blockading Charleston had to be particularly vigilant
not only for blockade runners but also for Confederate vessels or rams
attempting to attack their ships. "We are expecting nocturnal attacks by
ironclads and cotton-clads and are kept on the sharp lookout," Commander Enoch Parrott of the USS *Augusta* confided to his wife, Susan,
in a letter dated May 11, 1863. "The rebel navy have the advantage that
they can remain at . . . and without care behind their fortifications until
they are ready to attack, while we are kept constantly in a state of expectation." Referring to the need for constant vigilance, Parrott explained,
"I am generally up nearly the whole night. When the war is over I shall
be ready to turn Monk as far as nightly vigils are concerned." Concluding
his letter, Parrott wrote, "This morning a contraband paddled himself off
to us with one oar and I am now on the way to the senior officer to give

him the information and send this letter." The contraband had left from the shore opposite Charleston across the Ashley River, where he and eighty-five others had been engaged in constructing a fort for the rebels. The man claimed that he had worked at Fort Sumter, that it was "badly repaired," and that Confederate work on new forts on Morris Island had slowed. "Few contrabands are at work on the fortifications, they being just now most wanted on the plantations," he told Parrott.[31]

In addition to reports on Confederate blockade runners, during General George B. McClellan's spring campaign on the Yorktown peninsula, contrabands proved to be useful sources of information about Confederate ironclads, shore batteries, and other defenses. When the Army of the Potomac arrived in Hampton Roads, Virginia, in late March 1862, McClellan expected "by rapid movements to drive before me or capture the enemy on the Peninsula, open the James River, and press on to Richmond." At Fort Monroe, however, he learned that rebel batteries on the banks of the York River and the presence of the Confederate ironclad *Merrimac* and its consorts the *Yorktown, Jamestown,* and *Teaser* had closed both the James and York rivers to federal operations. Arguing that watching and neutralizing the *Merrimac* constituted his highest priority, Flag Officer Louis M. Goldsborough refused to detach any of his heavier warships to attack the water batteries at Yorktown and Gloucester. This quickly dashed McClellan's hope that the Union Navy would reduce the batteries and open both rivers, allowing his troops to outflank a skillfully constructed Confederate line of defense across the peninsula from Mulberry Island to Yorktown.[32]

McClellan blamed poor intelligence and inaccurate maps for his failure to realize that the Warwick River did not run northwest but actually ran across the Yorktown peninsula through a low-lying area, affording the Confederate commander, General John Magruder, a natural defensive advantage. The Union Army's lack of intelligence about Confederate defenses was particularly troubling given that General John E. Wool's command included the Fort Monroe area, where hundreds of contrabands had gathered who might have been good sources of information. Rather than interrogate a number of deserters and local blacks or test the rebel defenses, McClellan chose to rely on a single report by a deserter who claimed that Confederate general Joe Johnston's force would soon number 100,000 men, twice the actual number. McClellan then decided to bring up his siege artillery and lay siege to the Yorktown line.[33]

Goldsborough and Wool were far less concerned about rebel batteries at Yorktown and Gloucester Point than about the possibility of the rebel ironclad *Merrimac* (CSS *Virginia*) steaming up to Yorktown, blowing federal gunboats out of the water, and driving Union troops from Ship's Point. The appearance of the *Merrimac* on the morning of April 11, 1862, steaming toward Fort Monroe, accompanied by four gunboats and two tugs, only reinforced their fears. Federal ships fired warning shots to alert the *Monitor* and other blockaders, but the *Merrimac* remained out of range of Union gun batteries. In the early afternoon it took a long-range shot at the *Naugatuck*, which returned fire, but then returned to its anchorage under Craney Island. Other than this brief appearance by the *Merrimac* and a sortie by the *Jamestown* that snatched two brigs and one schooner, the Confederates did no more than hover harmlessly around Sewall's Point. Yet for two weeks the aging Goldsborough clung to the belief that at any moment the ironclad would sally forth and engage the federal squadron. A more likely Confederate strategy seemed obvious to the *Monitor*'s paymaster, William Keeler, who wrote to his wife on April 15, "I think the policy of the rebels to be to keep the *Merrimac* at Norfolk threatening us occasionally by appearing down here & in this manner neutralise the whole fleet in the harbour."[34]

Local contrabands only added to Goldsborough's fears. "Last night a contraband came on board from Gloucester in a canoe, at which they fired," Commander John S. Missroon wrote to McClellan. According to this contraband, "they expect *Merrimack* here, Colonel or General Magruder having written for her to come up, which is promised him, that the battery at Gloucester Point is commanded by Jeff Page, late of the U.S. Navy, a good officer." Missroon told McClellan that according to the black man, the rebel gunners are "very sanguine of sinking vessels." They had practiced their firing, the contraband noted, "which is very accurate; says Page (Jeff) can kill a dog at a mile." Suggesting that McClellan employ the contraband, Missroon explained, "He knows roads and creeks, I will send him P.M. If you want him, telegraph." Then Missroon posed a telling question, "Would it not be well to communicate with the Flag Officer, Magruder's expectation of *Merrimack* coming here?"[35]

Occasionally, Army of the Potomac headquarters passed on information to the navy obtained from runaway slaves about the *Merrimac* and Confederate activities. On May 1, 1862, for example, Wool sent Goldsborough a report obtained from five contrabands recently arrived at Portsmouth who claimed that Commodore Tattnall and the principal officers of the *Merrimac* had resigned and that the *Merrimac* lay off Craney Island, fast to a buoy. "She now mounts twelve guns. There are no other steamers there," Wool wrote. The five contrabands also relayed the important news that Union forces had taken Fort Macon, North Carolina, that Friday, "18 rebels killed, 27 wounded." Goldsborough welcomed the news of Fort Macon's fall, for the fort guarded the entrance to the fine harbor of Beaufort, which the Union Navy wished to secure for a logistical base. "Having a depot of supplies at Beaufort will greatly facilitate the maintenance of the Blockade off Wilmington," Goldsborough explained. Responding quickly to the report of Fort Macon's capture, Goldsborough ordered an ample supply of coal and provisions sent to Beaufort for the blockaders off Wilmington.[36]

Tattnall had not resigned, but in early May, Confederate forces abandoned their defenses at Yorktown and withdrew up the peninsula. "We have taken Yorktown," McClellan telegraphed Goldsborough on May 4, 1862. The following day Union forces marched off in a pouring rain in pursuit of the rebels. Five days later, learning that Union troops had landed on the bay shore, Tattnall decided to lighten the *Merrimac* and try to run upriver to protect Richmond. Although pilots assured him of sufficient water to navigate, the wind had changed; finding his ship unprepared for battle, Tattnall beached the *Merrimac* near the mainland, ordered the crew ashore, and set the ship afire to prevent its capture. After burning for an hour, it exploded.[37]

Two days earlier, at President Lincoln's request, Goldsborough had ordered Commander John Rodgers to take the *Galena, Aroostook,* and *Port Royal* up the James River. Rodgers set off, but fearing that his gunboats would ground on the bar and would not be a match for the five rebel gunboats reported to lie above him, Rodgers asked for reinforcements. To the delight of the *Monitor's* frustrated officers and crew, Goldsborough sent him the ironclad, which was no longer needed to bottle up the *Merrimac*. Rodgers's ships proceeded upriver on May 13 "under a sharp fire of musketry from both banks," and at City Point the five vessels dropped anchor. The squadron then departed City Point to ascend the narrow, twisting James River. In a letter to his wife, George Geer, an engineer aboard the *Monitor,* wrote: "We . . . left City Point and steamed up to here and found out by a Niger who came on Board that there was a very strong Fort some two miles above, so we anchored for the night." In his official report, Rodgers failed to mention the information provided by this black man, but curiously, in a notice to the *Petersburg Express,* Edmund Ruffin of Prince George provided readers with a detailed account of the passage of the federal flotilla to City Point on May 13, 1862: "The latest from City Point is, that after landing a few officers and portions of their crew, who cavorted about for awhile, and appeared to be on the best terms with a contraband or two who conde-scended to speak to them, the party re-embarked, and steamed up the river, with the prows of their vessels pointing Richmondwards."[38]

Although the contraband had warned of a heavy Confederate battery at Drewry's Bluff, just eight miles from Richmond, Rodgers resolutely continued past Harrison's Bar. At 7:35 A.M. a heavy battery on the 100-foot bluff opened fire on the federal squadron, and a hot fight ensued. "We've been fighting all day and have come out 2nd best," Geer told his wife. During the three-hour engagement, rebel gunners concentrated on the thinly armored *Galena,* striking the ship twenty-eight times and inflicting heavy casualties—thirteen men killed and eleven wounded. The *Naugatuck* had two men wounded, and the commanding officer of the *Port Royal,* George U. Morris, received a severe flesh wound in the right leg. Rebel shells also struck the *Monitor* three times but failed to inflict injury on the officers or crew.[39]

Confederate gunners at Drewry's Bluff had dashed Rodgers's hope of steaming boldly up to Richmond. When both the *Wachusett* and the *Galena* grounded in the narrow river on a falling tide, Rodgers ordered the entire squadron to anchor. A deserter gave the commander the discouraging news that the Confederates were still working on the obstructions, had placed another barrier about two miles above the first, strengthened their batteries on Drewry's Bluff, and placed a battery on the eastern bank of the river. From all he had learned of the batteries and barriers at Drewry's Bluff, Rodgers now concluded that to pass them with the steamers and the means at his disposal would be "a perfect impossibility."[40]

Goldsborough reacted quickly to the news of the Drewry's Bluff action, ordering the *Wachusett* and *Maratanza* up the James River to City Point and instructing Commander William Smith, who would assume command in the river, to assess the situation and, if possible, "reduce the enemy's works at Warren's (Drewry's) Bluff, break through the obstructions in the river there and get the *Monitor* up to Richmond." However, when Smith arrived and took command of the James River Squadron, he too concluded that Drewry's could not be passed without cooperation from land forces. Smith deployed his vessel to secure the river—the best he could do in lieu of a joint army-navy operation to attack the Drewry's Bluff batteries. On May 20, 1862, Goldsborough vis-ited McClellan to request the army's assistance in reducing the Drewry's Bluff defenses, but McClellan declined to divert any troops for that pur-pose, preferring to wait until he could get his army across the Chick-ahominy. The general assured Goldsborough that he would cooperate with the navy by sending an infantry column across the river to attack Drewry's when it was "expedient" and promised to communicate frequently and keep Goldsborough "fully informed of his operations and intentions." In return, Goldsborough agreed to keep the river open and support the army's campaign on the peninsula.[41]

Shortly after Smith took command of the James River Squadron, an incident involving a friendly contraband woman dealt a decisive blow to his career. Smith and Rodgers decided to visit the town of City Point, which, Rodgers claimed, was occupied by several Union families, all friendly. After calling at several of the homes, they discovered an ailing woman who asked for a doctor. In a compassionate response, Smith sent his gig ashore with Assistant Surgeon George D. Slocum, four officers, and eight sailors. "All the party were armed with pistols and swords," Smith wrote in his report. While Master's Mate Thomas Almy and five crewmen remained behind, the others went into the village. "In a few minutes after the party left to go up," Smith wrote, "a woman ran down to the beach and told the men to get into their boat immediately and go off, which they did." Although Smith did not specify her race, in a letter to his wife Keeler wrote, "I had been ashore but a few minutes & was looking for the officers of the *Wachusett*, some of whom I had agreed to meet on the dock, when a darkey came running to me saying 'Sojer men are coming jus' on the bluff dar.'" Keeler headed back toward his boat, ordered the men to shove off, and told the other boat crew to look out for their officers, as he believed the "Secesh" were coming. The crew waited for a few moments but then shoved off. However, Keeler wrote, they "had got but a short distance when a smart fire of rifles was opened on us from the brick ware house spoken of before. Half a dozen or so were all that were directed at us, as we were the furtherest off, but a shower of them fell around the other boat & I saw two men, fall." One uninjured man managed to row out to the *Wachusett*. "The *Wachusett's* boat was now picked up—one officer was found dead, two were fatally wounded, one badly so & one unhurt," Keeler wrote. "These were those who had remained by the boat, the others who had gone up the bluff were taken prisoner, with one exception & he escaped & got off in a little skiff he found on some other part (of) the beach." Taken prisoner were Acting Assistant Paymaster Levi S. Stockwell, First Lieutenant John W. De Ford of the U.S. Army, Dr. George D. Slocum, and six seamen. Keeler and his boat crew reached the *Monitor* just as it was getting under way, and had it not been for the warning of a friendly contraband, they too might have been killed or captured.[42]

The warning given by the anonymous black woman may have saved

Keeler and his boat party, but she could not save Smith's career. Navy Secretary Welles strongly disapproved of Smith's actions and particularly regretted the tragic loss of three men and the capture of another four officers and five men. Citing Smith's "neglect as commanding officer," Welles ordered Smith to detach himself from his flagship the *Wachusett* and take command of the steam sloop *Seminole*. Anticipating the launch of a long-awaited assault on Richmond by McClellan's army, Goldsborough chose a competent commander for the James River Squadron, Commander John P. Gillis, captain of the *Seminole*.[43]

On the last day of May 1862, before Gillis could reach the squadron and replace Smith, General Joe Johnston's Confederates struck McClellan's army. Prior to the rebel attack Smith had tried to obtain more information about the state of Confederate defenses and McClellan's movements, but he failed on both accounts. The *Maratanza* and *Aroostook* had gone up the James River, piloted by two free black fishermen, to reconnoiter at Farrar's Island, but Lieutenant T. H. Stevens reported that he had been unable to procure any reliable information "though making strenuous exertions to do so."[44]

Responsibility for the Union Navy's mission on the James River now fell to Commander John P. Gillis, who went upriver on June 2, 1862, in the USS *Delaware*. Writing from the *Wachusett* two days later, Gillis told Goldsborough that he intended to deploy the squadron in three divisions—"one at this anchorage, one at Turkey Island, where communication may be had occasionally through contrabands with Major-General McClellan, and one at City Point"—thus keeping them within supporting distance of one another.[45]

Gillis quickly learned that African Americans living or working along the banks of the James River represented a valuable resource, providing intelligence about Confederate movements and troop strength and serving as a means of communicating with the elusive McClellan. Two days after assuming command of the squadron, Gillis took the *Wachusett* downriver to Turkey Island, where, he explained to Goldsborough, he "hoped to be able to communicate through contrabands with General McClellan." According to the *Wachusett*'s log, rebels at the Watkins farm opened fire on them with muskets, and they returned fire. "Seeing some contrabands a short distance below, they were hailed and asked where the enemy's pickets were and how many of them," Gillis wrote. The contrabands replied that 300 rebels were hiding in the woods a short distance from the river. Determined to put an end to the annoying and ever-present threat of rebel sharpshooters taking potshots at his vessels, Gillis told Goldsborough, "I have sent Mr. W word by contrabands that if he permits the pickets to attack us while passing, his buildings will be destroyed." The *Wachusett* continued on to Turkey Island, but Gillis's report failed to mention whether he had established communication with McClellan. By then, McClellan's troops had repulsed Johnston's attack, only to be stalled by torrential rains that turned the roads to mud, swelled rivers and streams, and delayed any forward movement of the army toward Richmond.[46]

One of the most important bits of information gained from contra-bands coming into Union lines during the Peninsular Campaign was obtained by General Fitz John Porter. On June 25, 1862, Porter sent a disturbing message that a fugitive slave from Richmond had reported that General Beauregard's advance guard had entered Richmond and repeated a rumor that Stonewall Jackson would soon strike the Union Army's rear. This latest report confirmed tales from numerous other con-trabands, refugees, and deserters that the Confederates were gathering in large numbers to defend the Confederate capital, and it strengthened McClellan's ongoing belief, largely fed by Allan Pinkerton's intelligence-gathering efforts, that he faced an enemy of superior strength. That after-noon McClellan went to Porter's headquarters to warn the garrison and federal gunboats of a possible rebel attack. The rumors proved to be cor-rect, and the following day General A. P. Hill's Confederate troops struck Porter's corps at Mechanicsville. Over the next six days General Robert E. Lee's rebels pressed McClellan's troops as they withdrew toward the James River, supported by Union gunboats.[47]

On Sunday, June 30, the Army of the Potomac fell back to a more defensible position and repulsed Lee's troops in what became known as the battle of Malvern Hill. With the army's proximity to the James River, lines of communication between the James River Squadron and McClellan began to improve, but the Army of the Potomac made no fur-ther progress toward Richmond. The Peninsular Campaign was grind-ing to a close. After visiting McClellan at Harrison's Landing on July 25 and learning that he had abandoned plans for a direct assault on Rich-mond, General Henry Halleck ordered the Army of the Potomac back to Washington, leaving McClellan little choice but to begin planning a withdrawal down the James, assisted, of course, by the navy. By August 15 the entire Army of the Potomac had embarked save for a rear guard, and McClellan's troops then moved across the Chickahominy. The next day the *Wachusett, Maratanza, Sonoma, Tioga, Aroostook,* and six mor-tar boats departed to join the Potomac Flotilla, and the remainder of the James River vessels returned to Goldsborough's squadron. Within days of their return Goldsborough learned that the Navy Department had replaced him as commander of the North Atlantic Blockading Squadron with Rear Admiral Samuel Phillips Lee.[48]

McClellan's failed campaign did not end federal expeditions up southern rivers. Throughout the remainder of 1862 slaves continued to escape to Union Navy ships, many bringing vital information about Confederate blockade runners and ironclads. Contrabands reaching Union ships gave both Du Pont and Admiral Lee, the new North Atlantic Blockading Squadron commander, vital information about the rebel ironclad *Fingal* and other armored warships that posed a distinct threat to the less protected, wooden-hulled Union blockaders. For some time Du Pont had expressed concerned about rebel blockade runners and the effectiveness of the Union blockade. "The bad news is that a Negro told a colonel that the *Fingal* had got into Savannah—she is the vessel that we have had so many letters about from Washington," Du Pont had written to Sophie on November 23, 1861. "I hope it is not true. If it be so, it was done during the interregnum between the gale and the capture of the forts." Union blockaders kept a vigilant eye out for the *Fingal*, which would give Du Pont anxious moments for months to come.[49]

Du Pont also expressed particular concern about the status of ironclads under construction in sites up rivers and creeks, fearing that upon completion they would sail down and attempt to pass through the blockade into the open sea. In October 1862 Du Pont told Welles, "The idea seems to be to open the Savannah River, then come to Port Royal and thence off Charleston and raise the blockade." According to Du Pont, two recently arrived contrabands, one a stevedore who worked on the wharves, and "both more intelligent than the white man," had told him that the *Fingal* (called the *Atlanta* by the rebels) would soon be ready but that the ship would draw a great deal of water. These contrabands claimed that the rebels had two other ironclads under construction and had laid down a third but had ceased work on it. A month later Du Pont told his wife, "Contrabands keep coming in and we now and then get information of importance, or of interest rather. One the other evening we had in the cabin from Savannah, who told us a good deal about the *Fingal*—if he can be relied upon, they have her too deep." According to this contraband, the rebels intended to use the *Fingal* to retake Pulaski.[50]

Du Pont's concern about the *Fingal* and other Confederate ironclads continued into the new year, and he welcomed any tidbits of information about rebel ships from refugees white or black, especially men who had actually worked on these vessels. Understanding the threat posed by the rebel ironclads, Captain J. F. Green carefully questioned any contrabands picked up by his blockading vessels. On January 25, 1863, Green wrote to Commander John Worden with news that might bear on Worden's mission to run the *Montauk* up the Ogeechee River and shell Fort McAllister. In preparation for an attack on Charleston, Du Pont wished to test the newly commissioned Passaic-class monitor's guns against rebel forts and had chosen Fort McAllister. He instructed Worden to follow up a successful attack on the fort by sending gunboats past the fort's batteries to the place where the rebel privateer *Nashville* was anchored. "I have just finished catechising a contraband who left Savannah last Friday night, and who worked on the *Fingal* from the time work was commenced upon her to fit her as an ironclad until she was finished," Green wrote. According to this "very intelligent" contraband, the *Atlanta (Fingal)* had a draft of eighteen to nineteen feet and six rifled, breech-loading guns of six-inch caliber, but it leaked badly and was most vulnerable at the stern. He also claimed that the *Fingal* had dropped down to Augustine Creek the previous Monday for the purpose of taking advantage of the high tide to go through the creek or by Fort Pulaski and to sea to rescue the *Nashville*. "For some unknown reason she did not attempt it, as the contraband saw her off of the mouth of the creek last Friday," Green told Worden. This new report, however, confirmed Du Pont's suspicions that the *Fingal* posed a real threat.[51]

On January 26, 1863, the *Montauk*, followed by the *Seneca, Wissahickon,* and *Dawn* towing the *C. P. Williams,* steamed upriver and anchored three miles below Fort McAllister. The next morning they took up positions 150 yards below some obstructions and opened fire on the fort. Although struck several times, the *Montauk* suffered no damage. However, finding that the *Montauk's* solid shot had not seriously affected the enemy, Commander Worden ordered the firing to cease at 11:15 A.M. and stood downriver.

Du Pont advised Worden that unless he could get nearer than 700 yards from the fort by removing the obstructions, he could see no advantage in renewing the attack. Two days after the attack Worden obtained information that promised to alter the situation favorably. He later wrote that he had learned "through the medium of a contraband, who has been employed upon these waters as a pilot, the position of the obstructions below the fort and the location of the torpedoes placed upon the piling in the channel way." This information enabled Worden to take up a position nearer the fort for his next attack. On February 1, 1863, Worden took the *Montauk* upriver to bombard Fort McAllister a second time. He anchored the monitor 600 yards below the fort and opened fire. The enemy returned fire "vigorously for some time," Worden wrote. Just one fragment struck the *Seneca,* but Worden told the admiral in his official report, "We were struck by projectiles forty-eight times." Boastful Confederate reports that Fort McAllister's gunners had disabled the *Montauk* proved to be mere rumors.[52]

Despite being closer to Fort McAllister, Worden's second bombardment failed to neutralize the Confederate works, confirming Du Pont's long-standing opinion about a purely naval attack on Charleston, which he reiterated in a letter to Charles Henry Davis on January 4, 1863: "I have always been of the opinion that it should be a joint operation, carefully devised." Assistant Navy Secretary Gustavus Fox continued to turn a deaf ear to the admiral's arguments, however. Underestimating the unique defenses of the southern city in what he called "Satan's kingdom," Fox remained determined to take Charleston in a purely naval operation. Nor did this most recent bombardment of Fort McAllister put an end to Du Pont's concerns about the Confederate ironclad *Fingal.*[53]

The admiral continued to keep a close eye on Fort McAllister, the *Nashville,* and all the approaches to Savannah and to welcome any and all intelligence reports, such as the one received from Captain Percival Drayton on February 18, 1863. From two contrabands employed at the saltworks above Thunderbolt battery, one of a line of earthworks defending Savannah, Drayton had learned that the rebels had two batteries, each mounting four guns, and were extending the works. According to the contrabands, when they left, the *Fingal* lay between Fort Jackson and the city of Savannah. These two escaped slaves also informed Drayton that the rebels had taken all the blacks "up country," leaving none within the grasp of Union soldiers or gunboats. They "say that the blacks are still very uncertain as to how they will be treated by us, making believe the story of their masters about being sold to Cuba, as we are only fighting to get cotton and niggers. One says he was deterred from running away sooner than this," Drayton wrote.[54]

These recent contraband reports about the *Fingal* prompted Du Pont to order the monitor *Passaic* to Wassaw Sound, where its crew spent February on blockade duty, watching for signs of the rebel ironclad and the steamer *Nashville.* Then came astounding news. On the last day of February the *Passaic* crossed the bar into Ossabaw Sound, where the crew learned that the *Montauk* had succeeded in destroying the *Nashville,* "as well as having tested a torpedo in the river." Commander Worden had indeed destroyed the *Nashville* (or *Rattlesnake*). After observing the ship moving downriver, Worden had taken the *Montauk, Wissahickon, Seneca,* and *Dawn* up the river to attack. Early on February 28, 1863, he opened fire, and within twenty minutes the monitor's shells had set the *Nashville* on fire. The *Montauk* then retired, striking a mine in the river, but after repairs continued back down the Ogeechee.[55]

The destruction of the Confederate ram *Nashville* did not end the threat of attack from other rebel rams such as the *Fingal*, or, as it was now referred to in Union correspondence, the *Atlanta*. In June 1863 the *Atlanta* did come down to attack the federal monitors *Weehawken* and *Nahant*, but the *Weehawken's* first fifteen-inch shell stunned the Confederate gunners. After five shots the *Atlanta* surrendered. To his wife, Anne, *Weehawken* captain John Rodgers wrote, "The *Weehawken* took the *Atlanta* so quickly that the *Nahant* did not fire a shot."[56]

By mid-1863 the Union Navy had eliminated the *Atlanta* as a threat to the blockade, and federal blockaders had begun to substantially reduce the number of blockade runners going in and out of Charleston. The number fell from forty-five rebel steamers in the first half of 1863 to just six in the period from August 1863 to March 1864. Confederate blockade runners still endeavored to run out of other southern ports, however, especially Wilmington. To prevent blockade running into and out of Wilmington, Captain Scott's ships had been carefully watching the mouth of the Cape Fear River for months. This was no simple task, for the river had two entrances—one at New Inlet, and another to the south at the western bar channel that ran by Fort Caswell. In addition to the squadron's mission to enforce the Union blockade, both Lee and Scott had a keen interest in learning as much as possible about the Confederate defenses at Wilmington. The loss of the *Monitor* in a gale in December had postponed an attack on Wilmington, but Lee had not abandoned the hope of eventually attacking that Confederate stronghold.

Much of the responsibility for blockading Wilmington and planning to seize rebel works guarding the entrances to the Cape Fear River fell to Commander A. Ludlow Case, the senior officer off New Inlet, North Carolina. Case told Lee on March 12, 1863, that, "judging by the active movements of the rebels in getting their ironclads ready," they would soon try to lift the Union blockade. Offering Lee a bit of confirmation, Case wrote, "We have seen one ironclad in the river, and the contrabands taken on board *Cambridge* on the 23rd ultimo state that one ironclad was finished and [a] second nearly so." The contrabands to whom Case referred had been picked up by the USS *Cambridge* off New Inlet. In his diary, contraband-turned-sailor William B. Gould wrote on February 23, "About 1 bell pick'd up A Boat containing three colard Refugees from Masonboro." According to the *Cambridge's* commanding officer, Commander William Parker, they had escaped from shore. "I obtain but little information from them as they appear to be corn-field hands," he told Lee. The three contrabands informed Parker that a large portion of the troops at Wilmington and from the forts had been taken away and sent to Charleston. Furthermore, Parker explained, one of the rams had been finished and sent to Fort Fisher, "to run for the vessels here and destroy them." According to Gould's diary, the USS *Daylight* took the three black men on board and on Friday, March 13, 1863, sent them to Morehead City. Although Gould probably did not realize it, these three contrabands confirmed intelligence already obtained by federal authorities. On March 11, 1863, watch officers of the flagship *Iroquois* reported seeing a steamer passing out. "She was visible for an instant only, and not long enough to train a gun," Case related to Lee. The *Iroquois* got under way and steamed off in the direction of the steamer but, despite a nearly full moon and good visibility, could not find it. "I was under the impression that the officers were mistaken," Case wrote, "until yesterday, when some contrabands taken on board the *Daylight* off Masonboro Inlet, reported the sailing of a steamer on Sunday night, though they did not know which side she went out."[57]

Lack of accurate information about rebel blockade runners and rebel rams or ironclads waiting to escape into the open sea and drive off or destroy his blockade vessels continued to haunt Case. He admitted that he had heard contradictory statements about the rebel ironclads in the Cape Fear River. "We believe we have seen one, and the contrabands received on board the *Cambridge* on the 23d ultimo, and the *Daylight* on the 10th instant, confirm that belief, but those received this day, say neither is finished, though work is advancing rapidly on both, and they expected to have them ready soon." Whatever the status of these Confederate warships, Case assumed that with the coming of better weather and smooth seas, both rebel ironclads would eventually commence active operations against the blockade. Lee shared Case's concerns about the vulnerability of Union blockade vessels and ordered Acting Master W. D. Urann, in the brig *Perry,* to report to Case on board the USS *Iroquois* off New Inlet and assist him in maintaining the blockade.[58]

Throughout the spring and early summer of 1863 Lee kept a watchful eye on the shipbuilding at Wilmington. Fortunately, Captain Charles S. Boggs, now senior officer off Wilmington, received a steady flow of information from contrabands and free blacks about the city's defenses. One report from free blacks came to Boggs from Captain Benjamin F. Sands, the senior officer off the western bar, in a letter dated March 23, 1863: "I have to report that just before getting underway from my night station at daylight this morning three free negro men came on board, having escaped from Smithville and passed Fort Caswell in the dark. One had been captured by rebel pickets at Suffolk, Va. and brought here a prisoner." The three men brought information about a rebel battery being constructed at Smithville and about a rebel ram that had earlier appeared outside of New Inlet but had returned "because she could not stand the sea." According to these three black refugees, there were "three Whitworth guns (or, as they call them, 'the little guns that shoot so far') mounted at Fort Caswell. I had supposed four when I drew their fire on the morning of February 23rd last."[59]

In May 1863 Boggs reported that contrabands claimed the ironclad being built at Wilmington was "very large and of great breadth of beam, [and] is to carry 10 heavy guns." It had been taken some distance up the river to receive armor, they said, assisted by a large number of mechanics and material recently arrived in steamers that had run the blockade on the east side. Boggs estimated it would take the rebels two months to complete the ship, at which time, he warned, "we will all be driven off." This ironclad was most likely the CSS *North Carolina,* a 150-foot armored ram carrying six eight-inch guns. Equipped with poor engines, the *North Carolina* was relegated to a floating battery in the Cape Fear River and saw little or no action, sinking in September 1864. The Confederacy also built the iron-plated steam sloop CSS *Raleigh* at Wilmington, commissioned in April 1864.[60]

As the summer approached, Admiral Lee continued to hope that Union forces might mount an attack on Wilmington. He reminded Welles that summer was the best time for landing and supplying troops on the coast, but the Union Army's commanding general, Henry Halleck, told Lee that no troops could be furnished to assist in an attack on the defenses of the Cape Fear River until sufficient conscripts could be obtained. Every general was asking for more troops, Halleck explained. Lee's suggestions came to naught, and plans to attack Wilmington in a joint operation had to be postponed. Wilmington was clearly not a Union priority at the time.[61]

Rumors of a possible Union attack on Wilmington may have enticed blacks to flee to Union blockaders off the entrances to the Cape Fear River, bringing new information about the state of rebel defenses. One of the most important reports came to Lieutenant J. B. Breck, commanding the USS *Niphon,* on May 1, 1864, from a refugee named Charles Wesley, "a bright mulatto, who states that he left Fort Fisher about three hours before we took him off, and that he was servant to Colonel Lamb, commanding Fort Fisher." Wesley informed Breck that there were 800 Confederate troops now garrisoned at Fort Fisher, and General N. G.

Evans's division of 6,000 men had been ordered to Forts Caswell and Fisher. The refugee also claimed that the *North Carolina* intended to come out if it could get over the bar, but as the ship drew fifteen feet, he doubted it would be able to do so.[62]

Captain Sands took this information seriously. "The mulatto servant of Colonel Lamb, commandant of Fort Fisher, who escaped to the *Niphon* a few days ago," Sands wrote, "states that his master said that as the coast was now so strongly guarded by the Yankee gunboats, the runners must take their chance to run directly through the fleet in and out, and the light was to aid them in doing so." The rebels had located a "brilliant light" on a scaffolding at the Mound fort as a landmark for vessels entering or leaving that inlet. Noting this change of tactics by the enemy, Sands informed Lee that he was "altering somewhat the position of the vessels (endeavoring to keep the coast line strong, for they can easily make signal, when it is weak)." He enclosed a map that showed the position of each blockading vessel. The recent addition of more vessels to the squadron allowed Sands, and therefore Lee, to deploy sufficient ships off Wilmington to make the blockade more effective. By 1864 the squadron had three lines of blockading vessels—one close to the inlets to sight rebel vessels trying to run out and signal with rockets, a middle line tasked with actually chasing the blockade runners, and a third line farther out to sea to watch for incoming vessels and catch any that slipped past the other two lines.[63]

This new disposition of blockaders may have enabled the USS *Mt. Vernon* to observe the rebel ironclad ram *Raleigh* and two tenders when they steamed down the Cape Fear River into New Inlet on the evening of May 6, 1864. According to *Mt. Vernon's* commanding officer, Acting Volunteer Lieutenant James Trathen, at 6:30 P.M. they saw four steamers about three miles distant in New Inlet behind Fort Fisher, two of them seagoing vessels and one an ironclad ram. The *Mt. Vernon* then retired to its night station. The newly commissioned CSS *Raleigh,* under the command of Lieutenant J. Pembroke, accompanied by CSS *Yadkin* and CSS *Equator,* had come downriver to challenge the federal blockaders and gain their attention while six rebel blockade runners escaped.

Trathen did not report the sighting to Sands, but the *Britannia*, at No. 1 station, picked up the Confederate trio as they crossed the bar. In his report of the incident, Acting Volunteer Lieutenant Samuel Huse wrote that they sighted a "suspicious looking vessel" and ran in closer than usual. The vessel, which he thought to be an ironclad, turned directly toward the *Britannia*. Huse fired rockets and aimed his thirty-pounder Parrott at the ironclad, which returned fire. "Our course was

changed three times, hoping to elude him," Huse wrote, "but he followed and gained on us considerably, being within 600 yards when we
passed the buoy." The *Britannia* then headed northeast, and the rebel
ironclad steamed off to the east-southeast. After an uneasy night of waiting and watching, Huse and his crew sighted the *Raleigh* again at about
daybreak; it was located west-northwest and was engaging the Union
gunboat *Nansemond* and the screw tug *Howquah.* Both had sighted the
enemy ironclad and its consorts at about 4:25 in the morning. This was
the squadron's final engagement with the rebel ironclad, which grounded
on a sandbar returning to the protection of Fort Fisher's guns, breaking
its back.[64]

Union vessels operating in the James River in 1864 also had to con-
tend with Confederate gun batteries and mines, as well as rebel gunboats, rams, and even fireships. As they had so often in the past, Union
commanders anxiously sought information about these Confederate vessels and shared whatever they obtained. General Benjamin Butler, for
example, sent Lee two contrabands who, Lee acknowledged, brought
"useful" information. One of the two contrabands may have been Archy
Jenkins, a black refugee from Richmond. On June 1, 1864, he gave
Union officials fresh information on Confederate vessels in the James.
In a statement, Jenkins said, "I am a free man, a stevedore, employed
on the *Bonita.* I left Richmond on Monday. I gave a colored man $10 to
show me the batteries, past the pickets. I crawled through the bushes and
came down to Hill Carter's place." The Confederates, Jenkins warned,
"are putting two barges and a sloop lashed together, filled with shavings
and pitch and with torpedoes, which they intend to set on fire, and when
it reaches the fleet it will blow up and destroy the fleet. There is a vast
quantity of powder in it." Noting a freshet that was six or seven inches
higher than usual, Jenkins told Union officers that he doubted the rebels
would have any trouble bringing their ironclads over Trent's Reach, for
there was plenty of water close to the left bank. Jenkins, who claimed he
had been running on the river for five or six years, also told them, "They
all say they know 'they can whip you all; they are certain of it.'" The rebels preferred their torpedoes, Jenkins said, and they had told him, the
federals "haven't the sense to make a good torpedo; they reckon them
all else besides." In Jenkins's opinion, the rebels feared that if they came
downriver the federals would lead them over a string of torpedoes and
"blow them all up. They say that is all they care about."[65]

A white deserter from the CSS *Hampton* named John Loomis confirmed Jenkins's report that the rebels intended to attack the federal
fleet "in the night, first sending down fire ships, and following with rebel

craft." Loomis stated that the rebels had three ironclads—*Virginia II,
Richmond,* and *Fredericksburg*—below Fort Darling, six wooden gunboats partially plated with boiler iron, and six fireships with which to
make their attack.[66]

Lee judged the information provided by Jenkins and "from deserters from the rebel Army and Navy, and contrabands from Richmond" as
reliable. On June 1, 1864, he reported to Welles that the enemy was con-
templating "an immediate attack upon this fleet with fire rafts, torpedo
vessels, gunboats, etc. and ironclads, all of which carry torpedoes, and
that they are confident of being able to destroy the vessels here, principally by their torpedoes." Based on this information, Lee requested that
the Navy Department not send the *Tecumseh* to sea but, "considering
the importance of this river to the armies of Grant and Butler," to send
him one or more ironclads in addition to torpedo barges and torpedoes.
Welles agreed to send him twelve small tugs, to be used as picket boats,
and six acting ensigns to command them, but he ordered the *Tecumseh*
to proceed to sea. He then admonished Lee: "You have the best six ironclads in the Navy, and Admiral Farragut, threatened by a larger three
than is opposed to you, has not a single one."[67]

Both Lee and Butler were anxious to retain command of the James
River because they expected Grant to cross the river and operate against
Richmond from the south side. Despite information indicating that the
rebels might attack Union vessels in the James, most of the month of
June remained quiet. In fact, other than a rebel attack on laborers building a canal at Dutch Gap, naval forces along the James saw little action
during the summer of 1864, for neither Confederate nor Union vessels
could pass the obstructions in the river. Grant's troops failed to make
much headway against the Confederates around Petersburg, and the
year ended at a stalemate.

For most of the war a steady stream of black refugees—some, like Archy
Jenkins, free blacks; others, runaway slaves—had come to Union lines
and Union vessels, most of them bringing intelligence on Confederate
defenses, shipbuilding, troop movements, and the locations of mines,
obstructions, and blockade runners. From the earliest days of the war,
Union Navy commanders welcomed this information from friendly local
blacks and runaways. Although they occasionally reported the information to be unreliable, and although some local blacks remained hesi-
tant to share information with the Yankees for fear of being punished if
they were caught, naval officers came to rely on black informants. These
informants, most often expressing pro-Union sentiments, knew the local

landscape and waters; those who were servants sometimes overheard enemy conversations, and many could identify individuals carrying on illicit trade or supporting the Confederate war effort. Those refugees who had worked on or near Confederate works or in shipyards brought valuable firsthand knowledge of rebel gun batteries and ironclads under construction.

The majority of African Americans who sought refuge on Union vessels expressed loyalty to the Union, and many hoped the information they offered would encourage commanding officers to accept them on board and protect them. Throughout the Civil War, naval officers, including senior commanders such as Du Pont, Lee, Dahlgren, and Porter, not only welcomed such information but also eagerly sought it out. Repeatedly, reports from contrabands allowed commanders to identify persons carrying on illicit trade with the enemy, locate blockade runners up rivers and creeks or hiding along the shore, and learn when the rebels reinforced or abandoned key points along the coast.

The intelligence provided by contrabands about blockade runners and their routes enabled the Union Navy to tighten the blockade and gradually erode the Confederacy's ability to prosecute the war. Although the Union Army did not always act promptly enough to suit the navy on information offered by contrabands, and although some warnings of enemy troop movements or defenses went unheeded, Union Navy commanders continued to value African Americans as sources of intelligence about the enemy. Contrabands proved to be a useful means of communication between the navy and senior army officers, and in many cases these contraband reports prompted raids by federal gunboats or joint army-navy expeditions, resulting in successful operations to destroy enemy saltworks, depots, and defenses and to liberate hundreds of slaves. Friendly blacks contributed as well by informing Union Navy commanders of Confederate sharpshooters, gun batteries, and torpedoes (mines) laid in rivers and creeks, waiting to attack or blow up their vessels. These timely warnings saved countless Union sailors' lives during the war. Indeed, much of the intelligence gained by both Union services during the Civil War came from friendly local blacks and black runaways.

CHAPTER 5
CONTRIBUTING TO VICTORY

*I wanted to be free—and I wanted my race to be free—I knew this
could not be if the rebels had a government of their own—All the time
during, and before the war, I felt as I do now that, the Union people
were the best friends of the colored people.*

—*Alonzo Jackson*

The growing number of contrabands presented Union officials with a
difficult challenge. Able-bodied male contrabands were often enlisted as
crew on navy ships or worked for wages as stevedores, mule drivers, servants, or military laborers. Initially, however, the army and navy had less
use for women, children, and elderly runaways. Not wishing to clothe
and feed them at government expense, army officers offered the women
employment as cooks, laundresses, nurses, seamstresses, and servants.
Union naval commanders also sent dozens of contrabands to Union military posts or navy yards to be employed as laborers. Contrabands with
specific skills, such as machinists, caulkers, carpenters, and mechanics,
readily found work in Union Navy machine shops and repair facilities.

Union Navy commanders who rescued contrabands early in the war
often expressed uncertainty about what to do with the newly freed slaves
who no longer had owners to furnish them with clothing, housing, and
provisions. The presence of numerous contrabands on crowded Union
vessels taxed commanders' patience and threatened to reduce the ships'
rations and water supplies to dangerously low levels. Complaining about
the burden placed on his ships by the numerous African American refugees picked up along the Potomac, and frustrated by the need to provide for these fifty or so contrabands, Lieutenant A. D. Harrell wrote to
Captain Thomas T. Craven in November 1861, "These people have all
to be rationed, and it is becoming very embarrassing to me, short of pro-

visions as I am . . . I think it would be a good stroke of policy to return these negroes to their owners. It would tend to put a stop to the whole-sale desertion that is now going on, and relieve us of a most unpleasant difficulty."[1]

To relieve themselves of this burden, most Union Navy command-ers either employed the able-bodied males as crewmen on their vessels or sent them to military authorities at Port Royal or Beaufort. In Sep-tember 1861, for example, when commanders in the Potomac Flotilla rescued thirteen contrabands, Craven sent them to Commander John Dahlgren at the Washington Navy Yard with the suggestion, "I think the persons might be turned over to General McClellan who wants their labor." Craven carefully listed the names of the thirteen contrabands and their owners. One of the slaves was a female, Agnes Chew, the property of Charles Mason.[2]

Initially, the principal contribution of refugee slaves to the Union war effort was their labor. The military needed men to do fatigue duty; cut roads; build bridges, entrenchments, and fortifications; serve in ambu-lance corps and hospitals; work as teamsters, stevedores, and guides; and even act as spies. Although most contrabands did not work directly on Union Navy projects, their work at wharves unloading supplies, clearing rebel areas for entrenchments along rivers and creeks, and building gun emplacements and other defenses at vital points along waterways ben-efited Union gunboats and other vessels. Vincent Colyer, the superinten-dent of the poor for New Bern, North Carolina, reported that in the four months he had charge of contrabands, they built three first-class earth-works—Fort Totten, Fort Burnside, and a fort at Washington, North Carolina. "The negroes loaded and discharged cargo, for about three hundred vessels, served regularly as crew on twenty steamers, and acted as permanent gangs of laborers in all the Quartermaster's, Commissary and Ordinance Offices of the Department." He noted that a number of them were good carpenters, blacksmiths, and coopers and did effective work in bridge building and ship joining. Another fifty volunteers acted as spies and guides. According to Colyer, "They frequently went from thirty to three hundred miles within the enemy's lines; visiting his prin-cipal camps and most important posts, and bringing us back important and reliable information." The Confederates sent bloodhounds to pur-sue these brave contraband spies, and several barely escaped with their lives.[3]

Union operations along the southern coast often generated new sources of laborers. When a Union expedition captured Hilton Head

Island and Beaufort, South Carolina, in November 1861, white plantation owners fled, leaving hundreds of African American slaves with no means of support. Initially these newly freed slaves did not constitute a serious problem for the Union commander, General Thomas W. Sherman, for many of the plantations had supplies of food as well as unharvested corn and potatoes still in the field. Within weeks of the occupation, however, the general realized that when the blacks had consumed all the food left on the plantations, they would seek the protection of the government. "They will come in great numbers and no doubt will give us many laborers; but where we get one good able-bodied man, we have five to six women and children. They are a most prolific race," he wrote.[4]

The War Department favored a conciliatory policy toward southerners in the newly occupied Port Royal area, and at first, Sherman hoped the southern plantation owners would return to protect their plantations and property. When they remained in the interior, Sherman reluctantly decided to confiscate their property, including the cotton, and put the slaves to work. The War Department approved and on November 27, 1861, Adjutant General Lorenzo Thomas informed Sherman that four additional regiments would be sent to his command. He then instructed the general: "The services of negroes will be used in picking, collecting, and packing cotton, as well as in constructing defensive works, etc." With earthworks and defenses to build, ships to unload, teams of mules to be driven, and other fatigue duty, Sherman must have welcomed the additional laborers. He lamented to General Meigs, however, "Our labor here is enormous. Thus far the negroes have rendered us but little assistance. Many come in and run off. They have not been organized to an extent we desire. The large families they bring with them make a great many useless mouths." In another report to Thomas, Sherman explained the blacks' reluctance to work. "A sudden change of condition from servitude to apparent freedom is more than their intellects can stand, and this circumstance alone renders it a very serious question what is to be done with the negroes who will hereafter be found on conquered soil." He later noted that 329 contrabands had come in and offered their services, but only about 60 of them were able-bodied men, and some 320 had run off. "Every inducement had been held out to them to come in and labor for wages, and money distributed among those who have labored," he wrote. Sherman blamed this disappointing result on the blacks' "naturally slothful and indolent" nature, their joy at being freed which had unsettled their minds, and their present comfort on the plantations.[5]

In contrast to Sherman's experience, Commander Percival Drayton observed that slaves who were abandoned by their owners seemed "very friendly. They assisted us voluntarily, whenever we wanted their aid, and sometimes, as at Fort Heyward, worked very hard, and I overheard one of them say, 'that it was but fair that they should do so for us, as we were working for them.'"[6]

As General Sherman had accurately predicted, the Union occupation of Hilton Head and Beaufort continued to attract hundreds of black refugees. Private Elbridge J. Copp, who had enlisted in the Third New Hampshire Volunteers at age sixteen, described the arrival of slaves at his camp at Hilton Head: "There seemed to be an underground telegraph that took the news of the arrival of the northern troops to the slave population for miles around, and deserting their old masters and the plantation, they came into our camp for freedom and protection." Concerned about the large number of contrabands living on the Georgia Sea Islands, which were now in Union possession, on January 15, 1862, Sherman informed the War Department that some of them had come into camps with their families and obtained work. With rations issued to them by the army, he felt that the able-bodied males would be able to support their families, but he feared that those remaining on the plantations and living on corn and potatoes would soon be destitute, leaving them "in a suffering condition or thrown upon the commissariat of the Army for support." Therefore, Sherman urged the government to establish some kind of system by which these contrabands could sustain themselves, to send instructors to teach them the "rudiments of civilization," and to employ agents to take charge of plantations and superintend the blacks, who should be paid wages for their labor. As a white representative of the National Freedman's Relief Association explained in March 1862, freed people, both male and female, wanted to work and be independent. "All seemed anxious to provide for their own necessities, and implored us to give them seeds and let them begin at once. They are confident of their own ability to work and even manage estates on which they were left."[7]

Estimating that some 9,000 contrabands now resided on land controlled by his forces, Sherman issued Order No. 9 in February 1862 to subdivide his command into districts. He also appointed an agent to superintend the management of plantations, to enroll and organize willing blacks into working parties, and "to see that they were well fed, clad, and paid proper remuneration for their labor." In this order, the general took care not to interfere with the employment of blacks by the army or cotton agents, but called for benevolent and philanthropic organizations in the North to send suitable clothing and other necessities to the contrabands under his care.[8]

Union operations elsewhere along the coast replicated Sherman's situation at Port Royal. After the Union occupation of Roanoke Island in February 1862, Major General Ambrose Burnside's forces moved inland to occupy New Bern, North Carolina, an operation that freed a large number of slaves who then turned to the government for protection and sustenance. "They seem wild with excitement and delight— they are now a source of very great anxiety to us," Burnside reported to Secretary of War Stanton. "The city is being overrun with fugitives from surrounding towns and plantations." Fortunately, as Sherman had at Port Royal, Burnside quickly acknowledged the need for laborers to construct earthworks, forts, and other defenses and requested contrabands for the work. To oversee the task of caring for the 7,500 black refugees and 1,800 whites refugees at New Bern, Burnside appointed Vincent Colyer as superintendent of the poor. Colyer then offered work to both blacks and whites, paying whites $12 a month and blacks $8 a month. The opportunity to receive regular wages, even at a rate lower than that paid to whites, proved to be an important incentive for black refugees. When the Freedman's Commission asked Captain Hooper, the acting superintendent at Port Royal, "Do these persons work willingly for wages," he replied, "I never knew a case in which a colored man had reasonable security for getting wages—even moderate wages—that he was not ready to work." But Colyer at New Bern could provide only 2,000 of the 5,000 laborers requested by Burnside. "The truth was, we never could get enough of them; and although for a little while, there were a few more at Roanoke Island than were wanted there after the Fort was completed, they were brought to Newbern as soon as it was known."[9]

Although at New Bern, Roanoke Island, Port Royal, and Hampton Roads the army directed most contraband labor, the Union Navy regularly employed both contrabands and free blacks in navy yards. In 1862 Navy Secretary Gideon Welles reported that navy yards and naval stations were employing no fewer than 12,000 mechanics and laborers. Union naval commanders also occasionally hired contrabands as laborers. For example, on March 4, 1863, Commander Alexander Murray sent a creative request to Rear Admiral Samuel Phillips Lee for machinists and day laborers. "A machine shop and foundry and facilities for hauling up vessels are at Washington N.C., so, also, is Second Assistant Engineer Lay, of the Navy. These facts are suggestive," Murray told Lee. He wanted to employ ten machinists and ten day laborers (contrabands) and to buy the necessary material. "I wish to put the Government to a small expense with the promise of large returns," Murray explained to

Lee, suggesting that the new repair facility at Washington, North Carolina, "might be authorized as a branch of the Norfolk navy yard, subject to visitation from the commandant or his subordinate or entirely controlled by the senior naval officer on the spot." Murray's plans to use the repair facilities at Washington meant that extra precautions would have to be taken to secure the base. To defend the area, Murray drew on a valuable local resource—contrabands. "Now that I intend to do most of the repairs at Washington, N.C.," Murray reassured Lee, "an additional vessel will nearly always be there." Then he explained, "I have placed an old ferryboat with two guns and contrabands, which has added strength; she has become quite efficient. A two-gun battery is about to be erected, at the suggestion of Acting Lieutenant Renshaw, above the bridge, which will command the upper obstruction. Washington is secure."[10]

The Union Navy also employed contrabands in a machine shop that supported the South Atlantic Blockading Squadron. In a report dated May 1, 1863, the fleet paymaster, John S. Cunningham, noted a complement of thirteen contrabands at work at a machine shop that was listed as "part of our establishment." These contrabands probably worked at the Port Royal machine shops established by Du Pont soon after taking command of the blockading squadron in 1861. Realizing that he would need repair facilities at Port Royal to avoid having to send his ships north to navy yards, in the winter of 1862 Du Pont had the *India* and the *Edward* moored together in Station Creek—the former to serve as a floating blacksmith shop, and the latter as a machine shop. The *Edward* had facilities and workmen to make patterns and molds for castings, cast and forge items, and run five lathes. Both ships, which served the squadron for two years, contributed to countless essential repairs. In June 1863 the navy's chief engineer, Alban C. Stimers, chartered the screw steamer *Relief* and sent it south to Port Royal from New York with forty skilled laborers to repair monitors that had suffered damage from bombardments and to perform regular maintenance such as cleaning the boilers, a tedious, time-consuming task that could take up to thirty-five days to complete. Reluctant to send these monitors north to navy yards, where they might be out of service for months, Du Pont welcomed the opportunity to have ships repaired in the South. Although composed of skilled white mechanics, these working parties at Port Royal probably had the assistance of contrabands employed in the Hilton Head machine ship or the floating machine shop facilities. Contrabands also may have assisted in the improvements ordered to the monitors following the disastrous attack on Charleston in April 1863.[11]

When the Union Army returned to Tidewater Virginia in 1864, operations near Petersburg created a new demand for labor. To meet this demand, the army impressed contrabands by the hundreds from plantations and government farms in Virginia and North Carolina. Many of these black laborers went to work as stevedores unloading supplies at City Point or as laborers constructing a canal at Dutch Gap, a narrow neck of land connecting Farrar's Island to the mainland on the James River. During the summer of 1864 Union forces employed hundreds of other black laborers at the army's vital depot at City Point, where General Ulysses S. Grant had established his headquarters and the Union Army had built wharves and warehouses for supplies, including ammunition. City Point also served as an important departure point for passengers traveling to and from Washington and for Union wounded being brought to or evacuated from the hospital there.[12]

Protecting Grant's City Point base and the laborers digging the Dutch Gap canal from Confederate attack became an important mission for the Union Navy's Fourth Division on the James River. Union Navy vessels also convoyed transports up and down the James, dragged for torpedoes (mines) in the river and adjacent waters, supported troop movements, and occasionally dueled with rebel gun batteries or sharpshooters. On August 9, 1864, an ammunition barge carrying 20,000 artillery projectiles exploded at City Point, killing forty-three persons on the docks and all on board the barge. Just a mile away, Thomas Morris Chester, a black war correspondent, watched as "a terrible blaze was suddenly ascended, intermingled with dark objects which were thrown in every conceivable direction." Dust obscured everything within a half mile of the scene. "Then came toward me hundreds and thousands of civilians and soldiers, rushing from a terrible danger which, on account of its mystery, seemed to quicken their speed and their fears." The explosion had scattered debris in all directions and, Chester wrote, "Fragments of humanity were scattered around in the immediate vicinity of the tragedy in frightful profusion. Sorrow was depicted in every countenance that gazed on the ruins, but those loudest in their grief were the contrabands who mourned their relatives and comrades. Being employed in great numbers where the accident occurred, more of them were killed and wounded than any other class of individuals."[13]

On board the USS *Osceola*, Master's Mate Horatio Robinson heard the explosion. "I can't describe it but it was heavier than any Thunder ever I heard, and the air was filled with bursting shell & remains of vessels & Human Beings," he told his mother in a letter. "The explosion spread from the Barge to the immense Store house, some nine or ten hundred feet long and most filled with ammunition at the upper

half. This building is now a mass of ruins and hundreds of persons most
Negroes blown to pieces." The *Osceola's* second cutter had just gone
alongside the barge when the explosion occurred "ten feet from them,"
Robinson wrote. The explosion capsized the second cutter, but the first
cutter rescued six of the *Osceola* crewmen. "None of our men are hurt
very badly & it is nothing but a miracle that we ever heard of or saw them
again," Robinson wrote.[14]

Lieutenant Colonel Horace Porter, Grant's aide, confirmed that forty-
three were killed and another forty wounded in the explosion, which also
destroyed the boat and severely damaged the wharf. Grant appointed
Porter to head a board of officers to investigate the accident. "We spent
several days in taking the testimony of all the people who were in sight
of the occurrence, and used every possible means to probe the matter,"
Porter explained, "but as all the men aboard the boat had been killed,
we could obtain no satisfactory evidence." At the time, the explosion
was "attributed by most of those present to the careless handling of the
ammunition by the laborers who were engaged in unloading it; but there
was suspicion in the minds of many of us that it was the work of some
emissaries of the enemy sent into the lines." Many years later, Porter
met a man who claimed to have invented an explosive device, disguised
himself as a laborer, passed into Union lines, and placed the explosive
with a clockwork detonator on the ammunition barge. That man may
have been John Maxwell, a Confederate secret service agent. Maxwell
claimed that, having learned of "immense supplies of stores being landed
at City Point," he and another man, R. K. Dillard, had gone there with a
box containing a twelve-pound powder charge. Just before daybreak on
August 9, Maxwell cautiously approached the wharf and told the barge
sentinel that the captain had ordered the box on board. He then gave
it to a crewman and retired to a safe distance. An hour later the device
exploded, deafening Maxwell's companion.[15]

In his memoirs, Porter neglected to mention that most of those
killed in the explosion at City Point were contrabands; nor did he question the army's assignment of such backbreaking and dangerous duty
to black laborers. Chester noted that more contrabands were killed or
wounded than any other "class of individuals," but he did not go so far as
to suggest that the army was using black laborers to unload ammunition
because it considered contrabands expendable. In his follow-up report
to Major General Halleck, Grant's list of those killed and wounded confirmed Chester's observations: twelve enlisted men, two citizen employees, three commissioned officers, one citizen, and twenty-eight colored
laborers killed, and another three officers, four enlisted men, fifteen

citizens, and eighty-six colored laborers wounded. Eighteen additional soldiers and civilians who were near the wharf also suffered wounds. But neither the general nor his chief quartermaster, Rufus Ingalls, questioned the employment of black laborers to handle ordnance supplies, a reflection of the fact that the use of black laborers to build fortifications, load and unload stores, and do other fatigue duty was commonplace by 1864. One source claimed that one-fourth of all Union military laborers impressed in 1862 and 1863 died.[16]

The day following the explosion at City Point, Grant's and Lee's predictions about rebel rams threatening workers at the Dutch Gap canal project and Union positions along the James River proved accurate. Early on the morning of August 10, 1864, Confederate rams came down and, according to Captain Melancton Smith, the division commander in the James, the rebel rams fired six shells, "one exploding in the water below Dutch Gap and another striking the bank on the opposite side of the river, but doing no damage." Three days later a trio of rebel batteries, supported by two Confederate rams, opened fire on Union land forces and some 1,500 laborers digging the canal across Dutch Gap. The Confederates' attempt to drive soldiers from the gap failed, but according to John Grattan, "the brave fellows" defending the gap suffered "over thirty killed and wounded." Among the labor force working on the canal were a number of U.S. Colored Troops. The Confederates did not renew their attack on Dutch Gap, for as Flag Officer Jonathan Mitchell, CSN, reported, the day's experience had no serious effect on the enemy, and "it was a useless expenditure of ammunition." Undeterred by the rebel harassment of his troops, General Butler ordered them to continue digging the canal at Dutch Gap and on August 16, 1864, sent the Fourth and Sixth U.S. Colored Troops to the area for fatigue duty.[17]

In addition to providing the Union Army with laborers and the Union Navy with skilled workers, hundreds of newly freed slaves served the war effort by working as laundresses, cooks, hospital attendants, and servants to both officers and enlisted men. Although army officers usually employed male contrabands, the Union Army, Union Navy, and U.S. Sanitary Commission employed hundreds of African American women in hospitals and camps as nurses, laundresses, and cooks. Most of these women welcomed the opportunity to work for wages. These determined freedwomen, many of whom had been left without male providers owing to their men's conscription or enlistment in the Union Army, willingly accepted employment with the military to provide for their families. The wives of black soldiers, living on army pay that was often late or inadequate, had no choice but to seek wage work and cultivate garden plots to feed and sustain their families. This was also true for many black women in northern cities and Union-occupied areas, who were forced by wartime inflation and a lack of housing to accept wages offered by the government. On a more informal basis, Union sailors and soldiers paid contrabands to wash their clothes and serve as guides for hunting, fishing, or foraging expeditions. Enterprising contrabands who quickly realized that Union Navy crewmen made good customers came out in small boats to sell fresh produce. Others ashore sold baked goods, fruit, and fresh meat to hungry soldiers and sailors. Some even cooked meals for them.[18]

Union forces took advantage of the sudden availability of a labor force of thousands of former slaves who no longer had owners to provide them with food, clothing, and shelter. Faced with manpower shortages and the need to build roads, dig canals, erect fortification and entrenchments, and care for an unprecedented number of wounded men, the Union Army encouraged able-bodied black males to enlist or offered them gainful employment working for the war effort. At first, Union commanders seemed unsure what to do with newly freed black women, children, and the elderly, but they quickly realized that the women had experience as cooks or servants and in performing menial but difficult tasks. Their employment as cooks and servants was viewed by most white northerners as socially acceptable as well. The fact that many male contrabands had spent their lives working as field hands, servants, watermen, farmers, and mule drivers made their employment by the military an obvious solution. Initially, the Union Navy assigned black sailors to the rating of "boy" and often assigned them more menial shipboard duties than white sailors, but little evidence supports the argument that black sailors were given more difficult and dangerous duty on naval vessels. They served in engine and boiler rooms and in picket boats at night, but so did white sailors; when subjected to enemy fire, mines, or sudden storms, navy crews faced equal danger, regardless of race. Furthermore, many commanders chose not to assign black sailors to more dangerous duties in gun crews or armed landing parties.

Despite the War Department's policy of equal treatment of soldiers of equal rank, Union Army authorities frequently gave black troops inferior arms, clothing, and rations and often assigned black laborers and U.S. Colored Troops to menial tasks, fatigue duty, and unpleasant chores that white soldiers preferred not to do. One of the most egregious examples occurred during the siege of Petersburg, when military authorities ordered a black regiment to bury the bodies of soldiers who had been killed in an assault and left baking in the hot June sun for ten days. Because of the danger of rebel gunfire, the black troops had to work at night, "groping around for their bloated comrades in blue amidst the stench of decomposition and burning them quietly." In some cases, the military treated black laborers poorly, putting them to work in harsh or even dangerous conditions and depriving them of promised wages, clothing, and food rations. This mistreatment not only caused hardships for their families but also raised concerns about fraud in the quartermaster and commissary departments. As one historian noted, "Mistreatment reached such heights that a handful of officers in the Virginia theater accused the government of 'degrading' the freedmen to a 'lower level than before.'"[19]

Contrabands also worked in hospitals as nurses and orderlies. The Union Navy began the war with hospitals at Portsmouth, Virginia; League Island in Philadelphia; Portsmouth, New Hampshire; Chelsea, Massachusetts; and Brooklyn, New York, but within weeks of the fall of Fort Sumter, events in Virginia deprived the navy of one of its main hospitals. When Confederate troops took over Portsmouth Naval Hospital, the navy surgeon resigned and transferred medical care for officers and men to a hospital ship, the *Ben Morgan,* stationed off Old Point Comfort. Anticipating an increase in sick and wounded sailors, the Union Navy built a hospital at Washington, D.C., in 1861, and during the war it used the *Ben Morgan, Red Rover, Home, A. Houghton, New Hampshire, Valpraiso,* and other ships as floating hospitals. Women did not initially serve as nurses on these ships. Male nurses, formerly called loblolly boys, performed nursing duties. In 1862, however, sisters of the Order of the Holy Cross volunteered to be nurses on board the *Red Rover;* they were joined in time by five black nurses and several other contraband women who served as nurses and laundresses. The navy paid the nurses generously—$15 a month, compared with $12 for army nurses. In her research on women during the Civil War, however, historian Nina Silber found that black women employed by the military more often served as cooks or laundresses and were usually paid from $2 to $6 less than their white counterparts. Some black nurses, Susie Taylor King among them, never received any compensation for their work. Nonetheless, the navy's system of hospitals, which by 1865 included new hospitals at Memphis, Tennessee, and Mound City, Illinois, as well as its laboratory in Brooklyn, were manned by trained surgeons, nurses, and hospital stewards. As a result, the Union Navy's death rate during the war was far lower than the army's—just one in fifty men.[20]

Union soldiers and sailors occasionally mentioned these women in letters to family and friends at home. In the course of his duties as commander of the South Atlantic Blockading Squadron, Samuel F. Du Pont visited hospitals ashore and sometimes wrote home about his experiences. In a candid letter to his wife, Sophie, written in January 1863 from the flagship *Wabash,* Du Pont related the story of Jean Davenport Lander, an Englishwoman who had studied music in Paris, toured to much acclaim as an actress in Europe, and was the widow of explorer and engineer General Fredrick W. Lander. Mrs. Lander had come, he wrote, "to be the Florence Nightingale of the military hospital at Beaufort. Her first requisition for appliances to pursue her vocation was a carriage— 'a mounted orderly' (chassesur a cheval)—three female contrabands, a cook, and twenty washtubs." Du Pont found the story very amusing. "Of course she is in the way here; there is no sphere for that sort of thing," he told Sophie. Despite the admiral's obvious doubts about her usefulness, Mrs. Lander remained a supervisor of nurses at the military hospital at Beaufort for more than a year.[21]

Among the Sanitary Commission hospital ships serving the army during the Peninsular Campaign was the *Knickerbocker,* a 220-foot steamer built in 1843 by John Englis of Brooklyn. Before the war it had run from the foot of Robinson Street in New York City up the Hudson River to Albany. In June 1862 the *Knickerbocker* lay in the Pamunkey River at the terminus of the railway at White House, "in readiness for the reception of 450 patients, provided with comfortable beds and a corps of devoted surgeons, dressers, nurses, and litter-bearers." These supposedly clean, orderly accommodations promised to be a great improvement for the wounded, who often lay on muddy battlefields in the heat or at rail depots in the rain without food or shelter for days before being evacuated. However, all was not perfect on board Union hospital ships. When Amy Morris Bradley, a Maine woman serving on the *Knickerbocker,* found "several State rooms filled with soiled clothes," she immediately hired "four girls (colored) to wash the clothes and a crew to clean the boat." Bradley's solution to laundry and cleaning chores may have been typical, for in many Union-controlled areas, the availability of female contrabands to wash and clean spared white women from such menial chores. In certain locations along the coast, black women assumed duties originally assigned to white women. On Edisto Island, for example, white women gladly handed the job of delivering babies to skilled black midwives.[22]

Letters and diaries written by Union sailors attest to their desire to find laundresses, and some men apparently preferred wearing dirty clothes to doing laundry. In a letter to his wife, Martha, written in November 1862 from the USS *Monitor,* George Geer confessed that he had worn the underclothes she had washed for him for three weeks. "I think if I cannot send them to you I will have to pay a Counterband we have to wash them for me, as there is nothing I dislike so much as washing." The *Monitor*'s commanding officer had strict regulations about clean clothes. Geer observed, "The Captain is much stricter than he was before. He has all hands Muster every morning at 9 oclock in clean blue working clothes, but I am excused from muster and it saves me a great deal of washing and cleaning."[23]

Most sailors found doing laundry on shipboard a tedious chore. Bathing and washing clothes on sailing vessels had to be done in salt water using special soap, but even steam-powered ships with the ability to distill water had a limited supply of fresh water. According to Alvah Hunter, serving on the monitor *Nahant*, "We could buy salt water soap from the purser's steward aboard ship, but as I was able to get a bucket of hot fresh water from the condenser in the engine room at any time, I longed for fresh-water soap. I felt decidedly cleaner after having made that purchase." Hunter bought his "coveted" soap from the storekeeper with a $2 banknote sent by his father in the mail.[24]

During their trips ashore, officers and sailors alike searched for contrabands willing to take in laundry or sell produce. While strolling with the captain on Edisto Island on December 19, 1862, George Adams Bright saw the "numerous huts used by the soldiers who encamped here on the expedition to James Island." A considerable number of African Americans had once lived on Edisto in a colony, but by the time Bright arrived, the island had been all but abandoned by contrabands. "Saw the only two settlers on the island, Philip and Julia darkey refugees from Port Royal neighborhood," he wrote. "They are very civil and obliging and ready to do anything and having no use for money we pay them for services in gov't clothing etc. In return she does washing while he gets us oysters and goes with the officers hunting." Julia then roasted the oysters for them, and Bright noted that these oysters tasted better. The day before Christmas, men from the *South Carolina* went to the island to pick up both contrabands. In his journal, Bright wrote: "Dec. 24: This A.M. we sent boats ashore and brought off our two darkies Philip and Julia who were much gratified to go with us. While going out we discharged our battery into the woods lining the N. shore and then at the entrance and a very pretty splintering it made among the trees. Old Julia tried to get down through the deck into the Captain's pantry. Old Julia was perfectly beside herself with fear of the guns and tried to make Mr. Rowe share his pea jacket with her."[25]

In January 1863, when the *Fernandina* arrived off St. Simon's Island for blockade duty, the officers struck up friendships with contrabands at the old Thomas Butler plantation and discovered four or five elderly blacks willing to do their laundry. "Their prices are $.50 per dozen, you find soap, etc., or $0.75 per dozen, they find all the material such as soap, starch, etc.," Dr. Samuel Boyer noted. "There used to be, three months ago, upwards of 200 contrabands living on St Simon's Island, but they were all, with the exception of the few mentioned above, sent to Hilton Head, S.C., by orders of the commanding general stationed there." A contraband woman named Mary did washing for Boyer and probably many other officers. On April 20, 1863, he wrote in his diary that he had paid Mary's bill and then given another contraband named Harry some medicine for Old Sampson and some castor oil. The man named Old Sampson had a vegetable patch, which Boyer described: "The aspect is splendid around the place: the corn is growing beautifully; potatoes will be fit to eat in a week or two; watermelons, from the appearance of the vines, will be plenty in a month; there is every prospect of a large crop of peaches this season. In short, ere long we will live in clover as regards vegetables providing we remain in this station, which from all appearances seems likely." The doctor's observations are all the more compelling in light of the difficulty many Union warships on the blockade had in obtaining fresh provisions—so necessary to prevent scurvy and other diseases, not to mention improving the sailors' morale.[26]

When Du Pont visited St. Simon's Island in May 1862, Commander S. W. Godon took him on a carriage ride across the island. They visited Thomas Butler King's plantation, where, Du Pont told his wife, the contrabands were domiciled and the women did washing and ironing for the officers. One of the war's most famous black women, and a runaway slave herself, Harriet Tubman came to Beaufort, South Carolina, in 1862 to be a nurse and teacher for the Gullah people of the Sea Islands. Tubman initially received wages from the Union Army, which she used to build a wash house for the black freedwomen, and she taught them how to launder soldiers' clothes. When the army neglected to pay her regularly or issue her rations, the industrious Tubman baked and sold pies and gingerbread as well as root beer to survive.[27]

On one occasion, the officers of the USS *Fernandina* took up a collection of $30 to offer as a reward for information about the party or parties who had stolen the pocketbook of an African America woman named Lizzie who took in laundry. "The reward bill was written and posted on the mainmast," Boyer wrote, "where all hands had an opportunity of reading said reward." The suspects were put on the blacklist, he explained, and were not allowed to leave the ship. "I hope the thief or thieves will be found, for he or they deserve to be punished to the full extent of the law. It took the poor wench two weeks' hard work at the washtub to earn the above amount ($12), and she cannot afford to lose it."[28]

In between chasing rebel blockade runners and engaging in raids and expeditions up southern rivers, Union sailors endured long periods of monotony. It is no wonder that both officers and enlisted men on Union warships looked forward to mealtime. Commanding officers such as A. D. Harrell of the USS *Union* considered appetizing meals an important source of good morale and were always on the lookout for competent cooks. On November 21, 1861, Harrell gleefully wrote to his superior, Commander Thomas Craven, "I have a contraband on board this vessel who is a good cook, and I will thank you for permission to ship him, if not against the regulations."[29]

In addition to their shipboard meals, Union sailors supplemented their diets whenever possible by going ashore. With money in their pockets, these hungry sailors made good customers for home-cooked meals, as the contrabands on St. Simon's quickly realized. According to Boyer, on Sunday, February 15, 1863, the *Fernandina's* port watch went ashore for dinner. "Harry (one of ye intelligent contrabands) served them a dinner at 50/100 dolls [50 cents] per head, consisting of fresh pork, chickens, rice, greens, potatoes, etc. All were well satisfied with both their price and grub. From 16 to 20 dined at this table today. Harry done right smart. He intends to serve them dinner every Sunday. Bully for Harry and his dinners." Likewise, the contrabands on Sapelo Island served Union sailors with home-cooked meals. In April 1863 Boyer, Captain Moses, and the paymaster took a stroll on Sapelo, and the doctor wrote in his diary, "We found George and Mary having a gay and happy time preparing a dinner for the port watch, who were on liberty on shore today. The dinner consisted of beef steak; fried fish; stewed, fried and raw oysters; apple pie; and sassafras beer—the whole served up at 25/100 dollars per head. The boys enjoyed the dinner, and George and Mary put the 'greenbacks' in their pockets."[30]

Union Army commanders and ordinary soldiers also quickly discovered that black men and women made excellent cooks. To prepare their Thanksgiving dinner in November 1864, Sergeant Rice C. Bull and his fellow soldiers found an "old Negro aunty" named Susan in the slave quarters at Milledgeville and offered her $2 to cook their holiday meal. They gave her several hens, a goose, some fresh pork, a bag of wheat flour, and coffee and then gathered around a large open fireplace as she cooked. "We did what we could to help the old aunty, who was big, fat, and black as tar: we picked the fowls, brought the water and kept the fire while she did the cooking. With the wheat flour she made biscuits, baked them in an iron Dutch oven. All declared they had never eaten anything better than those biscuits and I don't think we ever had." Bull observed, "there were [not] many homes in the North who had their Thanksgiving Dinner on the 24th who were more thankful than we were in the Negro hut in Milledgeville."[31]

The contributions of these African American cooks not only improved morale but also eased the suffering of sick and wounded soldiers. Of sixty-five-year-old "Aunt Charlotte" of New Bern, who was the cook for the sanitary inspector of North Carolina, a correspondent for *Harper's Weekly* wrote, "Many a sick and wounded soldier . . . had reason to bless the culinary accomplishments of this venerable contraband cook, and to praise the alacrity with which, in times of their greatest need, she exerted her skill to save them from suffering."[32]

To supplement their rather monotonous diet, Union sailors also took small boats out to fish or went ashore whenever possible to hunt. Local African Americans often volunteered to act as guides for these navy foraging or hunting parties. During their time off St. Simon's Island, men from the USS *Fernandina* rowed ashore to hunt accompanied by black men who were undoubtedly more familiar with the area. "Our Nimrod, John E. Pickle, in company with two contrabands went in search of beef, venison, and turkeys," Dr. Boyer wrote on January 23, 1863. "Hope they may be successful." Although Pickle came back to the ship with only one hen and two ducks, he was unabashed by his hunting failure and immediately went off to clam and fish. Later, when he returned to the *Fernandina* with the cutter filled with clams and fish, the sailors cried, "Bully for Pickle, Pickle is the boy for us." In February, Pickle was able to kill a deer and a bullock. In fact, the *Fernandina* obtained sufficient supplies of fresh meat to send a deer to the admiral and a string of ducks to the fleet captain. Boyer's frequent references to these hunting expeditions attest to value the crew placed on fresh meat. However, on at least one occasion the doctor noted in his diary that the officers' mess had bought a cow from a contraband named King "for the sum of $5. which we intend to fatten so as to be fit to butcher by the latter part of April."[33]

These expeditions to obtain meat and other food could entail some risk, as a landing party from the USS *Mohican* discovered in March 1862 when they landed near Brunswick, Georgia, to look for fresh beef. According to Assistant Surgeon Archibald C. Rhoades, on the afternoon of March 11, he and Acting Paymaster John S. Kitchen took the second cutter to shore with ten men and a coxswain. They procured their beef supply, returned to the cutter, and were on their way back to the *Mohican* when, about twenty yards from the beach, they heard a musket shot coming from the direction of town. "This appeared to be a signal, for almost simultaneously with the report a force of 50 or 40 showed themselves within the thicket and fired a volley at our boat, killing 2 men and wounding 1 seriously," Rhoades reported. The rebels' first volley came without hailing the boat. When the rebels saw them pulling away they called out, "Surrender, you damned . . . ," but, Rhoades wrote, "as they had already killed two men and wounded others I replied, 'No, I won't surrender.'" Several of the men in the cutter jumped overboard, leaving fewer sailors at the oars to pull the boat out of harm's way. Rhoades pulled the stroke oar while Kitchen steered, and they gradually made their way into the stream, "being all the time exposed to a galling fire." The *Mohican* and *Potomska* then opened fire on the rebels, who "scampered towards Brunswick." The rebels' fire had killed sailors John Wilson and John Suter, mortally wounded two more, and wounded six others, including Rhoades.[34]

Despite the risks, Union Navy officers and men enjoyed these hunting expeditions ashore, but they benefited as well from contrabands who came to their vessels to sell meat and produce. In letters and diaries, Union sailors noted with relish the appearance of these contrabands, who lived on plantations or farms near the coast and could sail or row out to Union blockading vessels with a variety of foods to sell. Most often, these black entrepreneurs sought out customers on federal gunboats and ironclads patrolling up rivers or in sounds near the shore. During McClellan's Peninsular Campaign, for example, vessels operating on the James River benefited from their proximity to plantations whose slaves were eager and willing to bring them fresh produce. On the evening of June 4, 1862, William Keeler, paymaster on the ironclad *Monitor,* heard the watch cry, "Boat ahoy." He wrote, "I found a boat just coming alongside with three contrabands from 'Massa Carter's' plantation. They had in the boat a sheep, a couple of chickens, & some eggs, all of which we gladly bought asking no questions as to proprietorship. . . . Such things come off more plenty to us now than they did at first, the slaves finding in the present unsettled state of affairs that they are not liable to be detected & the trade is a profitable one to them."[35]

In July 1863 a middle-aged black man in a dugout canoe came alongside the monitor *Nahant* and beckoned for young Alvah Hunter to speak to him. After a brief discussion, Hunter recalled, the man "lifted up a white cotton cloth which was covering something in the bottom of the canoe and revealed a tin plate bearing a dozen or fifteen nice peaches, the first peaches I had seen." The man chose a nice peach and passed it up to Hunter, saying, "'Youse good to us niggers, Massa!' I begged him to sell me the whole plateful of peaches, and told him I'd give him a quarter for them." The man agreed, but when Hunter went below to get the money, one of the *Nahant's* officers "had bought the peaches and sent them down to be placed on the wardroom table, so the one that darkey had given to me was the only one of them I had."[36]

Union soldiers and sailors also commented on the availability of fresh produce to purchase from contrabands ashore. Writing from Drewry's Bluff, Virginia, Horace Henry Messenger, a hired substitute for a white man from Greenwich, Connecticut, wrote, "This land that we are on is raised a part of it by blacks now that was on it when the army come here. They raised potatoes and peanuts and sell them to the boys here but the boys are not allowed to go to their ground." Local blacks sold produce to hungry soldiers and sailors in marketplaces as well. In a letter to "Sister L" written on August 1, 1864, Oliver W. Norton described to a trip to Hilton Head:

> I was much amused while I was there at seeing the contrabands. It was market day (and is everyday) and they were coming to sell the melons and other vegetables. They came in boats, and the beach is so very flat that their boats cannot come near shore. The men come in every day costume, but the women put on their brightest bandanas and calicoes. Arrived at the end of their voyage, they run their boats up as far as they can, and then the men get out in the water and shoulder the women and carry them ashore and return for their cargoes.[37]

For Union sailors and officers, fresh provisions, especially fresh meat, constituted a delicious treat. "We had for Dinner this noon Rost Lamb; it was bully," George Geer wrote to his wife in early June from the James River. "Counterbands steel them and bring (them) off to us some times. They bring 2 or 3 sheep to a time, but the Officers have alwas taken them. This time they had more than they could eat, so they gave the Crew one Sheep."[38]

Supplying the Union Navy with fresh meat became a recognized trade during the Civil War. So important were these purveyors of fresh meat that on March 13, 1863, General David Hunter wrote to Du Pont regarding an exemption from the draft for certain "negroes who are employed in the business of supply in fresh meat to the Navy." He enclosed a copy of orders exempting these men and included their names: Tony Motcherie, January Small, Thomas Trickland, Robert Robinson, and Daniel Jenkins—all in employ of John Pitts, who furnished fresh meat to the navy.[39]

African Americans, in fact, availed themselves of every opportunity to assist Union sailors and soldiers while also making a little money or acquiring basic supplies. According to Du Pont, the contrabands on Ladies Island made baskets, presumably to sell. Edward Pierce sent Du Pont one that he in turn gave to his wife, telling her, "I am sending a basket which the sailmaker has put a neat cover over—it is made by the contrabands on Ladies Island." He suggested that she give the basket to Polly or to Anna Brinckle but wrote, "Do as you like best—it is very nice of the kind. I have the direction sewed on, so as not to hurt the linen cover."[40]

Even as the Union Army withdrew, contrabands and local African Americans took advantage of opportunities to sell to or barter with soldiers. Private Robert K. Sneden, marching with III Corps of McClellan's Army of the Potomac as it withdrew from Harrison's Landing on the James River on August 14, 1862, noted one such instance. In the sweltering summer weather, the soldiers of his unit stopped at Williamsburg en route to Yorktown. As Sneden walked through Williamsburg before dark, he wrote, "The inhabitants kept close to their houses, and peered cautiously at us behind shutters and doors. . . . The troops were bivouacked in the open fields on the outskirts of the town and not in it," he explained. "The Negro population were cooking 'corn pones' for the soldiers, who repaid them in sugar, coffee, and money."[41]

Many Union Army and Navy officers paid male contrabands to serve as valets and grooms. "Nearly all the officers here have contrabands as servants," Colonel Charles S. Wainwright of the First New York Artillery noted in the journal he kept during the war. "Hardly any of whom were house servants before they ran away, and consequently are as ignorant of their business as farm hands might be expected to be." On March 20, 1862, Francis Donaldson, a soldier serving with the 118th Pennsylvania Infantry camped near Bolivar Heights, Virginia, wrote to his brother: "Dear Jacob: Our camp is filled with contrabands and everyone now has 'George' to pull off his boots and to wait upon him." Union officers' and soldiers' views about these contraband servants varied. Wainwright held the contraband servants in contempt, decrying them as lazy and ignorant. "You may show them over and over again how you wish a thing done, but they will not learn, simply because they do not care," he lamented. "Their whole time is spent around the kitchen fire, talking or laughing, and playing cards." In contrast, Donaldson wrote, "My George has proved a treasure and by his conduct commands respect, not only from the soldiers, but from the nigroes, also, the latter, however, he is too swell a 'dark' to notice." Donaldson clearly valued his servant and in May wrote again to his brother from West Point, Virginia: "My man George continues to give me close attention and I fear that his usefulness has made it impossible to endure this life without him. He is faithful, honest, thoughtful and brave, and I am deeply attached to him."[42]

Union Navy officers quickly grew so accustomed to having personal servants, cooks, and wardroom stewards that they could barely manage without them. While serving on the USS *Florida,* William Keeler wrote to his wife, Anna, on April 7, 1864, to complain that their cook, steward, and boys "have all left, their time expired and each of us is left to shift for himself." He lamented that while the ship was being repaired they might have to stay in some private boardinghouse nearby or "hire some of the coloured women to keep house for us."[43]

The practice of employing contrabands as cooks and servants was common. On September 5, 1863, Rear Admiral Phillips Lee's wife, Elizabeth Blair Lee, wrote from her home at Silver Spring that she had been very busy as they were "short on servants." Several weeks later she wrote to her husband again, asking, "If you can pick up a good dining room servant, among your contrabands it would be a great benefit conferred on this domicile—we have a small house with two rooms where the man's wife can live if he has one & she can do the milking & some washing." Although she does not specifically mention obtaining any servants from among Lee's contrabands, Elizabeth wrote to her husband on March 20, 1864: "Charles does well & his wife better than at first—He is a good servant & will improve & seems very well content to be with us."[44]

Du Pont's wife, Sophie, also had the idea of obtaining servants from her husband's command. Alas, on May 29, 1862, Du Pont wrote, "In reference to a servant, I doubt if you can rely on my bringing one home . . . I might bring a contraband with me, but few domestic servants are found among them, the intelligent and likely ones being boatmen, pilots, and watermen." Du Pont, in fact, had a servant on his flagship *Wabash* and in this same letter told Sophie, "My boy Richard is a good servant and neat and understands silver, is young, *tres* blanc, too much so to be pleasant in a colored man."[45]

Many northern civilian women saw the influx of contrabands into Union lines as a source of servants as well. "I would like to get a good black girl to work for me," the mother of one soldier wrote to her son. Evidence suggests, too, that northern white women hoped the newly freed black women would remain subordinate and obedient to them, as they had to their former southern masters and mistresses.[46]

Contrabands served as cooks and servants for men of the U.S. Marine Corps during the Civil War as well. In August 1863 Rear Admiral John A. Dahlgren, now commanding the South Atlantic Blockading Squadron, received a contingent of 260 marines under the command of Major Jacob Zeilin. Dahlgren managed to find enough additional men to form a marine battalion, which he equipped with boats—four of them armed with a howitzer and a field carriage—to enable the marines to act as an amphibious strike force. In detailed instructions, the admiral specified that the marines would dress appropriately for the hot South Carolina climate, be prepared to move on an instant's notice, and carry cooked rations. He also ordered that "contrabands will be attached to the regiment whenever they can be had, so as to cook for the men, pitch and strike tents, and perform all the duties that can relieve the marines and leave them free for marching, fighting, etc." The assignment of contrabands to the newly formed marine battalion proved vital to its success, for, according to Major Zeilin, "Many of these men are raw recruits, and as I intimated, every garrison, receiving ship and even seagoing ships at the North, has been stripped to get these few together." Zeilin hesitated to undertake any "hazardous operation requiring coolness and promptness on their part" until the recruits had been drilled and had become acquainted with their officers. Few of the men had ever seen the enemy, he told Dahlgren. Furthermore, "Unaccustomed to living ashore, the men are very bad at caring for themselves in cooking and the various collateral duties of soldiers in this position, hence they are out of sorts, sick, and intractable."[47]

During the Civil War both the Union Army and the Union Navy relied heavily on contrabands to serve as laborers, cooks, laundresses, nurses, guides, personal servants, and purveyors of fresh meat and produce. In the final years of the Civil War along the southern coast, African Americans also played an important but little known role in assisting Union prisoners of war (POWs) who had escaped from Confederate prison camps. More than 400,000 Union and Confederate soldiers became POWs during the Civil War, confined in some 150 locations. Most of these camps were small (only twenty being of any size), and some quickly became overcrowded, unhealthy places. Confederate prisons such as Andersonville and Libby were notorious for their horrific conditions, but less well known Union prisons, such as the one at Point Lookout, Maryland, suffered from overcrowding as well. At the beginning of the conflict, both sides preferred to exchange prisoners on the battlefield and established a cartel agreement to conduct regular prisoner exchanges. In 1862, however, the Confederate government announced that it would no longer exchange African American POWs. Black military personnel taken prisoner would face punishment, including death or slavery. In response, President Abraham Lincoln issued an Order of Retaliation in July 1863 promising to put to death one Confederate prisoner for every African American Union prisoner executed and to sentence one rebel prisoner to hard labor for every black prisoner sold into slavery. When the Confederacy refused to give up its right to send black POWs back into slavery, Secretary of War Edwin Stanton ordered all exchanges to cease. This caused the number of prisoners confined in prison camps on both sides to increase dramatically.[48]

Although the majority of Union POWs remained in rebel prisons for the duration of the war, occasionally the Union Navy arranged a prisoner exchange. Thomas Morris Chester, a black war correspondent, witnessed one such exchange on October, 19, 1864, on the James River that included African American sailors. The truce boat *Mary Washington* brought 150 privateers to exchange for, he wrote, "the brave sailors who had been a long time languishing in Southern dungeons." Describing the rebel prisoners as well-dressed buccaneers, Chester noted that the Union sailors were "shivering under the cool breeze of the morning, many of them with nothing to wrap themselves up, while others were obliged to keep themselves as comfortable as possible with some very dirty blankets, of an inferior quality, furnished possibly by the rebels." Black soldiers greeted the Union prisoners when they came into view. "A large crowd of colored troops, those constituting the defence of this part of the line, with a very few white ones, were there to extend to them a cordial reception, and assure them that they had not suffered in vain," Chester wrote.[49]

These prisoners exchanged in the fall of 1864 were fortunate indeed, for most POWs languished in rebel prisons until the end of the war or succumbed to disease and malnutrition. Some, however, managed to escape Confederate prisons during the summer and fall of 1864 as hundreds of contrabands and other refugees, both white and black, followed General Sherman's army across Georgia. Escaping POWs naturally tried to reach Union lines or Union gunboats and vessels in southern rivers and creeks. Stories of such escapes almost always included the assistance of sympathetic blacks who offered food, shelter, directions, and even transportation. When First Lieutenant William H. Newlin of the Seventy-third Illinois Volunteers escaped with five others from a Confederate prison at Danville, Virginia, in the winter of 1863–1864, they came upon some blacks cutting wood. Upon being assured that no whites were around, Newlin and the other soldiers approached the men and asked for food. "They were quite willing, even anxious to respond to our call for food. They offered to divide with us at noon, when 'missus' brought their dinner out." In addition to food, the blacks gave the escapees advice on where to hide and then brought them a bucket filled with "eatables, consisting of fried ham, fried eggs, boiled beans, and corn-dodgers." Later the black men gave the federal escapees provisions, for which they gladly paid in Confederate dollars. "We could not pay them adequately, but hoped in the end they would have their reward in the results of the war," Newlin recalled.[50]

Whites and free blacks also gave aid to escaping Union prisoners. In Richmond, a remarkable white woman, Elizabeth Van Lew, used her Church Hill mansion as a safe house for refugees and guided their flights from Confederate prisons to Union lines or gunboats. One fugitive recalled, "Miss Van Lew told me the roads and where to take to the woods to escape the pickets and to go down to the James River, and I could, perhaps, before morning reach a place of safety where I could escape to our troops." According to Colonel David B. Parker, stationed at City Point, Virginia, "Miss Van Lew kept two or three bright, sharp colored men on the watch near Libby prison, who were always ready to conduct an escaped prisoner to a place of safety." Prisoners who managed to escape Libby prison later testified to the "heroism and patriotism of black Unionists who came to the timely aid of the escapees." Van Lew also had black men and women working inside the prison who, at great personal risk, informed Union prisoners that the woman who casually walked "nearly every Sunday" in front of the prison would assist them if they escaped.[51]

Many Union POWs escaping from Confederate prisons headed for the coast, taking advantage of the South's numerous creeks and rivers. On occasion, blacks living near the coast with access to small boats or canoes transported or assisted these fleeing Union prisoners to freedom. For example, when Morris C. Foote fled Camp Sorghum, he hoped to find a boat to take him down the Conagree and Santee rivers to the coast, where he might see a Yankee gunboat. After escaping, Foote approached some African Americans living in nearby cabins. "We confided in them fully," he recalled, "told them who and what we were and said we wanted some kind of a boat and provisions to enable us to go down the river and escape to a free land." The hour being late, the blacks told the escapees to hide for the night until they could find a boat. After spending the night in an old corn barn, the men, now rested, continued on their journey to freedom. Their experience was not uncommon.

Despite the danger of being discovered and given as many as 100 lashes, blacks willingly accepted the risk of aiding Union escapees. "We never get one who showed any disposition to betray us to the whites," one escapee recalled.[52]

Few of these African Americans could read and write, and even fewer wrote of their experiences during the war. One man, however, told interviewers about his wartime experiences, including his role in rescuing several "Yankee" soldiers who had escaped from the Confederate stockade at Florence. Alonzo Jackson, a black waterman living near Georgetown, South Carolina, provided an important eyewitness account of African Americans' assistance to escaped Union prisoners and others during the Civil War, and his story illustrated that black watermen were well informed about the presence and location of Union gunboats in southern waterways. "About 8 months before Georgetown was occupied by Union soldiers—while I was in the freighting business on my flat boat on 'Mingo' creek (up the 'Black river') about 30 or 40 miles from Georgetown by water, 3 white men came near my boat which was at the bank of the river," Jackson recalled. When the men saw that Jackson and his employee, Henry, were African Americans, they identified themselves as escaped prisoners and asked Jackson, "we are your friends can't you do something for us we are nearly perished." Jackson invited the men to come on board his boat and recalled, "I told them I would hurry and cook food for them, which I did and gave it to them in my boat." He then shoved off from shore about sixty feet and anchored. "They were very weak—and had no weapons. They had no shoes on—it was winter weather and cold—The 3 Yankees did not suggest anything for me to do for them except to feed them—and wanted to get to the gunboats— They did not know where the gunboats were—I did—and I told them I would take them where they could get to the gunboats unmolested." He said the soldiers did not threaten him or order him to take them, nor did they pay him or promise him anything for his assistance.[53]

Jackson hid the men in his boat and went downriver to Georgetown. "In about three days time we came to 'North Island' (about 12 miles from Georgetown) which I then knew was in possession of the Union forces—I did not pass Georgetown by day light for fear of being stopped by rebels who had 'pickets' all along the shore to stop all boats from going below." During the night he floated his boat on the ebb tide toward North Island unobserved. "I got there in the night and landed the 3 soldiers in my small boat—I showed them the direction to cross the Island so as to get to the gunboats—I knew there were many of the gunboat people on the shore there at that time." Jackson never saw the Yankee soldiers again, but through "a colored man named 'Miller' (who was on the shore near the gunboats) learned that the 3 soldiers had got to the fleet—'Miller' told me this about 2 weeks after I took the 3 soldiers—he saw them and described them so that I was certain he had seen the same 3 soldiers safe in the protection of the gunboats." Identifying himself as a Union sympathizer, Jackson said, "I wanted to be free—and I wanted my race to be free—I knew this could not be if the rebels had a government of their own—All the time during, and before the war, I felt as I do now that, the Union people were the best friends of the colored people." Although afraid to reveal his Union sentiments, Jackson said, "I always rejoiced over Union victories—I talked with a few white men at Georgetown and with such colored men as I could trust, in favor of the Union all the time during the war, but I knew my life would be taken if it was known how I really felt about the war."[54]

In at least one instance, and probably more, Union Navy commanders learned about escaped prisoners from contrabands. On November 30, 1864, Acting Master I. A. Pennell of the bark *Ethan Allan,* on station in St. Simon's Sound, reported that a contraband had come on board his ship from Brunswick, Georgia, claiming that about 300 Union prisoners had escaped from railroad cars while in transit from Savannah to Station No. 7. Flanked by Jekyll Island to the south and St. Simon's Island to the north, St. Simon's Sound led to the town of Brunswick on the Turtle River. These 300 Union POWs may have been some of the 5,000 who were transported in late 1864 via the Atlantic and Gulf Coast Railroad from Savannah to Blackshear, a makeshift camp in southeast Georgia. Although three of the escapees had been recaptured that morning while eating breakfast at a house, Pennell immediately sent word to Lieutenant Commander Chaplin of the *Dai Ching,* who dispatched his launch, the schooner *Mary,* and sixteen men led by Acting Ensign W. Walton "to assist in rescuing any which might have gotten to the coast." When this party arrived, Pennell, along with fifty men and three officers from the *Ethan Allen,* set out and landed at Belle Point soon after daylight. "On landing we discovered the pickets making a hasty retreat into the woods," he wrote. The Union landing party advanced cautiously, skirmishing with cavalry pickets for three miles, and then came to a house where a woman informed them that four Union soldiers had been recaptured that morning. Pennell's men continued to advance, encountering rebels in the nearby woods who were searching for the escaped prisoners. When the rebels began collecting in the woods in "considerable numbers," Pennell wisely decided to fall back to the boats.[55]

They had not given up hope of finding the escaped Union POWs, however. On December 3, 1864, the rescue party went thirty miles up the South Altamaha River to Hopeton Landing. After marching through deserted rice fields, the bluejackets reached Hopeton plantation and villa, where they found a crippled man named Poncell and his two sons. Pennell arrested the older son, a rebel soldier home on furlough, but left the other son, a ten-year-old, with his father. Unable to obtain useful information from Poncell, Pennell explained that he had "learned from a few old negroes that had been left on the plantation that there was a large number of cavalry sent down from station No. 7, to assist the coast guard in recapturing the escaped prisoners." The blacks told Penell that the rebels had encamped at Waynesville, but they had not seen any escaped prisoners there. On December 4 Pennell and his party returned empty-handed to his ship.[56]

This unproductive mission apparently whetted Pennell's appetite for boat expeditions, however. On December 20, 1864, acting on information from a contraband that there was a picket station at Troop's plantation twenty miles up the Altamaha River, Pennell fitted out another expedition. They left at dark with a launch, a howitzer, and several boats with three officers and forty men. Arriving at the plantation at two o'clock in the morning, Pennell sent for "an old negro" whom his guide said "would lead me to the camp." The elderly black man came down to the boats and informed Pennell that the rebels were encamped at a house about two miles inland. "He offered to lead me to them," Pennell reported, and performed the duty faithfully. An hour after landing, the sailors surrounded the house and captured seven of the pickets, along with their arms and seven horses. A corporal and one man on guard duty escaped. Pennell found a scow and intended to take off the horses at high water, but "while waiting, the whole force of the county, with Captain Hunter's company of cavalry, about 60 men, came down on us and attempted to drive us off; we had some sharp skirmishing with them for four hours." Pennell waited for the tide, then threw grape and shell into the house occupied by the rebels, forcing them to fall back into the woods. At high water he floated the scow out of the canal and embarked the rebel prisoners and horses, as well as "7 contrabands; one of them, the old negro who piloted me to the camp." At 1 A.M. on December 21 they were back aboard the *Ethan Allen*. Pennell's aggressive leadership impressed Dahlgren, and in early January 1865 the admiral recommended to the Navy Department that Pennell be promoted.[57]

Whether they remained with their masters or escaped to Union vessels or into Union lines, slaves and free blacks were important recruits in the

Union spy network. They often worked for Confederate commanders as stewards, as stevedores on wharves and blockade runners, or in yards building rebel ironclads. During the war, Union Navy commanders kept an eagle eye out for potential sources of information about the enemy and for individuals willing to seek out such intelligence. Occasionally, ambitious Union naval commanders actually created their own informal spy networks. Take, for example, the adventures of young Henry Phelon. In late May 1863, responding to a request from General John Foster to retaliate against the Whitford band of guerrillas, who had burned the coal schooner *Sea Bird* in the Neuse River, Commander H. K. Davenport sent the *Ceres, Shawsheen,* and *Brinker* to Wilkinson's Point. According to Phelon, his vessel, the 126-ton side-wheeler *Shawsheen,* went to Wilkinson's Point to "protect some 400 soldiers while they are building a battery." Phelon conned the *Shawsheen* down to the mouth of the Neuse River, closely following the shore, and then came back on the opposite shore, overhauling every suspicious-looking vessel. Occasionally he sent two boat crews ashore to buy eggs and chickens. "They are bitter secesh all up and down the river," he wrote. Phelon told his fiancée, Josephine (Josie) Brand, that he landed and "as quickly as they saw us coming, one of the young ladies ran into the woods as hard as she could go. I suspect to inform the guerillas that the 'Yankees are coming.'" When they went up to the house, Phelon discovered five or six "very pretty girls. We had quite a time. Oh how they hated the Yankees. I remained there some two hours bade them good bye and left." About half an hour before Phelon left, two of the young ladies went into the woods. Just prior to their departure, Phelon told "the old woman (who by the way has two sons in the rebel army) that if any of my men were injured by the guerillas I would shell her house and every house within two miles of hers. She said that, 'there were no guerillas around there as she knowed on.'"[58]

During June 1863 the *Shawsheen* continued to patrol the river, protecting commerce. In a letter to a woman named Stephanie dated June 21, 1863, Phelon wrote, "I had known of a party of guerillas (Whitford gang) that were engaged in burning her [the *Sea Bird*]. I know it would be a feather in my cap if I could capture them." Upon being informed "that a bee hive party was to be given at a house up south river, and that the guerillas were to be of the number at dark," Phelon took the *Shawsheen,* accompanied by the *Henry Brinker,* up Bay River and anchored at about 9:00 on the morning of June 22. "Took lunch with 15 soldiers and 18 sailors, headed by myself, and Mr. Ringot, arrived at the house at 11 P.M. got as close as I could and then gave the signal for one grand rush," he wrote to Stephanie. "And away we went pell mell. The house was surrounded in one minute capturing the whole boodle. 4 soldiers and rest citizens." The capture of the rebel soldiers pleased Phelon's superior, who, he told Stephanie, "complimented me very highly." Young Phelon then explained, "Do you see the reason for my gallant attention to the ladies? Having one of his slaves (Mr. Nelson's) as a spy for me. Ha ha. They have not captured me yet, and I have only captured four of them. Ha ha ha. I would like half a dozen ladies to wait upon. Do you see the point?"[59]

Acting Master Henry Phelon seems to have made good use of his "spy network," for on July 12, 1863, the *Shawsheen,* with Phelon in command, made a reconnaissance up Bay River. Phelon candidly described his recent activities to Josie. "I have made several expeditions since I wrote to you last, and have been successful beyond my expectations," he wrote. After relating some of these experiences to her, Phelon added, "I got underway and went over to Smith's Creek, landed a force on shore capturing the mail carriers, Mr. Dickson, and Mr. Salter also the mail, some 15 or 20 letters, and their mail boat." He sent Charles Ringot with the mail to New Bern. "Mr. Ringot has not been gone two hours when I was informed by one of my spys where a lot of sails, blocks, rigging, bolts, etc. were belonging to the burnt schooner. I took 6 armed men in my gig, went to the man's house, threatened to take him as a prisoner if he didn't tell me where the things were. I scared him so he showed me the place offering to cart them down to the beach for me which he did. Now they are all safely on board of my vessel, several hundred dollars worth." Phelon hoped this latest capture would elicit favorable comment from his superior. "Mr. Ringot will open his eyes as well as the Commander when he sees the lot, and will wonder how I find such things out. I have 7 or 8 spys that work for me all the time, am I not lucky Josie?"[60]

Phelon cleverly used young southern ladies and a slave as spies, but other Union commanders employed sympathetic whites and African Americans as spies and informants. The Union commander at Cape Hatteras, General Rush Hawkins, regularly employed blacks as spies. "If I want to find out anything hereabouts I hunt up a Negro; and if he knows or can find out, I'm sure to get all I want," he wrote. Other army commanders sent out spies, but espionage during the Civil War was, by and large, "an amateur exercise." Although no intelligence organization existed when the war began, both the Union and the Confederacy gradually developed intelligence units. Known as the Signal Bureau, the Confederate unit had agents in Washington, Baltimore, and other northern locations. The Union effort began at the State Department and then became a mission of the War Department. Much of the information obtained by both sides came not from a formal spy network, however, but from newspaper articles and from informants, both black and white. Furthermore, the need for wartime secrecy assures that the identity of many Civil War spies will remain unknown and the story of their contributions to the war effort incomplete.[61]

Although many white men and women spied for the Union, African Americans participated in intelligence-gathering activities during the Civil War as well. African Americans who spied for the Union included men such as George Scott, a fugitive slave who early in the war went behind the lines to provide General Benjamin F. Butler with information on rebel fortifications and troop movements. General George B. McClellan's chief of intelligence, Allan Pinkerton, debriefed former slaves and identified and recruited those who were educated or had good memories and other skills for intelligence work. One of these spies, W. H. Ringgold, a black crewman working on a riverboat on the York River, gave Pinkerton valuable information about Confederate fortifications, artillery batteries, and troop concentrations. Some argue that Ringgold's intelligence reports constituted the best information McClellan had prior to his famous Peninsular Campaign. As part of his intelligence-gathering activities, Pinkerton took advantage of leaders in the black community and also employed females agents, including Mrs. Carrie Lawton. Among her other wartime activities, Harriet Tubman served as a scout and an agent for the Union, gathering information. One of the Union Navy's most valuable African American spies was Mary Louveste, a freed slave who worked as a housekeeper in Norfolk, Virginia, for an engineer employed refitting the CSS *Merrimac* at the Gosport Navy Yard. From her vantage point inside the rebel yard, Louveste could report progress on the vessel to Navy Secretary Gideon Welles. Then, seizing the initiative, she stole plans for the Confederate ironclad and made her way to Washington, D.C. Mary met with Navy Department officials, showed them the plans, and convinced them that the Confederate ironclad was nearing completion, which prompted the navy to expedite work on its own ironclad, the USS *Monitor*. In his memoirs Welles wrote, "Mrs. Louveste encountered no small risk in bringing this information . . . and other facts. I am aware of none more meritorious than this poor colored woman whose zeal and fidelity I remember and acknowledge with gratitude." In Richmond, Elizabeth Van Lew organized agents to spy for General Butler. She recruited Samuel Ruth in October 1864 to use the railroad to set up a chain of communication between Richmond and another agent, Charles Clark, at City Point, Virginia. When the rebels grew suspicious and threatened to arrest some of the citizens of Charles County, Clark sent a "colored man" to meet with Ruth. By war's end, Van Lew and Ruth had established an effective spy ring.[62]

Unfortunately, African Americans did not author any of the twenty-four books written after the Civil War by persons claiming to have been spies or counterspies. The official records, however, offer glimpses of informants and agents—some of them African American, others not identified as black or white—used by Union naval commanders. In September 1862 Captain John Rodgers sent word to Rear Admiral S. P. Lee about a rumored attack on Suffolk, Virginia. "My informant brings me word that 8,000 more troops were bought from the direction of Petersburg to Zuni, near Suffolk, on Saturday last, making as near as can be calculated 14,000 troops there," he wrote. Rodgers referred as well to "other accounts" about rebel rams and troops moving down from Richmond to Williamsburg, but he did not specify where these accounts originated.[63]

Occasionally, Union commanders mentioned Confederate agents or guides in official correspondence. For example, in a letter written in October 1862 to Secretary Welles, Lee passed on information obtained through Captain Case, "by a person in the employment of the United States, and who has good opportunities for knowing about the matter, that recently a rebel agent came from Richmond to Norfolk and took away some fourteen or fifteen mechanics and ship carpenters, with their tools, to work on their ironclads." Union forces had occupied Norfolk in May 1862, so the rebel agent must have been very clever to infiltrate the city and take away so many valuable, skilled workmen.[64]

In his effort to intercept mail being carried between Norfolk and Richmond and goods from Norfolk, Commander John Gillis reported to Lee in late January 1862 that he had obtained "the services of a negro who is perfectly familiar with every portion of the country in Nansemond County along the Chuckatuck Creek and thus far he has proved more reliable than the intelligent contrabands generally do." Although Gillis did not specifically credit this black informant with providing information about the Confederate mail route between Norfolk and Richmond, he explained to Lee that goods and mail had been received from small boats in Chuckatuck Creek, "ostensibly employed in oystering and fishing," with passes obtained from Brigadier General Viele at Norfolk. Gillis acted on this information, taking the *Commodore Morris* up Chuckatuck Creek on January 22, 1862, and capturing several small vessels and boats.[65]

In another instance, Commander William A. Parker, who was actively seeking information about rebel defenses near Wilmington, was prepared to recruit the brother-in-law of an informer as an agent. As Parker explained to Lee, on December 25, 1862, three white men had come out from shore—two northerners and one North Carolinian named F. M. Savage, who was "fleeing for his life." From Savage, Parker learned that Savage's brother-in-law J. J. Orrell, a Confederate lieutenant "who is thoroughly Union and greatly desirous of aiding when the forts are attacked," was ready, "upon signals, to cut wires running to Wilmington and to immediately join the United States forces." According to Parker, Savage, who had escaped with Orrell's aid, was "willing to go as a guide, or remain as a hostage for Lieutenant's Orrell's veracity in his sincerity." A former lighthouse keeper at Campbell Island, North Carolina, Savage had been "proscribed for uttering Union sentiments."[66]

The Navy Department also obtained intelligence about Confederate activities and ships under construction from persons referred to as informants. The department passed these reports on to senior commanders such as Samuel Phillips Lee and Samuel Francis Du Pont, but unfortunately, these informants were seldom identified as African American, although some may well have been. However, in early 1864 Lee's correspondence with the Navy Department mentioned the organization of an army intelligence network that proved beneficial to the navy's operations along the southern coast. The operation in question involved federal gunboats supporting yet another successful raid into the interior, this one up the James River. At General Butler's direction, General Graham took three transports carrying troops and landed on a peninsula below Fort Powhatan, at a place known as Brandon Farms. According to the *New York Tribune*, this expedition "captured twenty-two of the enemy, seven of the signal corps, twenty-nine negroes, five Jews, together with large quantities of tobacco oats, corn and port—the latter three times of which were destroyed." Lee credited the information that led to Graham's successful expedition to a secret intelligence system organized by Butler. "I have several times urged upon General Butler to use his large civil fund to obtain exact intelligence about the ironclads in Richmond," Lee wrote, "and he has just told me that he is organising a secret intelligence system, and that the seizure made by General Graham at Brandon . . . was effected on information obtained." Butler's information may have come in part from Henry Moseby, a table servant to Confederate president Jefferson Davis. When Butler interviewed Moseby on January 26, 1864, the man told him that the Confederates had the ironclad *Richmond* at Drewry's Bluff and another unfinished one at Richmond. Moseby had not been aboard the *Richmond* but claimed that it would be completed in two months, with two guns mounted on each side as well as one in the bow and one in the stern.[67]

Evidence in senior naval commanders' official correspondence suggests that they authorized reward money for information and compensated spies or agents. In September 1862, for example, Lee, still anxious to intercept mail passing between Norfolk and Richmond, instructed Acting Volunteer Lieutenant Amos P. Foster, commanding the USS *Delaware* off Newport News: "You may give reasonable reward for information which may enable you to capture any important mail." Occasionally, other Union naval officers offered blacks compensation for information about Confederate defenses and ironclad construction. In an effort to learn more about two floating batteries rumored to be located at Hamilton and three gunboats at Halifax, Lieutenant Commander C. W. Flusser told Lee in October 1862, "I have offered a faithful and intelligent negro $100 to visit Halifax and Hamilton and bring me all the information he can obtain. I expect him to leave to-morrow." Flusser expressed fear that if the rebel batteries, partly ironclad, steamed down the Roanoke River and destroyed the *Commodore Perry* and *Hunchback,* they might gain possession of the sounds, "and our army will be captured or forced to evacuate North Carolina." He hoped that Lee could send him a light-draft ironclad better able to stand up to the Confederate ironclads nearing completion up the Roanoke River. Although the official records fail to reveal whether the black man succeeded in confirming the presence of the Confederate floating batteries, in early November 1862 Commander H. K. Davenport went up to Hamilton in the *Hetzel.* "With regard to this reconnaissance, I am satisfied that the rebels have as yet no ironclad boats in this river," Davenport told Lee, "nor do I think it probable that they will ever attempt the construction of any vessel of formidable character above Williamston."[68]

Union commanders also employed black men, both slaves and freedmen, as guides for expeditions. In mid-May 1862 General Foster obtained the services of one Samuel Williams, a "colored man," to guide three Union regiments on an expedition out of New Bern in the direction of Trenton. A freedman, Williams had come to Union headquarters with information about several hundred rebel soldiers and a plan to catch them. He "planned all the details, and made it as clear as possible," and in due time, General Foster agreed to the operation. Williams led the expedition on his horse with twenty cavalrymen, but unfortunately, the Union commander took another road, and Williams's party was ambushed; it was then rescued by the main body of troops. According to Colonel S. H. Mix of the Third New York Cavalry, Williams "performed effectual service for us, at the imminent risk and peril of his life, guiding my men faithfully and truthfully, until his horse was shot under him, and he was compelled to take refuge in a swamp." Another officer commended Williams by saying, "There was no a braver man in North Carolina, within our lines."[69]

On occasion, reports indicated that senior Union Navy officers dispatched spies to the interior to gather information about enemy activities. In mid-September 1864, for example, Dahlgren sent an intriguing message to the senior officer off Georgetown, South Carolina. He wrote: "I send the colored men, Fred Williams and Billy, by *Geranium* and desire you will land them at such a point and at such time as they desire. Furnish them with whatever they ask for to assist them. They will inform you where they will return, and have a boat about the spot every night the weather permits." That both black men were going ashore to engage in clandestine information gathering was clear from Dahlgren's next statement: "I desire that particular attention shall be given to the matter, as I expect these men, particularly Williams, will bring me useful information." The admiral then wrote, "I hear fugitives have frequently endeavored to escape, but have been unable to reach our vessels. You will give attention to this matter, and send boats at proper time along this shore and into the Santee to receive these persons." Dahlgren did not elaborate whether these fugitives were slaves, white refugees, Confederate deserters, escaped Union prisoners, or spies.[70]

Dahlgren obviously trusted Fred Williams and Billy, but other Union naval officers were suspicious of contrabands and occasionally accused them of being spies for their southern masters. In March 1863 Flusser, commanding the *Commodore Perry* at Plymouth, wrote to Commander Alex Murray about a "reliable contraband" who claimed to have deserted from the enemy. The man represented himself as an officer's servant and, Flusser wrote, "declares that he had heard of no boat building up this river, that he does not believe there is one there; that one was some time since under construction at Tarboro, but that work on her has been discontinued, etc." A suspicious Flusser told Murray, "I fear the 'reliable contraband' was sent in by Messieurs les Secesh. I do not think anyone can outlie a North Carolina white, unless he be a North Carolina negro."[71]

It was sometimes difficult for Union commanders to determine whether blacks picked up by Union ships were involved in blockade running or other wartime activities on behalf of the Confederacy by choice or by coercion. The experience of the federal gunboat *Zouave*, which captured a small sloop, the *J. C. McCabe*, on the James River on January 18, 1863, is a good example. The *Zouave*'s pilot, John A. Phillips, discovered six persons on board: two "white men, S. R. Durfey and Peter

Smith; one colored man, Tom Harris, and three white boys, John Lawrence, James Smith, and John Benson, aged, respectively, 16, 14, and 8." The two white men claimed that they had escaped from Petersburg to avoid conscription. In his official report, Phillips explained that the black man, Tom Harris, "alleges that he came away because he could get no pay for his work. I think from all the circumstances attending this case that it is only a scheme for getting to Norfolk, from whence they intended to run goods up the river for rebel use." Phillips surmised that the men were lying, for several reasons: "Durfey and Smith carried their families to Petersburg after the rebellion broke out; they left them there, although they could have been brought away in the sloop. The sum of $784.68 was found in their possession, notwithstanding they told me they had determined to leave what money they had with their wives and escape themselves." As further evidence, Phillips cited an order found in the lining of Harris's cap from J. E. Horner of Petersburg to Thomas Smith of Norfolk. It directed the latter to deliver a box of goods to Captain Smith or to Tom Harris. "This, of course, was to be taken to Petersburg," Phillips wrote. Lee agreed with Phillips's report and restated the details to Welles. Lee concluded that the men's objective "probably was to get the goods and information to Norfolk and run over the flats off the Nansemond and by the blockade here."[72]

Lee's suspicions were well-founded, for African Americans as well as whites acted as spies for the Confederacy. A correspondent wrote to the *Boston Herald* on March 17, 1863, "It has been found out for a certainty that some of the contrabands who have been liberated by Mr. Lincoln's proclamation have been doing us a great injury by passing our lines at Hilton Head, and conveying to the rebels information of the movements of our fleet and troops, for which they have been well paid by the rebels. Steps have been taken to put a stop to this by prohibiting the negroes from going beyond our lines." Union efforts to prevent contrabands from passing information to the rebels did not always succeed, however. In October 1862, for example, General Ormsby M. Mitchel organized an expedition up the Broad River to cut the railroad bridge at Pocotaligo, South Carolina. Supported by Commander Charles Steedman's eight gunboats, General J. M. Brannan's 4,448 federal troops left Hilton Head in transports on October 21 and went up to the mouth of the Broad River. From there, armed launches conveyed advance troops to the landing site, but missed signals, the grounding of one gunboat, and darkness threw the operation into confusion. When Brannan's men finally disembarked, swamps and burned bridges delayed their advance. The *Uncas* and navy howitzer gun crews attempted to cover the troops, but when they lost the element of surprise and the Confederate forces approached, Brannan called off the attack and ordered his men back on the transports. The expedition was, Du Pont had to concede to Assistant Secretary Gustavus Fox, "a complete failure, with heavy loss, the troops ventured out of reach of the gunboats, and, though behaving well, were thrashed by an inferior force, well posted, full of information of the movement having been carried to the rebels by faithless or spy contrabands." Although Steedman did not mention spy contrabands in his report, he did blame "the ignorance of the contraband guide who accompanied the *Wabash's* launches" for the party's failure to capture a rebel picket guard at MacKay's Point. The entire affair had taken place during Du Pont's visit to the Navy Department, but he returned to Port Royal in time to see the tragic remnants of the expedition. "I saw a portion of the poor, wounded fellows landing, said to be 400 in all, the killed amounting to 40." The expedition's failure came as a blow to the admiral, who told Fox that he regretted "such things were attempted in my absence by General Mitchel, absorbing my vessels from the blockade, which, of course, could not be refused him by the senior officer present." Even if successful, such expeditions could result in nothing more, he said, than "burning a wood pile or the wharf, to be replaced in a week."[73]

Despite this setback and other incidents caused, in part, by black Confederate spies or guides, intelligence gathered by African American spies and informants made valuable contributions to the Union war effort. Furthermore, without the labor of thousands of black military laborers and hundreds of laundresses, cooks, nurses, guides, and purveyors of fresh produce and meat, the Union Navy would have been hard-pressed to prosecute the war as successfully as it did. Although not all contrabands eagerly accepted employment from the government, preferring to live off either government or private charity, most freed people found that freedom left them without a means of subsistence. When the government would not or could not provide food and rations for them, many former slaves went to work at whatever tasks and for whatever wages they could get. For some enterprising contrabands and local blacks, the war offered gainful employment, and they quickly discovered that Union sailors and soldiers were ready customers for their goods and services. Many expressed a willingness to work for the Union cause, for as one Union Navy officer explained, "it was but fair that they should do so for us, as we were working for them." Nonetheless, not all black laborers received their promised compensation or rations; others lived in fear of being impressed by the military and sent far from their camps or homes and dependent families. Federal officials encouraged black women, an especially vulnerable group, to seek employment in the North as household servants, and some relief societies even established employment bureaus for black servants. Still, the Civil War created many employment opportunities for some enterprising African Americans, and the federal government provided much-needed food and sustenance for thousands of other newly freed people.[74]

CHAPTER 6
CONTRABAND PILOTS

We must have men of undaunted courage and great coolness, for much is at stake.

—Gustavus Vasa Fox

Of all the important contributions by African Americans to the Union Navy's North and South Atlantic Blockading Squadrons and Potomac Flotilla, none proved as valuable as that made by skilled black coastal pilots. Suddenly called on to enforce a blockade of almost 3,500 miles of southern coastline, much of it deprived of functioning lighthouses and stripped of navigational markers, the Navy Department quickly realized a need for experienced, loyal pilots. At the beginning of the Civil War, senior Union Navy commanders looked first to officers of the U.S. Coast Survey for assistance in piloting vessels in and out of harbors, surveying coastal waters, and other navigational missions. When the Blockade Strategy Board met in the summer of 1861, it recommended that a Coast Survey vessel be assigned to each of the principal blockading squadrons to complete surveys of portions of the coast not already done. In addition to providing or generating charts of the coast and adjacent waters, Coast Survey superintendent Alexander D. Bache and other Coast Survey personnel produced descriptions of coastal areas, obstructions to navigation, lighthouse locations, tides and currents, and other related information. The commanders of both the North and South Atlantic Blockading Squadrons benefited from the services of Coast Survey officers and men, and some 400 U.S. Navy officers who had served with the Coast Survey before the war fought for the Union, among them David D. Porter, John Dahlgren, Charles H. Davis, S. Phillips Lee, Stephen Rowan, John Rodgers, Benjamin F. Sands, C. R. P. Rodgers, Foxhall Parker, Alexander C. Rhind, and Charles Flusser, to name just a few.[1]

Early in the war Coast Survey personnel accompanied Union naval expeditions buoying channels and waterways, piloting naval vessels across bars, and conducting topographical surveys of the numerous islands along the southern coast. There were, however, too few Coast Survey officers to serve as pilots for every blockading vessel. Faced with the demands of a burgeoning fleet, the Navy Department anxiously sought qualified pilots who knew the rivers and creeks of the southern coast. John Dahlgren's discovery in late April 1861 that the rebels had removed buoys from Kettle Bottom in the Potomac River only added to their concern. Dahlgren asked the Navy Department for a "supply" of Potomac River pilots and told Navy Secretary Gideon Welles that he would pay them $50 to $80 per month, according to the value of their service. In response to Dahlgren's request for Potomac River pilots, Welles sent him six men: Captain Mitchell, J. T. Hilton, C. C. Pearson, H. Hayne, Robert Walter, and a man named Roberts. Dahlgren quickly sent Walter and another pilot, Stephens, to Lieutenant John Glendy Sproston and ordered him to take command of the USS *Powhatan* and proceed down the Potomac to replace and protect the buoys at the Kettle Bottom shoals.[2]

Not all these new pilots proved competent, as Commander John Gillis discovered. "Two of the pilots we received from *Powhatan* proving inefficient, and admitting they were only capable for vessels of 10 or 12 feet from Maryland Point up," Gillis wrote to Welles on April 27, 1861, "I took the lead in this vessel, and will convoy the transport to Washington." The following day Gillis arrived safely in Washington with the two transports and some 800 troops, but in other cases, the ignorance of pilots jeopardized or limited federal gunboat operations in the South's narrow, shallow rivers and streams. When Lieutenant Alexander Rhind mounted an expedition in the gunboat *E. B. Hale* with twenty men from the *Crusader* and attempted to ascend the Paw Paw River in late April 1862, the "ignorant" pilot ran it aground. Rhind got the *Hale* off and attempted to retrace his steps and pass through the South Edisto River, but finding the pilot "ignorant of the channel," he gave that up and returned by the Dawho to North Edisto. Anticipating a rebel attack in the narrow river, Rhind, according to Du Pont, "made all his crew lay down flat, put on all steam, and rushed by, receiving as he expected, very heavy volleys which struck the poor little craft all over." The *Hale* escaped "without having a single man hurt," Rhind reported, but the little *Hale* received numerous hits from rifles balls and canister and one solid shot that struck its thirty-two-pounder gun, rendering it useless. Had the pilot known the channel, the *Hale* might have returned by a safer route.[3]

As Union operations expanded and more blockade vessels came into service, the challenge of locating qualified pilots grew even more difficult. A year after the beginning of hostilities, Flag Officer Louis M. Goldsborough lamented to Welles, "I have great and constant difficulties and troubles about pilots." On the last day of June 1862 he explained: "They can make so much more money than we give them, $60 per month and found, by taking army vessels by the job, and otherwise get employed by the Army that scarcely any of them are willing to accept employment from us, and those we have all want to leave and do leave whenever they can on the slightest pretext."[4]

The need for competent pilots prompted the Navy Department to search for men with piloting skills among Confederate prisoners, deserters, and black runaways and to go to some length to obtain them. In late November 1862, for example, Welles wrote to Lieutenant Colonel Martin Burke, the commander of Fort Lafayette, New York, and asked if he could find among his prisoners "one or two Wilmington pilots, who, for a large reward, would pilot our men-of-war into that harbor." Two days later, Assistant Secretary Gustavus Fox wrote to George W. Blunt in New York requesting two pilots for the harbor at Wilmington. "There are no marks for the entrance and changes have taken place since the survey, yet the rebels have pilots who take a 12-foot vessel in at night," Fox explained to Blunt. "We must have men of undaunted courage and great coolness, for much is at stake. We can pay them $100. per month and board, and $5,000. if they take an ironclad to the town of Wilmington and back. We should like them in about a week." The Navy Department's generous offer proved effective, for less than two weeks after writing to Blunt, Fox sent Rear Admiral Samuel P. Lee the welcome news that Blunt had obtained the services of four pilots, obviating the need to employ prisoners from Fort Lafayette. "The pilots in Fort Lafayette are not to be trusted," Fox explained.[5]

Proof of that statement came when Rhind ordered his pilot to guide the *Keokuk* inside the Hatteras shoals and the man, Joseph H. Ryder, ran the ship into a buoy. Lee boarded the *Keokuk* on its return, and when Rhind expressed doubts about the pilot's fidelity, Lee ordered the man confined. Subsequently, Rhind had the pilot slapped in irons, but Lee countermanded that order, keeping Ryder in prison on the *Brandywine* until the incident could be investigated and resolved. After a time, Rhind decided that the pilot had not intentionally run into the buoy. From Captain Peirce Crosby, the admiral later leaned that the pilot claimed to be a U.S. citizen and a deserter from the *Tuscarora*.[6]

The *Keokuk* incident indicates the premium put on loyal pilots, but the search for skilled, conscientious, trustworthy pilots proved more difficult than the navy anticipated. This made the availability of local African Americans familiar with southern waterways even more important to the war effort. Veterans of many years spent fishing, oystering, piloting, or plying inland passages in small craft, these black watermen possessed intimate knowledge of the navigational features of the narrow, twisting, and often shallow creeks and rivers that flowed into sounds along the southern coast. Furthermore, based on the available evidence, African American pilots tended to be more loyal to the Union cause than many white pilots and watermen.

During the Civil War, Union Navy commanders secured the services of black pilots who guided federal vessels up rivers and creeks; provided vital information on tidal conditions, bars, and other navigational features; and risked their lives right alongside their navy counterparts. Although many African American pilots serving with the navy's blockading squadrons remain unidentified, seven black men have been recognized as professional pilots: William Ayler, William Debrech, Nicholas Dickson, Stephen Small, James Taliafaro, William Tulson, and a man calling himself Mazalina.[7]

In addition, five black pilots are named in official correspondence: Isaac Tattnall, Prince Coit, Robert Smalls, Nelson Anderson, and Thomas Mendigo. Anderson and Mendigo were specifically mentioned by Du Pont in a letter to Commodore Turner dated June 2, 1863: "Nelson Anderson and Thomas Mendigo, on board the *Lodona,* are pilots for Bull's Bay." Du Pont then instructed Turner, "When *Lodona* leaves that station you will please have them transferred, with their accounts, to the blockading ship which takes her place." As an afterthought, prompted perhaps by his suspicion that good pilots were sometimes "appropriated" by other vessels, the admiral wrote, "These contrabands, if not still on the *Lodona,* are on some vessel off Charleston. When found, please have them transferred to the blockading squadron off Bulls' Bay." A week later Du Pont sent a request concerning contraband pilots, probably Anderson and Mendigo, to Welles: "I desire to add that I have also made use of the services of certain contraband pilots, and have authorized the payment to them sometimes of $30. and sometimes $40. per month," he wrote. "May I hope that this course meets with the approval of the Department? They are skillful and competent."[8]

Occasionally, contrabands seeking refuge on Union vessels claimed to be qualified pilots. Such was the case when two men appeared off the *Keystone State* a little after daylight on Monday, March 1, 1862. According to Commander William E. Le Roy, a small sailboat with a white man and a contraband came alongside the *Keystone State*, which lay at anchor off Georgetown, South Carolina. Le Roy wrote in his report that the white person claimed to be Mr. J. N. Merriman of Georgetown, "a loyal citizen of the United States" who, from the time of the secession of South Carolina, had held the office of collector of the port of Georgetown. Merriman told Le Roy that he had escaped from Georgetown "in hopes of falling in with one of the blockading vessels and that he wished to go to Washington to communicate with the government." In addition to information about the rebel steamer *Nashville*, Merriman brought another precious commodity to the Union cause—an "intelligent negro" named Prince Coit who was a fisherman and "one of the best pilots out of Georgetown." Following his escape from Georgetown with Merriman, Coit became a Union Navy pilot.[9]

The contributions of black pilots to the Union war effort often proved vital to the success of joint army-navy expeditions along the coast. Nonetheless, in official reports many commanders neglected to credit their black pilots by name. One of the most glaring examples of this official reluctance to mention the contributions of African Americans to Union victory occurred in early April 1862 when General Ambrose Burnside's forces, assisted by black watermen, occupied the town of Beaufort, North Carolina, without a shot being fired. Fort Macon, located on Bogue Banks and controlling the channel leading to Beaufort, remained in the hands of a Confederate garrison under the command of Colonel Moses J. White, CSA, until daring exploits by an anonymous slave pilot resulted in its subsequent capture. Nevertheless, Union commanders never mentioned these African Americans by name.

Union commanders had detailed information about Fort Macon because, according to historian Paul Branch, the U.S. Army had built the fort and kept the original construction plans on file at the Office of the Chief of Engineers. Furthermore, one of Burnside's brigadiers, General John G. Foster, had spent three years as the engineer in charge of the fort. In April 1861 some sixty free blacks volunteered to strengthen the fort, and southern slave masters sent large numbers of slaves to assist in improvements there as well. Union officials may have obtained information about Confederate improvements to Fort Macon from these workers, but in December 1861 they also received valuable intelligence from three African Americans who escaped to the USS *Albatross*, on blockade duty off Beaufort. Commander George Prentiss questioned the three contrabands, who arrived at his ship on December 20. "One, a quite intelligent boy, employed as a servant in the fort, answers my questions this way: The fort is commanded by Colonel White, formerly of our

Army. There are about 400 men within the walls. There are casemates (describing them) with a curtain in front, but no guns mounted; they are used as quarters for men and officers, there being no others." The contraband told Prentiss he had counted about 2,000 regular troops at six different points near the fort, as well as militia training.[10]

Armed with this information about Fort Macon, in late March 1862 Brigadier General John G. Parke's troops began preparing to reduce the fort using naval gunfire combined with fire from well-placed land batteries. These included Parrott guns that Parke, a former topographical engineer, had brought in by rail over the recently repaired Newport Bridge. On March 23, 1862, Parke sent Colonel White a demand for surrender, which he declined. As White explained in his official report, "General Parke then, having collected a large force at Carolina City, took possession of Beaufort and Shackleford Banks, thus cutting us off from any communication without the range of our guns." By April 10 Parke had crossed his troops and artillery to the banks and established communication with the fleet. The following day the general, accompanied by Captain Williamson of the topographical engineers, Captain Morris of the artillery, and Lieutenant Daniel Flagler of ordnance, made a reconnaissance to within a mile of Fort Macon and selected sites for the batteries. Parke then had to arrange to convey the mortars with ammunition across Bogue Sound, a body of water so shallow that he could use only "the lightest draught flats and small boats" to bring troops, siege guns, ammunition, and supplies to his camp and depot at the head of one of the creeks. Because the road along the beach lay in full view of a rebel lookout at Fort Macon, Union guns, mortars, and ammunition had to be transported under the cover of night. Barges and scows brought these batteries to Carolina City by water, but Flagler wrote, "There were no men with the batteries to unload and move them, and the labor had to be performed by negroes, whom I obtained from Captain King, the division quartermaster." In his report, Flagler noted the difficulty of transporting the heavy artillery across the sound from Carolina City: "At the later point only one scow could be obtained suitable for carrying purposes across Bogue Sound to the Banks, and owing to the tides and the difficulties of a shallow, intricate channel not more than one trip could be made daily." The Union commander apparently called on one of Beaufort's slave pilots to guide craft bearing artillery across Bogue Sound. "The man who did take her through without an accident has never received a cent for his service; nor did he expect anything but his freedom," one journalist wrote. The black pilot remains nameless.[11]

On April 22 Burnside and his party arrived in several boats and anchored about four miles down the sound from the fort, but fire from a rifled rebel gun forced them to retire and take up a position near Harker's Island. The following day Burnside sent White another message demanding that he surrender the fort, but White refused. The two men met at 8 A.M. the next day. Burnside "then attempted by persuasion to produce a change in my determination," White wrote, "but was told that the fort would be defended as long as possible." By the evening of April 24 Parke had his land batteries in position, transported by men from the infantry regiments and from Captain Ammon's company, who dug them into the sand hills. At 5:40 the following morning Union gunners fired the first shots at Fort Macon, supported by Commander Samuel Lockwood's gunboats *Daylight, Chippewa,* and *State of Georgia.* Within a few hours Parke's mortars and Parrott guns had pounded the fort's masonry walls to pieces. The Confederate garrison suffered only a few casualties—nine killed, sixteen wounded—in the bombardment, but Union fire had opened a huge crack in a wall near the magazine, and Colonel White feared that another shell might detonate the tons of gunpowder stored there. At 4:30 P.M. he reluctantly ordered his men to surrender.[12]

The occupation of Beaufort and Fort Macon made General Ambrose Burnside and his men heroes. Union forces had now achieved all their major objectives along the North Carolina coast, except for the capture of Wilmington. Although Flagler acknowledged the contribution of black laborers in unloading the artillery from barges and other vessels, neither Burnside's nor Parke's report mentioned the role played by black watermen. Yet the Union capture of Beaufort and Fort Macon might not have been possible without the aid of the contrabands who hauled the army's artillery and the anonymous black pilot who guided the barges and scows across Bogue Sound.

On other occasions, Union Navy officers did specifically mention African American pilots, be they free blacks or contrabands, in official correspondence. Complicated joint army-navy operations to seize port cities such as Savannah, Wilmington, and Charleston generated a great deal of correspondence, much of it devoted to planning; this required detailed information about Confederate defenses as well as reliable descriptions of the approaches to these cities. In 1862, when General Thomas W. Sherman decided to attack Savannah, Georgia, he and Du Pont sought accurate reports on the three approaches to the city. Because Fort Pulaski guarded the most direct route up the Savannah River, Sherman and Du Pont were searching for other, less well defended routes. Both commanders and their subordinates turned to friendly contraband informants and, in one instance, to a black pilot, Isaac Tattnall, to provide these tidbits of information, including valuable additions to or clarifications of navigational charts and features of the coast and rivers.[13]

In early January 1862 Captain Quincy Gillmore of the U.S. Army Engineers and Commander John Rodgers made a reconnaissance of Little Tybee Creek or Freeborn's Cut. In their reports, both Rodgers and Gillmore mentioned Isaac Tattnall, "the colored pilot," whom they credited with being thoroughly acquainted with the channel. "The accuracy of his knowledge of the part under examination gives assurance that he may be perfectly relied upon as pilot for the rest of the passage." When Du Pont ordered Gillis to send the gunboat *Pembina* and pilot Tattnall to Port Royal, he enclosed a statement made by Tattnall on December 6, 1861, in which the contraband claimed to be a pilot along the Georgia coast from Wassaw to St. Mary's. Tattnall told Union officials that he had been on the packet *St. Mary's* and had seen the fight at Hilton Head. He claimed that on the day of the engagement, a heavy shot had struck his vessel, going through the galley.[14]

Carefully collating information about the unseen portion of Freeborn's Cut from Tattnall and other blacks acquainted with the passage, Rodgers and Gillmore concluded that gunboats might pass into the Savannah River through Freeborn's Cut "without meeting any artificial obstructions or any serious natural impediment." Both Rodgers and Gillmore recommended that Union forces enter the Savannah River and advance on the city, fighting vessels past Fort Jackson and reducing it from above to allow unarmed transports to pass up to the city. They surmised that rebel gunners manning batteries on Skiddaway Island and at the Thunderbolt would subsequently abandon their posts. Du Pont thanked Gillis for this report, which, he wrote, "I deem important."[15]

In the meantime, army officers investigating the approaches to Savannah from the northern side of the river had discovered obstructions placed by the rebels in Wall's Cut, which General Sherman ordered his men to remove. Du Pont explained that before attempting to carry gunboats and light-draft vessels through "these winding and intricate passages," he required another examination by professional seamen. On January 17, 1862, Du Pont ordered Rodgers to make a detailed reconnaissance of the approaches to Savannah under consideration. Unwilling to rely on Godfrey and Hatfards, the squadron's regular pilots, Du Pont instructed Rodgers to take the contraband pilot William, as well as Lieutenant Barnes of the *Wabash* and Captain James H. Wilson of the topographical engineers. In a letter to his wife, Rodgers explained that the boat party also included "picked men, Wabashes (white, and contrabands)." Three nights later, concealed by a dense fog, Rodgers conducted a boat reconnaissance of the channel and reported that the obstructions at Wall's Cut had been skillfully removed by the army, leaving a sixty-foot-wide passage containing "some 13 to 14 feet water at high tide." After Lieutenant Barnes had taken soundings, both Captain Wilson and the pilot Godfrey thought the gunboats could pass through the channel leading from Wright's River into the Savannah River at high tide, but Rodgers concluded that the passage needed to be examined more carefully under different circumstances. He also advised that the channel be staked or buoyed to prevent vessels from grounding and being subjected to the fire of rifled guns from Fort Pulaski. Indeed, on January 28, 1862, the *Unadilla* and *Henry Andrew* steamed through Wall's Cut at high tide, but the *Pembina* grounded on the soft bottom near the entrance. After more deliberation and another examination of the passage at low tide, Rodgers reported to Du Pont that Wright's River was "a practicable channel for most of the gunboats." However, he told the commodore, the five feet of water at high tide in Mud River made the passage of gunboats impracticable.[16]

By the end of the first week of February 1862, these reconnaissance expeditions and painfully slow deliberations had driven Sherman to exasperation. His infantry and artillery units had been kept waiting, and his troops in Wassaw Sound had been "huddled up on those little steamers some fifteen days." The army medical director feared the men would contract ship fever if they remained afloat any longer, prompting Sherman to ask Du Pont, "Can we not get into the Savannah River at once and effect our object?" In response, Du Pont ordered Rodgers to enter the Savannah River to support the army, regardless of the hazard that might entail. Rodgers did as ordered, and the army planted a six-gun battery on Jones Island at Venus Point. That very day, however, Sherman finally received a response from General George B. McClellan regarding future operations along the southern coast. Weeks of illness had prevented McClellan from reading Sherman's communiqués and making a decision, but now both McClellan and the War Department rejected the general's proposal for a siege of Savannah, preferring that Sherman use his forces to seize Fort Pulaski, Fernandina, and perhaps St. Augustine, Florida. The army thus began making plans to lay siege to Fort Pulaski and completing arrangements for a combined force to sail south to Fernandina.[17]

Although the proposed attack on Savannah had been canceled, Du Pont continued to value the services of pilot William. Writing from Port Royal on the last day of May 1862, he instructed Lieutenant Law, the senior officer in the Savannah River, to "immediately dispatch the *Henry Andrew* to this anchorage, sending in her the contraband pilot William." Although Du Pont did not specify why he needed the *Henry Andrew,* the following day General David Hunter requested that the ship be sent over to Hilton Head to take four or five companies of infantry to the Stono.[18]

Contraband pilots, or men working on pilot boats, also proved extremely useful to senior officers trying to enforce the blockade off Charleston. The new information obtained from these knowledgeable contrabands about the routes used by blockade runners to go in and out of Charleston allowed commanders to deploy their blockading vessels more efficiently. Black refugees seeking sanctuary on Union vessels also brought information about rebel privateers and other ships attempting to run the blockade. In August 1861 a boat containing four black men came alongside the USS *Penguin,* commanded by J. W. Livingston. The men were taken on board, and one of them claimed to have been a pilot on the steam tug *Uncle Ben.* He said the rebels intended to arm the tug and another propeller to go out to capture the *Penguin.* The man, whom Livingston described as a "negro pilot," also mentioned two other privateers at Beaufort. Officials responsible for bringing supplies across shallow Hatteras Inlet also turned to local contraband pilots to guide ships over the bar, which suggests that African American boatmen and pilots may have served the Union Navy on an informal basis in other locations along the coast.[19]

Union commanders valued their pilots, both black and white, so highly that they were willing to go to considerable lengths to assist them and their families, even sending federal blockading vessels to locate and rescue their wives and children. In early October 1862 Commander Maxwell Woodhull of the USS *Cimarron* left Mayport Mills, a small fishing village near the St. John's River entrance that served as a base for federal gunboats, for a mission up the river to Jacksonville, Florida. Pausing along the way to distribute copies of President Lincoln's "message relating to emancipation," he continued in the *Hale* to Palatka. To his surprise, Woodhull found Palatka deserted except for two persons on the landing, who introduced themselves as ex-governor Moseley and a "northern man" named Blood. They told Woodhull that, hearing rumors that the Yankees would seize every white man and either execute him at once or send him to a northern prison, all the men in Palatka had fled to the bush. When Blood insisted that his life was in danger and that he feared being taken by the rebels and "made to ornament a pine tree for his well known Union views," Woodhull sent armed boat crews to bring off Blood's family and property. He then sent Governor Moseley back to the town to tell the people they had been deceived by false rumors; Union forces had no intention of molesting them. Fifteen minutes after the boats left, Woodhull reported, "a good deal of confusion was observed among the blacks." Observing the scene more closely, he saw forty or fifty armed horsemen approaching the landing. The commander quickly recalled his boats and ordered the *Hale* to shell the rebels, forcing them to retire. The Union sailors then went back to remove Blood and his family. "Presently," Woodhull wrote, "some blacks informed us that the families of our black pilots would be hanged as soon as we left." Anxious to prevent "such a piece of savagery," Woodhull took off "all the family, wives, sons, and daughters, and even their grand children, to the number of about thirty persons."[20]

Several months earlier, in August 1862, Acting Master Edward McKeige, commanding the USS *Patroon,* had been instrumental in establishing a refuge for black river pilots on Batten Island, near the entrance to the St. John's River. In his report to Du Pont, McKeige explained that five or six Union families had come down to Batten Island, asking for his protection. The island had once been the home of black river pilots who guided vessels over the bar into the St. John's, but, as McKeige explained, "they were driven away by threats, and are now living in great distress in the woods." A sixty-foot-long bridge connected Batten Island to another island, Fort George, and the mainland. McKeige suggested to Du Pont that if he destroyed the bridge it would cut Batten Island off from the mainland and prevent guerrillas from harassing the loyal citizens who wished to live there. "The former bar pilots are willing to return with their families if the bridge is destroyed," he wrote. Determined to protect the loyal pilots and their families, on August 9, 1862, McKeige landed twenty bluejackets and a party of axmen, firemen, and coal heavers. In just three hours they had completed their mission of chopping down the bridge. "The inhabitants are now safe and feel more easy and comfortable," McKeige assured Du Pont.[21]

The Union Navy's concerns for the refugees at the Pilot Town colony on Batten Island, initially humanitarian, quickly became political. By early November 1862 the colony had grown and now consisted, according to Commander Woodhull, "of 5 men, 3 women, and some half dozen children and a number of blacks, fugitives escaping from the despotism of the rebel leaders in these parts." Woodhull believed that if the Union Navy could protect the refugees gathered on Batten Island, others would join them. He also surmised that the new Confederate conscription law was causing hardship for people along the river and that those who could flee conscription might do so. Four days later Woodhull again reported on the Pilot Town colony, which now numbered about thirty-five persons. "These people are generally destitute of almost everything, as they leave at night in small boats and are compelled necessarily, to confine their belongings to the smallest amount and the abandonment of other property." Woodhull told Du Pont that he had given them rations—four each of salt, beef, pork, and molasses for every four persons. "This, with the corn some of them brought with them and the fish they obtain, has been enough to keep these poor people in sufficient food." He had no bread or other rations to provide them and assumed that if they were sent north he would have to issue them clothing. "If the colony is broken up, we will lose the advantage of this nucleus for them to rally around, who might otherwise be compelled to give their services to the rebels," he argued.[22]

One month later the little Pilot Town colony had grown to 100 persons, both black and white. Encouraged by the growing numbers of refugees, Woodhull suggested that if the colony became a permanent post guarded by half a company of soldiers, the people would become so confident that, in his words, "there would be a rapid melting away of the armed men comprising the whole military strength of this part of Florida, which, so far as I can ascertain, does not average over 400 men." With the destitution in the region, the war weariness, and the recall of rebel troops from Georgia, Woodhull believed that many Floridians would join the Union cause. He assured Du Pont that he had engaged the men of the Pilot Town colony as guards and blocked all avenues of approach from Cedar Point and Trout Creek with heavy abatis, but he reminded Du Pont that his vessels had to furnish the refugees with food and asked the admiral's views on the colony's future. Du Pont passed Woodhull's concerns along to Brigadier General Rufus Saxton, who responded that he had nowhere to place the refugees except in tents. Once federal troops had occupied Edisto Island, Saxton thought he might have room there for the Pilot Town refugees and the contrabands from North Island. However, protected by Union Navy gunboats and the federal troops that had arrived at Mayport Mills on October 1, 1862, the refugees, including a number of slaves and bar pilots and their families, remained at Pilot Town until the cessation of hostilities in 1865.[23]

Commander Woodhull's rescue of pilots and their families and the establishment of a refugee colony at Batten Island may have gone beyond the call of duty, but other Union Navy officers also went to some lengths to rescue the wives and families of their faithful pilots. In the fall of 1863, a little over a year after the founding of the Pilot Town colony, Lieutenant Roswell Lamson attempted to bring the wife of the pilot of his vessel, the gunboat *Nansemond,* to safety. "When Capt. Case went home," Lamson wrote to his wife, Kate, "he gave me his Wilmington pilot, Mr. Bowen, who lived near Wilmington and had a wife and one child there." Bowen's wife had tried to join her husband in Beaufort but had been stopped by the rebels "and subjected to very harsh treatment," Lamson said. Although Captain Case had considered a rescue too dangerous, Lamson decided to try to bring the woman out. According to his superior, Captain B. F. Sands, "Lieutenant Lamson projected and carried out a plan for obtaining information and bringing off the wife of Mr. Bowen, the pilot of the *Nansemond,* by landing a contraband acquainted with the locality near the former pilot station of Mr. Bowen and residence of Mrs. Bowen." While the contraband searched for Mrs. Bowen, Lamson seized an opportunity to chase a blockade runner trying to reach Wilmington from Nassau and destroy it. In the meantime, the contraband sent ashore to find Mrs. Bowen gave a signal, and the *Niphon* rescued the pilot's wife. "We got his wife and child, and also a young brother who had just been drafted into the rebel army," Lamson explained.[24]

In some cases, Union Navy commanders unabashedly gave credit to their contraband pilots for contributing to the success of coastal operations or raids into the interior; others failed to mention their pilots at all. In at least one instance—a joint army-navy raid at Bear Inlet, North Carolina, in December 1863—commanders in the operation differed in their willingness to credit their contraband pilot. On the morning of December 24, 1863, two North Atlantic Blockading Squadron gunboats, the *Daylight* and the *Howquah,* along with a launch from the *Iron Age,* left Beaufort, North Carolina, carrying troops of the 158th New York State Volunteers, Ninth Vermont Volunteers, and a section of the Second Massachusetts Artillery with a twenty-four-pounder field gun. The success of their mission depended on the gunboat pilots' ability to navigate up the shallow inlet and find a schooner laden with salt and a rebel saltworks. According to the *Daylight*'s commanding officer, Acting Volunteer Lieutenant F. S. Wells, they proceeded to Bear Inlet and anchored within 800 yards of shore. The two gunboats then landed 200 soldiers and 50 sailors from the *Daylight,* the latter under the command of the executive officer, Acting Master J. H. Gleason. Although the troops and sailors went ashore without opposition, when they reached the schooner, the men discovered that all the turpentine and most of the salt had either been destroyed or removed by the enemy before their arrival. "Four extensive salt works in full operation were found at different points along the coast and near the inlet, which were all thoroughly destroyed by our men," Wells reported.[25]

Although Wells failed to mention the role played by their contraband pilot in this raid, Acting Master Charles B. Wilder, commanding the boats, did credit the pilot. Wilder left the *Howquah* with two cutters to cooperate with the men of the 158th New York State Volunteers. "I was sent with a contraband pilot to lead the way to Captain Saunder's salt works, followed by all the boats, eight in number," he stated in his report. Although low water allowed only four of the boats and twenty-eight soldiers to land that night, Wilder wrote, "We surprised the contrabands at work making salt and captured them." When the army commander, Colonel James Jourdan, came ashore, he sent Wilder with eighteen men to capture the local Confederate commander, a Captain Saunders, who lived about two miles from the saltworks. Not finding Saunders at home, Wilder decided to send the first and second cutters on to destroy saltworks owned by a Colonel Hawkins. "I landed at daybreak," Wilder reported, "and most thoroughly destroyed the salt works and a large number of spirits of turpentine barrels, which I found there, and returned to the colonel without being molested." The entire force then took their boats up Bear Creek to yet another saltworks owned by a Mr. Mills, which they destroyed together and 150 bags of salt. "We took with us on our return to the ship 12 contrabands who had been making salt on the works we destroyed," Wilder noted. In his report, Jourdan praised the assistance he received from Commander Benjamin Dove, the senior naval officer at Beaufort, and "the most hearty cooperation" from Lieutenant MacDiarmid, commanding the U.S. gunboat *Howquah;* Lieutenant Wells, commanding the U.S. gunboat *Daylight;* and their respective officers and crews. Not surprisingly, Jourdan failed to commend the contraband pilot, without whom Wilder's landing party probably would not have located the rebel saltworks.[26]

Black pilots accompanying Union Navy raids and expeditions sometimes became casualties. During the Union defense of Suffolk, Virginia, in April 1863, two pilots, one African American, suffered mortal wounds in a ferocious firefight between a Confederate artillery emplacement on Hill's Point and a federal flotilla under the command of Roswell Lamson. Confederate sharpshooters and artillery ensconced on Hill's Point found the small side-wheeler *Coeur de Lion* a conspicuous target. "As soon as we came within range the rebels opened fire upon us with artillery and sharpshooters," Acting Master Charles H. Brown wrote, "and when opposite the point a shot struck our pilot house, knocking the wheel and all our steering apparatus to atoms, mortally wounding the pilot and dashing him completely through the portside of the pilot house, one-half of which was carried away by the same shot." The *Coeur de Lion* swung toward the rebel battery, but Quartermaster James G. Burnett took the helm and kept it until the ship had passed all danger. A second shot then struck the *Coeur de Lion*, passing through the bow about three feet above the waterline, falling into the fore peak, and exploding, setting fire to the vessel. Fortunately, the crew had prepared for such an eventuality by placing buckets of water with a hose attached to the force pump, and they quickly extinguished the fire. Undaunted, the *Coeur de Lion*'s gunners gave the rebel battery its whole broadside as the ship steamed past.[27]

The *Coeur de Lion*'s feisty action against the battery at Hill's Point exposed many of the crewmen to enemy fire, including Brown, who directed the movements of the vessel from the exposed upper deck. "While there a rifle ball passed through my coat sleeve, bruising but not cutting my shoulder," he wrote. Brown commended Quartermaster Joseph Crawford and Boatswain's Mate William Horney for their coolness under fire. He then wrote, "The pilot, William Ayler, colored man, died at 8 P.M., but no others on board were injured." According to the assistant surgeon, G. S. Franklin, "William Ayler, the pilot, had his left leg completely amputated at the junction with the thigh by a 12 pounder rifle shot, died in thirty minutes afterward." Other casualties from the *Alert* and the *Coeur de Lion* included T. J. Hawkins, a pilot, who was struck in the head by a solid shot from a twelve-pounder rifle and killed instantly, and John Jones, a landsman severely wounded in the left arm by splinters of boiler iron.[28]

Not all the African American pilots killed or wounded while serving with the North and South Atlantic Blockading Squadrons fell victim to enemy fire, as an incident involving the gunboat *Penguin* aptly illustrates. In March 1862 Flag Officer Du Pont ordered the *Penguin* to cross the bar at Mosquito Inlet into Mosquito Creek and to establish an inside blockade and capture any rebel vessels found lurking in the vicinity. Union officials knew that Confederate blockade runners ran into Mosquito Inlet, only a twenty-four-hour trip from Nassau in the Bahamas. From the inlet, the rebels took contraband goods by wagon to the St. John's River and then shipped them to rail connections at Jacksonville. Complying with Du Pont's orders, Lieutenant Thomas Budd, commanding the *Penguin*, organized an expedition with five boats and forty-three men from his ship. Accompanied by Acting Master S. W. Mather of the *Henry Andrew*, they moved southward through the inland passage leading into Mosquito Lagoon on March 22, 1862, without incident. After going about fifteen miles, the boat party turned back and, within sight of the *Henry Andrew,* one boat landed under an abandoned earthwork near a dense grove of live oak and underbrush. Suddenly, a band of rebels hiding in the underbrush opened fire on the Union blue-jackets, killing Budd, Mather, and two sailors and wounding two others who were taken prisoner. When the other Union boats arrived on the scene, rebel gunners opened fire on them as well. A total of four men from the *Henry Andrew* died, and five fell wounded in the attack. "The negro pilot was shot through the foot," Commander C. R. P. Rodgers told Du Pont. Unable to escape from the rebels, the wounded pilot became a Confederate prisoner and was later hanged by his captors.[29]

Colonel W. S. Dilworth, the Confederate commander of the Department of East and Middle Florida, confirmed that seven Union men from the *Penguin* and the *Henry Andrew* were killed, about thirty wounded, and three men taken prisoner. "A runaway negro was also captured, who had piloted the enemy into the inlet to Smyrna, and who was to be hanged," Dilworth wrote. No one ever mentioned the pilot by name.[30]

Two months after the *Penguin* incident, Daniel Ammen of the USS *Seneca* informed Du Pont that he had sent him five contrabands but had kept and enlisted one contraband because of his local knowledge. "His master was one of the persons who attacked the *Penguin's* boats and boasts that he hung the negro pilot there captured," Ammen wrote. Incensed by the Confederates' treatment of the black prisoner, Ammen decided to seek revenge on those who had killed the pilot, Budd, Mather, and the other sailors. Three contrabands who arrived at the *Seneca* on the St. John's River near Black Creek provided additional information about the perpetrators. "They state they belong to a Captain Huston who commands a body of men . . . and have coverts near by for the purpose of picking off our men should we attempt to go up," Ammen wrote. On June 8, 1862, Ammen sent the *Seneca's* executive officer, Lieutenant John G. Sproston, with a three-boat expedition carrying forty men up Black Creek in search of George Huston, who had ordered the hanging of the black pilot. The party landed and advanced on Huston's house. In his memoirs, Ammen claimed that a "negro woman" saw them coming and gave the alarm. Sproston went to the house, and Huston "met him at the door with a double barreled gun, two pistols, and bowie knife," Ammen told Du Pont. When Sproston demanded that Huston surrender, "Huston fired at him with a pistol, the ball entering high up on the left breast and killing him instantly." In the blast of gunfire that followed, Huston was badly wounded, taken on board the *Seneca,* and then transferred to the *Isaac Smith.* Du Pont praised Sproston, whom he had

(*Above*) USS *Hunchback* (1862–1865). Ship's officers and crew on deck in the James River, Virginia, 1864–1865. *Naval Historical Foundation. (Below)* Beaufort, South Carolina. Group of African Americans on J. J. Smith's plantation. *Library of Congress.*

(*Above*) Arrival of an African American family in the lines. *Library of Congress.*
(*Below*) James River, Virginia. Officers of the USS *Monitor* grouped by the turret. *Library of Congress.*

James River, Virginia. Officers and men of the gunboat *Commodore Perry*. *Library of Congress.*

Aiken's Landing, Virginia (vicinity). Group of African Americans at Aiken's farm. *Library of Congress.*

Robert Smalls, pilot of the *Planter. Naval Historical Foundation.*

(*Above*) City Point, Virginia. View of the waterfront with federal supply boats. *Library of Congress.* (*Below*) City Point, Virginia. African Americans unloading vessels at the landing. *Library of Congress.*

James River, Virginia. U.S. gunboat *Massasoit. Library of Congress.*

(*Above*) Bermuda Hundred, Virginia. African American teamsters near the signal tower. *Library of Congress.* (*Below*) Alexandria, Virginia. The steam frigate *Pensacola. Library of Congress.*

Hampton Roads, Virginia. Rear Admiral David D. Porter and staff aboard his flagship, the USS *Malvern. Library of Congress.*

USS *Miami* (1862–1865). Members of the ship's crew on the forecastle circa 1864–1865. *Naval Historical Foundation.*

USS *Lehigh* (1863–1865). Crew members and a few officers pose on the monitor's deck in the James River, Virginia, 1864–1865. *Naval Historical Foundation.*

Group of contrabands at Foller's House, Cumberland Landing, Virginia, May 7, 1862. *Library of Congress.*

James River, Virginia. The monitor USS *Onondaga* with soldiers in a rowboat in the foreground. *Library of Congress.*

James River, Virginia. View of completed Dutch Gap Canal. *Library of Congress.*

USS *Monitor*. Crew members cooking on deck in the James River, Virginia, July 9, 1862. *Naval Historical Foundation.*

USS *Miami* (1862–1865). Black crew members sewing and relaxing on the forecastle, starboard side, circa 1864–1865. *Naval Historical Foundation.*

known on the China Station in 1858, as "an able, brave, and devoted officer from the State of Maryland." Ironically, although considered a "guerilla chief of desperate character," Huston's life was spared, Du Pont wrote, "by the sudden interposition of his wife."[31]

Despite the risk to men stationed in exposed pilothouses, the Union Navy continued to seek the services of loyal, conscientious pilots, and men with piloting skills continued to volunteer. Having a skilled, sober pilot remained of paramount importance to the war effort, for the penalties for employing careless or incompetent pilots included collisions and groundings of vessels on bars or sandbanks, which could make them vulnerable to enemy gunfire and even capture. A pilot's mishandling of a vessel might be attributed to a lack of skill or knowledge of the river or, on some occasions, to liquor. When the monitor *Nahant* entered Stono Inlet, surgeon Samuel G. Webber wrote to his wife, Nannie, "Our pilot had been on a coal schooner and came back decidedly worse for liquor. We had not gone more than a few ship's lengths when we struck fast in the sand." According to Webber, "The pilot was sent below & we waited til the tide rose when we started again. This time the Capt. directed her & in fifteen minutes we were aground again." When the tide rose and lifted the ship off the sand again, the *Nahant's* commanding officer, Captain William K. Mayo, again took charge and "directed us by the lead & we went two or three miles, more or less, without trouble."[32]

In a few cases, cowardly behavior by pilots, including African Americans, actually put Union vessels in jeopardy. One of the most notable examples involved the loss of the 520-ton, light-draft screw gunboat USS *Dai Ching*. In January 1865 Rear Admiral John A. Dahlgren's vessels had begun pushing up the Savannah and Combahee rivers in support of Sherman's army, brown-water operations that took them directly into harm's way. The navy sent the *Dai Ching* to the Combahee "to annoy the rebels as much as possible, to land and drive in their pickets." According to Lieutenant Commander James C. Chaplin, the *Dai Ching* went to St. Helena, secured a black pilot named Stephen Small from the USS *Stettin*, and proceeded up the Combahee River. The ship anchored at 5 P.M., Chaplin wrote, "because the pilot was afraid to go up after dark." The next morning a boat manned by white men came alongside and reported a schooner, the *Coquette,* loaded with seventy-four bales of cotton lying some two miles below the batteries at Tar Bluff. The *Dai Ching* steamed upriver followed by the tug *Clover.* Chaplin sent a cutter ahead to take possession of the schooner, but about a mile from the prize, the rebels opened fire on the cutter. The *Dai Ching's* howitzer and 20-pounder gun crews returned fire, but they could not bring their 100-pounder to bear. Chaplin quickly reversed engines, turned, and headed back down-river. "While turning a very sharp bend, the wind blowing fresh down the river, with a strong ebb tide, I perceived the ship would run into the bank on our starboard bow, and discovered that the pilot had deserted the bridge." Chaplin rang three bells, but before he could back up the *Dai Ching*, "she forged head into the bank where she remained fast." The tug *Clover* tried to tow the gunboat off the bank, but when the line parted for some inexplicable reason, the *Clover* deserted the *Dai Ching* and continued on its way. Chaplin sent a boat to contact the *Pawnee* and *Stettin* downriver. "Signals were again made recalling the tug," Chaplin wrote, "and though only a half mile below us, she took no notice of them." Exasperated, he then dispatched an officer in a cutter to bring the *Clover* to their assistance, but the tug continued down the Combahee.[33]

In the meantime, the *Dai Ching's* crew had cut the main rail, enabling the 100-pounder to get into the action. "Our battery was worked vig-orously all the while," Chaplin insisted, but the ship remained firmly grounded—a sitting duck for rebel gunners, who scored thirty direct hits. Chaplin then ordered all the crewmen except those working the 100-pounder to jump to the marsh and keep close under the bow, clear of the enemy's fire. At 2:30 P.M. rebel shot hit their only heavy gun, "disabling our only hope and wounding 4 men," Chaplin wrote. "The ship was now a perfect wreck, and we could make no reply to the enemy, who were playing on us with terrible effect." Explaining that "there was no hope of saving her," Chaplin decided to set the *Dai Ching* on fire. He sent Act-ing Ensign Walton ahead with two wounded sailors in the ship's gig, and Chaplin and the other crewmen walked four miles through the marsh, wading several creeks, until they saw the *Clover* and signaled it. The tug took all on board, and they arrived safely at the *Pawnee* at 11 P.M. Chap-lin blamed the *Clover* for not assisting them. "It is my opinion," Chaplin wrote, "that had they come to our assistance when ordered, and taken our hawser, the ship would have been saved, as sluing her stern a very little would have brought the tide on our inside quarter, which would have swept the ship off." Five members of the *Dai Ching's* crew were captured and nine wounded. The loss of the *Dai Ching* could have been prevented if pilot Small had not deserted the ship and if Acting Ensign Leach of the *Clover* had come to its aid. The navy punished the pilot and tried Leach at court-martial and found him guilty of disobeying orders and deserting his post, but a court of inquiry exonerated Chaplin.[34]

The cowardly behavior of the *Dai Ching's* pilot contrasts sharply with accounts of skillful, brave, loyal Union pilots, both white and African American. On May 2, 1862, a daring exploit by a black pilot captured the attention of the northern public and remains to this day one of the most well-known incidents involving an African American during the Civil War. The previous night, Robert Smalls and eight fellow slaves had commandeered the rebel tug *Planter* at a wharf in Charleston Harbor and sailed past Fort Ripley and Fort Sumter into the open ocean to freedom. With "palmetto and Confederate flag flying," Du Pont wrote, "she passed successive forts, saluting as usual by blowing her steam whistle. After getting beyond the range of the last gun she quickly hauled down the rebel flags and hoisted a white one." The blockade vessel *Onward* saw the flag, intercepted the *Planter,* and towed it to Port Royal. When Du Pont learned of the *Planter'*s capture, he sent for Smalls, whom he described in a letter to Sophie: "He soon came, a pleasant looking darkey, not black, neither light, extreme amount of wooly hair, neatly trimmed, fine teeth; a clean and nice linen check coat with a very fine linen shirt having a handsome ruffle on the breast, possibly part of the wardrobe of the Navy officer who commanded the boat, but fitting him very well if they were." Du Pont questioned Smalls, who informed him that the rebels had abandoned their defenses on Cole's Island. This vital information, confirmed by Commander John Marchand's reconnaissance of the Stono River, led to the Union attack on James Island (discussed in chapter 8). In recognition of his capture of the *Planter,* the Union awarded Smalls almost $1,500 in prize money and appointed him to command the *Planter.* The other black crewmen also received prize money from the *Planter,* which was subsequently valued at $9,000. In addition, Smalls's exploit made him one of the Civil War's most famous black heroes. He served the Union as a pilot on the *Crusader, Huron, Paul Jones,* and *Keokuk* during the war and later became a state senator from South Carolina and served in the U.S. Congress from 1876 to 1884.[35]

Describing the *Planter* as "a fine boat," Du Pont told Sophie that it "can carry seven hundred bales of cotton, has a fine engine, and draws but little water and will be of the greatest value to us." Indeed, the navy employed the 300-ton side-wheeler as a transport and on June 14, 1862, Du Pont observed, "I am glad the *Planter* has proved so useful a transport, and that we have again been able so materially to aid the army, especially at a critical time when their generals were almost helpless for want of transports." He added, "I understand there is a good deal of labor involved in supplying the *Planter* with wood, would it not be well to organize a body of contrabands for this work?"[36]

Du Pont's suggestion that contrabands be employed to supply wood for the *Planter* epitomizes the Union Navy's mutually beneficial relationship with contrabands during the Civil War. Faced with the need to maintain a blockade of the southern coast and to conduct operations in numerous rivers and creeks, the Union Navy required skilled coastal pilots, who were in short supply. As a result, blockade squadron commanders turned to African American watermen and pilots, many of them fugitive slaves. These black men had spent years fishing, oystering, piloting, and working as traders or ferrymen along the coast. Eager for gainful employment and often anxious to assist the Union war effort, these black pilots filled a vital need for the Union Navy. Whether planning major operations such as the attack on Wilmington or Savannah, seizing Beaufort and Fort Macon, conducting reconnaissance, identifying the routes of Confederate blockade runners, or merely enforcing the blockade and maintaining their squadrons, Union Navy officers came to depend on the skills of their loyal coastal pilots. Although commanding officers rarely named these black pilots in their official reports, and some failed to acknowledge their contributions at all, the navy recognized the value of these men. In some instances, naval vessels went to rescue their families, or the pilots were allowed to return home to bring their families out of bondage. Navy gunboats also protected the contraband colony of Pilot Town at the mouth of the St. John's River. Official reports attest to the fact that navy pilots faced considerable risk. Several black pilots died in the line of duty, and others suffered injuries when their vessels took enemy fire. The number of pilots employed by the Union Navy along the southern coast during the war is difficult to determine. It may have been as few as 100, meaning that African American pilots accounted for only about 10 percent; this figure may be considerably higher if temporarily employed black watermen are taken into account.

CHAPTER 7

CONTRABAND SAILORS

It seems strange to send negroes to garrison a fort in "Yankeedom," but
I have no doubt if properly drilled they will make very good sailors.
We have always had some on board every vessel in the Navy, and they
make valuable men for certain kinds of duty.

—*Roswell Lamson*

In September 1861 Navy Secretary Gideon Welles authorized navy recruiters to enlist African Americans, thus creating an opportunity for hundreds and eventually thousands of former slaves to serve in the Union Navy. African American sailors serving on navy crews was hardly a new phenomenon. Unlike the U.S. Army, the U.S. Navy had always accepted blacks in the enlisted ranks. Significant numbers of African Americans and other persons of color had served on navy warships prior to the Civil War, but in 1839 the navy limited African American enlistments to 5 percent of the monthly or weekly totals. Most if not all of these black men had been born abroad or as free blacks in northern states.

Soon after the fall of Fort Sumter, the Navy Department realized that the fleet's rapid wartime expansion would require thousands of sailors, and it sent navy recruiters out to recruiting stations, called rendezvous, in large eastern cities and small coastal and river towns to lure men into the service. Only about 300 African American men reported to these stations, and by the end of 1861 they accounted for only about 6 percent of Union Navy crews. These numbers soon grew, however. According to Howard University's Black Sailors Project, 18,000 African American men (and 11 women) served in the Union Navy over the course of the Civil War. African American sailors constituted about 20 percent of the enlisted force, nearly double the proportion of black soldiers who served in the Union Army during the war. The largest number of black men joining the Union Navy, a total of 5,000, listed their place of origin as either Maryland or Virginia. Of those recruited from states along the eastern seaboard, the majority came from states below the Mason-Dixon Line.[1]

As these figures indicate, the Union Navy recruited a generous portion of its African American sailors from slave states, but determining the exact number of contrabands or former slaves who joined the Union Navy during the war is a difficult task. As the Union Navy did not request an enlistee's race or his prewar status, free blacks from southern states had no way to indicate their free status. Only about 4 percent of the black men entering naval service identified themselves as "slaves," most of them enlisting in western states. Few recruits from southern coastal states gave their occupation as "slave," although most were probably former slaves or contrabands. According to historian Joseph Reidy, more than 11,000 black men enlisting in the navy were born in slave states, versus 4,000 from free states. Based on this figure and the fact that only a small portion of those born in slave states would have been free blacks, Reidy argues that "nearly three men born into slavery served for every man born free."[2]

Each Union Navy ship kept muster rolls, but many have not survived, and few specifically listed contrabands or their dates of enlistment. One of the exceptions is the muster roll of the USS *Housatonic*. As of January 1, 1863, its muster roll listed 20 contrabands, some of whom may have remained aboard as contract employees after their enlistments ended. The muster rolls of the store and receiving ship USS *Vermont* provide even more information. Of the 339 men in the *Vermont's* crew as of March 31, 1863, 175 were contrabands. By July 1, 1863, the ship had begun including the names, dates, ages, heights, and terms of enlistment of contrabands. Most of those contrabands who joined the *Vermont's* crew in Virginia were men in their twenties picked up in the Norfolk or Richmond area.[3]

Union Navy recruiters found African American recruits among the populations of small eastern coastal villages; in large urban areas such as New York, Boston, and Philadelphia; and among slaves and free black men seeking sanctuary on Union vessels, in contraband camps, and in Union-occupied areas. In the North recruiters put up colorful recruiting posters in places frequented by potential sailors and took out newspaper advertisements that offered travel expenses to a rendezvous and advance wages—three months' wages for former seamen and ordinary seamen, and two months' for landsmen. These advertisements, the promise of an attractive navy uniform, and, perhaps, prize money brought hundreds of young, free black men into the Union Navy. In addition, to attract young southern black men to the naval service, recruiters opened special rendezvous in eastern Virginia and North Carolina. Recruiters were not averse to employing some rather dubious tactics to lure young men into the navy. Shortly after joining the navy as an assistant surgeon in 1862, Dr. Samuel Gilbert Webber described to his future bride, Nannie Sturdevant, the actions of a man called a "runner." "A runner is one who goes around hunting up recruits. He usually, or quite often, makes them drink till they lose their money & are ready to do anything to get some more. Sometimes they are nearly drunk when they come to me." Among those recruits examined by Webber was a young contraband. "I examined one contraband 15 years old who said [he] liked the south and when his three years was up should return. He was a bright little fellow." The young physician's duties also included vaccinating recruits against smallpox. "We vaccinate all who pass," he told Nannie.[4]

Throughout the Civil War the Union Navy competed with the Union Army for white recruits, but at the beginning of the war, navy recruiters held an advantage in attracting black men to serve and fight for freedom because the army still refused to allow blacks to enlist. General David Hunter's efforts to recruit and train a regiment of black soldiers in South Carolina succeeded temporarily until President Lincoln refused to accept the regiment, forcing Hunter to disband it in August 1862. Unfortunately, Hunter's strong-armed recruiting efforts had alienated many blacks and discouraged others from volunteering to serve in the army in the future. Whether his experimental raising of a black regiment of Sea Island soldiers discouraged able-bodied black men from joining the Union Navy as well is difficult to ascertain.[5]

Some navy recruits in the North may have been contrabands, but the vast majority of former slaves who joined the Union Navy did so in Washington, D.C.; in southern cities such as Norfolk, Beaufort, Port Royal, Wilmington, or New Bern; or on board naval vessels in southern rivers and sounds. As previous chapters have already shown, Union Navy blockade vessels often served as "recruiting" stations for African Americans fleeing the South for various reasons. Most former slaves picked up by Union vessels along the coast had left their homes and plantations seeking freedom from bondage and protection from their former masters, but others confessed they had fled to escape deteriorating conditions in the South, service in the Confederate Army and forced employment on Confederate defenses, or the threats of their masters to take them into the interior. Undoubtedly, some of these contrabands escaped to avoid punishment or to locate and join friends, wives, and family members in the North. As William Keeler explained to his wife, Anna, in a letter dated October 28, 1863, the town of Beaufort was "filled with many Secesh, mainly females, who wish to go south but cannot leave. Many are encumbered with old worn out slaves too old & decrepit to run away & useless to hire out. Most of the blacks who were of any value to their masters have either left for parts unknown or have put on the uniform of the 'U.A.' [Union Army]."[6]

Almost all these contrabands expected to be freed, probably not realizing that Navy Secretary Welles's decision to allow contrabands to enlist and be compensated for their services did not technically make them "free" men. However, the new policy did enable black men to train and serve in the Union Navy, as historian Steven Ramold has pointed out, "in the same manner as free seamen." Whether the majority of contrabands who signed the shipping articles did so entirely of their own free will and fully understood the implications of enlisting in the navy is questionable. Although they may not have been coerced into enlisting, few able-bodied black male refugees had certain employment waiting for them ashore, and being in immediate need of shelter, food, and protection, they required little inducement to enlist. In explaining to Rear Admiral John A. Dahlgren why so many contraband sailors were being discharged from his ship in May 1865, William Reynolds noted that many blacks had left their families behind when they escaped to the USS *New Hampshire,* considering naval service "the only resource left to them." Now they came to him, Reynolds explained, saying that their families were in distress and asking to be discharged. As the war had ended, the admiral instructed Reynolds to discharge any of the contrabands from his crew who could be spared.[7]

Although specific information about contrabands, as opposed to other African Americans, is limited, the North Carolina–U.S. Colored Troops Project has gathered information about men born in North Carolina who joined the Union Navy. John B. McGowan has organized data on 933 African American sailors, both ex-slaves and freedmen, who listed towns and counties in North Carolina as their place of birth. My sample of these sailors, though small, indicates that they varied in age from thirteen to fifty-four years of age, with the majority being young men in their twenties. Although many listed their occupations as slave, farmer, cook, steward, waiter, or laborer, others listed skilled occupations such as carpenter, mariner, bricklayer, mason, barber, cooper, fisherman, shoemaker, or blacksmith.[8]

At the beginning of the Civil War the Navy Department authorized that contraband recruits, whether teenagers or middle-aged men, be given the rank of "boy," a rating usually reserved for youngsters under the age of seventeen. According to historian Michael Bennett, rating black sailors as boys reflected white prejudice, which condoned treating black men as children; it also conveniently allowed the navy to relegate blacks to "the lowest possible social stratum among sailors." In contrast to contraband enlistees, the navy ranked northern black men or free black foreigners according to their skills as seamen, carpenters, and so forth. Of the 900 contrabands, free northern blacks, and black foreigners who enlisted in the Union Navy in 1861, only 6.3 percent entered with a rating of boy; the vast majority were rated as landsmen. The navy paid boys $10 a month and landsmen $12. Although the allowance for first-class boys was the lowest on the navy pay scale, many contrabands welcomed the steady income, and they could have the navy allot a percentage of their pay to their families. In fact, according to Ramold, contraband sailors' families living in contraband camps often relied heavily on their allotment of navy pay.[9]

Within months of being authorized to enlist black men, senior Union Navy commanders began asking for authority to advance the ratings of contraband sailors to landsmen or seamen. In one instance, the request resulted from a daring and successful raid by Acting Master's Mate James J. Russell and two contrabands from the bark *Restless*, which won promotions for all three. Having obtained reliable information about a postal route near Palmetto Point, South Carolina, Acting Volunteer Lieutenant Edward Conroy ordered Russell to take a boat and try to intercept and capture the mail. Russell left the *Restless*'s anchorage in Bull's Bay at two o'clock on the afternoon of November 4, 1862, with a boat and two armed contrabands who were apparently familiar with the area. When the trio landed and went five miles inland, Russell met a contraband who "was acquainted with the two contrabands with me," he wrote, and from whom he learned that the mail was expected that night. They hid in the woods near the road, and when they spotted the mail carrier, Russell appeared and asked the man to halt. "He at once dismounted and told me he was glad, for he had long wished for an opportunity to leave that place." Russell searched the man and found two mailbags. Although they discovered four horses tied to a tree at the landing and had to avoid four pickets on lookout, Russell and his party made it safely back to the *Restless*. The mail carrier, a man named Milligan, accompanied them quietly and did not alarm the pickets. "The contraband (Jack Graddock) having proved himself of great service to me, and expressing a great desire to get off to the fleet, I brought him off with me," Russell told Conroy. The *Restless*'s mission gained Rear Admiral Du Pont's approval; he praised

Russell, writing, "This officer deserves great credit for the manner in which he carried out your orders, and I have shown my appreciation of his zeal by appointing him an acting ensign as from the 5th of November. The two contrabands who went with him are also, I think, deserving of an advanced rate."[10]

Based on their correspondence, few Union commanders hesitated to enlist contrabands as crew members. Beset by desertions and sailors leaving as their terms of service expired, Union commanders often found their ships short of manpower. With little hope of receiving additional enlisted men in a timely fashion, most commanding officers welcomed able-bodied black men who were willing to serve. By January 1862 the enlistment of contrabands had become a regular practice, although Commander John P. Gillis still found it necessary to justify doing so: "I presume there will be no irregularity in shipping Isaac (as ordinary sea-man), a colored refugee, or contraband, sent from the U.S.S. *Savannah* on board on account of his knowledge of inlets along the coast; he is somewhat intelligent and a quiet man," he told Du Pont.[11]

The commander of the North Atlantic Blockading Squadron, Flag Officer Louis M. Goldsborough, took a somewhat different approach to contrabands. In early 1862 he ordered his commanders not to accept all the contrabands seeking refuge on what he called "our crowded little vessels," but he encouraged them to ship able-bodied male contrabands whenever possible. The *Monitor*'s captain, Lieutenant William N. Jeffers, tried to adhere to Goldsborough's instructions, but while on duty in the James River in May 1862, the *Monitor* attracted many black refugees from farms and plantations ashore. "The Counterbands come off to us every night but we send them back in most cases, as we have no room for them," George Geer wrote to his wife. Jeffers must have retained at least one of these contrabands, for on May 20 Geer wrote, "We have one as Ships Cook. He is a likely, smart Darkey; Says his master owns 100 Slaves and is a Colonel in the Rebel army. We are laying in front of his farm, and a most splendid one it is." In fact, many naval officers took advantage of the numerous contrabands seeking sanctuary on their ships to procure cooks and personal servants for the wardrooms. For example, in his diary entry for February 2, 1863, the surgeon on the bark *Fernandina* wrote, "4 or 5 contrabands made their appearance having escaped from servitude. We intend taking one of them in the wardroom as one of our boys." The following day he noted, "The new wardroom mess boy came this morning. He looks more like a white boy than a contraband. I think he will make a good boy."[12]

South Atlantic Blockading Squadron commander Samuel F. Du

Pont favored recruiting and enlisting contrabands because he believed that local African Americans were in some way conditioned to the heat and humidity of southern summers. "The hot season on this coast, now approaching, renders it advisable that acclimated persons be employed on board the ships of this squadron," he wrote on May 15, 1862, "in such duties as involve much exposure to sun and heat, such as boat service and work in the engine rooms." Du Pont authorized his commanders to enlist contrabands, "with their consent," and rate them as boys at $8, $9, and $10 per month with one ration.[13]

Union vessels often encountered African Americans and others willing to enlist during expeditions or while patrolling rivers and creeks. On a foraging expedition upriver in February 1863, for example, the gunboat *Commodore Morris* acquired a young black boy. Paymaster Calvin Hutchinson explained that "a boy of 12 or 13 years smuggled himself under the canvas of the cutter after dark and was discovered too late to be set on shore. The *Morris* [was] going up river so he had to stay on board and was afterward enlisted as a 3rd class boy." As the boy's only possession was a tattered soldier's uniform, the gunboat's tailors made him a small navy blue suit and, Hutchinson wrote, "acted like proud parents when he came out at Sunday morning muster in a natty suit, black ribbons and a small pair of shoes which I got specially for him at Fortress Monroe." The boy's name was Henry Clark, and he told a pitiful story about having been a servant to an army captain who had just been killed, but "he proved to be a runaway from Pittsburg, Pa. and an awful liar." According to Hutchinson, the navy obtained permission from the boy's parents for him to enlist.[14]

One of the most unusual incidents involving the recruitment of black sailors occurred in September 1862 when Lieutenant Commander W. T. Truxtun, commanding the USS *Alabama,* received a note from a Mr. R. Stafford of Cumberland Island complaining that a number of "strange negroes" had returned from Fernandina and quartered themselves on his plantation. "A number of them being armed, several of their number by authority of Colonel Rich, commandant at Fernandina," Truxtun told Du Pont. When the blacks began killing cattle and overrunning private dwellings with arms and clubs and would not submit to any control, Stafford asked for the navy's assistance. Truxtun immediately steamed up the Brickhill River and sent an armed party ashore under Acting Masters West and Stimpson. According to West's report, he had arrived at Stafford's plantation to find the "old gentleman evidently very much frightened." He told Truxtun, "The darkies have most of them run away to Fernandina, and after obtaining firearms there, returned to the plantation and have done just as they pleased ever since until the old man no longer considered his life safe." To reassure Stafford, West stayed behind with six marines to guard the plantation and sent nine of the most "dangerous" blacks back to the *Alabama* with Stimpson. Taking no chances, Truxtun slapped the men in irons but later released them, explaining that their master had given up all claim to them. He then "placed them on the ship's books as a portion of the crew."[15]

Although procuring landsmen and ordinary seamen to fill out their ships' complements constituted a high priority for Union naval commanders, they especially valued skilled contrabands such as carpenters, caulkers, machinists, and coopers. Occasionally commanders made note of the arrival of skilled contrabands on board their vessels. When Commodore Stephen Rowan informed Welles that three contrabands had been picked up by guard vessels in the Stono River on the night of April 11, 1864, he took care to mention that "two of these men (Tony Bryan and Moses Bryan) are house carpenters by trade, and all of them have been shipped as first-class boys of the U.S. sloop *John Adams* for subsequent detail." According to Rowan, Tony Bryan had left his trade in January and had been employed on the side-wheel transport *Rebel,* which was used to carry Confederate troops from Charleston to Sumter, Sumter to Moultrie, Moultrie to Mount Pleasant, and Mount Pleasant back to Charleston. Tony Bryan also informed federal officials that the rebels had about 200 men in Charleston.[16]

In their official reports, Union Navy commanders usually noted the arrival of African Americans on their vessels but did not always provide their names, ages, or owners. When seven contrabands boarded the 655-ton screw gunboat *Monticello* in September 1862, however, its commanding officer, thirty-three-year-old Daniel Lawrence Braine, provided Commander Scott with a detailed list: Frank Clinton, age thirty-five years, belonging to Robert H. Cowan; Samuel Mince, age twenty-three, belonging to Mrs. Elizabeth Mince; Thomas Cowen, twenty-four, belonging to Mrs. J. G. Wright; Charles Millett, twenty-eight, belonging to Mrs. John Walker; James Brown, twenty-three, belonging to John Brown; Horace Smith, twenty-two, belonging to Mrs. William Smith; and David Millett, twenty-six, belonging to Mrs. John Walker. According to Lieutenant Braine, these young contrabands had given him a good deal of valuable information about rebel activities and the gunboat *North Carolina,* which they said was to be launched the next Saturday and "is to be clad with railroad iron down to the water's edge." He also told the commander that the contrabands, who were from the Wilmington, North Carolina, area, had informed him that the city was completely entrenched and that the rebels had mounted guns "at every half mile upon the works."[17]

Rear Admiral Samuel P. Lee directed Scott, the senior officer off Wilmington, to use as many of the contrabands from the *Monticello* as needed in squadron vessels, but he also asked Welles "to direct what disposition shall be made of those not wanted in the vessels." That same day Lee sent Scott the welcome news that 100 men had recently arrived at Newport News for the vessels off Wilmington and admonished him: "The occasion for a part of this draft might have been avoided by using such contrabands as available under circulars 13 and 14 of the general orders and circulations of this squadron, a copy of which is herewith enclosed."[18]

Within days of the arrival of the seven contrabands aboard the *Monticello,* eight more slaves found their way out to the USS *Cambridge.* Among these former slaves was William B. Gould, who kept a journal of his service in the navy—one of the few surviving written records by black sailors. On the night of September 21, 1862, Gould and seven others had left in a boat from Orange Street in Wilmington. Taking turns at the oars because they were afraid to hoist the sail and reveal their presence to the Confederates, they had rowed down the Cape Fear River and the next day sighted two blockading ships, the *State of Georgia* and the *Cambridge.* The *Cambridge*'s Commander William Parker wasted no time in taking advantage of the arrival of these eight black men. Illness and desertions had created eighteen vacancies in his crew, and Parker filled one vacancy by enlisting Gould as a first-class boy. On October 3, 1862, Gould wrote: "Off New Inlet. All of us ship'd to-day for three years taking the Oath of Allegiance to the Government of Uncle Samuel." The Union Navy issued all new recruits the standard navy ration and a uniform; the men had to purchase the latter, which usually set them back about three months' pay. Although Gould did not specifically mention being issued a uniform, on October 27, 1862, he commented, "Quite cold. Pea jackets quite comfortable."[19]

Like most black enlisted men, William Gould was assigned to primarily menial shipboard tasks. As historian Joseph Reidy has noted, a contraband sailor was "in, but not necessarily of," the crew with which he served. Contrabands "performed the manual labor necessary to keep a steam vessel functioning and the busywork that officers considered the foundation of good order and discipline on warships: holystoning, scrubbing, scraping, painting, and polishing." The *Cambridge*'s commanding officer quickly put Gould to work doing exactly that. On October 20 Gould noted, "Painted the Main Deck. Rattled down the Rigging.

Make preparations for painting outside." Whether Commander Parker allowed Gould to take part in gun drills is difficult to tell. He was more likely assigned to a general quarters station involving damage control or to a small-arms crew to repel boarders.[20]

Many contrabands enlisting in the Union Navy could not read or write, but those on board at least one ship had the opportunity to learn. "I am rejoiced to inform you that in our ship, all the contrabands can read, feel much interested in your paper, the [Christian] Recorder," contraband Ben R. Johnson wrote from the USS Vermont at Port Royal, South Carolina, where he served as a hospital cook. Johnson explained that he had left Boston in February 1862 and arrived in Port Royal after fifty-one days at sea, having experienced a fierce gale that claimed two crewmen. "There are nearly three hundred contrabands on board this ship," he wrote. "About one hundred of them can read." Nearly two years later, Johnson wrote again to the Christian Recorder, "informing us that he has been transferred to the U.S.S. New Hampshire. He states that many of the crew (contrabands) came on board unable to distinguish a from p, but when their term of enlistment expired, they could read and write. Who can say that colored men cannot study?"[21]

Ben Johnson's and William Gould's wartime naval service typified that of many contrabands, the majority of whom served as cooks or as stewards, waiting table for officers in the wardroom and cleaning their staterooms. "Navy officers often favored black cooks and servants, in part due to the common prejudices of the day—which held persons of African descent as naturally subservient—and in part due to their experience with black mess attendants at the U.S. Naval Academy." In a letter to Flora, written from the USS Nansemond in late August 1863, Lieutenant Roswell Lamson described his servant: "Charles Adams ('a fellow citizen and a brother') is my steward and cook, and James waits on the table and takes care of my room. Both of them are excellent servants, and Charles is a very fine cook. He has been at sea a good deal, and for some time waited on Admiral Du Pont. I am allowed three servants, but two are quite enough." Lamson's reference to "a fellow citizen and a brother" was a common abolitionist term denoting an African American.[22]

Even officers who did not attend the U.S. Naval Academy favored black servants, and the navy sometimes allowed them to bring their servants with them from one ship to another. In explaining the favored status of George Patterson, one of the black wardroom boys on the monitor Nahant, Alvah Hunter recalled, "Doctor Stedman was an intimate friend of Captain Downes and had served with him on the gunboat Huron. When the Captain and doctor were ordered to the Nahant, each had had his personal servants transferred also, and George considered himself as specially Doctor Stedman's boy, so went to him with any grievance."[23]

When William Keeler joined the Union Navy in early 1862 he was assigned to the newly built ironclad *Monitor,* lying at the time at the Brooklyn Navy Yard. Reporting for duty, Keeler discovered that the Navy Department had given the *Monitor's* commanding officer, Captain Worden, a clerk. This, he wrote to his wife, Anna, "will serve to make my duties still lighter, & more, they give me a *servant,* so I have spent a portion of two or three days in hunting up a contraband & finally found a good looking young darkey that came to me well recommended, but he wasn't of age & it was uncertain if his mother would let him go. I shall know tomorrow when I go aboard of the *North Carolina* (where the men are all sent when they enlist) & if I don't find him shall have to make another hunt." Paymaster Keeler evidently found a contraband to serve him, for on February 25, 1862, he told his wife, "My boy has made my bed but it has a full wheelbarrow load of books, blanks, paper, bundles, boxes, bottle of ink, &c, &c. deposited on top which has got to be removed to their proper places before I can turn in." In these letters to his wife, Keeler described the duties of his "boy," which were probably similar to those of dozens of wardroom servants or ship's boys in the Union Navy. After spending a cold, miserable first night between linen sheets in his stateroom on the *Monitor,* Keeler wrote, "Morning brought relief in the form of my darkey with a wash bowl of warm water. I made short work of my toilette & hurried into the engineroom to thaw out." The *Monitor's* wardroom thermometer, he explained, stood at thirty-five degrees. Keeler soon gave up shaving in his poorly lit room but told his wife, "Your suggestion as to having my boy black my boots is a very good one but was unnecessary for I find a pair of well blacked boots in my room every morning when I get up."[24]

In letters written to Nannie Sturdevant, Samuel Webber often mentioned the ship's boys as well his own steward. Although Webber did not identify them as African American, some undoubtedly were contrabands. In a letter written in October 1864 from his new assignment, the monitor *Nahant,* Webber provided a detailed description of the duties of wardroom boys. "Many members of the mess want me to cater for them. I have made up my mind not to do it till I can be sure of having a good cook, a pretty good steward and boys enough. There are thirteen officers with twelve rooms, besides the ward room to look out for. The ward room floor ought to be washed up every other day and the rooms every week; we have only three boys, five would not be any too many." Webber noted, if "I had the management [of the wardroom] I should have to keep the boys at work, all the time, and drive them pretty hard. I don't care to do that." He also told Nannie, "My boy takes tolerable good care of my room, but not as good as I should want if we had more boys. I get my shoes blacked two or three times a week & let the cobwebs go, spider ants and cockroaches are my daily and nightly companions." Earlier, while serving on the USS *Rhode Island*, Webber had found it difficult to find capable wardroom boys. "One of our wardroom boys has been put on deck for doing wrong," he told Nannie in July 1863. "He waits on me, was stupid & lazy. The one who took his place is better. I like the way he has done so far. I guess he will be better."[25]

Although Webber may not have verbally or physically abused his boys, other officers admitted losing their tempers with wardroom boys or stewards. In one letter written from the *Monitor* in early March 1862, for example, William Keeler confessed to his wife that he had lost his temper with his black wardroom boy over a misplaced letter. Keeler had gone to visit the *North Carolina* and wrote, "When I got back to my state room once more I found my darkey had been putting my room to right & as is always the case at such times, turned everything upside down & loosing your letter. I blowed up at him, found your letter, read that & felt better natured." There is no indication that Keeler expressed any regret about getting angry with the boy, who, being a servant as well as an African American, undoubtedly bore the brunt of white officers' wrath quite often.[26]

The Union Navy rated stewards as petty officers, but they were staff petty officers rather than petty officers of the line and did not traditionally have authority over other enlisted men. Few black men were promoted to petty officers of the line during the Civil War—"barely one hundred black men (0.6 percent of all black enlistees)," according to Reidy. In contrast, in U.S. Colored Troop regiments the senior noncommissioned officers were all black, although the officer corps remained mostly white. Not all contraband sailors served as wardroom stewards or servants, however. As Sherman Adams, assistant acting paymaster on the USS *Somerset,* wrote from Key West, Florida, in 1863, "On my muster roles are borne the names of about fifty 'contrabands' who having been received on board, were shipped in the Naval Service. They generally perform the duties of landsmen and Coal Passers, as well as the white men would perform them."[27]

Writing from Fortress Monroe on June 11, 1863, Lieutenant Roswell Lamson echoed Adams's opinion of contraband sailors. "It seems strange to send negroes to garrison a fort in 'Yankeedom,' but I have no doubt if properly drilled they will make very good sailors. We have always had some on board every vessel in the Navy, and they make valuable men for certain kinds of duty. I think we will have no difficulty in getting as many as we want here; we ship them as 'Landsmen' at twelve dollars per month, and rations; half of their pay can be paid to their families here, every month. It is the best prospect the negroes have had offered them." Lamson explained that he had just spent "three days making arrangements with Gen. Dix to ship some contrabands for the Navy upon the order of the Secretary. He wants one hundred for the Naval Battery at the Navy Yard, Portsmouth, N.H. and the same number for the 'Roanoke,' which will arrive in about ten days." General Dix sent the contrabands to Fortress Monroe, and Lamson shipped them to the receiving ship *Brandywine*.[28]

Despite the inclusion of black enlisted men in the U.S. Navy prior to the Civil War, racist attitudes persisted, and African Americans were treated as second-class citizens, if citizens at all. Letters and diaries written by both officers and enlisted men attest to their negative feelings about contrabands and African Americans in general, feelings that ran the gamut from annoyance to blatant dislike. In a letter to his future wife, Webber admitted that he did not like blacks. Describing a visit to Cape Haytien, Webber wrote, "We are again in this romantic and beautiful & ancient negro city. Although I think slavery wrong and would not countenance the institution, I cant say I like the negro. There are here some pleasant intelligent people who are colored, but they are not negroes. They are very light colored indeed." Though staunchly anti-slavery, Webber was not, by his own admission, in favor of giving African Americans equal rights. Nor were many of his fellow officers. On March 12, 1865, Webber described a discussion he had overheard from his room belowdecks. "I listened for a while & then I think Mr. R (Rodgers) made a remark rather sweeping in its character about the rights which he would & would not allow to the negroes. I answered him and we then had a general argument on the negro question which lasted till nearly dinner time."[29]

Other naval officers expressed strong opinions about contrabands. "We had another of the contrabands come on board this morning; he is very white. I wish they would send every one of them back as fast as they come. I am down on this Nigger stealing," George Geer wrote to his wife in May 1862. Charles Steedman, a career naval officer commanding the USS *Paul Jones*, candidly expressed his opinion about black troops in a letter written to his wife from Jacksonville, Florida. Steedman's gunboat had arrived in Jacksonville the previous week to find Colonel Thomas W. Higginson and his black troops "in quiet possession" of the town.

Steedman explained that the army force was too small to hold the town without the support of the navy's gunboats, *Uncas, Norwich,* and *Paul Jones.* "The duty has been by no means to my taste as the army force was composed entirely of niggers and . . . nigger-worshippers," Steedman wrote. "You can have no idea how annoying it has been to me to be obliged to work with these people, but as the old adage has it, 'Duty before pleasure.' It is probably I will have to remain here until all the reinforcements arrive which are on their way." The commander hoped to be able to go back to St. Simon's as soon as possible.[30]

Although there is little evidence that Union Navy commanders refused to accept African American crewmen on their vessels because of their race, officers often expressed annoyance with their black crews in letters and diaries. In recalling his service on board the USS *Pequot,* Calvin Hutchinson wrote that "a careless negro mess boy emptied overboard a bucket of dish water containing all the solid and plated silverware of the war-room mess and no doubt it is there near Powhatan now." In his memoirs Hutchinson also related an incident that occurred in March 1865. The *Pequot* had been cruising for months, and the officers' diet had been sorely lacking in fresh meat. When the ship got to Norfolk the wardroom mess officer told the caterer to buy the best fresh meat the market had to offer, and the officers would remain on board for a "good dinner." The caterer provided a pair of chickens and, Hutchinson wrote, "the handsomest young cock turkey that I ever saw, it weighed 30 lbs." Mr. Beattie, the *Pequot's* executive officer, "was an excellent carver," but when he "placed his fork in the breast and cut down the wish bone," Hutchinson recalled, "a horrid stench arose from the bird. . . . Calling the colored steward he said, 'George! Whats the matter with that turkey?' The steward removed the platter to the side-board, looked the bird over and answered—'Mr Beattie, de boys done cooked dat turkey without drawing it.' Mr. Beattie rose from the table, took the bird by its legs, and struck the poor darkey over the face with it as hard as he could." Rather than expressing surprise or outage at these actions, Hutchinson concluded his tale by writing, "A more disappointed crowd of 18 men compelled to dine off the two roast chickens cannot be imagined."[31]

Such meanness was not confined to the officer corps. In January 1863 the predominantly black crew of one Union warship, the USS *Constellation,* suffered abuse at the hands of three white sailors. Henry Martyn Cross recalled that although the ship had thirty-three African Americans in the crew, the three white sailors kicked, shoved, and cursed their black shipmates, calling them "God damn niggers," "black dogs," and "bitches." In fact, despite the common practice of segregating black sailors from their white counterparts, the influx of contraband and free black sailors on Union ships often strained relations between whites and blacks in the crew.[32]

On more than one occasion, white sailors' prejudice and their resentment of black sailors led to abuse or fights. Geer described one incident on the USS *Monitor* in May 1862: "This one [black sailor] I wrote you we had for a cook has gotten quite important already, and one of the saylors he had [given] some lip to gave him a smack over the mouth, which for the present has learned him his place. He began to think him self as good as a white man, and I must say he does know as much as some of these Saylors." A keen observer of the *Fernandina* crew's behavior, Dr. Samuel Boyer described a fight between sailors: "All hands were in the better of humour until 8 P.M., when two colored 'pussons' tried their skill at fisticuffing on the berth deck, but to their chagrin the master-at-arms soon heard the noise and politely handcuffed them, at the same time giving them a night's lodging in the brig." The doctor thought it "served them right." On another occasion, Boyer noted, *Fernandina*'s commanding officer, Captain William Moses, handed out severe punishment to two "gemmun ub culler," Austin Burroughs and John Brown, who were "bickering all day." Captain Moses "caused them to march the spar deck in the following manner: after being united together by means of a pair of irons placed on their right wrists by the master-at-arms, thus being back to back, they each shoulder a handspike so as to give them the appearance of soldiers." Moses then ordered the two men to walk for an hour and a half, one marching forward, the other backward—a "novel punishment" wrote Boyer. He noted, however, "They both appeared to be in good humor when they were released." Incidents of fighting, or "fisticuffs," were not uncommon among bluejackets living for long periods in confined quarters on shipboard.[33]

Some of these bouts occurred between white and blacks, others between black sailors. In his diary, Alvah Hunter described one case involving his fellow wardroom boy on the *Nahant*, George Patterson. "George Patterson and the captain's boy (Jerome Harris, also a colored boy) got to fighting and were put in double irons and sent to a coal bunker." According to Hunter, prejudice could go both ways. "Our wardroom cook was about the 'plainest' negro I have ever met, and, like most negroes, he had no love for an Irish boy, which Barney [the ship's cook] certainly was; but I was just plain Yankee, and cook and I had no frictions."[34]

Alcohol consumption ashore and afloat often led to arguments and fistfights on Union vessels. Although the Navy Department abolished the grog ration in 1862, many Union sailors and officers alike continued to have access to liquor smuggled aboard from shore. "Some despicable creature had smuggled some liquor into the navy yard," Hunter wrote, "and sold a quart or two to a group of our men, and half a dozen of our best sailors were fighting-roaring drunk." The master-at-arms, aided by two or three petty officers, slapped the inebriated sailors in irons. The sight of one of the men—a "model seaman," in Hunter's eyes—trussed up on deck caused Hunter to feel "a greater sorrow than I would have thought it possible to feel for a stranger." One of the most tragic incidents took place on the USS *Monitor* when a man either jumped or rolled overboard and drowned. "He was the Wardroom Stewart, and was very fond of liquor it seems," Geer explained to his wife. "He had been on shore to buy things for the wardroom when he got hold of a bottle of Whiskey and drank the whole of it. He was so crazy he took up an Ax and threw it at a Colord Boy, which if it had hit him would have killed him." When Captain Jeffers attempted to have the man put in irons, he "became Crazy as posebale, and it took 4 men to hold him while the Irons were put on him," Geer wrote. As soon as the men left, the steward "made a spring and eather fell or roled off the side." Weighted down by the heavy irons, he went under the water, and efforts to find him failed.[35]

For the majority of naval officers and crew, blockade duty meant long days at sea with little to relieve the monotony other than meals, shipboard routine, and, perhaps, smuggled liquor. When any suspicious light, smoke, or steamer came into view, all hands went to quarters, but more often than not, the blockade runner escaped. For those fortunate enough to be serving on a ship assigned to inshore blockade duty, opportunities arose to go ashore and take walks or go hunting, fishing, or oystering. These occasions often prompted comments in journals or letters home. On December 15, 1862, George Adams Bright's ship, the *South Carolina*, moved twenty miles to a new station off North Edisto Island. Bright recorded the change of assignment in his journal: "The station is spoken of as a comfortable one for a man can take a tramp on the shore (such as it is) beside getting oysters and shooting fowl or even a bullock occasionally and as we lie one or two miles from the bar we are tranquil enough." Two local African Americans, Julia and Philip, offered the *South Carolina*'s crew valuable services such as doing laundry and helping them obtain fresh meat and oysters.[36]

Boyer and other members of the *Fernandina*'s crew established a similar mutually beneficial relationship with contrabands on St. Simon's Island, Georgia, when the ship moved to its new station off St. Simon's in January 1863. Boyer took advantage of his proximity to shore to take long walks on the island, searching the beach for seashells and talking with local African Americans. "Taking exercise on shore is a great blessing to us naval officers and is a luxury that few on blockade duty enjoy," he wrote on a mild January day. The doctor and his assistant also went ashore to tend to a contraband named George and to offer ointments and other medicines to the local inhabitants. In turn, contrabands ashore prepared meals and served them to the *Fernandina*'s officers and crew, sold them local produce, and, on occasion, offered them entertainment. From their arrival on blockade duty, the *Fernandina*'s sailors had frequent and regular contact with blacks ashore.[37]

This social interaction between the *Fernandina*'s crew and the African Americans on St. Simon's Island continued a practice that had begun on Otter Island. On December 24, 1862, Boyer wrote in his diary: "On account of tonight being Christmas Eve, the captain gave forty of the boys liberty to spend a few hours on shore. So at 7 P.M. the captain, Paymaster Murray, Actg. Master Childs, Actg. Master James B. Henderson, and Actg. Asst. Surgeon Boyer with the above number of boys started for and landed at Ottar Island, the place occupied by King Ceasar." The sailors headed for one of the mansions on the island, to the "astonishment" of King Ceasar. "After the candles were all ignited, one John Brown (a darky) struck up a jig on his violin, the boys commended to dance, or rather make attempts," Boyer wrote. While Brown played, another man, Lewis Y. Close, tended bar, giving out ale and cigars. Boyer reported that the "fair sex" was also present, "represented by Aunt Peggy, aged 60 years, who danced every sett (at least 20 times); her daughters Maria and Rina; and Millie, Bailey's wife—all colored. The way the boys hugged the ladies was not slow." The sailors also danced and sang, and Boyer admitted that he danced "several times" himself. The liberty party returned to the *Fernandina* at 10 P.M., and "everything passed muster," Boyer wrote. "All enjoyed themselves." Two days after Christmas some of the contrabands from King Ceasar's settlement on Otter Island came out to the *Fernandina* to visit. Daniel Bailey, his father, wife, and son, and several others "all dressed in their best" came alongside. Bailey, Boyer wrote in his diary, was "munching peanuts," and Miss Grant "looked pleasant as a basket of chips." From the young physician's comments it appears that he was familiar with individual contrabands. He noted that Tom Mathers had on "his usual dry look" and that Old Man Bailey "showed himself to be the same good-natured old darky."[38]

Music and singing often relieved the monotony of blockade duty for Union bluejackets. On board the *Fernandina*, evening concerts delighted both officers and crew. Boyer wrote, "The crew are having quite a concert tonight under the hurricane deck. The colored portion are on the port side singing camp-meeting hymns, whilst the jolly portion are on the starboard side singing comic, Irish, sentimental, and patriotic songs—quite a contrast. Both parties are trying to make the most noise." Many Union ships boasted bands. "We have a Band of Music on board and we entertain all the officers who visit us," Stephen Chaulker Bartlett, the assistant surgeon on the USS *Lenapee,* wrote to his sister in February 1865. "[I]n the evening we sit on the quarter deck and smoke and listen to the music and have a good time generally." A week later he described the band in more detail: "We have a Band of Music composed of Contrabands and Banjos. They play well and we entertain on board." In a letter to his wife Nannie, Samuel Webber described the Fourth of July festivities on board the USS *Rhode Island:* "I have just come from deck. The fireworks did well. . . . Since then the men have been singing & one group of contrabands have been dancing their jigs, etc. It was pleasant to watch for awhile."[39]

The lively music provided by African Americans and enjoyed by Union Navy officers and sailors was not always confined to their own ships. Navy men wrote of attending worship services in black churches or listening to concerts aboard other vessels. On October 22, 1862, for example, George Bright, then serving on the *South Carolina,* wrote in his journal that he had gone to Hilton Head and then on to Beaufort on the *Gem.* While there, Bright met some acquaintances and noted in his journal, "So we had a most pleasant company. A choir of female darkies enlivened the passage by antiphonal singing, in a wild and weird strain, a sort of chant in part, with a sort of swaying of the body, and bobbing of the head, producing a peculiar effect in the calm twilight."[40]

Meeting acquaintances from home, dining or going ashore with fellow officers, and listening to shipboard concerts did much to relieve the monotony of blockade duty and to restore flagging morale. In his journal entry for September 15, 1862, Bright wrote candidly of the poor morale aboard his ship: "Things on the ship are getting to be intolerable and the Captain flies around as if his wits were gone." Noting a new regulation forbidding the men on the *South Carolina* to smoke or show lights after dark, Bright wrote, "Crew is unhappy." Bright blamed the new regulation on the excessive caution of the ship's captain and explained that theirs was the closest ship to shore, and Captain Almy feared that any lights could be seen from a distance of five miles. "So much for having an old granny for a captain," he wrote.[41]

The morale-building effects of the daily concerts given by black sailors are apparent in the memoirs of Paul Henry Kendricksen, an engineer serving on the double-ender *Conemaugh* off the South Carolina and Georgia coasts in late December 1862 and early January 1863. "When evening was approaching and before and after the sun went down (but still leaving its rosy shadow on the sky) the colored boys would get together and give some nice music; really, at times, good and sweet," he wrote. "In the early days of the blockade old songs used to be sung. These boys had instruments bought by the officers. When they sang 'Do They miss Me at home?' and all such songs every pleasant evening, it produced a cheery feeling."[42]

Minstrel shows with musical accompanists also offered diversions on Union ships, with the performers impersonating women, African Americans, and Irish characters. The USS *Braziliera*'s "Theatrical Company" used actors in blackface and, according to Joseph Reidy, relegated contrabands to the "Colored Gallery." On other Union vessels black sailors took part in minstrel bands, and black crewmen enjoyed the entertainment. Although minstrel shows did in some respects reinforce racial stereotypes, Reidy argues that they also "held the power to bridge racial and ethnic divisions by transporting both performers and auditors home, removed from harm's way and surrounded by loved ones."[43]

Black bluejackets formed friendships on board Union vessels and took pride in their ships. Contraband sailor William Gould, apparently not included in the *Cambridge* crew's raids or expeditions against the rebels, nonetheless joined other crewmen in watching and waiting for their comrades' safe return from these forays and took pride in his gunboat's fighting spirit. Shortly after his arrival, the *Cambridge* joined the *Mystic* and *Penobscot* in an expedition to find and burn the blockade runner *Kate*. According to Commander Parker, he had "an abundance of officers and men who have volunteered, in fact, everybody wants to go, including myself. It is perfectly safe."[44]

For Gould, the prospect of action against the rebels must have been, as his great-grandson suggested, "exhilarating." Buoyed by youthful optimism and enthusiasm, the *Penobscot*'s commanding officer, Lieutenant F. M. Bunce, left his vessel on the evening of October 7, 1862, with a boat crew and a contraband pilot from the *Monticello* and reported to Parker on the *Cambridge*. The following night two boats from the *Cambridge* and one from the *Mystic* attempted to cross the bar at New Inlet but were forced back by heavy surf. Gould recorded the events in his diary. On Thursday, October 8, he wrote: "Cruised as usual. Our Expedition faild to burn the steamer got lost in the fog, they will try again." In the next entry he noted: "Off New Inlet. Rained very hard last night the expedition did not go. Cruised until 3 O clock P.M. Cleard off. Made preparations to make another attempt at her. Wind strong, S.W." Finally, on Saturday, Gould explained: "About 7 O clock we got under- way and ran as near as we could to the shore, came to anchor. The Boats then left the ship (two in number) one in command of Lieut. Strong of the *Cambridge* the Lieut. Brannon of the *Penobscot*. When approach- ing the steamer they were discovered by the Batries when the expedi- tion returned but resolved to try again." Undaunted by these two failed attempts, Bunce tried again to enter the Cape Fear River on October 12 with two boats from the *Cambridge*. Once again they were unable to get across into the river by New Inlet, by a small inlet south of Zeek's Island, or by the beach. "The surf ran so high that after nearly losing the boats in the breakers the attempt was abandoned," Bunce told Commander Scott, the senior officer off Wilmington. In the end, even Bunce had to admit that absent calm weather or a southwest wind, the New Inlet entrance was "impracticable for small boats."[45]

Although Gould did not take part in any of these boat expeditions, he did witness one of the *Cambridge's* most daring engagements with the rebels. On November 17, 1862, Gould described the action in his journal: "About 1 bell A sail was reported close under the land right ahead. We gave chase. When within range of our Pet. we told them good morning in the shape of A shot for her to heave to. To this they took no notice. We sent another which fell under her stern. At this she about the ship and stood for the Beach. Shot after shot was sent after her but they heeded not. She pill'd high and dry upon the Beach." Parker, the *Cam- bridge's* skipper, then ordered Acting Master W. H. Maies to take ten men in a boat and burn the beached schooner, the *J. W. Pinda*. Gould recorded what happened next: "We immediately Man'd the first Cutter and sent her in charge of Master Mace to board and destroy her. We also sent two other Boats to lend assistance. The first got into the Breakers was capsized. Men and Boat was thrown apon the Beach. They boarded the Schooner and set her on fire, the crew having escaped to the shore." When Maies and the boat crew tried to return to the *Cambridge*, how- ever, heavy surf made crossing the bar impossible. "We attempted to float A line to them with Buoy's but faild," Gould wrote. "Act. Masters Mate Wells attempted to swim in with A line but when he got into the surf he was obliged to cut the line." Another officer, Acting Master's Mate Odiorne, managed to take a line into the beach. But before the boat could get out, twenty-five Confederate soldiers of the Third North Caro- lina Cavalry, in Gould's words, "dash'd over the Hill at the double Quick and all were prisoners. We could see them plane from the ship marching off our Men and draging the Boats after them. We lost Eleven Men and three Offercers." Gould's final comment was judgmental: "Rather A Bad days work."[46]

Although Gould remained safe and sound on board the *Cambridge* during his service off the southern coast, other black sailors found themselves in harm's way when their ships intercepted rebel blockade runners; engaged rebel rams, ironclads, and shore batteries; or took fire from enemy sharpshooters along riverbanks. Those serving in gun crews could fight back, but other bluejackets in engine rooms or at their battle stations could only do their duty and pray. Black sailors assigned to armed boat parties or to picket boats also found themselves targets of rebel infantry or cavalry and faced possible capture, injury, and even death; others acted as naval infantry in landing parties ashore. More became casualties when their vessels sank in storms or struck mines.

On numerous occasions, rebel gunners took aim on Union Navy vessels operating in southern rivers and creeks or participating in bombardments of Confederate fortifications, and in some instances the Union ships were forced to surrender. Operations in early 1863 in the Stono River just south of Charleston proved particularly dangerous to Union crews, for the Confederates had located gun batteries along the shore to discourage Union incursions up the river toward the city. Throughout January 1863 rebel gunners harassed Union gunboats patrolling the Stono, without measurable effect. Then, with just one day left in the month, Rear Admiral Samuel F. Du Pont learned from Commander Bacon that the rebels had not only fired on a Union gunboat but had actually succeeded in capturing one—the *Isaac Smith*. Bacon had sent the gunboat up the Stono River on the afternoon of January 30, 1862, for a reconnaissance. In his report of the incident, the *Isaac Smith's* commanding officer, Lieutenant Francis S. Conover, wrote, "At a little after 4 I anchored opposite what is known as Tom Grimball's plantation, about 4½ miles from the inlet, and although the signal quartermaster was at the masthead as usual, as well as one or two of the officers, nothing suspicious was seen in any direction." Not quite a half hour later, however, a battery of three twenty-four-pounder rifled guns on John's Island, masked by a thick clump of trees, opened fire on the gunboat. The Confederates had set a trap for the Yankees, mounting guns in the marshes and concealing them from the view of vessels in the Stono River. Conover immediately got under way, cleared for action, and within minutes had his guns returning fire. When other rebel batteries also began shelling the *Isaac Smith*, Conover wrote, "I saw immediately that we were trapped, and that my only course was to get the vessels below the batteries if possible and fight them with a more even chance of success." At the bend of the river, however, gunfire from what Conover insisted were eight-inch twenty-four-, eighteen-, and twelve-pounders raked the *Isaac Smith*. Although he had "high hopes of getting by without any very serious loss," Conover reported that one shot had struck the steam chimney, stopping the engine, and "with no wind, little tide, and boats riddled with shot, we were left entirely to the mercy of the enemy." At this point Conover decided to surrender and would have blown up the *Smith* had it not been for the wounded men covering the berth deck. "I hardly need say, sir, that the order to haul down the colors was the most difficult and heartrending one I ever gave," he told Secretary Welles in his report.[47]

"We took prisoners her entire crew consisting of 11 officers, 105 men, and 3 negroes," Lieutenant Colonel Joseph Yates, the Confederate commander, wrote in his version of the *Isaac Smith's* capture. He enclosed a list of prisoners that included three wardroom stewards: William Wilson, O. H. Brown, and W. H. Johnson. Conover's May 7, 1863, report on the capture of the *Isaac Smith* also mentioned that "Joseph Mays (colored)," a landsman, died in the attack. Colonel Yates credited their success in capturing the Union gunboat to the Confederate batteries on John's Island and at Legare's Point, which scored three direct hits on the gunboat's machinery, at which point the ship dropped anchor and surrendered. The rebels towed the *Smith* up the Stono and put it under the guns of Fort Pemberton. The *Isaac Smith* served the Confederates as the *Stono* until it was wrecked attempting to run the blockade with a cargo of cotton near Fort Moultrie, South Carolina, on June 5, 1863.[48]

On February 15, 1863, Commander Bacon sent Du Pont some additional and very illuminating information about the *Isaac Smith*. "I have just learned from an old negro who lives on the western end of Kiawah Island," he wrote, "that five of the enemy came over to the plantation on which he is living a day or two since and stated the following, viz. The capture of the *Smith* is principally due to the man that deserted from her about two months ago, and who, it appears, has joined the rebels and told them how easily she might be captured by having batteries placed in different positions on the river." According to the black informant, the rebels knew that the *Smith's* boiler, machinery, and steering apparatus made it vulnerable, so they planned to allow the gunboat to pass up the river and capture it on the return trip by "either disabling her wheel or throwing shot into her boiler." Bacon added, "I give this as the old negro told me, and I think that his story in the main may be relied upon."[49]

The *Isaac Smith's* capture engendered a heated controversy when the Confederates refused to parole its officers and crew. Brigadier General Thomas Jordan, chief of staff for the Confederate Headquarters, Department of South Carolina, Georgia, and Florida, informed Conover that he could not be paroled, citing the following reasons: "The Army and Navy of the United States, under the late proclamation of your President, are instructed to assist slaves in servile waters against their lawful masters, which is not only a high crime under the local laws of the State in whose waters you were captured, but is condemned by all people as means or appliance of war wholly illegitimate between civilized nations." Those naval officers and men "who incite our slaves to rebellion against their masters" would, Jordan stated, be punished. Jordan told Conover that he and the others would be issued the usual rations allotted to prisoners of war.[50]

Within days of the *Isaac Smith*'s capture and the death of at least one (possibly two) black sailor, the Confederate ironclads *Chicora* and *Palmetto State* left Charleston to attack vessels of the South Atlantic Blockading Squadron, an action that would claim the lives of more African American sailors. Early on the morning of January 31, 1863, the *Palmetto State* attacked and forced the USS *Mercedita* to surrender. Meanwhile, the *Chicora* had turned its attention to the gunboat *Keystone State*, a 1,364-ton side-wheel steamer that, like many Union blockaders, had a number of black crewmen. When the *Keystone State*'s skipper, Commander William E. Le Roy, became suspicious of an unidentified ship, he took his steamer alongside the approaching vessel and hailed it. Not satisfied with the rebel ship's reply of "Hallo," and by now able to identify the vessel as a ram, Le Roy ordered the starboard bow gun fired, and the *Chicora* returned fire.

In a letter to his wife the *Keystone's State*'s executive officer, Lieutenant Commander Thomas H. Eastman, described the engagement with the *Chicora:* "I fired into him seven guns, one after the other, hitting him at the distance of 50 yards, without hurting him. He fired into us without more words and tried to ram us, but we evaded him. His shot set us on fire and we had to run before the wind to put it out." They continued working the guns, but when the *Keystone State* came within 300 yards of the *Chicora*, the rebels put a shot through both the *Keystone State*'s boilers. "Then we were done. The ship fell on her side, she had four large holes in her bottom, we could not move any more, and one-fourth of our strong crew were killed or wounded—hors du combat," Eastman wrote. Hit by ten enemy shells, its power lost and the forehold on fire, the *Keystone State* began to take on water. "Captain Le Roy (God bless him), out of pity for the dying and the dead, hauled down our flag; the ironclad fired two more shots into us. Then Le Roy ran the flag up and we went to work at him again."[51]

Fortunately, the *Augusta* and *Quaker City* arrived on the scene and opened fire on the rebel assailants while the *Memphis* towed the *Keystone State* out of the enemy's range. Both the *Mercedita* and the *Keystone State* suffered casualties in the attack. Four of the *Mercedita's* men died and three sustained wounds, but according to Le Roy, the *Keystone State's* casualties "were very large, some 20 killed and 20 wounded." This represented about one-fourth of the 163-man crew killed or wounded, including "Robert McKinsey, second-class boy (contraband), Robert Willinger, second-class boy, (contraband) scalded to death." The wounded included "Rendy Gould, second-class boy (contraband): slightly scalded face and hands."[52]

Confederate rams and shore batteries inflicted casualties on Union Navy officers and men throughout the war, but rebel sharpshooters hidden in brush and woods along southern riverbanks could also wound and kill with deadly precision. In December 1862, for example, a joint army-navy expedition with General John G. Foster's troops up the Neuse River cost one black sailor from the USS *Ellis* his life. Commander Alex Murray commanded the naval vessels supporting this operation to destroy fortifications at Kinston and railroad bridges and track near Goldsboro, North Carolina. Although Murray's gunboats could push only about fifteen miles up the river because of low water, the light-draft *Allison*, with a crew of sailors from the *Hetzel* under Gunner E. A. McDonald, managed to get within shelling distance of the rebel batteries four miles below Kinston. When the gunboat, accompanied by the army transports *Ocean Wave, Port Royal,* and *Wilson,* rounded a bend in the river, it came under fire from a ten-gun rebel battery. Lieutenant Colonel H. A. Manchester of the Marine Artillery ordered the other three vessels to retire and positioned the *Allison* between the battery and the boats. "The enemy's shell exploded over and around us with but little damage," Manchester reported. "The *Allison* received three shots, one taking off the tip of the pilot house, the next passing through the roof and through the smokestack, and the third cutting off some fenders and light work." While the three boats backed down the narrow river, the *Allison* returned fire with its one Parrott gun, forcing the rebels to cease firing. Confederate sharpshooters on the riverbanks wounded three sailors on the *Ocean Wave* and, according to Murray, also wounded James Lloyd, "a colored boy of the steamer *Ellis* (since dead)." The *Allison* and the other army transports then took up positions for the night and proceeded downriver the next morning. Despite steady fire from rebel soldiers sniping at them from the riverbanks, Colonel Manchester never wavered, his boats continuing down the river as his gunners fired back on the enemy with grape and canister. Despite one man killed and three severely wounded, Murray reported that this Neuse River expedition "has been tolerably fruitful in results; the demonstration on the river was, according to contraband accounts, startling to the enemy."[53]

Chasing blockade runners, capturing prizes, and participating in river expeditions or armed boat parties ashore may have been risky, but it relieved the monotony of blockade duty and improved a ship's morale. Union Navy forays up southern rivers and creeks often called for boat crews to bring landing parties ashore or conduct reconnaissance in narrow, shallow creeks. Although most naval commanders' official reports failed to note the composition of these armed boat parties, they occasionally mentioned the inclusion of contrabands. When John Rodgers led a night boat reconnaissance of the small rivers near Savannah, Georgia, in early 1862, he told his wife, Anne, "Our boat crew was composed of picked men, Wabashes (white) and contrabands." The party also included pilot John W. Godfrey, Lieutenant John S. Barnes, and Captain James H. Wilson of the U.S. Topographical Engineers. Tossed by the waves in Tybee Roads and with no land in sight, Rodgers told Anne, "We could neither return nor advance. In this embarrassing position a contraband pilot came to the rescue—'I can take you in Massa I born about here—I know dem rollers—they aint no wuse dan you see—dis bank is all flat—I know I can take you in.'" True to his word, the contraband guided them safely into the Wright River in dense fog and then into the Savannah River. "We were within reach of the guns of (Ft.) Pulaski—and with only a boat's crew, part of them contrabands," Rodgers wrote. Using their compass to guide them in the fog, Rodgers's party completed their reconnaissance and returned to the *Wabash*. On board the flagship, Rodgers told Du Pont that, in his opinion, shoal water prevented boats from easily reaching the Savannah River via Wall's Cut and Wright River.[54]

These small boat operations could expose Union sailors to enemy ambushes, sometimes with devastating consequences, especially for African American seamen. For example, on March 3, 1863, Acting Master's Mate H. H. Savage, commanding the schooner *Matthew Vassar*, sighted a large boat on the point of the island at Little River Inlet and sent Acting Master's Mate George Drain and a crew of seven men and one contraband to either capture or destroy the boat, "if possible, without any risk," and then return to the vessel. Drain destroyed the boat as ordered but then proceeded up the Western Branch toward a saltworks.

After going about 200 yards he grounded his boat on an oyster rock. Suddenly, Drain saw a party of armed men approaching the beach. "The men having no sidearms or bayonets, and but ten spare cartridges for their rifles, I deemed it prudent to surrender rather than have the men all shot down, and there was no possible chance to get out with the boat, the wind and tide being against us."[55]

Savage's version of the incident varied from Drain's account. "They landed and destroyed the boat without any resistance, and then started to come back, when they turned back again and proceeded up the river behind the island, which was contrary to my orders." Savage sent another armed boat to assist the first boat crew, then had two guns fired to signal a recall and drive any rebel soldiers away. The *Matthew Vassar's* first boat crew landed, but the men disappeared into the woods and were not seen or heard from again. "It is my opinion that they are captured and taken prisoners, as this morning the boat is to be seen up the river with a quantity of rebels in her," Savage told Captain B. F. Sands, senior officer off Wilmington. In his report Savage listed the boat's officer and crew, which included one contraband by the name of Jesse Smith.[56]

Drain, among those men taken prisoner, explained in his report to Lee that the entire episode had been a trap. "The day before I was captured, the boat was sent ashore to take off two negroes that were seen on the beach, and Master's Mate Draper reported that a white man came down on the beach at the time and said he would like to go off to the blockade fleet and take the oath of allegiance, but his brother-in-law was up at the salt works and he wanted to do the same, and if the boat was sent there the next day, they would both come off." Draper took the man at his word and let him go. Later, Drain learned from one of his prison guards "that this man was a corporal in their company, and that they came on the beach after 4 o'clock that morning to catch anyone that might come to the beach."[57]

Although African American sailors such as Jesse Smith often found themselves in harm's way, few commanding officers singled out black sailors for commendation. One exception was the report submitted by Lieutenant Roswell H. Lamson following an engagement with rebel forces during the defense of Suffolk, Virginia, in April 1863. Lamson commanded a flotilla of small gunboats in the Nansemond River off the town of Suffolk, defended at the time by a large Union garrison of 25,000 troops under the command of General John J. Peck. On April 13 Confederate general Longstreet's men occupied Fort Huger, located batteries along the Nansemond River, and attempted to cut off river communications from Suffolk.[58]

When Lamson took the *Mt. Washington, Stepping Stones, Cohasset,* and *Alert* up the Nansemond to prevent the Confederates from crossing the river below the Western Branch and threatening Suffolk, they encountered fire from Confederate guns along the river. Lamson's vessels headed back toward Suffolk, but as they tried to run past a fresh rebel earthwork, "the enemy opened fire from seven pieces of artillery which they rolled into the work from the woods." The rebel guns raked *Mt. Washington's* bow and shot pierced the boilers, shutting down the engines. Then, Lamson reported, "the vessel drifted against the bank, and the escaping steam and hot water drove almost everyone out of the vessel, but at my order they returned and opened fire from all our guns." After *Stepping Stones* towed *Mt. Washington* off the bank, they steamed back downriver under steady fire from enemy sharpshooters. Near the mouth of the Western Branch *Mt. Washington* grounded again, and the enemy opened fire with ten pieces of artillery, "throwing a cross fire into our vessels." Fearing that the ship would be immovable until the next high tide, Lamson sent all his crew except for the gunners over to the *Stepping Stones,* which he ordered downriver to a safe position.[59]

Guns from the *Commodore Barney* and *Mt. Washington* silenced an enemy battery, but about 3 P.M. the rebels opened fire from a new position. Lamson reported that "his sharpshooters poured in a most galling fire from the trees and rifle pits." When the *Stepping Stones* arrived around 5 P.M. to tow the grounded *Mt. Washington* off, it was hit numerous times by enemy gunfire and survived only because of the *Commodore Barney's* "well directed fire," which forced the enemy to shift position. In his report Lamson praised *Mt. Washington's* captain, officers, and crew for their courageous conduct during the engagement and wrote that, according to Third Assistant Engineer John Healey, "the only men who remained at their posts in the engine room were William Jackson and James Lody, both colored." Total Union Navy casualties were five killed, fourteen wounded, and one missing in action. Slightly injured were two African American sailors on the *Stepping Stones:* Giles Scott, a twenty-seven-year-old North Carolina native who had enlisted for one year in February 1863 as a first-class boy, and John Down, only sixteen years old, who had signed on the *Stepping Stones* in November 1862 as a third-class boy.[60]

At sundown on April 19 the aggressive Lamson landed with 300 infantry and four twelve-pounder boat howitzers at the junction of the Western Branch and the Nansemond. After a brief firefight they captured five pieces of rebel artillery at Hill's Point and took 137 rebel prisoners. General Getty's men subsequently seized the ground at Hill's Point and began fortifying it. In his report of the action, Getty acknowledged the important services rendered by the naval forces in the river, calling for "a tribute which they have richly merited. Lieutenants Cushing and Lamson and the officers and men of their command have shown that in their country's service they know no fear, and that the old breed of naval heroes is not extinct." Among those heroes were William Jackson and James Lody, the two black sailors who braved the shot and shell and stuck to their station in the *Mt. Washington* engine room.[61]

Union gunboat operations exposed navy officers and men, especially small boat crews, not only to the risk of attack from sharpshooters and rebel batteries but also to the possibility of capture by Confederate troops or guerrillas. Although evidence on the number of black sailors sent on such missions is scanty, reported incidents testify to the danger to contraband sailors, who faced abuse, a return to slavery, and possible death if captured. One of the most dramatic and tragic examples occurred in December 1863. In reporting the loss of three officers and twelve men, Acting Master Samuel Gregory of the brig *Perry* explained that he had sent two boats to Murrell's Inlet, South Carolina, to destroy a schooner reportedly being fitted out to run the blockade. After ordering the *Perry* to shell around the schooner, Gregory sent Acting Ensign Arrants, Ensign George Anderson, and a party of men to the beach to set fire to the schooner. He instructed the ensign to send one person ahead to scout and one or two men to set fire to the schooner and to keep the remainder in the boats. To Gregory's surprise, Arrants disobeyed his order, landing all but two of the first cutter's crew. In a matter of minutes, rebel cavalry "rushed down and surrounded them to cut off their retreat." The *Perry* scattered the attacking rebels with gunfire, but "after some hand to hand fighting our men surrendered, there being more than sixty in number of the cavalry." Expressing amazement that Arrants could have made "so great a mistake," Gregory told Rear Admiral John A. Dahlgren that his "precious son, a lad of 17 years of age, was among the number captured."[62]

Almost a year later Ensign Anderson provided important additional details about the Murrell's Inlet expedition. He had landed at Magnolia Beach, near Murrell's Inlet, on December 5, 1863, with two boats and twenty-two men accompanied by Arrants and two other officers. Gregory had ordered Arrants and Anderson "to take with us George Brimsmaid (colored landsman) to land on Magnolia beach, and to send him ahead unarmed, as a scout." Anderson landed with his men on the beach as instructed and stationed a landsman, Samuel Gregory Jr., with a signal flag and told him how and when to use it. The landing party then started for the schooner lying in Murrell's Inlet, but after only a short distance, Anderson saw young Gregory running toward them, "crying out that the enemy's cavalry were approaching from the southward." In his excitement, however, Gregory forgot to signal the *Perry*, so Anderson quickly seized the flag and tried to alert the ship. Before he could do so, he wrote, "we were charged by a company of cavalry and forced to retreat." While Anderson's men took refuge at the foot of a sand hill, one company of rebel cavalry charged the *Perry*'s boats and then rushed the bluejackets on the beach. After what he called "a brisk resistance," during which five men were wounded, Anderson chose to surrender. The rebel captain ordered one of the wounded sailors, John Pinkham, to stand up. "On replying that he could not, the captain shot him with his revolver, inflicting a wound from which he died a short time after." The rebels then marched Anderson and his men to their camp in the woods. There, Anderson reported, "George Brimsmaid (colored landsman) was taken from our party by two of the rebel cavalrymen and a man in citizen's dress. One of the rebels was seen to strike Brimsmaid over the head with his saber as they were taking him from the camp." A few minutes later the Union prisoners heard a loud yell and two gunshots. "The two rebels who took Brimsmaid soon returned, and stated that they had hung him and then shot him." Several officers of the Confederate command confirmed this shocking news.[63]

Stinging from the loss of the *Perry*'s boat crews at Murrell's Inlet and the earlier capture of a boat crew from the *T. A. Ward*, Admiral Dahlgren decided to retaliate. Two days before Christmas he ordered Captain J. F. Green, the senior officer off Charleston bar, to organize a retaliatory expedition to Murrell's Inlet "to administer some corrective to the small parties of rebels who infest that vicinity." Dahlgren detailed the steamers *Nipsic, Sanford, Geranium,* and *Daffodil;* the sailing bark *Allen;* and the schooner *George Mangham* with 100 marines, four howitzers, and as many boats as needed for the expedition. Dahlgren gave specific orders to "take possession of whatever arms and ammunition may be within reach, and afford every facility to the colored people for the enjoyment of privileges held out by law and the proclamation of the president."[64]

On the afternoon of December 30, 1863, as ordered, Captain Green went to Murrell's Inlet with a landing force of 250 men. The schooner *George Mangham,* commanded by Acting Master John Collins Jr., joined them at the inlet. To everyone's disappointment, poor weather canceled their first retaliatory boat expedition and forced Green's vessels to retire to a safe anchorage some twenty miles distant. On New Year's Day 1864, however, the *Nipsic* returned to Murrell's Inlet to find a rebel schooner "loaded with a cargo of turpentine, awaiting an opportunity to evade the blockade and proceed to Nassau." The *Nipsic* shelled the schooner but could not set it on fire because a sand spit concealed its hull. Determined to destroy the schooner, Commander Spotts sent the *Nipsic's* executive officer, Master Churchill, with an eighty-man party that included a contingent of marines to finish the job. When the marines opened fire with a howitzer on the turpentine-filled schooner, it burst into flames. The landing party returned to the *Nipsic* to report "mission accomplished." The success of this retaliatory expedition to Murrell's Inlet pleased Dahlgren, who wrote to Welles, "I trust this correction will serve to moderate any gratification which the rebels may have derived from the capture of our boat's crew."[65]

At the time Dahlgren ordered this retaliatory raid, he knew that one of the *Perry's* African American crewmen, George Brimsmaid, had been captured, but he was apparently unaware that the rebels had hung him. Two days later, perhaps in response to rumors, the admiral fired off a letter to Gregory, asking for information about the capture and hanging of a black man belonging to the *Perry*. Gregory promptly replied, "I beg leave to state that there was 'a colored' man captured belonging to the boat's crew, but I have no evidence that he was hung. All that I have in regard to him was a rumor, coming from the U.S.S. *Nipsic,* that he was hung immediately after capture." Gregory followed this report with a second one written the same day informing Dahlgren that "Brimsmaid, captured at Murrell's Inlet, was a colored man from New London, Conn., shipped on as a landsman on board the *North Carolina* September, 24, 1863, was transferred to this vessel *(Perry)* from there October 29, 1863, aged 23 years. Had been interrogated as to whether he was a slave, and he said he never had been one. He had no arms when captured."[66]

Few Civil War letters from black sailors have survived, but several letters to the *Christian Recorder* from George W. Reed, an African American drummer serving on board the USS *Commodore Read,* offer detailed accounts of raids conducted by his ship in 1864. When he enlisted at Washington, his birthplace, in October 1863, Reed told the navy he was twenty-one years old, five feet four inches tall, and a barber. In a May 14, 1864, letter to the *Christian Recorder,* Reed described the actions of a landing party from the *Commodore Read.* Being the ship's drummer, Reed's duty included beating the call for all parties to go ashore. "No sooner than I had executed the order," he wrote, "than every man was at his post, our own color being first to land." Reed also made an insightful comment about race relations: "At first there was a little prejudice against our colored men going on shore, but it soon died away." Few Union Navy reports included information about African American sailors in landing parties or boat parties, so Reed's observations are of particular interest. "We have been on several expeditions recently," he wrote. "On the 15th of April our ship and other gunboats proceeded up the Rappahannock River for some distance, and finding no rebel batteries to oppose us, we concluded to land the men from different boats and make a raid." According to Commander Foxhall Parker, the expedition left on April 18, 1864, in search of rebels rumored to be establishing a ferry at Circus Point a few miles below Tappahannock and collecting boats there for the purpose of attacking federal blockading vessels. Parker's flotilla visited both banks of the river and all its various creeks from Circus Point to Windmill Point, remaining in the area until the evening of April 22. Pleased with the results of the expedition, Parker reported to Navy Secretary Welles that they had broken up two ferries and a number of smaller craft, destroyed 300 barrels of corn, and brought away twenty-two boats, 1,000 pounds of bacon, two horses, sixty bushels of wheat, and many other articles, including "five refugees and 45 contrabands (men, women, and children)." They landed these refugees in Maryland, the commander stated, "with the exception of five stout fellows, whom I shipped."[67]

In his letter to the *Christian Recorder*, Reed provided additional details of the raid, including the fact that the *Read* had "succeeded in liberating from the horrible pit of bondage 10 men, 6 women, and 8 children. The principal part of the men have enlisted on this ship." According to drummer Reed's account, "The next day, we started up the river, when the gunboat in advance struck a torpedo, but did no material damage." Reed then described their next action: "We landed our men again, and repulsed a band of rebels handsomely, and captured three prisoners. Going on a little further, we were surprised by 300 rebel cavalry, and repulsed, but retreated in good order, the gunboats covering our retreat." Parker estimated the rebel cavalry force to be around 500 men, "kept at bay by the fire of the *Eureka*," he wrote, "commanded by Acting Ensign Isaac Hallock, and a howitzer launch in charge of Acting Master's Mate Eldridge." The skirmish resulted in a very personal loss for Reed, who wrote, "I regret to say that we had the misfortune to lose Samuel Turner (colored) in our retreat. He was instantly killed, and his body remains in the rebel hands. He being a fifer, I miss him very much as a friend and companion, as he was beloved by all on board. We also had four slightly wounded."[68]

Although the navy assigned a large number of black sailors to duty as cooks, wardroom boys, and officers' servants, others served in the engine room as coal heavers or as carpenters and deck hands. Their station during general quarters varied, but some commanders assigned black sailors to gun crews on their ships. In his memoirs, Lieutenant Daniel Ammen specifically mentioned the assignment of contrabands to gun crews on the USS *Sebago,* one of the first "double-ender" gunboats. Ammen had assumed command of the *Sebago* in August 1862 and lamented that although the gunboat had been in commission seven or eight months, it had had several indifferent commanders. As a result, the neglected crew had become inefficient and unhappy, but Ammen set about improving conditions on board. "I applied for and obtained four additional nine-inch broadside guns," he wrote, "with 'contrabands' equal to the complement of men for them. In six weeks the men were anxious to go into a fight."[69]

On one occasion the commanding officer of a federal gunboat specifically mentioned the contribution of a contraband sailor in his ship's gun crew. When two rebel batteries of field and siege artillery on St. John's Island in the Stono River celebrated Christmas 1863 by taking potshots at the screw gunboat *Marblehead,* Lieutenant Commander Richard W. Meade Jr. ordered his crew to open fire and reply "vigorously to the enemy." Closing the range, the *Marblehead* slugged it out with the rebel gunners for an hour. After the engagement, Meade commended his officers and men for their "gallantry and good service," specifically mentioning the officers of the gun divisions and Boatswain's Mate William Farley, Quartermaster James Miller, Joseph Bouden (the sailmaker), and "Robert Blake, a contraband, [who] excited my admiration by the cool and brave manner in which he served the rifle gun." The *Marblehead* suffered three men killed and four wounded. Four of the *Marblehead's* crew won Medals of Honor for bravery in the engagement, including Blake, who was born a slave in Santee, South Carolina, and enlisted in the navy while on North Island. He was serving as steward for Meade and during the engagement was knocked down by the explosion of a rebel shell, which killed a powder boy at one of the guns. Blake could have gone below to safety but chose to take the powder boy's place, bringing powder boxes to the gun loaders. Although Blake was the first African American to actually receive a Medal of Honor, Sergeant William Harvey Carney's Medal of Honor action took place before Blake's, but he did not receive his medal until 1900.[70]

Not all Union Navy casualties occurred during engagements with enemy batteries or rebel sharpshooters. Dozens of Union sailors died or suffered injuries when their ships sank or struck "torpedoes" in rivers and sounds. One of the most famous losses occurred on December 30, 1862, when the ironclad *Monitor* sank during a storm off Cape Hatteras. The *Rhode Island,* which had been towing the ship, launched its boats and rescued forty-seven of the *Monitor's* crew, but another sixteen drowned. Eight men from the *Rhode Island's* cutter also went missing. Among the *Monitor* crewmen listed as missing was an African American, Robert H. Cook, a native of Gloucester County, Virginia. Cook, rated a first-class boy, had enlisted for three years at age eighteen in September 1862 at Hampton Roads. Robert H. Howard, an African American officer's cook, was also reported missing.[71]

Although storms battered and sank Union ships and Confederate shellfire, musketry, shrapnel, and mines inflicted hundreds of casualties in the North and South Atlantic Blockading Squadrons during the Civil War, accidents and disease incapacitated or killed even more bluejackets than combat did. In his journal, Dr. Samuel Boyer recorded many observations about his patients, both sailors on the bark *Fernandina* and African Americans ashore. On May 1, 1863, he wrote, "I placed Alexander Jackson, a contraband, on the binnacle list for the night, he suffering from the effects of a swollen gum, hence not fit for duty in the night air. Jackson as a general thing is a good-natured sort of a darkey, consequently a favorite with all on board."[72]

Similarly, surgeon Ashael Sumner Dean, who served of the USS *Harvest Moon,* noted that in addition to those on the ship he had "to look for the sick on the tugs who hang about us as tenders." He wrote, "We have two or three always and we are a headquarters for all the refugees, prisoners and contrabands. So usually more than half my practise is outside the Ship's Company." Dean's comments about his African American patients are most interesting. "You ought to be disabused of the notion that Negroes stand the climate and exposure better than our men," he wrote to Virginia. "Nothing is farther from the truth. The mortality among them both in the Army and Navy is three times greater than with the whites. Negroes can't go where white men can, can't do so much hard work. Half of them are either consumptive or scrofulous, out of 24 plantation Negroes I found only 7 who would be able to do service as Lands Men in the Navy and they were quite an average lot. More Negroes die than white sailors and they have the same food and clothing." There is some evidence supporting Dean's assertion that the mortality rate was higher among black sailors than among white. In one sample of sailors recruited from several northern states, 8 percent of the black sailors died during their term of service, compared with 5 percent of the white sailors. According to historian Steven Ramold, the greatest difference in mortality between black and white sailors occurred in Illinois—14 percent versus 10 percent. He attributes this figure to the large number of slaves enlisting from Illinois and to their service in the Mississippi Squadron, which saw a number of casualties from "close-in fighting" engagements with the rebels.[73]

On occasion, army officers visiting Union vessels treated contrabands and sailors. For example, John Chipman Gray wrote to his mother on December 14, 1864, from headquarters at Hilton Head, South Carolina: "On the 11th I went on aboard the *Canandaigua,* a sloop of war and dined. . . . The night was very cold, the thermometer being at 25 degrees at seven in the morning and almost all the servants were taken sick in consequence, and when a darkey is sick he always thinks he is going to die. But by a liberal but somewhat indiscriminate use of whiskey, ginger, castor oil and hot flannels prescribed by me, they have mostly recovered from their various head, tooth, chest and stomaches."[74]

Union Navy surgeons treated a variety of serious illnesses, including scurvy, yellow fever, typhus, and smallpox. Cases of scurvy appeared on blockading vessels from time to time despite the knowledge that the condition resulted from a lack of vitamin C in the diet. The navy had a supply system to replenish stores for both the North and South Atlantic Blockading Squadrons, but once the supplies were delivered to ports such as Port Royal, they had to be distributed to the individual ships. This distribution process kept ships well supplied in many but not all cases. When vessels grew low on provisions, the lack of fresh fruits and vegetables contributed to numerous cases of scurvy. In January 1862 Welles brought the problem to the attention of Secretary of the Treasury Salmon P. Chase. "The crews of some of our vessels at Port Royal and that vicinity are suffering from scurvy," he wrote, and requested that a license be granted to responsible parties to trade with vessels taking the fresh supplies to his ships.[75]

During McClellan's Peninsular Campaign, cases of scurvy occurred among officers and men on Union gunboats and ironclads of the James River Flotilla. Fleet Surgeon William Maxwell Wood, surveying the men of the flotilla in late July 1862, reported that personnel were suffering from diarrhea, dysentery, typhoid fever, and scurvy. Noting that the navy had the ability to supply the ships with fresh provisions, Wood recommended that fresh vegetables be sent to the flotilla twice a week. To promote better health and discourage cases of diarrhea, Wood also suggested that the practice of using river water for drinking be discontinued in favor of distilling water from ships' condensers. In an endorsement, J. C. Spear, the assistant surgeon, reported several mild cases of scurvy.

"The persons attacked are contrabands and convalescent patients," he wrote. Spear attributed the scurvy to the men's dislike of fresh canned beef and desiccated vegetables. He recommended that the crews be provided with more canned tomatoes, which "are specially good, and one of the very best anti-scorbutics."[76]

Knowing the value of vitamin C in preventing the scurvy, on at least one occasion naval surgeon Samuel G. Webber took the opportunity to purchase citrus fruits: "I bought 160 limes today for 50 cts and then sold half to a messmate for a quarter. So I can have lemonade every day for twenty days," he wrote to his wife in July 1863. Although Webber did not identify the source of these limes, they may have been purchased from local African Americans coming alongside his ship, the USS *Rhode Island*, or from vendors ashore.[77]

Not all naval officers were as fortunate as Webber in obtaining fresh supplies. By midsummer 1862, for example, vessels of the James River Squadron were getting very low on provisions. "Calling upon our Steward for edibles is like calling spirits from the vasty deep—they don't answer the call," William Keeler told his wife in a letter dated July 30, 1862. Furthermore, the diet of *Monitor*'s crew had been woefully lacking in fruits and vegetables for months. Keeler confided to his wife that he "had hardly had a taste of anything green this summer. When I came up from Old Point Comfort I brought with me a bbl. filled with a mess or two of well ripened, well wilted peas, a few cucumbers, some cabbage, lettuce & beets, these for a mess of Sixteen did not last long. This is the extent of my vegetarian experience this summer." Yet, along the banks of the James River, the sailors could clearly see the estates and plantations of wealthy southerners and fields of corn and wheat.[78]

Although navy store ships such as the *Massachusetts* brought ice, fresh food, and other supplies to the blockading squadrons, fresh fruits and vegetables could be a scarce commodity. Writing to his wife from the monitor *Nahant* off Charleston Harbor in October 1864, Webber shared a bit of good news: "Dr. P received a basket of peaches by the *Donegal*. He gave me two or three. They are the only peaches except canned I have had for two years."[79]

For some fortunate Union gunboat crews, patrolling southern rivers and creeks meant opportunities to go fishing or to venture ashore to hunt or to procure fresh produce or livestock. In one instance, however, a foraging expedition ashore by men from the USS *Lenapee* resulted in a near tragedy. In mid-March 1865 the ship had gone up the Cape Fear River past "many fine plantations," Assistant Surgeon Stephen Bartlett wrote to his parents. "We landed several times and helped ourselves to sheep cattle hogs &c for the country up here is full of them and we certainly don't go hungry." On a trip ashore about fifteen miles from town, the *Lenapee's* executive officer was accidentally shot by one of the men. "I was near him at the time and the first to reach him," Bartlett told his parents. "He was struck in the neck and fell like a dead man." Fortunately, Bartlett was able to stop the bleeding. "Got him on board and removed the Ball," he reported. "He is not dangerously hurt, but I recommended he be sent home to recover. We did not stop to take our stock on board, they are left for the crows and negroes." In this case, the hasty departure of the *Lenapee's* foraging party benefited local blacks, but in many other instances, sailors undoubtedly took produce and livestock from whites and blacks living along the riverbanks or near the coast that likely caused deprivation and resentment among local planters and slaves.[80]

More than any other illness, Union Navy doctors feared smallpox. By the mid-nineteenth century the smallpox vaccine had substantially reduced outbreaks of the disease, but cases did occur, and the possibility of smallpox spreading among soldiers in army camps and prisons or sailors on shipboard represented a distinct threat. Smallpox was more common among African American troops and contrabands. Statistics for the Union Army from May 1861 to June 1866 indicate a higher incidence of smallpox among black troops—12,236 reported cases among white troops, or 5.5 per thousand men annually, versus 6,716 cases among U.S. Colored Troops, or 36.6 per thousand men annually. When the war began and states rushed to send troops into the field, Union physicians discovered that many of the recruits had not been vaccinated against smallpox. Although army regulations called for the vaccination or, if necessary, revaccination of troops, not all states managed to comply. Smallpox appears to have been more prevalent among contrabands because owners did not always vaccinate their slaves. The necessity of vaccinating contrabands became apparent early in the war when Union forces occupied areas of the South populated by large numbers of African Americans. Smallpox spread easily in the less-than-sanitary conditions of contraband camps. Secondhand shops also sold contraband clothing infected with the smallpox virus, which could live for eighteen months, spreading the disease even farther.[81]

To prevent the spread of the disease, Union Navy and Union Army physicians took the precaution of vaccinating contrabands whenever possible. George Harlan, a navy surgeon who resigned his commission in August 1861 to join an army cavalry unit, wrote to his wife from Camp Hamilton at Fortress Monroe: "I vaccinated eight or ten little contrabands in a house near the hospital the other day . . . they were the cutest little . . . I ever saw. Their owner, a large property owner near Hampton left them behind in his flight to secesh and their mothers are making a living washing for officers. One of the women was very pleased and said her 'old marster was a great hand for vaccination.'"[82]

Serious diseases such as smallpox occasionally spread from the civilian population to crewmen of Union vessels, most often to black sailors exposed to the disease while visiting friends or relatives ashore. Cases of smallpox, for example, kept the USS *Keystone State* at Hampton Roads in January 1862, preventing it from rejoining the South Atlantic Blockading Squadron until the disease, in Secretary Welles's words, "disappeared from among her crew." On October 19, 1863, Captain B. F. Sands, the senior officer off New Inlet, reported a similar outbreak to Admiral Lee and stated that the *Dacotah* would have to leave the inlet "for a time, to seek a harbor where my sick may be nursed, having this morning 33 cases of varioloid, or smallpox, among the crew. The cases are not now very violent, but there is apprehension of its increase. Should it spread more, or increase in virulence, I will be obliged to seek Beaufort, or probably Norfolk, to recuperate." Sands assured the admiral that he would remain as long as possible on station, "as I should regret very much the necessity to leave the blockade, where every vessel, and more if we can get them, is so much needed."[83]

Other cases of smallpox occurred in late 1863, prompting Lee to write to Fleet Surgeon Wood on board the USS *Minnesota.* "I am informed by General Butler that the varioloid, or smallpox, is prevailing among the contrabands in this vicinity," Lee told Wood on December 9, 1863. "It has further been reported to me that there were four cases (two decided) among colored men on board the *Commodore Barney,* which has just come from the navy yard." In view of these facts, Lee asked for suggestions regarding sanitary regulations, because smallpox is spread not only by airborne virus-laden droplets but also by contaminated clothing and bedding. Lee told Wood that General Butler could provide vaccines if necessary, but as a precaution, he ordered the *Barney* to the naval hospital at Gosport. The next day Lee forwarded this correspondence to Welles to inform him of the measures being taken to deal with smallpox, "which has appeared in this neighborhood among the contraband camps and of which four cases have occurred on board the *Commodore Barney* among colored men." Lee then assured Welles that precautionary measures advised by the fleet surgeon had been ordered. In his reply Wood told Lee that the surgeon at Gosport had refused the smallpox cases, so he had sent them to the pest house at Fort Monroe. Wood carefully

explained to the admiral that he had ordered the entire squadron vaccinated during November, "so there are no other precautions to be taken
than to prohibit intercourse with Newport News, and to prohibit, for ten
days at least, promiscuous visiting or traveling to the *Barney*."[84]

In view of the outbreak of smallpox in 1863, the North Atlantic Blockading Squadron issued new guidelines in 1864 for handling cases of this
highly contagious disease. These guidelines instructed commanders to
order sailors determined to have smallpox into a three-week quarantine
at an army smallpox hospital. Despite precautions, smallpox continued
to break out occasionally on Union Navy vessels for the remainder of the
war. "Cases of smallpox among the negro mess boys were reported to
the Doctor and we put into Beaufort NC on Feb 17, 1864," wrote Calvin
Hutchinson, serving on the USS *Pequot* at the time. "No white men had
the disease but we were sick with mumps, measles, frostbite, and colds
from watches in wet clothes. We were put in quarantine and all were
vaccinated, the small pox cases were sent to a shore hospital where two
of them died. . . . The *Dacotah*, anchored near us, was also quarantined
with the same disease."[85]

An incidence of smallpox at Port Royal in 1864 prompted Webber
to take precautionary action. "Today I vaccinated the crew, all except six
who were on duty," he told his wife in a letter dated August 16, 1864.
"I believe I mentioned that there is smallpox at Port Royal & as there
is constant communication between here and there I thought it safest
to do this. It took me about two hours." In a later letter Webber told
Nannie, "The small pox is no longer here. You were mistaken though
in supposing that the disease was on shore. It was among the vessels. A
quarantine was established & there are no more cases in the harbor now.
At least I was told so and the yellow flag (sign of contagious disease) is
only on board the quarantine ship."[86]

During the Civil War the Union Navy provided both black and white
sailors with similar medical care, whether they suffered from smallpox,
typhus, yellow fever, or other illnesses or from injuries sustained in accidents or combat. Black bluejackets also received the same uniforms and
rations (including the grog ration, until it was abolished in 1862) as their
white counterparts. The navy's equal treatment of African Americans
and other persons of color stemmed in part from the antebellum navy's
practice of recruiting and enlisting black men, largely free blacks and
those from foreign ports. The wartime need to fill crews for an increasing number of vessels prompted the Union Navy to eliminate quotas and
to recruit as many free blacks, former slaves, and foreign persons of color

as could be induced to enlist. By 1864 African American sailors, many of them contrabands, made up a significant portion of Union Navy crews. In some federal ships, such as the *Commodore Read,* blacks composed the majority of the ship's complement. Reluctant at first to rate them higher than "boy," the Union Navy assigned black sailors to menial tasks as wardroom boys, servants to officers, cooks, and picket boat crews. These were traditional roles for African Americans, whether free northern blacks who listed their pre-enlistment occupations as waiters or laborers, or former slaves who had been field hands, house servants, and cooks. However, during the Civil War the Union Navy discovered that blacks could also serve as skilled mariners, carpenters, caulkers, machinists, pilots, and guides. The navy welcomed and employed these individuals and gradually promoted black sailors to landsmen and even petty officers. In a policy similar to that of the Union Army, which assigned white officers to black regiments, the navy did not commission any African Americans as officers.

In addition to serving the navy as servants, wardroom stewards, cooks, and stokers, black sailors played a role as entertainers and morale boosters to Union officers and crews, who enjoyed and often commented on their singing and dancing. Contraband sailors familiar with the local waterways and countryside also served as guides for hunting and fishing parties and foraging expeditions ashore, providing Union officers and crewmen with fresh meat and local produce.

Black sailors carved out roles for themselves as warriors, serving in gun crews, in armed boat parties, and as guides during raids ashore. In addition to these raids and armed expeditions up southern rivers and creeks, Union Navy vessels participated in major operations against Charleston and Wilmington, which entailed serious risks to gunboats and ironclad monitors alike. They also conducted joint operations with Union Army units, including regiments of U.S. Colored Troops. In these bombardments and engagements, African American sailors were no more immune to injury or death than their white counterparts.[87]

CHAPTER 8
JOINT ARMY-NAVY OPERATIONS

I tol' him [General Benjamin F. Butler] *it would be a black man's war 'fore dey got thru.*

—*Henry Jarvis*

Enforcing a blockade of the southern coast constituted the Union Navy's principal Civil War mission, but federal gunboats and other vessels frequently supported Union Army operations by providing gunfire support, convoying and landing troops, defending army depots and supply bases, and participating in joint army-navy expeditions or raids into the interior. In addition to previously discussed joint operations, Union Navy vessels cooperated with the army in attacks on James Island and Fort Fisher, the capture of Fort Pulaski and Plymouth, North Carolina, and dozens of smaller operations. African Americans provided intelligence that prompted or supported these operations, contributed to them by acting as guides, and served as crewmen on navy vessels or as rank-and-file soldiers in U.S. Colored Troop units. On more than one occasion these missions included liberating slaves as a means of recruiting able-bodied men for the newly formed black army regiments. As more of these black regiments were created, these expeditions increasingly included African American infantry units, accompanied occasionally by cavalry or artillery. Transporting black soldiers up the narrow rivers and creeks of the South could be a risky endeavor, but it gave naval officers and sailors an opportunity to become acquainted with their army counterparts both white and black. Furthermore, these joint operations offered black sailors a rare chance to meet and fight with their African American counterparts in the Union Army.[1]

The first of these army-navy expeditions with black troops came shortly after the announcement of the Emancipation Proclamation on

January 1, 1863. About this time, the commander of the First South Carolina Volunteers, Colonel Thomas Wentworth Higginson, wrote that General David Hunter had consented to send his black troops on an expedition up the St. Mary's River "to pick up cotton, lumber, and, above all, recruits." The raid was supposed to be a secret, and Higginson had asked General Rufus Saxton to be "as mum as I am and not a soul in the regiment has dared to ask me about it." The St. Mary's expedition may have been the idea of Corporal Robert Sutton, a former slave and now a member of the First South Carolina Volunteers. The corporal had reason to believe that a large supply of lumber could be found up the St. Mary's River, where, before his escape to Union lines, Sutton had been employed. In his memoirs Higginson related the story of Sutton's escape using a dugout canoe to leave a plantation at Woodstock and travel down the St. Mary's River; he later returned to take his wife and children out of bondage. "And up this river he was always imploring to be allowed to guide an expedition," Higginson wrote.[2]

On January 23, 1863, Higginson embarked 462 black soldiers of the First South Carolina Volunteers at Beaufort on three steamers—*Ben De Ford,* the army gunboat *John Adams,* and the captured *Planter.* They stopped first at St. Simon's Sound, where Higginson met with Acting Lieutenant William Budd of the *Potomska* and Acting Master Moses of the bark *Fernandina.* In his memoirs Higginson noted that Budd and Moses "made valuable suggestions in regard to the different rivers along the coast, and gave vivid descriptions of the last previous trip up the St. Mary's undertaken by Captain Stevens, U.S.N., in the gunboat *Ottawa,* when he had to fight his way past batteries at every bluff in descending the narrow and rapid stream." Budd and Moses warned the colonel to expect enemy opposition on his return downriver and cautioned him about underestimating the Confederates, who had dug rifle pits along the banks from which it was all but impossible to dislodge them.[3]

When the *Planter* arrived, Higginson's little flotilla left for Fort Clinch, where he transferred 200 of his men to the *John Adams* before proceeding to the St. Mary's River, hoping to catch the enemy by surprise. The colonel had planned more than a mere foraging expedition for his unseasoned black troops. He wished, he wrote, "to get them under fire as soon as possible, and to teach them, by a few small successes, the application of what they had learned in camp." Just below Township Landing, Higginson sent an advance detachment ashore under Captain Sutton. When Higginson finally went ashore, Sutton met him and informed him that a black man in a neighboring cabin had just come from the rebel camp and could provide them with "the latest information." At midnight they set off into the pine woods with Sutton and "his captured negro guide whose fear and sullenness had yielded to the magic news of the President's Proclamation, then just issued." Governor Andrew had sent Higginson a large printed supply of the proclamation and, he recalled, "we seldom found men who could read it, but they all seemed to feel more secure when they held it in their hands." After marching a distance they ran into rebel cavalry. The two groups exchanged fire before the Confederates disappeared. With the element of surprise now lost, and under orders from Saxton "to risk as little as possible in this first enterprise" with his black troops, Higginson decided to withdraw his men. They returned to the landing, taking with them the wounded men and the body of Private William Parsons of Company G, who had been killed in the encounter. Although the expedition had not liberated any local blacks, Higginson was pleased with his men's reaction to their first, if brief, "stand up fight." He later wrote, "Hereafter it was of small importance what nonsense might be talked or written about colored troops; so long as mine did not flinch, it made no difference to me."[4]

Higginson's First South Carolina Volunteers made a second trip up the St. Mary's River at the end of January 1863 to a brickyard, where they intended to obtain bricks reportedly made for Fort Clinch. Corporal Sutton, the former slave, piloted them up the river. In his journal the colonel wrote that the men took a flock of sheep, a cannon, and a flag but left $50,000 worth of southern pine. "I did not injure anything except the feelings of the inhabitants," he wrote, "who did chafe at the complexion of my guards and blackguards, though the men behaved admirably [and] even one who threatened to throw an old termagent into the river took care to add the epithet 'madam.'" Higginson noted, "We found but few colored people in this vicinity," some of whom they brought with them, but "an old man and woman preferred to remain." The expedition located the brickyard, loaded as many bricks as possible, and went back downriver. Rebels on the Georgia side of the river fired on the *John Adams* during the return trip and killed the captain, but in Saxton's mind, the mission had accomplished every objective he had in mind. In fact, although Higginson's two expeditions with the First South Carolina Volunteers had no direct Union Navy support, they did a great deal to vindicate the use of black troops and encourage future joint operations. Eventually, army-navy operations with black infantry units became commonplace for vessels in both the North and South Atlantic Blockading Squadrons.[5]

Several months after Higginson's raids the Union established the Bureau for Colored Troops and, except for three regiments of state

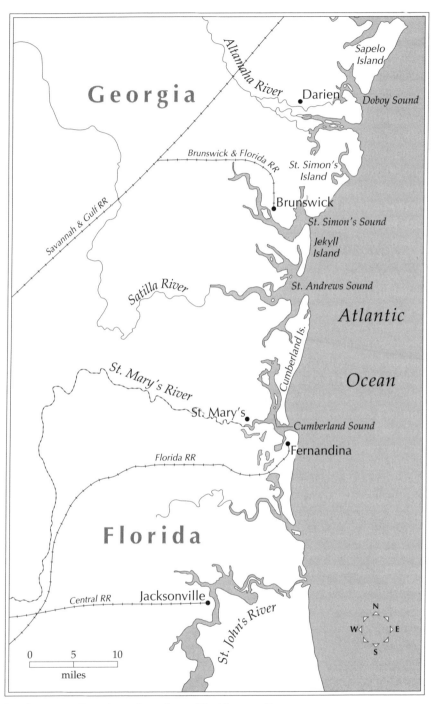

Southeastern Georgia and northern Florida coastline

troops, redesignated all black regiments as United States Colored Troops (USCT). Among the first units to join the Union Army in May 1863 was the Second Infantry Regiment, South Carolina Colored Volunteers, organized at Beaufort and Hilton Head and commanded by Colonel James M. Montgomery. This unit later became the Thirty-fourth U.S. Colored Troops. The first regiment of black troops to be raised in the North was mustered into federal service on May 13, 1863, as the Fifty-fourth Regiment of Massachusetts Volunteers. In early June 1863 the Fifty-fourth went south and arrived in Port Royal after a seven-day voyage from Boston. Among its members was twenty-seven-year-old James Henry Gooding, a native of Troy, New York, who had gone to sea in 1856 with the New Bedford whaling fleet. Instead of joining the Union Navy, Gooding walked into the Bedford recruiting office on Valentine's Day 1863 and enlisted in the Fifty-fourth Massachusetts Regiment. An educated, well-traveled black man, Gooding recorded his experiences in letters sent to the *New Bedford Mercury*.

After landing on June 8, 1863, at Beaufort, South Carolina, the Fifty-fourth Massachusetts marched to a campground about a quarter mile out of town. "Our reception was almost as enthusiastic here in Beaufort, as our departure from Boston was," Gooding recalled. Their arrival caused a quite a stir. "When the 54th marched through the streets of this town, the citizens and soldiers lined the walks, to get a look at the first black regiment from the North," According to Gooding, "The contrabands did not believe we were coming; one of them said, 'I neber bleeve black Yankee come here help culer men.'" Noting that the Copperhead press had spun tales "that the slaves were better satisfied in their old condition than under the present order of things," Gooding told readers that the contrabands "appear to understand the causes of the war better than a great many Northern editors."[6]

In reporting the safe arrival of the Fifty-fourth to Governor Andrew of Massachusetts, General Hunter referred to a dispatch he had received from Montgomery of the Second South Carolina Volunteers. Hunter then revealed to the governor his overall strategy: "Col. Montgomery's is but the initial step of a system of operations which will rapidly compel the rebels either to lay down their arms and sue for the restoration to the Union or to withdraw their slaves into the interior, thus leaving desolate the most fertile and productive of their counties along the Atlantic seaboard." Montgomery had just returned from a raid up the Combahee River into the interior with 250 soldiers of the Second South Carolina Volunteers and a section of the Third Rhode Island battery. They had advanced twenty-five miles into the interior, burned a bridge across the Combahee River, and liberated a vast amount of cotton, rice, and other property. Montgomery had also brought back with him 727 slaves and five horses. These former slaves, still clothed in "their field suits of dirty gray," were accompanied by a tiny black woman, known to some as "Moses" but to most as Harriet Tubman. According to sources, the slaves had come running to the river at the sound of the gunboats' whistles. Among the slaves "carried off by the Yankees" were 199 men, women, and children from Cypress Plantation.[7]

Hunter included the newly arrived Fifty-fourth Massachusetts, commanded by Colonel Robert Gould Shaw, in his plan to reclaim coastal counties for the Union. On June 9, 1863, the men of the Fifty-fourth reported to Montgomery on St. Simon's Island. The following day, leaving two companies to guard their camp, the Fifty-fourth boarded the *John Adams* with five companies of Montgomery's Second South Carolina Volunteers. "We landed on the main land, at a small town, named Darien, about 50 miles from here by water, but only about 20 miles over land," Corporal Gooding wrote. The rebels had fled, warned perhaps by the arrival of the regiment at St. Simon's. "After our forces landed, there was not more than 20 inhabitants to be seen in the place, the most were slaves and women; so there was no chance to show what sort of fighting material the Fifty-fourth is made of." Finding Darien deserted, Montgomery sent out foraging parties, which soon returned with a quantity of loot. According to Gooding, they burned books, pictures, furniture, and household property. "The town of Darien is no more," Gooding wrote to the *Mercury* on June 14. "The flames could be distinctly seen from the camp on the Island from three o'clock in the afternoon til daylight the next morning."[8]

The Union Navy was not responsible for the burning of Darien. Orders to set fire to the town had come from Montgomery, who said, "Southerners must be made to feel that this is a real war and that [they] are to be swept away by the hand of God like the Jews of old." When Shaw questioned Montgomery's slash-and-burn policy, Montgomery replied that he and his men were outlawed and thus not bound by the rules of warfare. This provoked Shaw to write to Governor Andrew and Hunter's adjutant, Colonel Halpine, reminding them of their promise that the Fifty-fourth Massachusetts would have honorable work. In fact, the Fifty-fourth Massachusetts did not accompany Montgomery's troops on anymore raids but settled in to a pleasant camp life on St. Simon's Island. Then, on June 24, 1863, they were shipped north to St. Helena Island, across Port Royal Sound from Hilton Head.[9]

Joint army-navy raids into the interior were not the exclusive mission of the South Atlantic Blockading Squadron. Ships and gunboats of the North Atlantic Blockading Squadron also supported army movements ashore and engaged in operations designed to liberate slaves and to suppress the activities of rebel boat expeditions and guerrilla bands. On one occasion, Union troops took part in a daring operation to seize a large supply of cotton—an operation proposed and led by a black man. "A large, six foot negro, came into camp one day, and said he had been hard at work in the enemy's camp, but by good luck had got away," Vincent Colyer wrote. The man, named Charlie, had discovered a large pile of cotton, "high as a house, covered with brush. 'If you give me a flatboat and some men, we can get that cotton,'" he argued. So they "took a boat, twenty negroes, and one hundred men, every thing depending on Charlie's caution and skill, and in three days the steamboat came back laden with cotton, which was of great value to us as protection to our men in the gunboats. Its cash value was over $26,000."[10]

Many joint army-navy operations were aimed at guerrilla bands because, as the war went on, their activities in the South became more than a mere nuisance. Recent scholarship suggests that these guerrillas and other irregular units caused hardship for many local inhabitants as well as soldiers and that "this low-level conflict was widespread and lethal."[11]

In early June 1863 Major General E. D. Keyes informed Lieutenant Commander John Gillis that a combined expedition of land and naval forces would leave Yorktown on a mission to destroy a foundry at a point on the Mattapony River, about ten miles above Walkerton. The general's information indicated that the rebel foundry manufactured shot, shell, guns, and other "instruments of rebellion." He did not specifically mention liberating slaves, but he might have expected them to be working at the foundry. On the evening of June 4 Gillis's vessels—the *Commodore Morris, Commodore Jones,* and *Winnissimet,* along with the army gunboat *Smith Briggs*—went up the York River carrying 400 infantry troops from the Fourth Delaware, 168th New York Infantry, and 169th and 179th Pennsylvania Drafted Militia under the command of Lieutenant Colonel C. Carroll Tevis. In the early morning they landed the troops at Walkerton, and when the men reached Aylett's, where the foundry was located, they found "an immense amount of machinery of all kinds, and a very large quantity of flour and grain, which was in a large flouring mill belonging to the rebel Government," according to Gillis. After destroying the equipment and the mill, Tevis and his men headed back to the river, stopping at different places to destroy grain and to capture horses, mules, and cattle. In their official reports, neither Gillis nor Keyes mentioned that the expedition liberated any slaves, but Calvin Hutchinson, the *Commodore Morris*'s paymaster, claimed that they freed more than 100. Hutchinson, in a letter dated June 6, 1863, described the expedition to Aylett's and what happened next: "A negro came in at noon on Friday & said that the rebels were trying to obstruct the river below us in a narrow place at Mattapike & so prevent our return." Gillis ordered the *Smith Briggs* down "to shell the banks and keep the channel Open," Hutchinson recalled, and the *Commodore Morris* waited for the soldiers to return. "They began to straggle in at about 3 o'clock & reported that the main body was skirmishing with rebs about three miles off. They all got in at last except one killed, two wounded & two missing, all of the 168th N.Y."[12]

The *Commodore Morris, Commodore Jones,* and *Winnissimet* then went back downriver. Although they "kept up a terrific storm of shell grape and canister along the banks and cliffs for twenty or thirty miles down," Hutchinson wrote, rebel sharpshooters fired at them just a few times, "& fortunately no one was hit." They found only silence at West Point—no rebel gun batteries. "After we got by we were startled by a terrible doleful yell from the water alongside. It was very dark & we could see nothing & we hailed 'Hello! Who's there? What do you want?'" Hutchinson described "a poor darkey voice" that replied, "'I wants to get aboard massa.' We were in ticklish waters and couldn't stop to take to the poor fellow & he may be drifting yet in his canoe towards freedom." According to Hutchinson, the expedition succeeded not only in destroying the rebel foundry but also in freeing a large number of slaves. "We brought off between one and two hundred negroes & a lot of horses. We had to leave behind some sixty head of cattle & a flock of sheep for want of transportation."[13]

This expedition to Aylett's was composed of all-white infantry troops, but on occasion, joint army-navy expeditions included landing parties of Union Navy bluejackets fighting alongside U.S. Colored Infantry troops. In mid-June 1864, for example, a company of 100 sailors from the *Fuschia, Anacostia, Read,* and *Sophronia* cooperated with 500 soldiers and 50 cavalry under Colonel Alonzo G. Draper, commanding the Thirty-sixth Regiment, U.S. Colored Troops, in a joint army-navy expedition to Northern Neck, Virginia. Draper's black troops were hardened veterans. Formed originally as the Second Regiment, North Carolina Colored Volunteers, on October 28, 1863, at Portsmouth, Virginia, they had been redesignated in February 1864 the Thirty-sixth Regiment USCT. Before embarking on their June 1864 expedition, Draper's men had participated in a raid into Westmoreland County in April and one from

Point Lookout to the mouth of the Rappahannock River on May 11–14 to search for enemy mines. During the May raid they had struck out into rebel territory to seize cattle, horses, mules, and farm carts for contraband farms they had established on the Patuxent River. Shortly after arriving for duty at the Union camp for Confederate prisoners of war at Point Lookout in April 1864, Draper's men had appropriated 2,000 acres of abandoned rebel land on which to settle their families, and the colonel obtained permission from General Butler to make these raids whenever necessary to support these "government farms."

Lieutenant Edward Hooker, who commanded the First Division, Potomac Flotilla, for Draper's June raid, telegraphed cryptic but clear instructions for the expedition to the *Fuchsia*'s skipper, Acting Master William Street: "Use your judgment, burn grain and other things you think proper, take boats, etc, nets, seines, etc. I see lots of canoes below us. I think we had better clean them all out." Trusting his subordinate, Hooker added: "Be expeditions [expeditious] as possible. [The] darkies, bring off etc. You know what to do. Again use your own judgment."[14]

On the morning of June 12, 1864, Colonel Draper's Thirty-sixth USCT infantry, some cavalry troops, and Street's sailors landed at Pope's Creek on Virginia's Northern Neck and swept through the countryside, rounding up cattle, horses, and farming implements. The next day Street sent fifty sailors ahead with Draper while he and the remainder of the naval party went to Machodoc to secure it as an embarkation point for Union vessels. The following day, a Monday, the *Commodore Read* joined them, and for two days the sailors labored driving the cattle on board the transports "and examining the various estates about Machodoc." By sunset on Wednesday the energetic Street had rounded up 150 head of cattle, 33 horses, 20 sheep, 8 prisoners, and 50 contrabands. According to Street, the sailors "behaved better on this than on any former occasion, and have become quite efficient on shore duty." Transports took all the livestock and contrabands to Point Lookout. The *Commodore Read*, with the *Eureka* in tow, then proceeded into St. Inigoes to load coal, while Street and his sailors returned to their respective vessels. On Thursday, June 16, Hooker went by Point Lookout to land a large number of contrabands and then on to the Union wharf at Rappahannock, where he found the *Freeborn* and *Jacob Bell*. By then, Draper's black troops had arrived at the wharf with a large number of cattle, which they herded on to the transports. "The sailors on shore were also taken on board this ship," Hooker wrote, "they being very footsore, etc."[15]

For four days the rebels had not opposed Hooker's expedition, but during the afternoon a small body of cavalry attacked, and from their "persistence," Hooker concluded they had reinforcements nearby. Hooker and his men braced for a nighttime attack, but the night passed peacefully. Early the next morning, however, Lieutenant Colonel Meriwether Lewis's 300 Confederates renewed their attack, pushing Hooker's men back into the woods before pulling back to Burnham Church and throwing up breastworks. "The fighting was but little more than a sharp skirmishing in the woods with 150 men on our side, but lasted until 1 o'clock P.M., when the enemy fell back with considerable loss," Hooker reported. When the rebels rallied again, Hooker ordered the *Commodore Read*'s gunners to open fire on them; guided by a cloud of dust, they continued to shell the rebels until they were out of range. At dark Hooker began loading the soldiers on to the transports, but the rebel cavalry made a last-minute dash for the wharf, only to be stopped short by a broadside from the *Read*. According to Hooker, the rebels "skedaddled in confusion." After fending off yet another cavalry charge and loading and reloading troops and cattle, on June 21, 1864, Hooker's vessels headed for Point Lookout. Their successful joint expedition to Northern Neck, Virginia, had been achieved at a small price—two soldiers killed, one sailor seriously wounded, and one missing. In his report to Commander Foxhall Parker, Potomac Flotilla commander, a satisfied Hooker summed up the expedition known as the Draper raid: "The raid has been a success. Between 400 and 500 head of cattle, nearly 200 horses, as many sheep, and several hundred Contrabands have been obtained, besides a steamer load of farming utensils to go to the 'contraband farm.'"[16]

Although successful, the Draper raid became the subject of controversy when accusations surfaced about the behavior of some of Hooker's sailors and officers, who were accused of entering houses or behaving improperly toward unarmed or unprotected women. Hooker staunchly defended his men, responding, "I am unable to learn that any improprieties were committed by our sailors, nor do I think that they are guilty of such conduct. I am aware that such things were done by the negro soldiers, and some of them were severely punished by Colonel Draper for it. The sailors, however, I believe to be guiltless."[17]

Not all joint Union operations included the liberation of slaves, but they still affected the lives of African Americans living in areas targeted by federal troops and Union gunboats. Nowhere along the southern coast was the status of local blacks more in question, and the political climate more complex, than in Jacksonville, Florida, and along the St. John's River. In March 1862, hearing of the pro-Union sentiments prevailing at St. Augustine, General T. W. Sherman directed Brigadier General Horatio Wright to take one or two regiments to Picolata and land in the rear of St. Augustine to seize Fort Marion and the St. Augustine barracks. In a surprise move, however, Wright sailed two troop transports thirty miles up the St. John's River to Jacksonville, escorted by the Union gunboats *Pembina, Seneca, Ottawa,* and *Isaac Smith.* Neither he nor Samuel F. Du Pont, commanding the South Atlantic Blockading Squadron, intended to permanently occupy Jacksonville; the goal was merely to conduct a reconnaissance. The occupation of Jacksonville, though brief, had tragic consequences for a number of pro-Union white citizens and local blacks.

The Union vessels under Lieutenant T. H. Stevens crossed the bar on March 11, 1862, and, after stopping briefly at Mayport, reached Jacksonville. When they appeared, Judge S. L. Burritt came out with a flag of truce and surrendered. Many of the white inhabitants, hearing rumors of a large Union force headed for Jacksonville, had panicked and left town, according to one historian, "without a destination and guided and protected only by their faithful servants." Other citizens remained loyal to the Union but, fearing retribution from the Confederates, had concealed their true sentiments. In his report, Stevens told Du Pont that he thought many of the town's white citizens would return, but those who remained feared rebel harassment and sought Union protection. Encouraged by Sherman's declaration that the government had come to protect loyal citizens and their property from further mistreatment by the rebels, a committee of five met on March 24, 1862, hoping to organize a Florida state government under the jurisdiction of the United States. That same day Wright arrived to assume command of troops in Jacksonville.[18]

A week later Wright's situation in Jacksonville changed dramatically, and with it, the fate of pro-Union families in town. On March 31, 1862, General David Hunter, the new commander of the Department of the South, abruptly decided to evacuate the town. At the time, Hunter had 17,000 troops in his department, with preparations under way to attack Fort Pulaski and take Savannah. Explaining his reasoning to Secretary of War Edwin Stanton, Hunter wrote, "It is my opinion that this force is entirely too scattered and is subject to being cut off in detail. I shall order an abandonment of Jacksonville, Fla., and the re-enforcement of Forts Marion and Clinch."[19]

Responsibility for evacuating Union troops from Jacksonville naturally fell to Du Pont. In a letter to Commander Percival Drayton, commanding the USS *Pawnee* at Fernandina, he expressed concern for the remaining loyal citizens who had committed themselves to the Union cause and told Drayton that he had directed Lieutenant Stevens to protect them. "Word of the impending withdrawal of Union forces from Jacksonville produced great distress among the Union people," Stevens later explained, "many of whom are fleeing for their lives for protection against the Confederate Government, and are on board of the transports and naval vessels."[20]

Union troops had begun loading public stores on April 7, 1862, and by about two o'clock the following afternoon, all the soldiers had boarded the transports. Convoyed by the *Ottawa, Pembina,* and *Ellen,* the transports left Jacksonville and steamed downriver to Mayport, took aboard a company of the Fourth New Hampshire Regiment, and then proceeded to St. Augustine and Fernandina. With him, Wright had a number of loyal Union families wishing to leave Jacksonville. "These persons could not remain behind with their families with any safety, the enemy having threatened the lives of all who should show us the least favor or even remain in town after our occupation," Wright wrote in his report. Concerned about providing for these loyal Floridians, who had left Jacksonville without any funds save for "worthless paper currency," Wright instructed the post commander at Fernandina, Colonel H. Bisbee Jr., to assign them vacant houses as temporary homes and to furnish them with government provisions at the post, "not to exceed one ration to each person over twelve years of age and half ration to those under twelve."[21]

Under orders to protect the property of those deemed or believed to be loyal citizens, Union Navy officers in Florida walked a fine line as they tried to ascertain the loyalty of the local inhabitants. Because the occupation of Jacksonville took place months before Congress passed the Second Confiscation Act, this proved especially difficult when it came to making decisions about accepting fugitive slaves or returning them to their owners. On April 1, for example, Lieutenant Daniel Ammen accepted aboard the gunboat *Seneca* three slaves belonging to a Mr. Byar. The slaves assured Ammen that although their master was too old to serve, two of his sons were in the rebel army. At noon, when Byar came to the *Seneca* to retrieve his slaves, Ammen explained that, "having satisfied myself that his sons in rebel service were not minors, I remanded the men to him." The following day, however, eight more men arrived at Ammen's ship from the vicinity of Palatka. This time, he told Stevens, "having satisfied myself that their masters were rebels in arms, I gave them passage and they now await your orders." When Ammen found that the water over the bar was too shallow to proceed to sea and back to Hilton Head as ordered, he decided to return to Jacksonville. Suddenly, about twelve or fourteen miles below the city, rebels opened fire on the gunboat from Yellow Bluffs. "About fifty balls struck the ship," Ammen reported. "The man at the masthead, John Built (ordinary seamen), was shot through the calf of left leg, and Andrew Webb (coal heaver) through the thigh, a negro man (contraband passenger) was shot in the back." The *Seneca* returned fire with its howitzer and then proceeded to Jacksonville, where Ammen picked up four men and their families who wanted to leave the city. The lieutenant then took this party of twenty-two whites and eight contrabands (including the wounded man, who was well enough to walk) and landed them at Hilton Head.[22]

These eight contrabands were indeed fortunate, for fifty-two other African Americans evacuated from Jacksonville met a different fate. In explaining the situation during the Union evacuation, Stevens wrote, "Captain Bankhead heard General Wright give the order to put all the negroes on shore before leaving, and that afterwards they were enticed on board by the soldiers." Rescued by Union soldiers against Wright's orders, the contrabands were taken downriver, probably to Fernandina. Their southern masters had not forgotten them, however. On April 13, 1862, Stevens informed Drayton, commanding naval forces in the St. Mary's, that Judge S. L. Burritt and several "prominent citizens" of Jacksonville had gone to Fernandina "to endeavor to secure some property which has escaped from them in some of the transports which were at Jacksonville." Referring to Burritt as a "personal friend" and the others as peaceable and unoffending citizens who had taken no active part in the rebellion, Stevens asked Drayton to assist Burritt in retrieving this "property," by which he clearly meant slaves. He noted that Burritt "has been of great service to me in the attempt I made, and was doing so well in his efforts to bring back people to their senses." Burritt and his family had earlier boarded Stevens's gunboat the *Ottawa,* seeking protection. On April 10, 1862, Stevens directed Acting Master William Budd of the *Ellen* to take Burritt and his family back to Jacksonville and send a boat to shore with a white flag. If the Confederates agreed to allow them to land, Budd could put the judge and his family ashore. Budd did as ordered, landing the judge and his family under a flag of truce on April 11, 1862. He reported that Jacksonville was occupied by a provisional force of about 300 rebels. In asking Drayton to aid Burritt and the others in retrieving their slaves, Stevens admitted, "Of course, our relations to the subject are very delicate, but at the same time it appears an easy matter for the commanding officer, without taking any active part in remanding them, to allow owners to take them." He then assured Drayton that their policy of noninterference with property was "rapidly producing a reaction of feeling, which would, in a short time, have

converted the majority of the citizens of the State to the Union cause."
Stevens argued that by refusing to carry out this policy, any advantages
gained in securing the confidence of the people of Florida would be
lost. Union authorities must have honored Stevens's request, for Colonel
W. S. Dilworth, CSA, commanding the District of East and Middle Florida, reported that after evacuating Jacksonville, "the enemy returned
under a flag of truce, and were permitted to land 52 negroes, which were
taken in charge by the commander of the post."[23]

Although the official correspondence indicates that Stevens made
honest efforts to comply with federal laws governing the return of slaves
to loyal citizens, he nonetheless felt compelled to defend the actions of
his men to the Confederate officer commanding the provisional forces
in east Florida, Colonel W. G. M. Davis. Stevens wrote, "Rest assured,
sir, no encouragement or inducement has been offered on my part, or
on the part of any officer or man under my command, to entice slaves
away. My orders are stringent upon this subject and I know of no violation of them."[24]

The evacuation of Jacksonville by federal troops and Union gunboats
proved tragic for some of the city's slaves, but another joint army-navy
operation along the southern coast had adverse effects on contrabands
and blacks living on the Sea Islands under the protection of Union
troops. In May 1862 a black pilot named Robert Smalls escaped and
informed Du Pont and his staff of recent developments that suggested
that Charleston might be vulnerable to attack via the Stono River. "From
information brought by the *Planter* the rebels are abandoning a portion,
certainly, of their defenses in Stono," Du Pont wrote to Commander
John Marchand on May 15, 1862. "The battery on Cole's Island I have no
doubt has been left, and I deem it highly probable they are abandoning
Old Battery opposite Legareville." Du Pont recommended that March-
and conduct an immediate reconnaissance with his gunboats to confirm
Smalls's report. When the *Pembina* arrived that evening with Du Pont's
message, Marchand moved quickly to organize an expedition to explore
the Stono River. If it lay undefended, federal vessels might bypass rebel
fortifications guarding the entrance to Charleston Harbor and attack
and capture that "Cradle of the Confederacy." While boats sounded the
bar, Marchand had his gig rowed into Stono Inlet, within grapeshot distance of the rebel fort on Cole's Island. To his surprise, he found the fort
abandoned. "From information received from Contrabands and other
sources, 48 cannon had a short time ago defended the place," he wrote
in his journal entry for May 16, 1862.[25]

Until Smalls's escape and Marchand's reconnaissance of the Stono,

Union officials had no idea that General Robert E. Lee's successor, General John C. Pemberton, had taken Lee's advice and abandoned numerous exposed points along the coast within reach of federal gunboats. The Confederates had withdrawn their forces to interior positions where they could meet Union forces on more equal terms. For this reason, the rebels had evacuated Cole's Island and removed all their defenses along the Stono, except for a few troops and batteries instructed to withdraw at the sight of a federal flotilla. After this discovery, a joint army-navy operation up the Stono to attack Charleston was attempted in early June 1862; however, it was unsuccessful, forcing Hunter to abandon these plans and to focus on a future frontal assault on the harbor's main approaches.[26]

The withdrawal of federal troops from the Georgia Sea Islands for the Stono operation had negative consequences for Union Navy commanders trying to enforce the blockade and protect contrabands gathered on these islands. On June 13, 1862, just prior to the assault at Secessionville, Du Pont received a letter from Lieutenant William Truxtun, commanding the USS *Dale* in St. Helena Sound, alerting him to the new dangers facing contrabands along the Georgia coast. Du Pont, in turn, forwarded Truxtun's "very graphic letter" to the Navy Department; it described "in strong and earnest words" the condition of many of the Sea Islands following the withdrawal of the army's forces. Du Pont explained that with the withdrawal of Hunter's troops from the fort on Otter Island and his pickets from many of the adjacent islands, that left "only the *Dale*, a sailing vessel, to protect the contrabands remaining of choice on the plantations, where many of them had been born."[27]

Unfortunately, the *Dale*'s thirty-two-pounder guns could not prevent a Confederate attack on Hutchinson's Island, which resulted in the deaths of African Americans living on a plantation owned by a Mrs. Marsh. On June 13, 1862, the Confederates made one of their most serious attacks on the Sea Islands. At four o'clock that morning, Truxtun received a report of a fire on Hutchinson's Island and then a signal from the home of the pilot, indicating the presence of rebel troops in the vicinity. With the tender *Wild Cat,* Truxtun set out in the direction of the fire. "Soon after leaving the ship a canoe containing three negroes was met, who stated that the rebels, 300 strong, were at Mrs. Marsh's plantation killing all the negroes," he told Du Pont in his report. As the party continued up Big River Creek, they encountered more canoes filled with panic-stricken blacks. Two and a half miles from Mrs. Marsh's plantation, shallow water forced Truxtun to anchor the *Wild Cat* and continue with the cutters and launch. "On arriving at Mrs. Marsh's the scene was most painful," he wrote. "Her dwelling and chapel were in ruins, the air heavy with smoke, while at the landing were assembled over 100 souls, mostly women and children, in utmost distress." Truxtun immediately threw out pickets but soon learned that the rebels had left the neighborhood and returned to the fort. Local blacks told him that the rebels had landed during the night, guided by a black man who had been employed by the army for a long time on Otter Island. They surrounded the house and chapel, where a large proportion of the blacks were housed, and murdered the occupants in cold blood. The rebels then posted "a strong guard to oppose our landing," Truxtun wrote. "At early dawn," he explained, the rebels "fired a volley through the house. As alarmed people sprang nearly naked from their beds and rushed forth, frantic with fear they were shot, arrested or knocked down." After snatching a number of chickens, the rebels set fire to the buildings and fled.[28]

These Confederate raiders might have inflicted more damage or taken the slaves away had they not sighted the *Dale*'s boat party approaching. According to Truxtun, the rebels exclaimed, "Be quick, boys, the people for the ship will be up." In his report of the attack on Hutchinson's Island, the Confederate cavalry commander, Major R. J. Jeffords, explained that he had landed on the north end of the island on the night of June 12 in three boats with 105 men. Hearing drums and confident that Union troops were present, Jeffords approached a settlement and deployed skirmishers. When a black watchman gave the alarm and men rushed past his skirmishers, ignoring a proper warning to halt, he wrote, "I ordered men to fire before I discovered they were negroes." Before he could order a cease-fire, ten men had been killed and ten or fifteen wounded. Jeffords explained that "high bush, corn waist high and the darkness of the night" had made it difficult to identify the blacks. When he got closer, Jeffords found "some 125 negroes there, with various kinds of provisions, say corn, bacon, beef & c, doubtless left them by the enemy." Jeffords and his men set fire to the buildings. Then, as "gunboats were just below and three of them moving up, and my retreat could have been cut off," he ordered his men to depart Hutchinson's Island.[29]

When Truxtun's party arrived, he filled his boats with all the remaining slaves who wished to leave and sent them back to the *Wild Cat*. "I returned to the ship," Truxtun wrote to Du Pont, "bringing with me about seventy, among them one man literally riddled with balls and buckshot (since dead) another shot through the lungs and struck over the forehead with a clubbed musket, leaving the bone perfectly bare [and] one woman shot in the leg, shoulder and thigh; one far gone in pregnancy, with dislocation of the hip joint and injury to the womb, caused by leaping from a second-story window, and another with displacement of the cap of the knee and injury to the leg from the same cause." The lieutenant told Du Pont that he was at a loss to account "for their extreme barbarity to the negroes, most of whom were living on the plantation where they had been born, peacefully tilling the ground for their support, which their masters, by deserting, had denied them, and who were not even remotely connected with the hated Yankee."[30]

The *Wild Cat* left the area with its refugee passengers, whom Truxtun had sent to Hilton Head to alleviate the demand for provisions. However, thirty more had arrived from the mainland on Tuesday, and "scarce a day passes without more arrivals," he wrote. Since the withdrawal of federal troops, Truxtun had been urging the contrabands to move to Edisto or St. Helena, but the majority wanted to stay because it was their home, and "all have the most perfect faith in the protection of the ship." The lieutenant reminded Du Pont that for months the contrabands had been cultivating crops on the island under Union protection and offered his opinion that "the Government is bound by every principle of justice and policy to shield them from these barbarian inroads." Although the *Wild Cat* returned and shelled some Confederates sighted near the Ashepoo River, Truxtun urged the Navy Department to send more light-draft steamers and troops to defend that portion of the coast against rebel attack. Du Pont, in turn, wrote to Welles, "The Department will perceive by the narrative how much the gunboats are looked up to by the contrabands for their defense and how much they are feared by the enemy for attack." In this report, Du Pont reminded the Navy Department that for months the army had enjoyed some measure of control of many of the Sea Islands in the vicinity, extending to North Edisto. He then reiterated Truxtun's words, telling Welles, "The contrabands have remained quietly here, cultivating the plantations under our protection, and it seems to me that the Government is bound by every principle of justice and policy to shield them from these barbarous inroads." He praised Truxtun's zeal and earnestness, requested that the department send him more light-draft steam vessels, and called to the government's attention "the urgent need of more troops on this part of the coast."[31]

Coastal blacks certainly suffered when federal troops left the Georgia Sea Islands for duty elsewhere, but in other instances, Union raids against Confederate forces or irregulars caused many frightened African Americans to flee to safety. Take, for example, the well-intentioned efforts of a joint expedition into Mathews County, Virginia, in October 1863. That autumn, a troublesome band of rebel guerrillas known as the "Coast Guard" and led by Captain J. Y. Beall had created a commotion by raiding shipping in Chesapeake Bay. "The party appeared to have no organization, and were not dressed in uniform," Lieutenant Commander John H. Gillis reported to Captain Guert Gansevoort, senior officer at Newport News. Concerned about losses to Beall's bandits, Admiral Samuel P. Lee asked General John G. Foster to organize an expedition to curtail these rebel boat incursions from Mathews County to the eastern shore of Virginia. Foster agreed to send an expedition from Yorktown that was composed largely of 744 men from Colonel Duncan's Fourth U.S. Colored Infantry, a regiment organized in Baltimore beginning in July 1863. They would embark in both army and navy gunboats under Gillis's command for a mission to find and capture the guerrilla Coast Guard.[32]

On the morning of October 5, 1863, Brigadier General Wistar left Yorktown with his troops and Colonel John S. Spear's cavalry. At daylight on the sixth, the cavalrymen fanned out, and for the next three days, "every work, corner, creek, and landing place was visited." About 150 boats and sloops were destroyed, some eighty head of cattle en route to Richmond were captured, and four persons were brought in. Although this joint operation of black troops and Union gunboats took a few horses, arms, and about 100 prisoners "more or less connected with illicit trade," the notorious Captain Beall escaped. The rebel Coast Guard had fled to the eastern shore in their boats.[33]

In his report of the expedition, Gillis explained that he found it "to be a very difficult matter to break up the organization (of rebels), for the reason that as soon as our cavalry is seen approaching, they, the rebels, take to the woods, and knowing every path, find no difficulty in eluding pursuit in almost every instance." The rebel Beall proved elusive indeed, but in mid-November 1863, Lieutenant John W. Conner and Sergeant Robert R. Christopher of Company B, First Eastern Shore Maryland Volunteers, captured Beall and fourteen of his bandits.[34]

Union expeditions chasing after rebel guerrillas in Mathews and Gloucester counties had unintended consequences for the African American population. According to Lucy Chase, a white native of Worcester, Massachusetts, who had gone south to teach the contrabands, hundreds of blacks fled to Norfolk, Virginia, after these expeditions. "Two or three days ago," she wrote to Anna Lowell in a letter dated November 29, 1863, "4 hundred negroes followed on the heels of a force sent out from Norfolk in search of guerillas, and now we find them at our doors. Two weeks ago, four hundred other negroes, accepting a cordial invitation from colored soldiers, came to town. Not to spend the winter, not to tarry but a night, but with their faces firmly turned forever and a day from their homes? Such a flood we look for all through the winter." Lucy begged Anna to send her clothing for these refugees—stout colored shirts, dresses, baby clothes, and sewing materials, which were in great demand among the contrabands at Norfolk.[35]

In January 1864 Captain Riley of the Sixth Regiment USCT returned to Mathews County. "I was sent by General Butler, with one hundred picked men, to rescue some Union families from Matthews Co., Va., which country was at that time held by a strong force of Rebel Cavalry," Riley told readers of the *Christian Recorder*. The troops boarded the USS *Morse* on Friday, January 22, 1864. According to the *Morse's* captain, Charles Babcock, he had gone to New Point Comfort at Butler's request to protect the mission. Babcock ordered the *Crusader* to follow him, and at nine o'clock that morning the vessels anchored in Mobjack Bay and lowered their boats. "Our raid was a success," Riley wrote. "Three Union (white) families were brought off, and about thirty five slaves." While ashore the soldiers came upon a man named White who implored Riley not to let his soldiers destroy his property or take his chickens. When Riley noticed two black children "clad in rags, barefooted and covered with filth," shivering in the cold, he asked White where their mother was. "She is dead," White replied. Thinking of his own children at home in Ohio, Riley told the man, "Take good care of the little colored children; they will be free when this war is over." When the soldiers returned to the gunboats, the contrabands on board told Riley that the children's mother was not dead but that "old White" had "bound her down to a cart and sent her off" to be sold. Riley regretted not taking the children with him, as did his soldiers.[36]

Fortuitously, a few days later Riley received orders to return to that part of Mathews County to capture a blockade runner. "I was more than glad of the opportunity that this expedition might afford me to get the children, and visit some kind of punishment on their cruel and heartless master," he wrote. Although the presence of rebel cavalry made this mission more dangerous than the last one, Riley and his men landed at midnight, surrounded the blockade runner's home, and easily captured him. At two o'clock in the morning Riley went to White's house and, he said, lectured him "severely for the falsehood he had told me about the mother of the children, and his treatment of his slaves in general." He then ordered the five children he found there to come with him and told his soldiers to kill the poultry. When they returned to Yorktown, Riley gave the children to Eliza Yates, who sent them to the orphans' shelter in the city. "I called at the shelter," Riley told readers, "and saw the children yesterday. They are happy and well cared for. The boy, Douglas White, is about eight years old. The girl, Ella, is six. O, how I was delighted to hear them sing."[37]

Riley's mission to rescue white Union families saved not only them but also their slaves, and it gave Riley the opportunity to save five black children from a cruel master. Though sometimes risky and not always as rewarding as Riley's mission, these joint missions conducted by navy gunboats transporting U.S. Colored Infantry units gave Union sailors both black and white an opportunity to become acquainted with black troops. Few surviving letters or diary entries mention the relationship between black soldiers and sailors, but in his correspondence to the *Christian Recorder*, George Reed, a black sailor serving on the *Commodore Read*, recalled one such incident in May 1864. "On Thursday, the 12th inst., we were notified that wounded soldiers were drifting in the river near Aquia Creek, having been driven there by guerillas in their retreat from the front," Reed wrote. His gunboat proceeded to the area and remained there to aid some of the 20,000 casualties of the fighting in the Wilderness. "I had the pleasure of conversing with some of the colored soldiers who were wounded in the late battles," Reed told readers. "I am told by them that their officers could not manage them, they were so eager to fight. Whenever they caught a rebel they cried out, 'No quarter! Remember Fort Pillow!' 'No quarter for rebs, & etc.'" Reed assured readers of the *Christian Recorder* that the wounded black men had distinguished themselves. "They are doing as well here as can be expected, and are being properly cared for. They seem principally to belong to Burnside's division, and many who were slightly wounded have gone back to the front. They are all eager to go back to retaliate for the Fort Pillow massacre."[38]

During the last years of the Civil War, Union forces took advantage of the navy's ability to provide increased mobility by transporting troops and small artillery pieces up southern rivers and creeks into the interior. These brown-water operations involved an element of risk but allowed the army to strike unexpectedly at Confederate forces, especially irregular or guerrilla units, and to destroy enemy saltworks, foundries, depots, and other works. Union raids and expeditions boosted morale, especially among African American soldiers and sailors, giving them the chance to assist or rescue family and friends who were still in bondage. Furthermore, fighting alongside black troops allowed Union Navy officers and men, both black and white, to see that contrary to white claims that blacks would not fight, U.S. Colored Infantry soldiers were capable, brave, and enthusiastic warriors.

CHAPTER 9
THE FINAL MONTHS

The people are sullen and will not speak to us if they can help it. Not so with the Negroes. I went into several of their shanties and found them in great glee. They say, "why did you stay away so long? We've been praying and praying for you to come."

—*Ashael Sumner Dean*

As December 1864 came to a close, General William T. Sherman's army approached its objective: Savannah, Georgia. During the army's movement across Georgia to Savannah and on toward Columbia, Union soldiers frequently encountered and interacted with African Americans. Although many northern soldiers manifested varying degrees of racial prejudice, historian Joseph Glatthaar concludes that "most of the soldiers treated blacks reasonably well." There were minor incidents, of course, and some serious cases of mistreatment of blacks by soldiers. The most famous of these involved the Fourteenth Corps on its march from Augusta to Savannah, with Wheeler's Confederate cavalry in pursuit. The Union troops crossed safely over a pontoon bridge spanning Ebenezer Creek, but the corps commander, Jefferson C. Davis, ordered the pontoon removed, denying its use to hundreds of black men, women, and children following his troops. Trapped on the wrong side of the creek, many drowned attempting to swim across; others were shot or captured by the rebels.[1]

Despite this tragic incident and other less well known or undocumented cases of cruelty, Sherman's march across Georgia afforded many Union soldiers the opportunity to become acquainted with and befriend black civilians. Young northern soldiers hired black men as servants, teaching them to read and offering them tips on how to survive in their new world of freedom. In letters home, soldiers wrote of their admiration for blacks who assisted escaping Union prisoners and guided Union soldiers on foraging parties in search of food. In one instance, an elderly black man offered his shoes to a barefoot forager, reasoning, "Soldier, honey, doan't you know dat I'se glad to go barefooted to help you fight de battle of freedom?"[2]

On December 21, 1864, Sherman's troops occupied the city of Savannah, which had been abandoned by Confederate forces. Reporting the good news to Navy Secretary Gideon Welles, Rear Admiral John A. Dahlgren wrote: "I have walked about the city several times, and can affirm that its tranquility is undisturbed. The Union soldiers who are stationed within its limits, are as orderly as if they were in New York or Boston." On January 4, 1865, Dahlgren returned to Savannah to confer with Sherman, who had already begun moving his troops out of the city, sending 30,000 men from his right wing for transport to Beaufort. The admiral offered Sherman the navy's assistance and hoped that Sherman's troops would move on toward Charleston and attack that city, which had long been an objective of the Union war effort.[3]

To Dahlgren's disappointment, three days later Sherman informed him that he had ordered four army corps, General John G. Foster's 5,000 men at the Tulfinney, and a regiment at Boyd's Neck to move out toward Florence, not Charleston. Although clearly displeased with Sherman's decision, Dahlgren supported the army's operations by ordering the *Pontiac* to the Savannah River, the *Mingoe* to cooperate with General Foster's force, and the *Dai Ching* and *Sonoma* to operate in the Coosaw or the "nearest rivers to assist the advance of troops." Dahlgren told Welles that any further cooperation would be confined to assistance in attacking Charleston or in establishing communication at Georgetown.[4]

According to Charles P. Ware, hundreds of blacks who had accompanied Sherman's army to Savannah followed it northward, many of them arriving in the Port Royal area. "They are said to be an excellent set of people, more intelligent than most here," he wrote, "and are eager for work. They will get distributed onto the plantations before a great while." Referring to them as "the Georgia refugees," Harriet Ware wrote on January 6, 1865: "Miss Towne gave us quite an interesting account of the Georgia refugees that have been sent to the Village. The hardships they underwent to march with the army are fearful, and the children often gave out and were left by their mothers exhausted and dying by the roadside and in the fields." One couple who had twelve children carried one child each and tied the rest "all together by the hands and brought them all off safely, a march of hundreds of miles." Harriet Ware also noted, "the men have all been put to work in the quartermaster's department or have gone into the army, and the families are being distributed where they can find places for them."[5]

One group of Georgia refugees went to the Morgan Island plantation. On January 8, 1865, E. S. Philbrick, who supervised a dozen plantations, wrote, "drove over to Mr. Well's house on Wednesday. He had gone to Morgan Island to receive and stow away some one hundred and fifty Georgia refugees, which were expected by a steamer from Beaufort." They arrived at sunset, and Wells "spent half the night there in the rain, stowing them in houses and getting their baggage up from the steamer, which lay at anchor discharging into small boats." According to Philbrick, these refugees came "from the shore counties near to Savannah, and brought a good deal of truck, beds, and blankets, and some rice and peas." Wells gave them rations for a week because they could not get anything to eat "till next harvest in any other way."[6]

African Americans from all over Georgia continued to pour into the vicinity of Port Royal. "The Georgia refugees are coming along by hundreds and thousands, and General Rufus Saxton, visiting St. Helena, "wanted to make room for them," Philbrick, noted on January 22, 1865. Philbrick wrote that the refugees had gone to work for York at Fripps Point and that "George Wells has got over a hundred Georgians on Morgan Island, doing well, and I guess the rebels, won't trouble him, they are too busy."[7]

Contrabands filled the streets of Beaufort, South Carolina, and their encounters with white troops from Sherman's army varied from harassment to encouragement. William Waring, a chaplain with the 102nd U.S. Colored Infantry Regiment stationed at Beaufort, described these very different experiences in an issue of the *Weekly Anglo African* newspaper. "Up the street a little farther the negro-hating element shows itself. One of them takes a colored woman's pies and then slaps her over because she complained. Another one inflict a wound on an already wounded colored soldier. . . . Around the corner another one interferes with a colored woman in her own yard, and she, like a true South Carolinian, falls back on her 'reserved rights' and cuts his head with an axe." In striking contrast to these abuses, Waring wrote, "Here comes a soldier full of fun, and meeting an old contraband lady of fresh arrival, throws his arms around her, with a 'hurrah, old woman, bully for you!'" A recently arrived contraband saw a soldier carrying some loaves of bread and asked him for one. "'Oh! Yes, Aunty, we will fight for you and feed you, too,' and with that shares his commissaries with her," Chaplain Waring told his readers.[8]

Many able-bodied male slaves who followed Sherman's troops across

Georgia enlisted in the Union Army in December 1864. They filled out the ranks of the Twenty-first U.S. Colored Infantry Regiment, which had been formed from the Fourth and Fifth South Carolina Volunteers as well as the Third South Carolina Volunteers, a unit originally composed partially of black men recruited in June 1863 on Ossabaw Island, at Fort Pulaski, and in Fernandina.[9]

The advance of Sherman's army across Georgia to Savannah and then northward encouraged thousands of slaves to seek freedom and start new lives. For many more African Americans along the southern coast or in Union-occupied areas inland, the final months of the war brought a measure of peace and stability. For other African Americans, especially those in the path of Sherman's advance, 1865 brought turmoil. When slaves found themselves at the mercy of Union foraging parties or saw their women sexually assaulted by white soldiers, they began to question the abolitionist sentiments of Union soldiers. Although Sherman's troop movements across the Carolinas gave many blacks the opportunity to achieve freedom, according to historian Jacqueline Campbell, in the face of prejudice and abuse by white soldiers, some African Americans began to "question the benefits of leaving the plantation."[10]

In addition to the thousands of refugees who followed Sherman's army across Georgia, others, both black and white, continued to find their way into Union lines or out to Union vessels. As they had since 1861, these fugitives brought valuable information about Confederate morale, troop deployments, ship movements, the location of mines, and the state of rebel defenses. Until the end of the conflict, former slaves and free blacks supported the Union cause. Men served as soldiers and sailors, informants, spies, pilots, guides, laborers, and mechanics. The women gained employment as laundresses, cooks, and servants.

Men serving on the vessels of the North and South Atlantic Blockading Squadrons and the Potomac Flotilla spent the first months of 1865 on routine patrols and blockade duty. Navy gunboats and other vessels supported Sherman's advance by undertaking demonstrations or feints to distract the rebels from his real movements and, in the process, often became targets for rebel gunners and sharpshooters; others on routine duty fell victim to mines lurking in inlets, rivers, and harbors. At dark on the night of January 16, 1865, for example, the Passaic-class monitor *Patapsco,* scheduled to accompany the *Lehigh* on advance picket duty in the Charleston River, got under way and proceeded up the harbor. Having spent much of the war off Charleston, including operations against Morris Island, the *Patapsco's* officers and crew, among them a number of African American sailors, were familiar with the area and knew the necessity of watching for "torpedoes." Despite their vigilance, the *Patapsco* struck a mine when approaching a buoy, "and in less than half a minute the *Patapsco*'s deck was under the surface." The commanding officer, Lieutenant Commander Stephen Platt Quakenbush, gave the order to start the pumps, but as he wrote later, "In an instant more I discovered that the whole forward part of the vessel was submerged, and, there being no possible chance to save the vessel. I then gave the order to man the boats, but before even an effort could be made to do so the vessel sunk to the top of the turret." The *Patapsco*'s officers and crew had survived the lengthy Union campaign to capture Fort Sumter, including the attack on Charleston, during which the ship took forty-seven hits from Confederate gunfire, as well as two more years of blockade duty, only to see their ship sunk during a routine mine-clearing operation just three months before the war finally came to an end.[11]

Surgeon Samuel Gilbert Webber sent his wife, Nannie, news of the *Patapsco*'s loss. "There were 43 saved from the *Patapsco* & 58 missing. Of these five officers were saved and eight are among the missing. It is barely possible that some of the missing are with the rebels. One person was picked up on the ice box drifting towards Charleston." Quakenbush, the *Patapsco*'s fourth commanding officer during the war, survived the sinking. Six African American sailors—two landsmen, two cooks, and two first-class boys—died or went missing when the *Patapsco* sank.[12]

The *Patapsco*'s loss curtailed any efforts by the South Atlantic Blockading Squadron to force its way into Charleston Harbor, but Dahlgren continued to follow the movements of Sherman's army as best he could and anxiously awaited any word about the Confederate garrison at Charleston. On February 1, 1865, a message arrived from Commander George Balch that must have been music to the admiral's ears. Balch wrote that a contraband had brought a Union prisoner from the Fourteenth Illinois Cavalry on board the *Daffodil*. "From him we get some interesting intelligence of affairs in Dixie," Balch wrote. "Among other items he expressed the opinion that the rebels are evacuating Charleston, and he heard that they were removing heavy guns from Sullivan's Island and James Island." The escaped prisoner claimed that the rebels were discussing falling back on Summerville, some twenty miles from Adams Run. Indeed, by mid-February General Beauregard had decided to save his garrison by abandoning Charleston. The white Union prisoner, presumably helped to freedom by the unnamed contraband, probably returned to his unit or to civilian life. As Union Navy commanders had done so often during the war, however, Balch retained the contraband on board his vessel. Almost four years of war seemed to have changed Balch's attitude toward contrabands, for he told Dahlgren, "[I] will, if occasion offers, permit him to return and bring off his family. His wife is employed washing at the rebel hospital at Adams run, and has been enjoined to bring all information of affairs there." Like so many other anonymous black women, the laundress had been supplying the Union with intelligence about the Confederates.[13]

On February 7, 1865, Sherman sent Dahlgren a message that he was on the railroad at Midway, South Carolina, and "would break 50 miles from Edisto toward Augusta and then cross toward Columbia." Explaining that the weather was poor "and [the] country full of water," Sherman told the admiral that he might be forced to turn against Charleston. Dahlgren did his best to support Sherman's army in its movements, and his commanders continued to seek information and assistance from local African Americans. In the meantime, however, the admiral had not forgotten about the wreck of the ill-fated *Dai Ching*. When Lieutenant Commander James Stillwell took the USS *Ottawa* up the Combahee River on February 8, 1865, to within 200 yards of the *Dai Ching*, he found that the ship had been burned to the water's edge and that the rebels had been working on it, "but with little success." Stillwell also sent the ship's executive officer, W. H. Winslow, in the cutter and Acting Master E. H. Sheffield in one of the *Winona*'s boats upriver. En route they found two escaped Union prisoners on a raft and took them with them. "We landed below Tar Bluff," Winslow reported, "and leaving a boat guard, scouted along the high bank about two miles, discovering fresh horse trails and footprints, a high water battery with three casemates," but no guns in it. Retreating by a main road three miles to "a negro settlement," they communicated with three local blacks. "They said 30 cavalry ran from our fire upon the bluff and passed at noon, going to Chiselville, 15 miles back, to return in a day or two, that the fort above was still armed and manned, though the principal force had left." After encountering and firing on some rebel cavalry, Winslow's party returned to the ship.[14]

Sheffield's report gave additional details, including that the two escaped Union prisoners on the raft were from the Fourth Massachusetts and Fourth New Hampshire Regiments. "They informed me they had been taken care of for a number of days by negroes who live about a mile from where we then were," Sheffield wrote. He decided to seek them out for information and arrived at their huts about noon. "They seemed very friendly, and informed us that about 30 cavalry had left there that day and gone back 15 miles." Satisfied from the testimony of the blacks and his own reconnaissance that they would not be attacked at Tar Bluff, Sheffield and his party returned along the left bank of the river. When about a mile and a half from the fort, they spotted men on a bluff observing them. Expecting a fight, Sheffield ordered his men to "take good aim and fire rapidly, letting their shots go just above the bluff." Both boats began firing, and the men thought they heard screams "such as men would give when badly wounded." They pulled quickly downriver and arrived back at the *Ottawa* at 3 A.M. with the Union prisoners. According to Sheffield, the prisoners reported that the blacks had told them the *Dai Ching's* crew "were captured and not killed, as was supposed"—welcome news for their family and friends.[15]

During February, Sherman's army advanced through South Carolina, across rivers and creeks swollen with winter rains. The record rainfall promised to make the 425-mile journey to Goldsboro, North Carolina, almost impossible, but Sherman organized pioneer battalions of soldiers and contrabands to construct roads of felled trees and to build bridges and causeways over these obstacles. On the morning of February 16, 1865, Sherman reached a point near Columbia from which he could see the city. "I could see the unfinished State-House, a handsome granite structure, and the ruins of the railroad depot, which were still smouldering," he wrote in his memoirs. When Sherman spotted a number of blacks carrying off bags of grain or meal piled up near the burned depot, he ordered his artillery to fire a few shots nearby "to scare away the negroes who were appropriating bags of corn and meal which we wanted." After Sherman's soldiers entered Columbia the following day, fires broke out in the city. Some said they were set by the army, but more likely they started from bales of hay left smoldering during the Confederate evacuation. A high wind spread the fires and, despite efforts to control them, "burned out the very heart of the city, embracing several churches, the old State-House, and the school or asylum of that very Sister of Charity who had appealed for my personal protection." Sherman insisted that the fires were not deliberately planned or set.[16]

While the South Atlantic Blockading Squadron supported Sherman's advance from Savannah, Rear Admiral David D. Porter's North Atlantic Blockading Squadron had finally accomplished a long sought after goal— the seizure of Wilmington, North Carolina. On New Year's Day 1865 Lieutenant Essex Porter, the admiral's son and an aide-de-camp on General Ulysses S. Grant's staff, brought the first word of plans to resume the attack on Wilmington. "It then became known that the troops brought away from Fort Fisher would be returned and under the command of Major General Alfred Howe Terry, who was directed to cooperate and *fight* with the navy. They were expected to arrive on the 4th of January,"

John Grattan wrote. For this important joint army-navy operation, Terry had been ordered to replace General Butler, whose December attack on Wilmington had ended in dismal failure.[17]

Union forces—including a 2,000-man naval landing force, Butler's original 6,500 troops, and an additional 2,000 reserve black troops—resumed their attack on Wilmington in mid-January 1865, following a joint amphibious plan carefully devised by Terry and Porter. The iron-clad *New Ironsides* opened fire on Fort Fisher on January 13, 1865, and this time, Porter ordered his commanders to concentrate their fire on the fort's guns. While the fleet pounded Fort Fisher, Terry's federal troops landed and advanced near the fort. The *Pequot's* captain, Daniel L. Braine, noted that on the morning of the first day of the operation, his ship was anchored close to the beach and shelled the woods to cover the troops' landing. The *Pequot* sent its launches to shore with troops, both black and white, but "a heavy surf on the beach . . . rendered the landing extremely difficult. Many boats were swamped and I fear that some soldiers were drowned," Paymaster Calvin Hutchinson wrote. The launches were "very fortunate and only got half full of water several times, but the 2nd cutter got struck by a roller swept broadside on & rolled over & over up the beach soldiers sailors officers & all, luckily no one was lost." According to Hutchinson, "the scene was a very lively and comic one in some of its features. . . . The black troops were especially hilarious and jolly with less modesty than the white soldiers they stripped & waded ashore 'in puris naturalibus' Keeping their clothes & accoutrements bag in a bundle at the end of their bayonets."[18]

Porter's ships bombarded the forts defending Wilmington for two days, and on the afternoon of January 15 a force of marines and sailors led by Lieutenant Commander K. Randolph Breese came ashore. At 3:30 in the afternoon Breese's men, mistaking a feint for the infantry attack, rushed the fort, only to be cut down by rebel fire. "We advanced at a double quick, under very severe fire, and charged up to within about 100 yards of the fort," reported Anthony Smalley, who commanded forty-two of the *Pequot's* sailors in the attack. "The enemy's fire then became so severe that, in spite of the efforts of the officers, the men fell back and retreated down the beach in some confusion." Two *Pequot* crewmen died in the attack, and another three were wounded. At 10:20 P.M. Braine learned that the fort had surrendered. "The fort is ours," Hutchinson wrote. "The soldiers charged in rear & sailors and marines in front. We have three men killed & several wounded but no officers hurt on this ship."[19]

Although Hutchinson did not specify whether any of the sailors par-

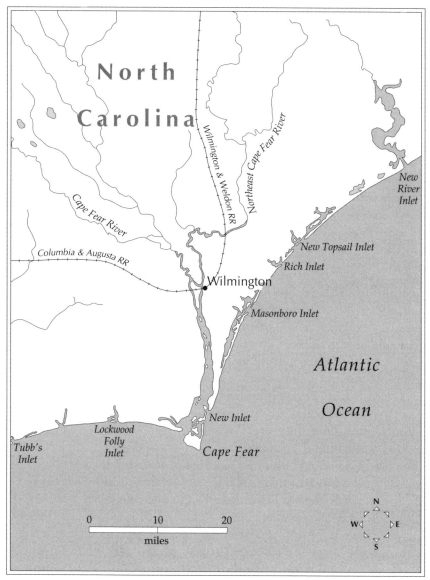

Wilmington and approaches to the Cape Fear River

ticipating in the attack on Fort Fisher were African American, the commanding officers of the *Pontoosuc* and *Minnesota* both acknowledged the contributions of black crewmen. These two vessels offer an excellent example of the role of the Union Navy in the attack on Fort Fisher and provide a glimpse into the experiences of the officers and crew, including black sailors, many of whom were probably contrabands. Among the crewmen on the *Pontoosuc,* a 1,173-ton double-ender, side-wheel gunboat, was a black sailor named Clement Dees, a seaman. Born in San Antonio, Cape Verde Islands, Dees enlisted for a two-year term in the Union Navy at Eastport, Tennessee, in June 1864. According to his enlistment record, the twenty-seven-year-old mulatto stood five feet four inches tall and listed his occupation as mariner.

The *Pontoosuc's* mission during the bombardment of Fort Fisher was to cover and assist the landing of federal troops. Some of its sailors also took part in the assault on the fort on January 15, 1865. On that day the *Pontoosuc* anchored close under the stern of the *New Ironsides* and opened fire on Fort Fisher with eleven-inch guns from 1,700 yards. It shifted to near the beach at noon and fired until 2:15 P.M. In the meantime, forty men armed with cutlasses and revolvers under the command of Acting Ensign Louis R. Chester and Acting Master's Mate Thomas Brown went ashore to participate in the assault on the fort. All returned to the ship, but Ensign Chester and six men were wounded, four severely. Commander William G. Temple told the admiral that his men had behaved admirably throughout the whole affair and that the detachment sent ashore "displayed coolness and courage under a withering fire of grape, canister, and musketry from Fort Fisher, and that several of them were prominent in bringing off the wounded."[20]

Temple recommended Medals of Honor for eight of the men under his command for their gallantry, skill, and coolness in action during operations in and about the Cape Fear River from December 24, 1864, to February 22, 1865. He specifically listed a boatswain's mate, a sailmaker's mate, James W. Verney, the chief quartermaster, the captain of the forecastle, a cabin boy, John Angling, and "Clement Dees, seaman (colored)." Although the navy awarded all eight men Medals of Honor, Dees never received his and later deserted. Ironically, in his official report of the engagement, Porter wrote that the awarding of medals was a "most popular thing," and he wished them to be given to officers also. "Anyone who has seen the pride with which sailors wear the medals bestowed upon them for gallant conduct can readily imagine how grateful it would be to officers. Trifling as such a mere bauble may be in intrinsic value, yet the history of war tells how valuable they are as inducements to perform gallant deeds."[21]

Also participating in the bombardment of Fort Fisher was the screw frigate *Minnesota,* a longtime veteran with the squadron. According to the muster roll for January 1, 1865, the *Minnesota* had 17 African Americans among its crew of 562; many had been transferred to the navy from

the army partway through their enlistments. The *Minnesota* contributed
240 officers and crew to the assault on Fort Fisher, including at least one
black sailor, and probably more. Lieutenant Commander James Parker,
who led the *Minnesota's* assault party, stated that they went ashore
around 11 A.M. "The sailors were divided into four companies, to which
proper sergeants and corporals were assigned," he wrote. "Very many
of the men had been in the Army, such as had been were armed with
Sharps rifles, and the rest with cutlasses and revolvers or pistols." On
the beach about a mile and a half from the fort, Parker's men joined
other sailors from the fleet who were divided into three divisions; the
marines formed a separate division. "The men were formed in column
and advanced up the beach toward Fort Fisher some distance," Parker
reported. "The enemy opened upon us with shell and grape, and it was
deemed advisable to form in line. This was done, the marines in front,
and then the march toward the fort resumed by the right flank of companies." When they realized that the beach offered some protection, the
assaulting party re-formed and marched close to the water's edge.[22]

About half a mile from the fort, they received word to take cover
under the crest of the beach and await the order to storm the fort. "The
enemy kept up the fire with their rifles and occasionally treated us to a
stand of grape," Parker wrote, "while the shells of the fleet passing over
us, on their way to the fort made horrid music, and some few, bursting prematurely, scattered their fragments rather nearer than was agree-
able." At about three o'clock they observed federal troops moving, and
the order came to advance. "This they gallantly and rapidly did, under a
very heavy fire of musketry and occasional grape from the enemy, which
became very hot as soon as the fire from the fleet ceased." Parker's column "pressed forward" to the palisades of the fort where it met the beach,
and a few of the officers and men advanced a few yards beyond them.
By now, however, intense rebel fire prevented the sailors and marines
from going forward, so they changed direction. "Many officers and men
had been killed," the commander told Commodore Joseph Lanman, the
Minnesota's captain, "and large numbers wounded." Fortunately, Parker
was among some 200 attackers who had reached the palisades. "Very
nearly all our sailors were there, and some of our marines," he reported,
but a mass of sailors and marines had halted a quarter mile to the north
and taken cover on a crest of beach.[23]

Parker then observed some enemy soldiers on the fort's parapet
"without arms in their hands, waving their hats to us as if desirous to surrender." Taking his cue from them, Parker ordered the men to advance,
and a large number followed him to the top of the sand hill and partway

through the breach in the palisades. "As I did so I turned to see if the others were following, and to my surprise I saw that, seized with a panic, the men were retreating on the run. Only about 60 remained with me. I tried, and so did others, in vain to rally them, and finding that the enemy were concentrating their fire upon those who remained, I ordered these behind the palisades and went [there] myself." They hid from enemy fire until nightfall, when darkness allowed them to safely carry off the wounded, their arms, and the colors. Parker had nothing but praise for the gallant conduct of those officers and men who remained with him, noting the coolness and bravery of Captain George Butler of the marines, Lieutenant E. T. Woodward, Ensigns James Birtwistle and Frederick A. O'Connor, and Acting Master's Mate Joseph M. Simms, as well as a number of sailors. Seven in the *Minnesota*'s assault party died in the attack on Fort Fisher, and twenty-five men suffered wounds. In a correction to his report of casualties, Commodore Lanman included two men as missing, one of them Charles H. Thomas, a black seaman. He may have been the same Charles Thomas, a fireman and farmer from Long Island, New York, who enlisted on the *Minnesota* as of May 6, 1864. Thomas claimed to be forty-eight years old and five feet six inches tall. Although not officially designated "colored" in the casualty report, at least one other black crew member was wounded in the attack: William Johnson, age nineteen, who was listed on the muster roll as "negro." Johnson, who described himself as a waiter, was five feet six inches tall and gave his birthplace as Baltimore. He enlisted in the navy in August 1864 and served on the *Minnesota* in 1864 and 1865. The *Minnesota* also reported seven men killed and one wounded in an explosion.[24]

Porter's fleet had accomplished what other naval forces had failed to do—capture Fort Fisher and close off the entrances to Wilmington. Following the capture of the fort, General Braxton Bragg chose not to defend Wilmington. Instead, he blew up Fort Caswell, causing an explosion heard as far away as Fayetteville. The capture of Fort Fisher and the demise of Fort Caswell left Wilmington vulnerable to attack, but Bragg merely withdrew his troops to the vicinity of Fort Anderson.

In anticipation of their advance on Wilmington, Porter's ships vigilantly watched for Confederate rams up the Roanoke River and for rebel ships bottling up the Cape Fear River. Reports of rebel rams being built at Edwards Ferry on the Roanoke River had caused Grant considerable concern, but in a soothing letter Porter reassured him that "no ram can get into the sounds if officers do their duty and carry out my orders." He told the general that he had taken ample precautions but noted that the current had opened a gap in the obstructions at New Bern and suggested that it be filled by cobwork and stone.[25]

As they had for most of the war, Union Navy commanders endeavored to gather intelligence about the rebels' rams from local African Americans. On February 19, 1865, Commander John C. Febiger, in charge of affairs at Plymouth, told Commander W. H. Macomb that the latest information he had about rebel ram building up the river "was received from a negro and was to the effect that the frame of the ram was not yet entirely up." He also assured Macomb that all the rumors and information obtained over the last month indicated that the rams were not near completion and "the rebels despair of ever being able to finish both from want of material and proper workmen." In fact, the Confederates had only one small sixty-six-ton screw steamer, to be named the *Fisher*, under construction at Edwards Ferry.[26]

The following day Macomb sent Admiral Porter a telling letter that speaks volumes about the changing nature of the war and the willingness of Union Navy commanders to rescue fleeing blacks. "Since the rebel Congress has decided to draft the negroes into their Army, the contrabands have been pouring into our lines at such a rate that there will be very few left to cultivate crops next year," Macomb wrote. He had received information that a number of runaway blacks were waiting a short distance upriver for a chance to reach Plymouth, so, he told Porter, "I sent up six boats from this ship and the *Mattabesett* and brought them all off. There were about 120 or 130 of them." Confederate conscription of blacks had been long in coming. Although the Confederacy had been suffering from manpower shortages since 1862, President Jefferson Davis had steadfastly refused to consider drafting and arming blacks and allowing them to serve as soldiers. In the winter of 1865, however, General Robert E. Lee urged the government to conscript blacks, and on March 13, 1865, the Confederate Congress passed General Order No. 14, authorizing the Confederacy to draft up to 300,000 African Americans as soldiers. Based on Macomb's correspondence in February, however, rumors of black conscription had already reached many African American men and their families, prompting numbers of them to flee.[27]

In the meantime, Union forces continued to defend their hold on the entrances to Wilmington. General Terry's troops dug in while Porter's vessels began sweeping the river for mines. Grant immediately ordered General John Schofield's Twenty-third Army Corps east from Tennessee, and shortly after their arrival on February 9, 1865, they began to advance against Wilmington from two directions. Porter ordered sixteen of his vessels up the Cape Fear River to support the attack, including the USS *Pequot*. When the army's first maneuver from Masonboro Inlet failed and the second met stiff resistance from Confederate artillery, Schofield transferred 8,000 of his men across the Cape Fear River to the west bank, requesting naval gunfire support for an attack against Fort Anderson. On February 17, 1865, Porter placed the *Montauk* close to the fort and ordered the *Pequot, Lenapee, Unadilla,* and *Pawtuxet* to enfilade the fort. Porter knew that the rebels had planted the river with torpedoes, but just before the attack on Fort Anderson, "a veracious 'contraband' paddled alongside the *Malvern* in a canoe and informed me that that enemy had a powerful ram and torpedo-vessel ready to come down upon us after dark that night." Porter ordered every vessel to keep two boats ready with crews armed for boarding and equipped with a heavy net on a pole to foul the rebel boat's propeller.[28]

The *Pequot*'s paymaster had gone off on a duck-hunting expedition, assuming there would be no fighting that day. But when he returned and got near the ship, Hutchinson wrote, "the Officer of the Deck sung out, 'Hurry up your boat and get on board and get your signal book, that's our number flying on the flagship!'" Hutchinson "looked astern and there was a boat with a colored pilot getting on board, the signal read '*Pequot* get underway and proceed up river, abreast of Monitor & began firing on Fort Anderson.'" Braine quickly got the *Pequot* under way, but at 3:30 P.M. a solid shot struck the port davit, wounding five men. "There was a flood tide, the channel was narrow, the pilot frightened, the bow struck aground on starboard hand and the stern swung quartering toward the fort," Hutchinson recalled. He stood to the port side of the quarterdeck and, seeing "a flash and a puff of smoke," stepped to his left. At that moment, he wrote, "a shell exploded at the boat davit and a fragment took off [Lyons's] hand at the wrist." Hutchinson escaped unscathed, as did Braine and the black pilot, but Quartermaster William Brian died of his wounds. Jeffrey Lyons lost his left arm, Carl Poelstrom his leg, and two others suffered minor wounds. The *Montauk* and four other Union ships enfiladed the rebel works. "The fort answered pretty briskly, but quieted down by sunset," Porter wrote.[29]

Although Schofield's troops planned to assault the fort the following day, February 18, 1865, they were delayed, John Grattan wrote, by "dense woods, cane brakes, briars, and almost impassable swamps" and could not get into position before darkness fell. Porter's ships, however, moved in closer and, with the monitor *Montauk* in the lead, kept up a heavy fire throughout the day, dropping downriver for the night. At daylight they discovered that the Confederate defenders had "hastily evacuated both Fort Anderson and their position before General Terry during the night." Union soldiers went in and hoisted the flag on the ramparts of Fort Anderson. "We lost but 3 killed and 4 wounded," Porter reported. After going ashore and inspecting the earthwork, Porter ordered his vessels to advance up the river, preceded by fifty boats equipped with grappling irons to drag for torpedoes. They snagged several mines, allowing the Union vessels to pass the obstructions. The *Malvern* then led the way upriver past Fort Anderson, directed by a rebel pilot who had deserted to the Union cause. The pilot informed Porter of the location of mines in the river, including, he claimed, many in front of the fort "only a few feet under the water." The fleet then passed safely through the area and went upriver to within five miles of Wilmington.[30]

The final push to capture Wilmington was a joint army-navy operation involving Porter's ships and federal troops, including a number of black regiments. After the evacuation of Fort Anderson, Porter sent his gunboats up as far as the water would permit, while Union troops worked their way up on both banks of the river. Steady gunfire from Porter's ships drove the Confederate defenders from Fort Strong, and the next day General Ames's division took the fort after a sharp fight and opened the road to the city. Sergeant N. B. Sterrett of the Thirty-ninth USCT served in the leading regiment of the black brigade entering Wilmington. "I would have loved for you to have a sight in the City of Wilmington on February 22nd, as we marched through. Men and women, old and young, were running through the streets, shouting and praising God. We could then truly see what we had been fighting for, and could almost realize the fruits of our labors," Sterrett wrote to the *Christian Recorder*. In his memoirs Porter recalled that after the fort's fall, a contraband informed him that the rebels intended to let a hundred mines drift down the river and blow the federal ships to pieces. The admiral ordered a double line of fishing nets spread across the river. "It was a bright moonlight night, and although we had little faith in the negro's story, we kept a good lookout all the same," Porter wrote. The contraband's information proved correct when, at about eight in the evening, Porter saw a barrel drifting downstream. He ordered a boat out to inspect it, but when the ensign in command of the boat fired on the barrel, it exploded, "dangerously wounding the officer and killing two and wounding several of the crew." Later, another mine caught in the *Osceola*'s wheel and knocked the wheelhouse "to pieces." Giving credit to his African American informant, as too few officers had done during the war, Porter explained, "But for the information given by the contraband which led to the precaution of setting the nets, I might have lost several of my vessels that night." The fall of Wilmington freed up a number of federal vessels, which Porter sent to the James River or to Hampton Roads for further orders.[31]

While Porter's ships were securing the approaches to Wilmington, Dahlgren's attention was focused on Charleston and on rumors that the Confederates might, at last, be evacuating the city. He instructed Captain Scott, the senior officer at Charleston, to remain vigilant, carefully watch rebel movements at all points of the harbor, and signal him immediately "of the first appearance of any abandonment of the city or harbor or defenses." A Union demonstration at Bull's Bay by a joint army-navy expeditionary force under Commander F. Stanly may have hastened the Confederates' decision to abandon Charleston. On February 16, 1865, federal troops escorted by the *Pawnee, Sonoma, Ottawa, Winona, Potomska, J. S. Chambers,* and *Wando* landed at Bull's Bay "without loss of one man." While an armed launch "dashed up a creek and drove in the enemy from their rifle pits," Stanly reported, Ensign Macgregor accompanied the Thirty-second Colored Regiment with a fieldpiece and destroyed bridges in the rear. In his report, Stanly noted that he had found "large numbers of slaves, but every one of them refused our offer to accompany us or the army." Obtaining a firm foothold in Bull's Bay "added much to the fear caused by General Sherman, which has caused the abandonment of Charleston on the 18th."[32]

The Confederate withdrawal from Charleston's forts and defenses had indeed left the city wide open to Union forces, and on February 18, 1865, the USS *Gladiolus* steamed into Charleston Harbor. Acting Ensign Napoleon Broughton sent a boat to Castle Pinckney and "hoisted the stars and stripes, and brought off a rebel flag." When Broughton sent a boat crew over to the blockade steamer *Syren* to take it as a prize, they discovered that the steamer was on fire. "I got on board of her as soon as possible," Acting Master's Mate Sydney W. Byram wrote, and "found the flames gaining rapidly, the hatches broken open, and about twenty negroes engaged in loading their boats from the cargo." Byram wasted no time in dealing with these looters. He quickly organized the blacks into a fire party and "set them to work putting out the fire, which we succeeded in doing after a while." The *Syren* was later towed into shoal water.[33]

In describing the Union occupation of Charleston, an astonished Dahlgren told Welles, "Not a shot was fired for the place, not a blow struck." He explained that the rebels "went unheralded by a shot, and today I quietly steamed up the wharves and walked through the town." Then a vindicated Dahlgren added, "I have just walked over the city, every house is shut up, the few persons in the streets were foreigners and negroes. . . . As they have made their beds, let them lie."[34]

The *Harvest Moon*'s surgeon, Ashael Sumner Dean, enjoyed several hours in Charleston and described the city in glowing terms, telling his wife of the oranges, the oleanders, the magnolias, and the warm spring weather. "The people are gone, their furniture and servants are gone. I mean the wealthy. Those who were too poor to go had to remain," he explained. Charleston's African American population reacted with joy to the arrival of federal troops. "The next thing was the colored people," Dean wrote. "They shouted and danced and sang and prayed and when the first troops marched down the street . . . their joy could not be constrained. They followed them in a mob whose only desire seemed to be to exult and dance and sing." According to an article in the *Walton Reporter*, when the 144th New York Volunteer Infantry Regiment arrived in Mount Pleasant, a suburb of Charleston, on the morning of February 20, 1865, "A colored woman gave one of the men of the 144th a United States flag which she had secreted. 'Bress de Lawd, bress de Lawd!' she cried with joy and tears mingling on her face."[35]

With Charleston in Union hands, federal vessels began going up the Cooper River into the interior to support the army. Fleeing Confederates gave them a "warm" reception, however. When Acting Master F. M. Montell took the USS *Potomska* up the Cooper River on the morning of February 20, 1865, rebels fired a volley of musketry at the vessel from a plantation on the riverbank. The *Potomska* returned fire with its port broadside guns and rifle and discharged "several stand of grape and a few 5-second shell." As had happened so often during the war, most noticeably after the fall of Port Royal, the plantation's owners had fled, taking with them as many slaves as possible. "The slaves, as I understand, were herded together the night previous for the purpose of being transported to Georgetown by way of the Georgetown and old ferry road, but several succeeded in escaping from their masters," Montell reported. This plantation belonged to a Colonel Singleton, he told Dahlgren, "a rank secessionist, and who has often boasted of going on Long Island and shooting our pickets."[36]

Although Georgetown, South Carolina, had not yet been secured, Dahlgren had not forgotten about the city. On February 19, 1865, he sent the *Harvest Moon* to scout up the Santee River and two gunboats to Georgetown Harbor. He then fired off a note to Commander J. Blakeley Creighton of the USS *Mingoe*, asking him whether he had taken the battery at Georgetown and stating that if not, he would send Creighton 150 marines. "*Pawnee* is on the way up," he assured Creighton.[37]

The next morning Creighton learned from rebel deserters that Fort

White had been abandoned. Anxious to confirm these reports, Creighton decided to go upriver, but he had no pilot. Like so many other commanders, he turned to a local black waterman for assistance. "I got underway and stood up the river, moving very slowly," he wrote, "for I had no other guide than a contraband that had been upon the river here, Prince, my pilot, being with the *Geranium* for the purpose of sounding out Santee bar." Prince Coit, a former fisherman and reputed to be the "best pilot out of Georgetown," had arrived at the USS *Keystone State* on March 1, 1862, with J. N. Merriman, a former collector at the port of Georgetown. Sending boats out to search for mines and finding none, Creighton pushed on and fired three rounds into Fort White. When he got no response the commander sent his executive officer with a boat party to occupy the fort.[38]

With Fort White in Union hands, the occupation of Georgetown soon followed. Captain Stellwagen ordered the little tug USS *Catalpa*, Acting Ensign Allen K. Noyes commanding, to go upriver toward Georgetown early on February 25. Noyes arrived at the Georgetown dock, asked for keys to the town hall, and then sent a party to raise the American flag above that building. However, he wrote, "as soon as the flag was raised, the rebel horsemen made a dash in the town, and engaging the men of this vessel sent by me to scout the outskirts of the town, after some fifteen minutes fighting, they captured one man, Morris Sullivan, an ordinary seaman." As soon as the alarm was given, armed boats from the *Catalpa* and *Mingoe* were sent to shore, and the sailors drove the enemy out of town. Dahlgren proudly reported to Welles that his forces had occupied Georgetown, South Carolina: "The town is being held by six companies of marines under Lieutenant Stoddard, and the battery (15 guns) by one company of marines under Lieutenant Breese. *Mingoe* flanks the town and commands it with her guns."[39]

On that same Sunday, February 25, 1865, the *Harvest Moon* set sail for Georgetown. Arriving offshore, surgeon Dean sent a description of the newly occupied port to his wife, Virginia: "Georgetown is a port of entry at the head of Winyaw Bay. Exports rice, turpentine and lumber chiefly. An old place, has some fine residences and stores. . . . The people here are chiefly Negroes. The Whites are Secesh." Dean explained, "The Admiral has put the City under martial law and issued a proclamation, a part of which reads thus: 'In accordance with an Act of Congress, etc. Slavery no longer exists within the limits of the Union and every man is entitled to the fruits of his own labor' and so forth. The Negroes seems to anticipate this proclamation for hundreds came down and wanted to 'ship.'" Knowing that the navy was always short of manpower, Dean saw the arrival of so many contrabands as a boon for his ship. "I examined and passed 15 and they are now in service."[40]

Dean went into the city of Georgetown and told Virginia, "The people are sullen and will not speak to us if they can help it. Not so with the Negroes. I went into several of their shanties and found them in great glee. They say, 'why did you stay away so long? We've been praying and praying for you to come.'" Union gunboats had twice before sailed up the river to Georgetown but had not attempted to seize the city, giving rise to this lament by the city's black population. From Dean's description of the vibrant spirituality of the town's African American population, their faith had sustained them as they waited and prayed for liberation. He wrote, "Theirs is a religion of the heart—I got our guides to sing wrestle Jacob and I'm Bound to the Land of Canaan . . . nothing pleases me more than to see their strong faith helping them when their Wives and Children are run off and in difficulties which would appall even you and I. These people gave us their chickens, pigs, and ducks, etc. saying, 'We wish we had more to give you, you are welcome.'" The blacks' heartfelt prayers touched Dean, who told his wife that all those he had examined "were scarred badly and have suffered terribly." Dean also learned that "more than twenty of them have been hung for trying to reach our lines."[41]

The advance of Sherman's army into areas formerly controlled by the Confederacy and the Union occupation of Charleston, Georgetown, and Wilmington freed large numbers of slaves and gave others the opportunity to escape. Some African Americans took refuge in the Virginia Tidewater, but many, fearful of being caught and punished by their masters, remained on plantations and simply waited for a Union victory.

Fortunately for many African Americans in the South, the tide was turning in the Union's favor, and none too soon for the war-weary sailors in the Union Navy. From the monitor *Nahant*, still on station in Stono Inlet, surgeon Samuel Gilbert Webber anxiously followed the progress of the war and sent news to his wife, Nannie. In late February he informed her, "Sherman is said to be advancing towards Virginia & there is almost nothing to oppose him. Wilmington is evacuated. I trust that now so near the end nothing may happen adverse to our arms." Weary of the war and the monotony of blockade duty, Webber wrote, "May God bless our generals & give them wisdom & may this war soon cease." He told his wife that for months he had been praying for the war to end, "& I thank God that He has heard me in giving us so much success." An avowed abolitionist, Webber concluded, "And we shall henceforth be a nation without the curse of slavery. I doubt not that the amendment to the constitution will pass and that source of discord will be removed & in so far we shall be righteous." Webber was referring to the impending passage of the Thirteenth Amendment, abolishing slavery throughout the nation. The original amendment had been completed by the Senate Judiciary Committee a year earlier, on February 10, 1864, but had failed to gain the two-thirds vote necessary for passage in the House of Representatives. On January 31, 1865, the House finally passed the amendment to the cheers and acclamation of those present, but the amendment awaited ratification by the states. Maryland and Missouri had already enacted legislation to abolish slavery.[42]

When the Confederates retreated from Wilmington, Porter sent many of the squadron's vessels back to the sounds of North Carolina and to the James River, where the war was far from over and the rebels continued to keep navy crews vigilant. Union vessels in the James had been on alert since New Year's Day, reacting to rumors that a rebel squadron might come down the river and either pass Union ironclads or attack and destroy Grant's supply base at City Point. These reports had a basis in fact, for on January 16, 1865, Confederate Navy Secretary Stephen Mallory had ordered Flag Officer Mitchell to take the *Virginia II, Richmond, Fredericksburg,* and *Drewry,* along with smaller vessels, down the James River through a gap in the obstructions caused by winter rains.[43]

After a week's delay, Mitchell finally took his Confederate squadron down the James, but only the lighter-draft *Fredericksburg* managed to get over the obstructions. Just one Union vessel, the USS *Onondaga,* blocked the rebel ironclad's path. Rather than steaming to meet the enemy, however, Commander William Parker ordered the *Onondaga* downstream toward a pontoon bridge, where he thought he would have more room to maneuver and engage the rebel ships. Exasperated by Parker's lack of initiative, Grant telegraphed him on January 24, "What fleet have you collected or ordered to the front? You ought to have every gunboat you can get in the river up with you." Grant reminded Parker that it was his duty to attack any rebel vessels coming downstream and to defend the supply base at City Point. When a disgruntled Grant telegraphed Welles and told him that Parker "seems helpless" and that Grant was sending direct orders to navy commanders, the Navy Department moved swiftly to relieve Parker. Welles ordered Admiral David G. Farragut down to the James River and ordered the commandant at Norfolk to send all ironclads "within your reach" up the James.[44]

In the meantime, Union batteries at Trent's Reach had fired on the rebel ironclads, one shell hitting the *Drewry* and blowing it to pieces. The *Onondaga* finally got into the action, and its big fifteen-inch guns dealt the *Virginia II* a direct hit. The USS *Massasoit,* Lieutenant Commander G. Watson Sumner commanding, supported the *Onondaga,* falling in behind the monitor and taking fire from a rebel gun battery. In this, the *Massasoit's* first action, there were five casualties among the ship's crew. One of those who escaped injury was a sixteen-year-old black landsman named Lewis Latimer. The son of escaped slaves, Latimer had enlisted for three years at Boston in September 1864, giving his occupation as waiter. After the war Latimer became a draftsman, then an inventor who worked with Alexander Graham Bell and Hiram Maxim. Bested by the *Onondaga* and *Massasoit,* the Confederate ships retired upstream, and after one more cautious effort that night, Mitchell decided to call off his attack. Grant's troops and supply depot at City Point remained wide open to attack, however, still defended by just a single vessel, the *Onondaga.* Despite Grant's and Porter's fears, the Confederate naval squadron remained above the obstructions and never tested them again.[45]

At the end of February Porter's attention shifted back to the Cape Fear River, Wilmington, and the progress of Sherman's army. Anxious to learn Sherman's whereabouts, on March 1, 1865, Porter sent Lieutenant Commander Chandler in the USS *Lenapee* up the Cape Fear River to the West Branch in search of information from rebel deserters, local African Americans, or sympathetic whites. Chandler took the *Lenapee* up the river and reported, "I remained there until 1 o'clock P.M. to-day. During the night some negroes came down, and, on questioning them, they informed me that they had been told General Sherman's forces were at a town called Robeson, 20 miles from Fayetteville."[46]

Two days after Chandler's reconnaissance, General Schofield handed a cipher dispatch to Acting Master H. Walton Grinnell with instructions to locate Sherman and deliver the dispatch to him. On the evening of March 4, 1865, Grinnell left the USS *Nyack* in a small dugout with a volunteer party consisting of Acting Ensign H. B. Colby, seaman Thomas Gillespie, and Joseph Williams, the ship's painter. They carried rifles, revolvers, and two days' rations. After going upriver about twelve miles, Grinnell's party encountered a rebel advance picket post and passed it without being discovered. At a point near Livingston's Creek, however, Grinnell wrote, "I found the picket so strongly posted that I deemed it the more prudent course to abandon my boat and to attempt to communicate with General Sherman's forces near the Pedee River." The following morning Grinnell's party struck out on foot for the Wilmington and Whitehall road passing through the village of Summerville, where they destroyed some arms. Learning that a party of rebel cavalry intended to cut him off at Livingston's bridge, Grinnell reported, "I was reluctantly compelled to secrete myself and party in negro hut near by." He stayed there two days until the rebels grew tired of searching for him and recrossed the river. "At dark on the 7th instant, having secured the services of a negro guide, I started in the direction of Whiteville, advancing with caution and moving only by night." Led by their black guide on a tedious journey through the swamps, on the morning of March 9 Grinnell and his party reached a point near the town of Whiteville, which was held by a strong enemy force. Their slow progress on foot frustrated Grinnell, so he decided to travel faster by impressing some horses and, "by a bold dash break through the pickets on the Lumberton road." His plan worked perfectly. They reached a crossroads, dashed through the pickets, and captured and disarmed two rebels of Company A, Fifty-first North Carolina Infantry. Grinnell made the rebels follow him for five miles, then paroled them. "After hard riding night and day," Grinnell wrote, "I reached Downing Creek, at a point near the town of Lumberton, on the afternoon of 11th. Here I first learned of the whereabouts of General Sherman's forces." Grinnell and his men finally met the rear scouts of Sherman's army at Lumber Bridge Road, about twenty miles from Fayetteville, but as wagons and artillery blocked the road, he did not reach the general's headquarters until 1 P.M. on March 12. "General Sherman received the dispatch and expressed himself much surprised at receiving it through the Navy and by such a route," Grinnell reported to his superior, Lieutenant Commander George Young. Grinnell praised the conduct of Ensign Colby and his two sailors, Gillespie and Williams, "who were every ready to encounter any dangers or hardships that came in their way." He did not, however, elaborate on the assistance of his African American guide or the inhabitants of the hut, if there were any, where his party had spent two nights. Neither the guide nor any blacks who may have sheltered his party along the way were in Union service, which may explain why Grinnell failed to acknowledge them. This is yet another example of the valuable but often unheralded contributions of anonymous African Americans to the navy's war effort.[47]

In the meantime, while Grinnell's party was searching for Sherman, Commander Young had gone up the Cape Fear River in an army tug and reached Fayetteville on the evening of March 12. In a letter to his brother, Major Thomas W. Osborn noted the arrival of Young's tug: "A little river steamer from Wilmington arrived here this morning and will return at noon," he wrote. "The boat left Wilmington at 2 P.M. yesterday and ran the gauntlet of rebel musketry from both sides of the river, for several miles. The officer in charge is deserving of great credit for coming up so promptly." Also noting the arrival of Grinnell's boat party,

Osborn wrote, "A naval boat is below us, some of the officers having landed and come through on foot. They are considerably chagrined that the tug beat them in coming through."[48]

Summing up the campaign to date, Major Osborn explained that they had come from Beaufort, marching through Pocotaglio, Hickory Hill, Midway, Orangeburg, Columbia, Winnsboro, and Cheraw to Fayetteville. "So far this campaign has been a great success and will be of great value in the final closing of the war. We have marched 400 miles, destroyed some 20 miles of railroad and all the factories of three large manufacturing cities. Columbia, Cheraw, and Fayetteville, where supplies were produced for the southern armies." Sherman's troops cut a swath of destruction according to William Craig, who wrote to his wife from Goldsboro, North Carolina, on April 3, 1865: "We burned the houses and the women and children standing outside crying. Neither clothes nor nothing to eat. We traveled about 4 hundred miles through the center of South Carolina and we cleaned everything in the distance of 80 miles wide and we are doing the same in this country." Osborn noted the many white refugees and contrabands who had followed Sherman's troops from Columbia and estimated that they numbered about 7,000 persons. He told his brother they had captured "a moderate steamer, which will be sent down, loaded with refugees, who came from Columbia, with us." Sherman complained that these refugees "have clung to our skirts, and impeded our movements, and consumed our food." Anxious to rid himself of these refugees, both white and black, Sherman ordered them collected and sent to Wilmington. Osborn observed them as they moved past headquarters. "A majority of them were women and children though there were a good many able bodied men. A few house servants were well dressed, the great majority of them were very scantily clad, if clad at all. The field hands were in field dress which by the way, most of them had worn since the breaking out of the war, and patched and mended till the present time." According to Osborn, "This troop of negroes is of all ages, sexes and colors, the black however, predominating." General O. O. Howard saw the column of refugees as well and described them in a letter to his wife dated March 16, 1865: "Bundles on their heads, children in arms, men on mules, women in old wagons, all poorly clad & many with little to eat. They will do anything! Suffer anything for freedom. They go they know not where. I can only think and say to myself God will care for them." Indeed, their fate is not well documented.[49]

Although peace was just weeks away, these final Union operations of the Civil War proved risky to officers and men of both blockading squadrons, including Admiral Dahlgren. On the morning of March 1, 1865, his flagship the *Harvest Moon,* which had recently enlisted eighteen contrabands as landsmen, was steaming from Winyah Bay to Charleston. "It was nearly 8 o'clock, and I was waiting breakfast in the cabin," Dahlgren recalled, "when instantly a loud noise and shock occurred and the bulkhead separating the cabin for the wardroom was shattered and driven in toward me." The explosion did not injure the admiral, who at first thought "that the boiler had burst, as a report had been made the previous evening by engineer that it needed repair badly." According to the *Harvest Moon's* log, the ship ran into a mine that "blowed a hole through the starboard quarter tearing away the main deck over it which caused this ship to sink in 5 minutes in two & half fathoms of water." The tug *Clover* came to assist the stricken ship and took off Dahlgren and his staff. It also picked up landsman Patrick McGrath, who had been thrown overboard. Remarkably, there was only one casualty, John Hazzard, a white wardroom steward who had been in the hold at the time of the explosion.[50]

"Torpedoes" or mines strewn in rivers and creeks continued to plague ships of both blockading squadrons until the end of the war.[51] Federal vessels probing rivers and streams in March 1865 also ran afoul of rebel troops and guerrillas. Fortunately, friendly blacks warned some of these Union vessels of danger. On the evening of March 7, 1865, for example, Lieutenant Commander George Morris took the side-wheel steamer USS *Chenango* up the Black River from Georgetown, searching for a small rebel steamer rumored to be there. Morris anchored for the night in the narrow river and proceeded the next morning to a plantation owned by a Mr. Perkins. When the pilot decided they could go no farther, Morris landed. Here, he wrote, "I learned from negroes that the little steamer I was in search of had been carried 30 miles farther up the river." The blacks, some of whom lived at the Perkins plantation, also warned Morris that about thirty mounted cavalry "armed with rifles" lay in wait to attack Morris's boats should they venture farther upriver. In addition, they reported that the rebels had a company of mounted troops at Brown's Ferry, which the *Chenango* had passed earlier that morning. After nearly four years of war and countless accurate reports by local blacks and contrabands, it is no surprise that Morris believed this information to be true and decided to revisit the plantations as he went downriver, keeping all hands at general quarters. As predicted, near Brown's Ferry the rebels opened fire on the *Chenango* from behind a levee or bluff. "We immediately responded with broadside guns and riflemen stationed in the tops," Morris reported. His officers, who were

aloft, claimed that some of the rebels had been hit. Thanks to the warning by the friendly African Americans, the *Chenango*'s crew was ready
for the attack, and only one seaman, a man named Charles Wilson, suffered serious wounds.[52]

In yet another expedition on March 16, 1865, the *Don, Stepping
Stones, Heliotrope,* and *Resolute,* vessels assigned to Commander Foxhall Parker's Potomac Flotilla, pushed up Mattox Creek, Virginia, and
landed armed parties to search houses in the area and along the left side
of the creek. The following day the *Don*'s commanding officer, Lieutenant Commander T. H. Eastman, went ashore with seventy sailors
and marines to clear the right side of Mattox Creek and sent Ensign
Summers in a launch up the creek's left prong. Summers's boat crew
destroyed three schooners but came under fire from 300 or 400 rebels.
Within just a few moments the rebel fire had cut away half the launch's
oars and cut the barrel off the musket Summers was firing. Miraculously,
only one man, Robert Lee, was slightly injured in the action. This boat
expedition, one of dozens completed during the spring of 1865, would
not have been particularly notable except for one important comment
in Eastman's report: "The crew of the boat were all black but two," he
wrote, "and P[atrick] Mullen, boatswain's mate of the U.S.S. *Don,* and
Aaron Anderson, landsmen (colored), of the *Wyandank,* are reported to
me by Acting Ensign Summers as having assisted him gallantly—Mullen
lying on his back while loading the howitzer and then firing so carefully
as to kill and wound many rebels, besides driving them away." Eastman
recommended that Summers be recognized for his gallant action and
promoted to master. Anderson, the black landsman, received a Medal of
Honor for bravery, as did white crewman Mullen.[53]

In addition to visiting plantations along the river and destroying boats
and vessels belonging to the Confederates, Union gunboat officers and
crews occasionally assisted white families by restoring order during this
socially unstable time. In one such case, four naval officers went to a
plantation with good intentions but unfortunate consequences for themselves. As Acting Master's Mate Thomas Newton of the *Jonquil* reported
to Dahlgren, officers from his ship and from the *Philadelphia* and *John*
went ashore on March 21, 1865, "for the purpose of assisting some of
the white families against the negroes at Lewis-field." According to Acting Ensign Charles Hanson of the USS *Jonquil,* he, Henry Lynch, William Barclay, and John Ryan had set off toward the plantation of a Mr.
Ebough "to restore order amongst the negroes on his farm." The well-
intentioned foursome never made it to Ebough's plantation, however.
At a fork in the road leading to the house, they ran into a band of rebel

pickets or perhaps guerrilla troops and succeeded in driving them back to their main force. However, Hanson wrote, "we were obliged to retreat and take cover behind the trees on the roadside," where they made a stand until completely surrounded by twenty-three rebels. "I am sorry to say that after four years of fighting, I was obliged to surrender myself a prisoner of war to the so-called Confederate States of America." The rebels marched Hanson and his three fellow officers to Orangeburg, where guards stepped in and prevented the local citizens from hanging them. After being sent to Augusta and confined, they were paroled on May 1, 1865. Hanson failed to mention his reaction to being captured by rebels while on a mission to protect a white plantation family, possibly with Confederate sympathies, from blacks who were probably reacting to their new status as free people.[54]

During the spring of 1865 rebel pickets and guerrilla bands threatened not only the crews of Union gunboats but also ordinary citizens, white and black alike. Hearing of guerrilla threats against the plantations and settlements along the Waccamaw River, and noting the "great alarm . . . felt on the whole route by blacks and whites," on March 27, 1865, Captain H. S. Stellwagen dispatched the *Mingoe*, towing ten armed boats, up the river as high as Buck's Mills. Stellwagen followed with the steam tug *Catalpa*, a steam launch, and two large row launches from the Santee. A shore party continued by land, and "after incredible labor and difficulty," Stellwagen's party made it to Conwayboro at nightfall. "The people of the town were glad to see us, even those having relatives in the army professed their joy at being saved from the raiding deserters," he wrote. The townspeople hoped the Union force would prevent the guerrillas from returning to that neighborhood. Reporting to Dahlgren, Stellwagen stated that he had permitted several Union people to come down to Georgetown and had "met many negroes coming down in flats." Fearing famine if they did not begin to plant crops, Stellwagen had encouraged both blacks and whites to do so and told Dahlgren that he hoped these efforts might save hundreds of lives.[55]

Concerned about preserving order and providing future sustenance for the population, the next day Dahlgren wrote to Welles from Charleston: "Our own military force is generally limited to the city lines. The gunboats are advanced up the Cooper River, and the officers use their efforts to preserve order as well as they can and to extend the United States laws to white and black." He explained to Welles that the "chief danger is from probable lack of food, the season for planting is at hand, and the freedmen have not generally agreed on terms with landowners." Work had commenced on some of the plantations, the admiral wrote, adding, "The negroes have generally proved docile and well disposed, and a little judicious action would put the new system into full movement." The new system of free labor would be put to the test when the war ended and the Reconstruction began.[56]

The war was rapidly moving to a conclusion. By mid-March 1865 Union troops had taken possession of Kinston, and following an engagement with the Confederates at Bentonville on March 24, Sherman's troops entered Goldsboro, North Carolina. When Sherman's army met Schofield's corps at Goldsboro, their combined strength spelled doom for Confederate general Joseph Johnston's army, which would be hard-pressed to keep Sherman's and Schofield's troops from joining Grant's in Virginia. Seizing the moment, Grant's troops began a movement to turn Lee's flank southwest of Petersburg on March 29, 1865, and the weakened Army of Northern Virginia fell back. General Philip Sheridan's men cut the railroad into Petersburg, and as the infantry began to push through rebel lines, General Robert E. Lee saw the handwriting on the wall. On April 2, 1865, Confederate forces withdrew from Petersburg, and Lee telegraphed President Jefferson Davis, stating, "I think it is absolutely necessary that we should abandon our position tonight." The rebels evacuated Richmond, and the Confederates blew up their ironclads in the river. "The *Patrick Henry* was in flames at rockets, and the Navy Yard and all public buildings therein situated were in process of destruction. Several of the smaller vessels were burned at the city wharves," the *Richmond Whig* reported. The city officially surrendered at about ten o'clock to Major General Godfrey Weitzel. "We took Richmond at quarter past eight this morning," Weitzel telegraphed Secretary of War Edwin Stanton. "I captured many guns. The enemy left in great haste. The city is on fire in one place. Am making every effort to put it out. The people received us with enthusiastic expressions of joy." He also wrote that Grant had started toward Danville to cut off Lee's retreating army and that President Lincoln had "gone to the front."[57]

That same day Porter accompanied Lincoln up to Richmond, where, Porter wrote, "he was received with the strongest demonstrations of joy." In his recollections of the war Porter related that neither he nor the barge crew bearing the president knew where to land in Richmond, so they found a small landing. "Behind it were twelve negroes digging with spades. The leader of them was an old man sixty years of age. He raised himself to an upright position as we landed, and put his hands up to his eyes. Then he dropped his spade and sprang forward 'Bress de Lord,' he said, 'dere is de great Messiah! I knowed him as soon as I seed him He's bin in my heart for' long yeahs, an' he's cum at las' to free his chillun from deir bondage. Glory, Hallelujah!'" The twelve men then joined hands and sang a hymn. Soon a crowd of jubilant blacks gathered near the president, nearly overwhelming him and the admiral's barge party. Lincoln told them they were free and spoke to them of liberty: "Liberty is your birthright. God gave it to you as he gave it to others, and it is a sin that you have been deprived of it for so many years." Porter also noted, "We found the rebel rams and gunboats had all been blown up, with the exception of unfinished ram, the *Texas,* and a small tug gunboat, the *Beaufort,* mounting one gun." Within the week, in a practice established earlier in the war by army forces, the army quartermaster had employed hundreds of contrabands to collect abandoned rebel ordnance, naval stores, and machinery along the Richmond docks. On April 10 the chief quartermaster of the Army of the James, John B. Howard, instructed the acting quartermaster, Captain J. C. Slaght, to "employ all colored men who make application, or are sent to you" and to take possession of a large empty building near the steamboat wharf and have it fitted as quarters for the contrabands. Howard told Slaght to arrange for cooking facilities, quarters, and an eating room and to find another small building for a hospital. Then Howard noted, "Quite a number of the contrabands in the Quartermaster's employ are women. These are now engaged as cooks and laundresses." He claimed that they were well clothed and were getting all they wanted to eat "and appear as happy as they possibly can be." According to the *New York Herald* on April 13, 1865: "In all there are employed along the docks about one thousand negroes. Some are engaged in loading and unloading government vessels, others in carting, hoeing and shoveling, more in carrying, collecting and storing, and all to a good purpose."[58]

In Hampton Roads, officers and men of the Union Navy greeted the news of Richmond's fall with joy and celebration. From Hampton, Commander E. T. Nichols wrote to Porter, "Upon receipt of the glorious news yesterday all naval vessels in the roads dressed with flags and a salute fired from *Sabine.*"[59]

Though hailed as a great Union victory, the fall of Richmond did not mark the end of the war for Union soldiers or for the men of the blockading squadrons. Just three days after President Lincoln's entry into Richmond, Welles sent an alarming report to Parker, commanding the Potomac Flotilla, that rebels had captured the steamer *Harriet De Ford* at Fair Haven in the Chesapeake Bay, some thirty miles below Annapolis. The rebels then used the ship to chase another steamer. Initial reports about the seizure of the *Harriet De Ford* indicated that a rebel party of twenty-seven men, led by a Captain Fitzhugh, had taken the one-masted propeller; released the captain, mate, and white passengers; and sailed down the bay. "Use your best exertions to recapture the steamer or overtake the rebel party," Welles urged Parker, who immediately ordered Acting Volunteer Lieutenant Edward Hooker of the *Commodore Read* to overhaul all steamers and be prepared to sink the *Harriet De Ford* "should you fall in with her."[60]

Suspecting that the steamer might be lurking somewhere on the eastern shore, on April 6, 1865, Parker also instructed Hooker to send the *Putnam* to Mobjack Bay to join the *Western World* in searching for the captured steamer. "During the day send your vessels out into the bay and overhaul everything passing," he told Hooker. With information supplied by two of the captured steamer's crew, Simon Brown and James Hudson, the *Commodore Read, Coeur de Lion,* and *Heliotrope* quickly found the *Harriet De Ford.* "We have holed the rat, but can't get at him, he is in Indian Creek," the lieutenant told Parker that same day. To reinforce Hooker's three vessels, Parker sent him the *Mercury, Freeborn, Currituck,* and *Yankee.*[61]

Joined by the *Freeborn,* the *Commodore Read* and *Coeur de Lion* entered Indian Creek, but the latter soon went aground hard and fast. The *Read* managed to pull the *Lion* off, and Hooker found a pilot on board the *Heliotrope* who knew the channels of the creeks well. The pilot guided them up about five miles, Hooker explained, "all of us shelling woods and suspicious places. While there we took on board a number of contrabands, among them one of the crew of the captured steamer." When these contrabands informed Hooker that the *Harriet De Ford* had gone to Dimer's Creek, not Indian Creek, he ordered the *Freeborn* and *Coeur de Lion* to Dimer's Creek. The *Commodore Read* followed, guided by the *Heliotrope*'s pilot, whom Hooker applauded for "a service which was most satisfactorily performed, the pilot carrying me to a higher point in each creek than other gunboat of equal draft has ever before attained." At Dimer's Creek Hooker found the wreck of the captured steamer, which had been set on fire by the enemy and burned to the water's edge. "She was still burning when we boarded her," he reported. The Union vessels fired into the steamer's boiler and machinery to destroy it and returned to the Rappahannock River. Hooker concluded his report with distressing news: "Contrabands which I have report that the negroes captured in the steamer were taken to Kilmarnock and sold at auction yesterday afternoon. I would respectfully suggest that there are many rank rebels, male and female, within our reach who might be seized as hostages for these negroes."[62]

A week later Hooker sent Parker further information about the capture of the *Harriet De Ford* provided by two black crewmen from the steamer. They told Hooker the names of two of the men responsible for the *Harriet De Ford's* capture: John Turpin and Robert Hudgins. The black crewmen recognized the former as the son of Sewell Turpin of Worcester County, Maryland, for whom they had worked. This did not, however, end the affair of the *Harriet De Ford*. On April 10, 1865, Parker steamed up the Rappahannock in the USS *Don,* where he captured a boat "containing four persons, three of whom proved to be rebel soldiers and the fourth a blockade runner." In a carpetbag found in the boat, Parker discovered "two orders from T. Fitzhugh, leader of the gang of guerillas who captured the *Harriet De Ford,* to a Captain Henderson, to deliver certain goods belonging to said vessel to the blockade runner." Parker immediately sent an expedition to find and arrest Captain Henderson, who was then turned over to the provost marshal at Point Lookout, Maryland. After Henderson's arrest, Parker reported, the people in the neighborhood of Kilmarnock "expressed a desire to return the stolen property from the *Harriet De Ford*." According to Hooker, he recovered a brass six-pounder trunnion piece from the *Harriet De Ford* and assisted the vessel's owner to salvage whatever he could from the wreck. Neither Parker nor Hooker mentioned whether any action had been taken with regard to the African Americans sold at auction.[63]

The *Harriet De Ford* affair offers a fitting conclusion to this examination of the relationship between the Union Navy and African Americans during the Civil War. Throughout the war along the East Coast, Union Navy commanders organized expeditions and raids to follow up on information provided by local African Americans, Confederate deserters, and other refugees. Hooker's expedition up the Rappahannock into several small creeks in search of a steamer seized and burned by a band of rebel guerrillas represents just one of many such small actions. Like many of these brown-water operations, Hooker's expedition attracted African Americans who approached the federal gunboats seeking sanctuary. In this case, one of those contrabands proved to be a member of the crew of the captured *Harriet De Ford*, and he offered valuable information about its actual location that allowed Hooker and his vessels to find and destroy the steamer. After Parker's capture of Captain Henderson, Hooker succeeded in retrieving property taken from the vessel but, sadly, not the black crewmen seized by the rebel guerrillas and sold at auction. Following the cessation of hostilities they may have been freed, but their fate remains unknown.

At the end of July 1865 Parker ordered that some of the boats seized in the Patuxent River be returned to claimants, among them Ezekiel

Daniels, who represented himself as an agent for "colored" people who had lost their boats. Daniels was told that "if colored men came and identified their property, it would be returned to them," Parker wrote. "No colored men appeared, but Mr. Daniels brought with him to the depot a number of white men not willing to take the prescribed oath," one of whom claimed that he had lost his boat many months earlier in the Potomac River. "Under these circumstances," Parker wrote, "I directed that the boats should be distributed among officers, seamen, and pilots who had served faithfully during the rebellion, and to some contrabands who had acted as guides." They were given to these persons without charge.[64]

In his farewell to the officers and men of the Potomac Flotilla, Fox-hall Parker wrote the following:

> In taking leave of those with whom I have been so long associated, my heart is filled with various emotions—with sorrow at parting, gladness that our beloved country no longer has need of us, and pride, just pride, that when I reflect upon the past and remember the taking up of the torpedoes from the Rappahannock with the destruction or capture of the whole rebel force engaged in placing them there, thereby making Fredericksburg a secure base of supplies for General Grant's vast army, the burning of the schooners at Mattox Creek under the severe musketry fire of the enemy, and the almost daily expeditions up the rivers, in the creeks, and through the marshes of the northern neck of Virginia—all requiring skill and nerve—I can truly say "The Potomac Flotilla has not been unmindful of the traditional honor and glory of the Navy."[65]

These eloquent words are fitting tribute to all the officers and men of the Union Navy's Potomac Flotilla and to those of the North and South Atlantic Blockading Squadrons as well. His words honor, too, the contribution of the Union Navy's African American sailors, but they fail to acknowledge the vital contribution of thousands of African American men and women who served as informants, spies, pilots, guides, laborers, laundresses, nurses, mechanics, and purveyors of fresh meat and produce. Their service and loyalty to the Union cause helped make a Union victory in the Civil War possible.

NOTES

ABBREVIATIONS

ORA   R. N. Scott et al., eds., *The War of the Rebellion: A Compilation of the Official Records of the Union and Confederate Armies,* 70 vols. (Washington, D.C.: Government Printing Office, 1880–1901).

ORN   Richard Rush et al., eds., *Official Records of the Union and Confederate Navies in the War of the Rebellion,* 31 vols., series 1 (Washington, D.C.: Government Printing Office, 1894–1927).

SFDP Letters John Hayes, ed., *Samuel Francis Du Pont: A Selection of His Civil War Letters,* 2 vols. (Ithaca, N.Y.: Cornell University Press, 1969).

INTRODUCTION

1. Litwack, *Been in the Storm So Long,* especially chap. 4. Ward's recent study *Slaves' War* offers numerous experiences of slaves on plantations during the war.

2. Cecelski, *Waterman's Song,* 123–27; Gara, *Liberty Line,* chap. 1.

3. Cecelski, *Waterwan's Song,* xvi, 53. Abraham H. Galloway, a slave who escaped from the village of Smithville to Philadelphia on a schooner in 1857, returned to New Bern during the war as a Union spy and abolitionist leader.

4. Gara, *Liberty Line,* 28–29, 192–94; Cecelski, *Waterman's Song,* 8–11, 58, 65–66; Hoag Levins, "New Jersey's Underground Railroad Myth-Buster," June 4, 2001, http://historiccamdencounty.com/ccnws11.shtml; Fladeland, *Men and Brothers,* 343. See also Pacheco, *The Pearl.* Gara argues that fewer slaves escaped along the so-called underground railroad than was previously thought.

5. Litwack, *Been in the Storm So Long,* 23; Cecelski, *Waterman's Song,* 123; Levins, "New Jersey's Underground Railroad Myth-Buster."

6. Ramold, *Slaves, Sailors, Citizens,* 39–41; A. D. Harrell to Commander Potomac Flotilla, November 8, 1861, in Berlin et al., eds., *Freedom,* 1:78; Goodwin, *Team of Rivals,* 369–70; Wartman, "Contraband, Runaways, Freedmen."

7. The most recent studies of the blockading squadrons are Browning, *Success Was All That Was Expected* and *From Cape Fear to Cape Charles.* See also Trotter, *Ironclads and Columbiads;* Roberts, *Now for the Contest;* and Reed, *Combined Operations in the Civil War.* Personal memoirs by African Americans include King,

Reminiscences of My Life in Camp, and Gould, *Diary of a Contraband*. For black sailors, see Ramold, *Slaves, Sailors, Citizens*.

CHAPTER 1. UNION NAVY POLICY TOWARD CONTRABANDS

1. S. H. Stringham to G. Welles, July 18, 1861 enclosure, Commander Oliver S. Glisson to Flag-Officer Silas Stringham, July 15, 1861, *ORN*, 6:8–9. See also "Blockade!": The Blockading of the Southern Seaports in the Civil War," www civilwarhome./blockade.htm. A replica of Stingray Lighthouse is displayed at Stingray Marina, near Deltaville in Mathews County; see www.cheslights.org/heritage/stingraypt .htm.

2. Glisson to Stringham, July 15, 1861, *ORN*, 6:8–9; Glisson to Stringham, July 17, 1861, *ORN*, 6:9; "Silas Horton Stringham," in Virtual American Biographies, ww.famousamericans.net/silashortonstringham/. Oliver Glisson, who became a commodore in the U.S. Navy, returned to Norfolk, Virginia, after the war. His house at 405 Duke Street in the historic district is now a retirement home for men.

3. Stringham to Welles, July 18, 1861, *ORN*, 6:10–11; Welles to Stringham, July 22, 1861, *ORN*, 6:10.

4. W. R. Palmer to Prof. A. D. Bache, June 8, 1861, *ORN*, 4:505–6. In this June 8 report, Captain Palmer wrote that he was indebted to Commander Stephen C. Rowan, commanding the sloop *Pawnee* on station off Aquia Creek, for his assistance and protection. Alluding to the *Pawnee*'s unusual hull design, which enabled it to carry heavy armament on a shallow draft, Palmer wrote, "The proximity of her guns may have had a good influence on the rebels there, as, although I landed and scoured the woods at these places with an escort of two officers and twenty men only, I was not disturbed by them."

5. S. C. Rowan to Welles, June 12, 1861, *ORN*, 4:508. The commander of the Potomac Flotilla, James H. Ward, had ordered Rowan in the *Pawnee* to keep a watchful eye on rebel activities in the Potomac and to organize rowboat patrols at night off Maryland wharves and creeks.

6. Rowan to Welles, June 18, 1861, *ORN*, 4:521–22; Schneller, *A Quest for Glory*, 181–83. Later, however, Secretary Welles ordered the goods returned to the man, informing Dahlgren that "reliable parties" had given the department statements about his character.

7. Dahlgren to Welles, June 18, 1861, *ORN*, 4:522–23; Rowan to Welles, June 25, 1861, *ORN*, 4:535; Dahlgren to Welles, June 23, 1861, *ORN*, 4:532. In a sad footnote to this story, on June 27, 1861, Confederate soldiers repulsed a shore party led by Commander J. H. Ward attempting to land at Mathias Point and clear it of trees to prevent the enemy from erecting batteries there. Ward's party had gone to Mathias Point despite the warning of a black informant that 200 rebels actively patrolled the beach. When some 400 or 500 rebel soldiers suddenly came up over a hill, Ward ordered Lieutenant Chaplin to take the boats and lie offshore while he went aboard the *Freeborn* and fired on the enemy. Ward made it to the *Freeborn* but suffered a gunshot wound in the abdomen while sighting the ship's thirty-two-pounder bow gun. He died an hour later, the first Union Navy officer to be killed in action during the Civil War. See Rowan to Welles, June 27, 1861, enclosure, Chaplin to Rowan, June 28, 1861, *ORN*, 4:539–40; Rowan to Welles, June 27, 1861, *ORN*, 4:537.

8. Welles to Stringham, July 22, 1861, *ORN*, 6:10.

9. Butler, *Autobiography and Personal Reminiscences*; Aptheker, "The Negro in

the Union Navy," 169–200; Ramold, *Slaves, Sailors, Citizens,* 38–39; Gerteis, *From Contraband to Freedman,* chap. 1; Wegner, "The Union Navy, 1861–1865," 108. The Union Army's relationship to slaves seeking refuge even before the Port Royal experiment is explored in Wartman, "Contraband, Runaways, Freedmen." Wegner argues that at the beginning of the conflict, "faced with confusion," the small Navy Department was "understandably slow and deliberate in reacting to events that demanded quick and decisive action." The Navy Department did acquire an assistant secretary, Gustavus Vasa Fox, in July, and Congress passed an act to reorganize the department into a new system of eight bureaus.

10. Stringham to Welles, August 17, 1861, *ORN,* 6: 91, endorsement by Welles, *ORN,* 6:92.

11. Rowan to Welles, July 23, 1861, *ORN,* 4:584; Welles to Rowan, July 26, 1861, *ORN,* 4:584.

12. Valle, *Rocks and Shoals,* 161–62; Niven, ed., *Diary of Gideon Welles,* 324–25; Paullin, *History of Naval Administration,* 297–98; William S. Dudley, "Going South: U.S.A. Navy Officer Resignations & Dismissals on the Eve of the Civil War" (Naval Historical Foundation, 1981); Wegner, "The Union Navy, 1861–1865," 107–8; Symonds, *Lincoln and His Admirals,* 54–55. The U.S. Navy officer corps in 1861 totaled 571 officers, 253 of them southern born. Dudley notes that sectional loyalties motivated many officers, a large number of whom were of southern birth.

13. Manning, *What This Cruel War Was Over,* 13, 43–44; Symonds, *Lincoln and His Admirals,* 163–64. As Symonds has pointed out, Lincoln and many northerners were confused about "how or if, freed blacks could be integrated into white America." Could they be granted citizenship, allowed to vote, serve on juries, bear arms?

14. Keeler to Anna, March 25, 1862, in Daly, ed., *Aboard the USS* Monitor, 61.

15. Du Pont to Mrs. Du Pont, December 30, 1861, *SFDP Letters,* 1:294.

16. Du Pont to Mrs. Du Pont, April 8, 1862, *SFDP Letters,* 1:413. Willard Saulsbury, a former attorney general of Delaware, defended slavery but supported the preservation of the Union. James A. Bayard Jr. served in the Senate from 1851 to January 1864.

17. Sophie to Du Pont, April 29, 1862, *SFDP Letters,* 2:85n27; Du Pont to Mrs. Du Pont, June 1, 1862, *SFDP Letters,* 2:86–87.

18. Webber to Nannie, May 24, 1863, Samuel G. Webber Papers, South Caroliniana Library, University of South Carolina; Manning, *What This Cruel War Was Over,* 84.

19. Webber to Nannie, May 24, 1863; Manning, *What This Cruel War Was Over,* 84–85.

20. Donald, *Lincoln,* 314–15; Goodwin, *Team of Rivals,* 91–92, 206–7, 369–70; Lee, *Wartime Washington,* 14n, 151n, 189.

21. Berlin et al., eds., *Freedom,* 2:107; Ramold, *Slaves, Sailors, Citizens,* 39.

22. Chaplin to Goldsborough, October 27, 1861, *ORN,* 6:363; Parker to Goldsborough, November 3, 1861, *ORN,* 6:390. This congressional action also prompted Goldsborough to send the following instructions to Commander William A. Parker of the USS *Cambridge* off the Rappahannock River on November 6, 1861: "You are advised that none of the contrabands received on board the blockading vessels in the Rappahannock come from the state of Maryland or any other State not in rebellion." Goldsborough to Parker, November 6, 1861, *ORN,* 6:409.

23. Major General Benjamin F. Butler, special order, August 6, 1861, *ORN,* 6:63; Crosby to Butler, August 12, 1861, *ORN,* 6:73–74.

24. Welles to Goldsborough, September 25, 1861, *ORN*, 6:252; Ramold, *Slaves, Sailors, Citizens*, 40–41; Ringle, *Life in Mr. Lincoln's Navy*, 13. Recall that on July 15, 1861, Glisson had told Stringham he had been issuing rations to the contrabands on the *Mt. Vernon*. Welles wrote later, "They should be cared for and employed in some useful manner, and might be enlisted to serve in our public vessels or in our navy yards, receiving wages for their labor."

25. Valle, *Rocks and Shoals*, 20–21; Quarles, *Negro in the Civil War*, 229; Langley, *Social Reform in the U.S. Navy*, 92–93; Welles, circular, December 18, 1862, *ORN*, 5:201, 8:309; Ramold, *Slaves, Sailors, Citizens*, 35, 42–43, 45, 50. Seafaring tribesmen called Kroomen had also temporarily filled out the complements of ships stationed along the African coast that had been reduced by desertions and illness.

26. American Freedman's Inquiry Commission Preliminary Report, 1863, sec. II, 13–14, Samuel J. May Antislavery Collection, Cornell Library online. This report found that black refugees from the District of Columbia, eastern Virginia, and North Carolina were, "with rare exceptions, loyal men, putting faith in the government, looking to it for guidance and protection, willing to work for moderate wages if promptly paid, docile and easily managed, not given to quarreling among themselves, of temperate habits, cheerful and uncomplaining under hard labor, where they are treated with justice and humanity, and (in the Southern climate) able and willing, on the average, to work as long and as hard as white laborers, whether native or foreign born."

27. Drayton to Du Pont, April 4, 1862, in Berlin et al., eds. *Freedom*, 1:122.

28. Browning, *Success*, 114–15; Berlin et al., eds., *Freedom*, 1:22; Rodgers to Du Pont, July 19, 1862, *SFDP Letters*, 2:164; Lee, *Wartime Washington*, 166, 173n6; U.S. *Statutes at Large* 12 (1863): 61–67. For an excellent documentary history of the bill to forbid military and naval officers from returning fugitive slaves, see Moore and Everett, eds., *Rebellion Record*, 22–24. The Senate passed the bill by a vote of twenty-nine to nine, and the president approved it on March 13, 1862.

29. Craven to wife, June 3, 1862, Craven Letters, Naval Historical Center, Washington, D.C.; also reproduced in *ORN*, 18:528–29.

30. Craven to Porter, June 24, 1862, Craven Letters; Porter to Craven, June 24, 1862, *ORN*, 18:571–72. Prior to receiving this order, Porter had written to Craven with regard to an order he had received on the USS *Octorara*. A midshipman from the *Iroquois*, Porter wrote, had come "with verbal orders to take any contrabands he may find on the Mortar Flotilla or anywhere else." Porter asked Craven whether he should give them up. He enclosed a written regulation from the Navy Department issued by Flag Officer Goldsborough to the effect that contrabands claiming protection should be enlisted at $8, $9, or $10 a month. Porter then pointed out that when vacancies occurred in the flotilla, they were being filled by able-bodied contrabands picked up on the river. "I should be very glad to get rid of some of those on board, could I do so without violating the law, which enacts that contrabands belonging to rebels shall not be given up [by] officers of the Army or Navy." Then he asked, "Will you please give me a written order to this effect. I would not, of my own accord, give up these people (who came to us for protection) to brutal overseers, or to parties who claim to be Union now, though at the same time the difficulties of keeping them are very great and there is no knowing how many may come hereafter." At first he had sent them away to other vessels or just passed them on the river, Porter explained, "but they come on board now at night, and I can not, according to my

understanding of the law and wishes of the Government, refuse to receive them."
See Porter to Craven, June 24, 1862, *ORN*, 18:571–72.

31. Lewis, *David Glasgow Farragut*, 101–2; Schneller, *Farragut*, 57–58; Farragut to Bell, July 1, 1862, *ORN*, 18:606; Farragut to Welles, July 1, 1862, *ORN*, 18:714; Craven to Farragut, July 1, 1862, *ORN*, 18:604–5; Farragut to Craven, July 1, 1862, *ORN*, 18:605; Craven to Welles, July 11, 1862, *ORN*, 18:607; Farragut to Craven, *ORN*, 18:602–3; log of *Brooklyn*, July 2, 1862, *ORN*, 18:764. Farragut asked Craven to explain why he had not gone upriver as ordered and was clearly displeased with Craven's response. In correspondence with Farragut, Craven also complained about the assignment of the attack on the Vicksburg forts to a commander junior to Craven. He asked to be relieved of command and hoped the Navy Department might take proper steps to ascertain the fairness of the reprimand. Craven departed on July 4 for Washington, D.C., but, citing "an attack of illness," went first to Geneva, New York. For details of this incident, see Farragut's biography by Charles Lewis, who explains that Craven blamed Porter for his failure to follow the flagship. He claimed that Porter's steamers had obstructed the river, delaying his progress, and that the mortar boats had ceased firing, leaving his ship unsupported. When Craven confirmed that he had permitted claimants to search for runaway slaves and requested that officers deliver them to their rightful owners, Secretary Welles condemned Carven's actions as "not warranted by instruction, by usage or by law [and] in derogation of each." Welles to Craven, July 16 and 26, 1862, cited in Berlin et al., eds. *Freedom*, 3:658.

32. Niven, ed., *Diary of Gideon Welles*, 70–71, 313, 417–18; Buker, *Blockaders, Refugees, and Contrabands*, 44. Welles's biographer John Niven called it a "momentous change." As late as 1863, enforcement of the Fugitive Slave Law continued to divide Lincoln's own cabinet. In his diary entry for May 26, 1863, Welles wrote, "There is a sharp controversy between Chase and Blair on the subject of the Fugitive Slave Law, as attempted to be executed on one Hall here in the district. Both were earnest, Blair for executing the law, Chase for permitting the man to enter the service of the United States instead of being remanded into slavery."

33. Lee, *Wartime Washington*, 168–69; see also Guelzo, *Lincoln's Emancipation Proclamation*.

34. Welles, September 22, October 1, 1862, in Nivens, ed., *Diary of Gideon Welles*, 142–44, 158. On October 1, 1862, Welles confided in his journal that the announcement of the Emancipation Proclamation "has, in its immediate effects, been less exciting than I had apprehended it would. It has caused but little jubilation on one hand, nor such angry outbreak on the other."

35. James Himrod Papers, 1861–1864, South Caroliniana Library, University of South Carolina; Daly, ed., *Aboard the USS* Monitor, 224; Manning, *What This Cruel War Was Over*, 88–89. Manning argues that the troops reacted strongly both for and against emancipation, but many blamed the army's poor morale not on the proclamation but on poor leadership, battlefield reverses, and the removal of McClellan.

36. Drayton to Du Pont, December 20, 1862, *SFDP Letters*, 2:306–7.

37. Webber to Nannie, January 19, 1865, Webber Papers. Webber also told his wife that he did not consider himself radical but would be glad when the amendment to the Constitution was passed by Congress.

38. Du Pont to Mrs. Du Pont, May 1, 1862, *SFDP Letters*, 2:24; Du Pont to Mrs. Du Pont, May 21, 1862, *SFDP Letters*, 2:65–66; Du Pont to Mrs. Du Pont, May 11, 1862, *SFDP Letters*, 2:44–45; Weddle, *Lincoln's Tragic Admiral*, 148–49; Miller,

Biography of David Hunter, 98–102; Doc. 24, Proclamation by the President, in Berlin et al., eds., *Freedom,* 1:123–25. Although Du Pont confessed that he laughed out loud when he saw the order, his flag captain, C. R. P. Rodgers, "looked aghast—thought it premature, would do harm." By allowing Hunter to form his regiment of blacks in South Carolina, Secretary of War Edwin Stanton had, in effect, encouraged the recruitment of African Americans.

39. Rose, *Rehearsal for Reconstruction,* 188–89; House Exec. Doc. No. 143, 37th Cong., 2nd sess., ser. 1138; Sprout, "Blueprint for Radical Reconstruction."

40. Rose, *Rehearsal for Reconstruction,* 190–91. General Saxton's plan included sending units into coastal areas to destroy saltworks and other rebel property and to recruit slaves for black regiments. Although the recruited blacks were supposed to receive the same pay and rations allotted to white volunteer soldiers, they often did not receive equal compensation. As historian Willie Rose has pointed out, classifying blacks as volunteer laborers "provided a very shabby foundation for consistently underpaying the Negro soldier organized in the Department of the South."

41. Du Pont to Steedman, September 15, 1862, *ORN,* 13:327–28; Flusser to Davenport, September 19, 1862, *ORN,* 8:78; Flusser to Davenport, October 12, 1862, *ORN,* 8:129. Squadron commanders continued to have questions about contrabands. See Scott to Lee, September 25, 1862, *ORN,* 8:87–88; Lee to Welles, October 20, 1862, *ORN,* 8:137. In his letter to Welles, Lee refers to an answer from the Navy Department dated October 18, 1862, but this letter concerning the disposition of contrabands is not in the *ORN.*

42. Boggs to Lee, March 24, 1863, *ORN,* 8:625.

43. Lee to Welles, March 28, 1863, and enclosure, Lee to Captain C. S. Boggs, March 28, 1863, *ORN,* 8:632–33. Feeling it necessary to reiterate these instructions to Boggs, on April 13, 1863, Lee wrote, "Regarding the disposal of white and colored persons from the insurrectionary region taking refuge on board any of the vessels of this squadron, and of the masters and crews of prize vessels, you will hereafter be governed by the following rules (authorized by the Department in communications to me of April 4 and 9), which you will communicate to the commanding officers of the blockading vessels: All white and free colored persons taking refuge on board any of the blockading vessels, if there is good and sufficient reason to suppose that they are bonda fide refugees, can be landed at Beaufort, N.C. Refugees known as 'contrabands' not willing to enlist can be turned over to the United States military authorities at Beaufort."

44. Du Pont to Welles, June 15, 1863, *ORN,* 14:260.

45. Welles to Dahlgren, July 24, 1863, *ORN,* 14:395; Welles to Dahlgren, July 28, 1863, *ORN,* 14:401. The 1863 draft law meant that men could no longer indicate a preference for the Union Navy. This seems to have had a negative impact on recruitment and the supply of seamen for the navy.

46. Dahlgren to Lieutenant Commander Breese, November 19, 1863, *ORN,* 15:128–29.

CHAPTER 2. GOING TO FREEDOM

1. McPherson, *Battle Cry of Freedom,* 284–85; Ward to Welles, May 22, 1861, *ORN,* 4:475; Welles to S. Breese, April 27, 1861, *ORN,* 4:430; Breese to Welles, May 1, 1861, *ORN,* 4:443;. Breese to Welles, May 12, 1861, *ORN,* 4:458; Sproston to Gillis, May 16, 1861, *ORN,* 4:467–68; Welles to Rowan, April 23, 1861, *ORN,*

4:423; Welles to Gillis, April 23, 1861, *ORN*, 4:423; Gillis to Welles, May 21, 1861, *ORN*, 4:472–73. The *Resolute*, with Acting Master William Budd and a sixteen-man crew, joined the reconnaissance effort in mid-June. See W. R. Palmer to Bache, June 8, 1862, *ORN*, 4:505–6; Budd to Rowan, June 9, 1861, *ORN*, 4:507. The navy had acquired the 775-ton screw *Pocahontas* in 1855 and rebuilt it as a second-class sloop in 1859 at Norfolk.

  2. Rowan to Welles, June 12, 1861, *ORN*, 4:508; Rowan to Welles, June 21, 1861, enclosure, statement of John Dowling, June 22, 1861, *ORN*, 4:530–31. Rowan wrote of Dowling, "Added to this his exposure during the night on the beach naked, and a walk of 2 miles up the beach opposite the ship, and another swim of a mile to the ship, all bespeak of character and energy."

  3. Pattison to Craven, September 10, 1861, *ORN*, 4:667; A. G. Harris to R. B. Lowry, August 1, 1861, enclosure to R. B. Lowry to Welles, August 1, 1861, *ORN*, 4:594; Rowan to Welles, June 12, 1861, *ORN*, 4:508. For the number of vessels searched in June, see N. Collins to Dahlgren, June 12, 1861, *ORN*, 4:515. White southerners also approached Union gunboats, many of them trying to escape service in the Confederate Army. See J. W. Livingston to Captain T. Craven, August 26, 1861, *ORN*, 4:637; Livingston to Craven, September 2, 1861, *ORN*, 4:653. These Union vessels' efforts to enforce the blockade were impressive. In the course of two days, June 7 and 8, 1861, the USS *Anacostia* stopped and examined or searched thirteen schooners.

  4. Norton to Craven, September 23, 1861, *ORN*, 4:687; Gillis to Welles, September 25, 1862, *ORN*, 4:688–89; enclosure, McCrea to Gillis, September 25, 1861, ORN, 4:689. Hoping, perhaps, to prove themselves useful to the Union and secure their freedom, the contrabands told Norton that a 400-man Confederate unit had started erecting a battery on Freestone Point. Acting on the contrabands' information, Lieutenant Edward P. McCrea took the *Jacob Bell* and the *Seminole* to the point, found the battery, and shelled it. The rebels retuned fire, but, McCrea wrote, "No one was injured during the action, the officers and men firing deliberately and coolly."

  5. Mohr, *On the Threshold of Freedom*, 72–77; George A. Bright Journal, August 29, 1863, Bright Papers, Huntington Library, San Marino, Calif. In his research on Georgia slaves, Clarence Mohr compiled a table of escapes from coastal Georgia in the period 1861–1864. Of the 290 escapes, 249, or 86 percent, involved groups of three or more persons. The number of individuals successfully fleeing to freedom increased dramatically, from 6 in 1861 to 302 in 1862; another 55 blacks escaped in 1863, and 198 in 1864. Although the duty was arduous, many bluejackets preferred bombardment duty off the Charleston forts to the monotony of blockade duty. Furthermore, the Navy Department had authorized a temporary pay increase for enlisted men on monitors involved in the bombardment. See Welles to Dahlgren, August 3, 1863, *ORN*, 14:414–15.

  6. Naval correspondent off Charleston, *New York Herald*, June 3, 1862, and June 17, 1863, Letters of the Civil War Web site (no longer functioning).

  7. Berlin et al., eds., *Freedom*, 3:9; Gray to Craven, July 18, 1861, *ORN*, 4:577; Craven to Welles, August 11, 1861, *ORN*, 4:603; enclosure, Budd to Craven, August 10, 1861, *ORN*, 4:604. Gray's schooner welcomed other runaways. On November 5, 1861, he wrote, "My hands are full. I have fifteen negroes, which I caught last night, and as soon as I get them regulated will come up." *ORN*, 4:746.

  8. Blassingame, *Slave Testimony*, 699–702; Drayton to Du Pont, June 19, 1862,

ORN, 13:116; Marchand to Du Pont, June 20, 1862, *ORN,* 13:120–21; Lanier to Welles, June 26, 1862, *ORN,* 13:121. At Port Royal, Summerson wrote, "Captain Elwell, Chief Quartermaster, gave me a piece of land, and I built me a little house. I waited on Capt. Elwell, and my wife washed for him and other officers. My wife used to sew for Gen. Hunter's wife, and about a week before we came North Gen. Hunter gave me paper that made me forever free."

9. Baxter to Du Pont, June 16, 1862, enclosure, Baxter to Du Pont, June 5, 1862, *ORN,* 12:734–37. The South Carolina Plantations Web site does not list a Blake plantation, but it is a useful source for others; see http://south-carolina-plantations.com.

10. Jordan, *Black Confederates and Afro-Yankees,* 72–77.

11. Berlin, et al., eds., *Free at Last,* 61–63. These Georgia planters estimated the value of the 20,000 slaves who had fled at from $12 to 15 million.

12. Harlan to Margaret, May 24, 1862, George Harlan Papers, Huntington Library, San Marino, Calif.

13. Gillis, abstract of reconnaissance of Wilmington Narrows and Turner's Creek, March 26, 1862, *ORN,* 12:661.

14. Dove to Dahlgren, August 3, 1861, *ORN,* 4:599; Welles to Stringham, August 3, 1861, *ORN,* 6:50–51.

15. Mygatt to Craven, August 12, 1861, *ORN,* 4:599.

16. Craven to Welles, August 30, 1861, *ORN,* 4:645; Parker to Craven, September 4, 1861, *ORN,* 4:661; Jordan, *Black Confederates and Afro-Yankees,* 57–58. See Brewer, *Confederate Negro.* The Confederacy enacted legislation to register and enroll free blacks for military work, and in 1862 the Old Dominion's General Assembly authorized the impressment of 10,000 Virginia slaves for up to sixty days' service at $16 a month. One of the four men, James Scott, may have enlisted in the navy on September 21, 1861, at Washington. Scott told the navy he was fifty years old, a carpenter, and had been born in Virginia. He enlisted for one year as a first-class boy and was on the muster roll of the USS *Brandywine* on October 1, 1862.

17. Boyer, *Naval Surgeon,* 103–4; Ward, *Slaves' War,* 29–30. Slaves prayed frequently for freedom. Laura Abromson recalled, "They had places they met and prayed for freedom." Other slaves expressed ambivalence. "If freedom come, 'what will we do?' they wondered. 'We have no home, no money, no clothes, nothing,'" Robert Anderson wrote. Quoted in Ward, *Slaves' War,* 29–30.

18. Du Pont to Mrs. Du Pont, November 8, 1862, *SFDP Letters,* 2:295–96.

19. Henry Jarvis interview, in Blassingame, *Slave Testimony,* 606–11.

20. John J. Almy to Captain Thomas Turner, May 25, 1863, *ORN,* 14:217; Turner to Du Pont, May 25, 1863, *ORN,* 14:216–17.

21. Allen Parker, "Recollections of Slavery," in McCarthy and Doughton, eds., *From Bondage to Belonging,* 316–18.

22. Sam Mitchel interview, in Rawick, *American Slave,* 200; Rose, *Rehearsal for Reconstruction,* 12; Browning, *Success,* chap. 2. The fifty-ship convoy carrying General T. W. Sherman's troops left Hampton Roads on October 29, 1861. After a several-day delay caused by a storm off the South Carolina coast, Du Pont's ships arrived off Hilton Head on November 4. The following day Commander John Rodgers's gunboats crossed the bar and dueled with Confederate defenses, but a stiff breeze delayed Du Pont's main attack on Forts Beauregard and Walker until November 7. The battle lasted until early afternoon, at which time the rebels abandoned their works and the attackers hoisted a Union flag over Fort Walker.

23. Browning, *Success*, 44; Rose, *Rehearsal for Reconstruction*, 5, 9; Johnston, ed., *Him on the One Side*, 67, 69; Dr. Frank O. Clark, "The Battle for the Coastal Islands of South Carolina," www.sciway3net/clark/civilwar/coast/html. According to one estimate, by 1860 the population of Beaufort County was 83 percent African American, with some 11,000 slaves serving on plantations owned by the Hayward, Elliot, Coffin, Fripps, and Barnwell families. All these white families fled at the arrival of the federal fleet, taking some of their slaves with them but abandoning many more.

24. Vagabond, "The Results of Our Naval Victory," November 13, 1861, 21–22; "From the Army in South Carolina," November 16, 1861, 2; "The Capture of Beaufort," 6–7, 11, newspaper clippings in Andrew Dickson White, *Great Naval Expedition*, Samuel J. May Antislavery Collection, Cornell Library online. For example, according to Dr. Frank O. Clark (see note 23), "On Datha Island, Dr. Berners Barnwell Sams ordered his slave Cupid to gather the slaves on the island at the 'big landing' to be transported to the mainland, but Cupid and the other slaves instead took to the woods."

25. Ammen, *Old Navy and the New*, 33–45. The *New York Herald* correspondent painted a similar picture of Beaufort, telling his readers, "They found the place entirely deserted of its white population, and the negroes in full possession. They were plundering left and right, breaking open stores of all kinds, and having things their own way, and the officers are of the opinion that in a few days a negro rebellion will be in full blast in the region."

26. *New York Herald*, November 9, 1861; Du Pont to Mrs. Du Pont, November 13, 1861, Journal Letter No. 6, *SFDP Letters*, 1:235; Johnston, ed., *Him on the One Side*, 67, 69.

27. Rose, *Rehearsal for Reconstruction*, 17.

28. November 8, 1861, clipping, in White, *Great Naval Expedition*, 17–19.

29. Drayton to Hoyt, November 30, 1861, in Drayton, *Naval Letters*, 9; Drayton to Du Pont, December 21, 1861, *ORN*, 12:405–6. Drayton did not mention this incident in his official reports for November or December, but on December 20, 1861, he told Du Pont that 150 blacks, "all [in a] great state of alarm," had collected on different vessels.

30. Du Pont to Biddle, December 17, 1861, *SFDP Letters*, 1:181. "The plantations were all abandoned by the whites," Du Pont wrote to James Stokes Biddle. When they landed at Dr. Morrill's plantation, they found the mansion much as its owners had left it, "not an article removed and, until the Negroes began to plunder, there they were, showing every evidence of an instantaneous desertion."

31. From a Lutheran chaplain, November 26, 1861, in *Christian Recorder*, December 28, 1861, item 44370, www.accessible.com. "Three companies of our regiment have taken possession of St. Helena island, and are quartered at the large and elegant mansion of Dr. John J. Jenkins, about ten miles up Station creek." Explaining that hundreds of blacks had flocked to the Union standard, the chaplain wrote, "They tell us, that their masters said, 'Follow us, or hide yourselves in the woods, for the Yankees will either kill you, or carry you to Cuba for sale.' But they did not believe these masters, and say they have now found out that Yankees are their friends."

32. Du Pont to Mrs. Du Pont, November 13, 1861, Journal Letter No. 6, *SFDP Letters*, 1:235–38, Du Pont to Mrs. Du Pont, November 18, 21, 1861, Journal Letter No. 8, *SFDP Letters*, 1:255; Rose, *Rehearsal for Reconstruction*, 7–8, 16–17.

Rose referred to one fugitive planter who advocated burning the crops to prevent the North from harvesting the cotton. Without the cotton, he surmised, the hungry slaves would be forced to return to their owners or starve.

33. Rose, *Rehearsal for Reconstruction*, 18–21; 23; Du Pont to Mrs. Du Pont, December 12, 1861, *SFDP Letters*, 1:275; Grimsley, *Hard Hand of War*, 55. "Small wonder it was that (Secretary of the Treasury) Chase turned his first attention to contraband cotton rather than to contraband Negroes," Rose wrote. The War Department instructed General Sherman to "seize all cotton and other property which may be used in our prejudice" and ship it to New York. The sustenance and protection of these contrabands are covered in more detail in the next chapter.

34. Abbot, "The Navy in North Carolina Sounds," 567–84.

35. Ibid.

36. D. L. Day, "My Diary of Rambles with the 25th Mass. Volunteer Infantry, with Burnside Coast Division; 18th Army Corps, and the Army of the James," January 31, 1862 (Milford, Mass.: King & Billings, 1884), www.digital.lib.ecu.edu/historyfiction/document/dam/entire.html.

37. Schafer, "Freedom Was as Close as the River," 157–85.

38. Day, "My Diary"; Rowan to Goldsborough, March 15, 1862, *ORN*, 7:117; McCook to Rowan, March 15, 1862, *ORN*, 7:117–18; Browning, *Cape Fear*, 32–34, chap. 2, n. 54; Trotter, *Ironclads and Columbiads*, 121; Burnside to Stanton, March 21, 1862, *ORA*, 9:199–200; Redkey, ed., *A Grand Army of Black Men*, 202–1; Burnside's report, April 10, 1862, *ORA*, 9:210–17; Kurtz to Captain S. Hoffman, March 15, 1862, *ORA*, 9:216–17. General Burnside blamed the blacks for these incidents. "Nine-tenths of the depredations on the 14th, after the enemy and citizens fled from the town, were committed by the negroes before our troops reached the city. They seemed wild with excitement and delight. They are now a source of great anxiety to us." Burnside explained that fugitive slaves from surrounding towns and plantations had overrun New Bern. Two had been hiding in the swamps for nearly two years. "It would be utterly impossible, if we were so disposed, to keep them outside of our lines, as they find their way through to us through woods and swamps from every side."

39. *Boston Evening Express*, May 10, 1862; Wert, *Sword of Lincoln*, 81.

40. "From the Rappahannock," April 19, 1862, *Christian Recorder*, item 24481 (www.accessible.com); Virgil Mattoon to brother, April 22, 1862, ms. 71834, Connecticut Historical Society, ww.chs.org/afamcoll/mss.htm; Ward, *Slaves' War*, 99.

41. Marvel, ed., *Monitor Chronicles*, 78–81.

42. Daly, ed., *Aboard the USS* Monitor, 147, 138–39.

43. Sneden, July 31, August 1, 1862, *Eye of the Storm*, 107–9.

44. Ibid.; Daly, ed., *Aboard the USS* Monitor, 208–9; Marvel, ed., *Monitor Chronicles*, 80, 94–95.

45. Woodhull to Wilkes, August 19, 1862, *ORN*, 7:658; Woodhull to Wilkes, August 28, 1862, *ORN*, 7:687. Jeffrey Wert's *Sword of Lincoln* does not cover African Americans during the final days of McClellan's Peninsular Campaign.

46. Marchand to Du Pont, June 5, 1862, *ORN*, 13:77. Percival Drayton sent eight contrabands to Du Pont from the Stono River area; see Drayton to Du Pont, July 24, 1862, *ORN*, 13:210. Commander J. M. B. Clitz picked up seven contrabands in September 1862; see Clitz to Scott, September 23, 1862, *ORN*, 8:89. One of the contrabands taken aboard the *James Adger* did, in fact, enlist. According to enlistment records, Thomas Hamilton, five feet one inch tall, age twenty, was born in Christ

Church, South Carolina, and enlisted at Port Royal on June 13, 1862. He was rated a second-class boy and may have served on the USS *Flambeau*. Hamilton reenlisted in 1863, 1864, and 1865, ending his Civil War service aboard the *Proteus*.

47. Calvin Hutchinson, "Service on a Ferry Gunboat," 17, Calvin Hutchinson Papers, HM41742, Huntington Library, San Marino, Calif.

48. Wilder testimony, American Freedman's Inquiry Commission Preliminary Report, 1863, sec. II, 13–14, Samuel J. May Antislavery Collection, Cornell Library online.

49. Dahlgren to Welles, off Morris Island, January 26, 1864, *ORN*, 15:253–54; Harrison, "Conscription in the Confederacy," 11–16, 40. In the spring of 1862, when the number of southern white males flocking to volunteer decreased dramatically, the Confederacy passed a conscription act. Under its provisions, males already in the military serving one-year terms had to remain for another two years, and those aged eighteen to thirty-five would become eligible for the draft. Although the act provided for substitutes, and another act was passed five days later, exempting a long list of men in civilian occupations, conscription was very unpopular in the South.

50. Welles to Dahlgren, February 6, 1864, *ORN*, 15:316; J. F. Green, USS *John Adams*, to Dahlgren, July 14, 1864, *ORN*, 15:568; Rose, *Rehearsal for Reconstruction*, 305–8, 318. Captain Green, the senior officer off Charleston, wrote to Admiral Dahlgren, "There are on board this ship 15 contrabands, 10 males and 5 females, that escaped from Bull's Bay and came off to the *Blunt* on the 11th instant. I shall send them by the first opportunity to Port Royal."

51. Boyer, *Naval Surgeon*, 44–45, 103–4, 125; Moses to Le Roy, June 1, 1863, *ORN*, 14:227. At the end of May the *Fernandina* welcomed more contrabands escaping deprivations in the South. "One of ye intelligent contrabands from Macon, Ga. arrived on board, having left Secesh two days ago," Dr. Boyer wrote in his diary. When asked by Captain Moses where he was from, the contraband answered, "'From the southern States.' 'Oh!' says the captain, 'I thought you were from Maine.'" The boy "reports hard times in Secesh, people starving for want of the necessaries of life."

52. Babcock to Lee, January 24, 1864, *ORN*, 9:414.

53. Frailey to Lee, February 2, 1864, *ORN*, 9:436; enclosure, Saltonstall to Lee, February 2, 1864, *ORN*, 9:436–37. Saltonstall directed that the contrabands be sent north in the *New Berne*.

54. Wild to General G. F. Shepley, September 1, 1864, *ORA*, 42(2):653.

55. Pearson, ed., *Letters from Port Royal*, 293–94.

56. Ibid.; "Cases and Claims of the Emancipated Slaves of the United States, Being the Address of the Central Committee of the Society of Friends in Great Britain and Ireland, to Their Fellow Members of the British Public, London, 1865," in Samuel J. May Antislavery Collection, Cornell Library online. "Please find enclosed 7,000 contrabands, the first installment of 15,000," Sherman told General Rufus Saxton.

57. H. G. Judd to Saxton, August 1, 1865, Records for the Assistant Commissioner for the State of South Carolina, Bureau of Refugees, Freedmen and Abandoned Lands, 1865–1870, National Archives Microfilm M869 Roll 34, Freedman's Bureau online; J. M. M'Kim, "Forty Thousand Slaves in Washington," a letter to the Edinburgh Ladies Emancipation Society, October 30, 1864, in Samuel J. May Antislavery Collection, Cornell Library online. M'Kim explained that he had come to the city to superintend the construction of two new buildings—one for a school, and the other for a dormitory for teachers, storeroom, and kitchen.

58. Ward, *Slaves' War,* 77, chap. 15. Whites took slaves inland, and this "refugee-ing," as it was called, gave some slaves an opportunity to escape. Ward argues that in "large parts of the South, turning on one's owner and running away was at least as risky as it had been before the war." However, the chance of capture lessened, and the number of "potential havens" grew.

59. Ramold, *Slaves, Sailors, Citizens,* 182.

CHAPTER 3. CONTRABAND CAMPS

1. Berlin et al., eds., *Freedom,* 3:87–88; Sherman to General Lorzeno Thomas, December 14, 1861, *ORA,* 6:204; Sherman to General Meigs, December 15, 1861, *ORA,* 6:201.

2. Dispatch from Hilton Head to *New York Tribune,* December 23, 1861, in Blassingame, *Slave Testimony,* 359–62; "Testimony of the Former Superintendent of Contrabands at Hilton Head, South Carolina before the American Freedman's Inquiry Commission, June 1863," in Berlin et al., eds., *Freedom,* 3:113–14, 121. There were some 200 plantations near the Port Royal area.

3. Edward L. Pierce to Hon. Salmon P. Chase, February 3, 1862, in Berlin et al., eds., *Freedom,* 3:146–47.

4. Sherman to Du Pont, December 2, 1861, *ORN,* 12:383; Du Pont to Welles, December 4, 1861, *ORN,* 12:382; Du Pont to Rodgers and Du Pont to Missroon, December 1, 1861, *ORN,* 12:382–83; Du Pont to Welles, December 6, 1861, *ORN,* 12:384–85; Sherman to Du Pont, December 7, 1861, *ORN,* 12:387; Rodgers to Du Pont, December 6, 1861, *ORN,* 12:385–86; P. Drayton to Du Pont, December 9, 1861, *ORN,* 12:388–90; Sherman to Du Pont, December 6, 1861, *ORN,* 12:390; Du Pont to Rodgers, December 2, 1861, *ORN,* 12:388–89. Du Pont complied with Sherman's request by ordering Captain C. R. P. Rodgers down to Wassaw Inlet in the gunboat *Ottawa,* accompanied by the *Pembina,* to confer with Commander Missroon, who had previously reconnoitered Tybee Island and reported it defensible with a small force and a few heavy artillery pieces. Tybee Island, a promontory of land between Wassaw Sound and the entrance to the Savannah River, occupied a strategic location guarding the approaches to Savannah.

5. Percival Drayton to Heyward Drayton, January 10, 1862, in Percival Drayton Papers, Pennsylvania Historical Society.

6. Nicholson to Du Pont, December 13, 1861, *ORN,* 12:392–93. A career naval officer, Lieutenant Nicholson had joined the U.S. Navy as a midshipman in 1838. The 566-ton sloop of war *Dale* had made three extended cruises in the 1850s to suppress the slave trade along the African coast and had been recommissioned in June 1861 and sent south to join the Atlantic Blockading Squadron. The *Dale* was 11 feet long, with a 32-foot beam and 15.8-foot draft; it could make 13 knots and carried a crew of 150 officers and men. It was armed with fourteen 32-pounders and two 12-pounders.

7. Drayton to Du Pont, December 21, 1861, *ORN,* 12:405–6.

8. Ammen, *Old Navy and the New,* 356–57; Drayton to Budd, December 19, 1861, *ORN,* 12:412; Berlin et al., eds., *Freedom,* 1:116–17, 125–27, 128.

9. Du Pont to Welles, February 1, 1862, enclosure, Ammen to Du Pont, December 29, 1861, *ORN,* 12:430–32; Ammen, *Old Navy and the New,* 357.

10. Lieutenant T. A. Budd to Du Pont, January 14, 1862, and enclosure to W. B. Wright to T. A. Budd, January 9, 1861, *ORN,* 12:463.

11. Ammen to Du Pont, January 8, 1862, *ORN,* 12:464–65.

12. Ammen to Du Pont, January 21, 1862, *ORN,* 12:516–17. In concluding his January 21 report, the lieutenant noted that a party of black men, anxious to obtain work, had asked for passage to Port Royal. "I have brought them and their families, numbering perhaps fifty persons," he told Du Pont.

13. Report of Colonel Stevens, January 27, 1862, *ORA,* 6:78–80.

14. Ibid.; Ammen to Du Pont, January 21, 1862, *ORN,* 12:517–18; report of Brigadier General Nathan G. Evans, January 25, 1862, *ORA,* 6:77–78. "The negroes have evidently been incited to insurrection by the enemy," Evans wrote. "I have now as prisoners several negroes, who say they can identify the men who attacked the pickets." Evans stated that he had the captured black men under guard at headquarters, but "the women and children I have sent to the workhouse at Charleston." He felt it unsafe to return to their master five men who had confessed to attacking rebel pickets on Jehossee Island. There is a discrepancy in the dates; Ammen's letter was written on January 21, but Stevens said the attack took place on January 22.

15. Du Pont to Welles, February 15, 1862, enclosure, Rhind to Du Pont, February 7, 1862, *ORN,* 12:520.

16. Du Pont to Truxtun, February 3, 1862, *ORN,* 12:533–34; Du Pont to Rhind, February 5, 1862, *ORN,* 12:536; Du Pont to Welles, February 15, 1862, enclosure, Rhind to Du Pont, February 7, 1862, *ORN,* 12:520–21; Holmes, *Voyage of a Paper Canoe,* chap. 12. Although he may not have informed Rhind of recent intelligence regarding rebel movements on Edisto, Du Pont had received word in early February that the rebels appeared to be gaining confidence and had returned to South Edisto Island and to Governor Aiken's rice plantation on Jehossee Island on the South Edisto River. As a young man, William Aiken had received the 5,000-acre plantation as a gift from his father. In 1874 he told Bishop Holmes that it "required four stout negro oarsmen" to row Aiken around the property. Aiken employed 873 slaves on Jehossee Island, and after making many improvements, he earned $50,000 a year from his rice crop.

17. Enclosure, A. C. Rhind to Du Pont, February 7, 1862, *ORN,* 12:520–21; Edward Pierce to Secretary of the Treasury, February 3, 1862, in Berlin et al., eds., *Freedom,* 3:124–25.

18. Du Pont to Rhind, February 10, 1862, *ORN,* 12:540; Du Pont to Welles, February 15, 1862, *ORN,* 12:520. "I am pleased to find that you are giving proper and kind attention to the contrabands," Du Pont wrote. "I will see the general as to removing them from Botany Bay Island."

19. Du Pont to Fox, February 10, 1862, *ORN,* 12:541–42; Berlin et al., eds., *Freedom,* 3:90–93. Edward Pierce estimated in February 1862 that the Union would have to care for 10,000 to 12,000 contrabands who had come to Beaufort, Hilton Head, and North Edisto Island. Pierce criticized the cotton agents sent from the North, who collected a 6 percent commission; appropriated wagons, carts, mules, and horses from the former slaves; and tried to force them to pick the cotton. He preferred that the freed people be supervised by benevolent white northerners with no interest in financial gain from the plantation.

20. John M. Head Diary, 1861–1862, South Carolina Historical Society; H. Moore to Lorenzo Thomas, February 15, 1862, *ORA,* 6:89–90. See *ORA,* 6:91, for an army report on reconnaissance using several black guides. In the margins of his diary Head noted, "Capt. Eldredge, Penn 55th." This appears to be a reference to

the Fifty-fifth Pennsylvania Volunteers, which transferred to Edisto Island on February 25, 1862, after serving on some small islands off Hilton Head.

21. Cecelski, *Waterman's Song,* 157–58; rough notes of the naval expedition to Roanoke Island, etc., by Henry Van Brunt, secretary to flag-officer, *ORN,* 6:581–82.

22. Vincent Colyer, "Union Army in North Carolina, pt 1. of *Brief Report of the Services Rendered by the Freed People to the United States Army in North Carolina in the Spring of 1862,* 4–5, www.rootsweb.ancestry.com. On January 12, 1862, the *New York Times* reported that in December, 1861 a number of contrabands had actually escaped form Roanoke Island and had been fired upon by rebels in the process.

23. Colyer, *Brief Report of Services Rendered;* Berlin et al., eds., *Freedom,* 2:91; Elizabeth James, December 19, 1863, in "Letter from Miss E. James," 39–40; Click, *Time Full of Trial,* 38; Roanoke Island Special History Study, 28; Roanoke Island Freedmen's Colony Web site, www.roanokefreedmenscolony.com; Reid, *Freedom for Themselves,* 217–18, 223–27. The colony was only a partial success. Although it helped attract recruits for Wild's regiment, it also attracted many black refugees who were not related to soldiers. Conflicting white views about the contrabands also led to problems. Blacks on the island worked for wages, but they were not always paid, and in the final months of the war the colony increasingly suffered from illness and a lack of clothing. For more on the Roanoke Island colony, see Reid, *Freedom for Themselves,* 227–37.

24. Lucy Chase to Sarah, January 12, 1865, in Swint, ed., *Dear Ones at Home,* 134–36.

25. Godon to Du Pont, March 30, 1862, *ORN,* 12:633–34; Symonds, *Lincoln and His Admirals,* 170–71. Lincoln and his cabinet were divided over the fate of the contrabands and the contraband colonies. Chase wanted a military government with authority over the Sea Islands, but Bates objected. According to Symonds, Lincoln knew he would eventually have to decide the issues of emancipation and colonization, but in April 1862 he deferred the matter to the War Department.

26. Du Pont to Welles, May 28, 1862, enclosure, Prentiss to Du Pont, May 25, 1862, *ORN,* 13:21–23.

27. Prentiss to Du Pont, June 12, 1862, *ORN,* 13:92. Du Pont did send Prentiss more vessels and a contingent of marines; see Du Pont to Drayton, June 18, 1862, Du Pont to Lieutenant Lawry, USMC, June 18, 1862, and Du Pont to Prentiss, June 18, 1862, *ORN,* 13:112–14.

28. Symonds, ed., *Charleston Blockade,* 174–75; Assistant C.O. Boutelle to Du Pont, May 22, 1862, *ORN,* 13:16–17. Marchand's reconnaissance was prompted by his belief that Charleston could be taken by first capturing Fort Johnson, which he deemed "the key of Charleston." Boutelle also wrote that he sent the *Bibb's* second cutter with five contrabands as crew out to buoy the channel and survey the work abandoned by the rebels. Neither Marchand nor Du Pont mentioned this incident in the official correspondence.

29. Symonds, ed., *Charleston Blockade,* 183; Marchand to Du Pont, May 26, 1862, *ORN,* 13:36. In his diary entry for May 24, 1862, Marchand wrote that Captain Downes had reported that "so many Contrabands had received their protection they did not know what was to be done with them."

30. Evans report, May 23, 1862, *ORA,* 14:18–19; Ball, *Slaves in the Family,* 334; Symonds, ed., *Charleston Blockade,* 192. Ball reports the date as May 23, 1862;

Evans's report is dated May 23, but he says the raid took place the day before. Confederate units included eight companies of infantry, an artillery unit under the command of Captain Edward Parker, and two companies of cavalry.

31. Marchand to Du Pont, May 28, 1862, *ORN*, 13:51.

32. Du Pont to Mrs. Du Pont, May 11 and 24, 1862, *SFDP Letters*, 2:48, 70. Describing the *Uncas* incident to Sophie, Du Pont wrote, "Away they went with great panic, more frightened than hurt—for they were afraid of firing into the huts (our officers were afraid of firing directly on the rebels lest their balls should strike the Negroes' huts)."

33. Du Pont to James Stokes Biddle, December 17, 1861, *SFDP Letters*, 1:281.

34. H. C. Eytinge to Du Pont, August 11, 1862, *ORN*, 13:249. The *Knapp* was a 160-foot, 838-ton ship acquired by the Union Navy in August 1861. It had a complement of 93 officers and men.

35. Prentiss to Flag Officer Du Pont, July 2, 1862, *ORN*, 13:121–23.

36. Baxter to Du Pont, July 15, 1862, *ORN*, 13:192–93.

37. Du Pont to Pierce, April 25, 1862, South Atlantic Blockading Squadron Letterbook 4, ms. 9–3273, Manuscript Division, Library of Congress, cited in *SFDP Letters*, 2:29–30n11.

38. S. W. Godon to Flag Officer Du Pont, June 26, 1862, enclosure, "Notes on the colony at St. Simon's," *ORN*, 13:144–45.

39. Ibid., 142–45.

40. Ibid.

41. Ibid.; Mohr, *On the Threshold of Freedom*, 79–80; Rose, *Rehearsal for Reconstruction*, 112–13. Mohr argues that Godon's "heavy handed" tactics eroded the mutually beneficial relationship of the navy and the former slaves.

42. Du Pont to Goldsborough, June 18, 1862, *ORN*, 13:110; Du Pont to Godon, June 11, 1862, *ORN*, 13:92; J. R. Goldsborough to Du Pont, July 16, 1862, *ORN*, 13:195–96; Berlin et al., eds., *Freedom*, 3:32–33. For everyday life in contraband camps, see Berlin et al., eds., *Freedom*, 2:17–18, 60–61, 72–74.

43. Charles Steedman to Roxanna, July 17, 1862, in Steedman, *Memoirs and Correspondence*, 311; abstract log of *Paul Jones*, *ORN*, 13:188–89.

44. J. W. A. Nicholson to Du Pont, June 17, 1862, *ORN*, 13:108–10, enclosure, Nicholson to Rodgers, June 17, 1863, *ORN*, 13:109–10; Nicholson to Du Pont, June 27, 1862, *ORN*, 13:147; Ward, *Slaves' War*, 139–44. The term *refugeeing* was coined to describe this forced migration of slaves into the interior.

45. Du Pont to Mrs. Du Pont, June 19, 1862, *SFDP Letters*, 2:124.

46. Truxtun to Du Pont, July 13, 1862, *ORN*, 13:185–86; Du Pont to Truxtun, July 15, 1862, ORN, 13:192; Wright to Captain A. C. Rhind, June 3, 1862, ORA, 14:348. The Fifty-fifth Pennsylvania Volunteer Infantry arrived at Port Royal on December 12, 1861, and remained until February 22, 1862, when it went to Edisto Island. For a history of the Fifty-fifth Pennsylvania, see www.unionsonsoflillywashington .info/55thpennsylvaniavolunteerinfa.htm.

47. Rose, *Rehearsal for Reconstruction*, 182–83n30.

48. Steedman, *Memoirs and Correspondence*, 313; Du Pont to Mrs. Du Pont, July 10, 1862, *SFDP Letters*, 2:162; Du Pont to Mrs. Du Pont, August 2, 1862, *SFDP Letters*, 2:162; Pierce, "The Freedmen at Port Royal," 299. On August 2, 1862, Sophie Du Pont wrote to Henry Winter Davis, a member of Congress and a Du Pont supporter, that the admiral "extremely" regretted the abandonment of "such valuable property to the raids of the secessionists."

49. Baxter to Du Pont, July 15, 1862, *ORN*, 13:192–93; Baxter to Balch, July 24, 1862, *ORN*, 13:202–3. In the process of destroying the saltworks, which belonged to Ward and John La Bruce, they received fire from a party of about twenty-five rebels hiding in the woods. Two of Baxter's men suffered wounds in the attack.

50. Du Pont to Fox, August 21, 1862, *SFDP Letters*, 2:260; Du Pont to Balch, July 21, 1862, *ORN*, 13:203–4.

51. Balch to Du Pont, July 24, 1862, *ORN*, 13:208–9; Balch to Du Pont, July 25, 1862, *ORN*, 13:212–13. Robert Blake later served on the USS *Marblehead* and was awarded the Medal of Honor for his actions during an engagement with a rebel battery on John's Island in June 1862.

52. Balch to Du Pont, August 15, 1862, *ORN*, 13:256–59, enclosure to Du Pont to Welles, August 21, 1862, *ORN*, 13:257; Balch to Du Pont, August 22, 1862, *ORN*, 13:272. In a postscript, Balch explained his reason for not continuing upriver to find the *Nina*. Contrabands had told him that the machinery had been removed from the steamer, including the boiler. Both Balch and Baxter believed that at least some of the machinery had been removed and that it was not worthwhile to risk detention in the narrow river during the sickly season.

53. Baxter to Du Pont, September 20, 1862, *ORN*, 13:337–38.

54. J. R. Goldsborough to Du Pont, July 16, 1862, enclosure from Pen Watmough to Goldsborough, July 9, 1862, *ORN*, 13:195–97. The report from Acting Lieutenant Watmough "evinces at least that the knowledge of the existence of a large colony of fugitive negroes on the island has attracted the serious consideration of their owners and possibly with an idea of soliciting military assistance for their recapture."

55. Du Pont to Goldsborough, August 7, 1862, *ORN*, 13:244; Goldsborough to Du Pont, August 13, 1862, *ORN*, 13:251–52; Du Pont to Goldsborough, August 11, 1862, *ORN*, 13:248. Du Pont was installed as an admiral in a ceremony on August 10, 1862.

56. Du Pont to Eytinge, August 18, 1862, *ORN*, 13:264–65.

57. Saxton to Stanton, August 4, 1862, in Berlin et al., eds., *Freedom*, 3:209–10; Cornish, *Sable Arm*, 53–54.

58. Saxton to Stanton, August 16, 1862, *ORA*, 14:374–76; Stanton to Saxton, August 25, 1862, enclosure, Stanton to Saxton, August 26, 1862, *ORA*, 14:377–78; Westwood, "Generals David Hunter and Rufus Saxton," 86. Hoping, Saxton wrote, "by this arrangement to increase a little at least the efficiency of our noble Army in its mighty struggles for the integrity of our bleeding country, I beg leave submit it for your consideration and such action as you may deem proper." Saxton also reported that in some cases slaves had been employed by the government at high rates, but their wages were given to the agents of their slave owners. Saxton also noted that 600 people had been transferred from Georgetown and 175 from Hutchinson's Island.

59. Stanton to Saxton, August 26, 1862, *ORA*, 14:377–78; Symonds, *Lincoln and His Admirals*, 166. In March 1862 General Hunter declared martial law and liberated slaves in the Union-occupied area of the Department of the South. He also began raising a regiment of black troops from among the contrabands, promising them freedom at the war's end as an inducement to enlist. The secretary carefully confirmed the instructions given to Saxton at the time of his appointment "to enlist into United States service for three years or during the war, in order to fill up the regiments in the Southern department, as many able-bodied white persons as may be required." This enabled him to do as requested.

60. Du Pont to Steedman, October 28, 1862, *ORN,* 13:420. Union forces were not, however, able to protect blacks on St. Catherine's Island from a Confederate raid in October 1862 by rebels under the command of Captain William Brailsford, a wealthy cotton planter. In July 1862 Brailsford and a party of men had gone out to the USS *Potomska* in Sapelo Sound, claiming they had the sanction of General Mercer to request the return of fugitives. Lieutenant Pen Watmough, commanding the *Potomska,* refused and suggested that they take their case to John Goldsborough, now the senior commander of the district. In October Brailsford took thirty armed men and raided St. Catherine's, killing two black refugees and taking four others prisoner. See Mohr, *On the Threshold of Freedom,* 79; Watmough to J. Goldsborough, July 9, 1862, *ORN,* 13:196–97.

61. "The Civil War, Hilton Head, and the Evolution of Mitchelville," www .sciway.net/hist/chicora/mitcheville; Reed, *Combined Operations,* 267–68. Hunter had fallen out of favor, especially with Du Pont, after the failed landing on James Island in June. Reed argues that Mitchel was a favorite of the Joint Committee, that he was in favor of a joint attack on Charleston, and that Du Pont's powerful friends in Congress had urged his appointment to replace Hunter.

62. Dr. O. Brown to the committee, February 8, 1863, "Second Report of the Committee of the Representatives of the New York Yearly Meeting of Friends upon the Condition and Wants of the Colored Refugees" (1863), 6, 7, in Samuel J. May Antislavery Collection, Cornell Library online. The Society of Friends reported sending eight cases of garments to refugees at Point Lookout, thirty-four cases to Washington, D.C., and fifty-one cases to Fortress Monroe and Craney Island. In addition, this chapter sent boxes of shoes and more cases of clothing to Alexandria and Cincinnati and appropriated $1,000 for blankets.

63. Du Pont to Steedman, April 1, 1863, *ORN,* 13:803; Du Pont to Beaumont, April 1, 1863, *ORN,* 13:802; Du Pont to Beaumont, March 24, 1863, *ORN,* 13:783. In ordering Beaumont to remove the contrabands, Du Pont explained: "After diligent enquiry I am induced to believe that it will be to the advantage of that station and of benefit to the people who are there that the colony on North Island should be removed."

64. Rose, *Rehearsal for Reconstruction,* 240–41; Pearson, *Letters from Port Royal,* 155–56; Schultz, *Women at the Front,* 93; Hawks, *Woman Doctor's Civil War;* Ward, *Slaves' War,* 235–37. These were not isolated incidents of abuse by Union troops. According to Esther Hill Hawks, "No colored woman or girl was safe from the brutal lusts of the soldiers, and by soldiers I mean officers and men." Ward cites one case in which black vigilantes in Yorktown, Virginia, "shot a Union sailor to death for forcing himself on a black girl."

65. Dutch to Du Pont, May 19, 1863, *ORN,* 14:205; Dutch to Du Pont, May 20, 1863, *ORN,* 14:206–7; Du Pont to Dutch, May 21, 1863, *ORN,* 14:211.

66. Woodson, *A Century of Negro Migration,* citing Levi Coffin, *Reminiscences,* 671. Another 72,500 contrabands, Coffin testified, had located in cities, on plantations, and in freedman's villages. Of these, 62,300 were entirely self-supporting, employed as planters, mechanics, barbers, hackmen, and draymen, "conducting enterprises on their own responsibility or working as hired laborers." The remaining 10,200 received government subsistence; of these, 3,000 belonged to families whose heads of household worked cash crops, and 7,200 were indigent, elderly, crippled, or sick in hospitals. See Eaton, *Grant, Lincoln, and the Freedmen.*

67. Ramold (*Slaves, Sailors, Citizens,* 46) claims that by 1863 the navy was super-

vising thirteen contraband camps and some 8,000 contrabands. Unfortunately, he does not cite sources to support these claims. I found no evidence to support his labeling of these camps as a "system." These camps appear to have been established out of necessity and informally maintained by individual navy commanders in the vicinity.

68. Ward, *Slaves' War,* 286. "Many of the slaves who fled to Union lines were never seen again," Ward writes. Others were killed in battle or in ambushes as they returned home, or they died of disease.

CHAPTER 4. INFORMANTS

1. Rowan to Welles, June 25, 1861, *ORN,* 4:535; Rowan to Welles, June 18, 1861, *ORN,* 4:521–22; Welles to Dahlgren, June 29, 1861, *ORN,* 4:523; Craven to Welles, August 11, 1861, *ORN,* 4:602–3. Rowan had local blacks to thank for details about the smuggling activity of a man named Carpenter. That information led to the seizure of a wooden schooner and some hogsheads at a fish house opposite Aquia Creek. Later, Union officials determined that George W. Carpenter had not engaged in illicit trade, and Rowan had to return the articles.

2. Craven to Welles, August 11, 1861, *ORN,* 4:602–3. During the first months of the Civil War, from May to December 1861, the Potomac Flotilla consisted of the *E. B. Hale, Pocahontas, Pawnee, Satellite, Union, Valley City, Jacob Bell, Freeborn, Iceboat, Seminole, Resolute, Dana,* and *Yankee,* as well as the *Harriet Lane,* which served as Craven's flagship.

3. Ibid., enclosure, Budd to Craven, August 10, 1861, ORN, 4:604. Colonel Brown had been the receiver and forwarder of supplies and recruits, so his property used for that purpose was confiscated. "The foreman of the contrabands, who is a remarkably intelligent negro, informs me that an expedition is organized in Machodoc to capture any of the schooners that are anchored or becalmed in that vicinity," Budd reported.

4. Dahlgren to Welles, August 25, 1861, and Dahlgren to Navy Department, telegram, August 25, 1861, *ORN,* 4:636; Moses to Major J. S. Williams, August 19, 1861, third endorsement, McClellan, August 24, 1861, *ORN,* 4:634.

5. Ely to Craven, August 18, 1861, *ORN,* 4:620–22; Dove to Rowan, July 5, 1861, enclosure, Ely, July 5, 1861, *ORN,* 4:563.

6. Craven to Welles, August 30, 1861, *ORN,* 4:640–41; Welles to Craven, August 31, 1861, *ORN,* 4:641; Craven to Welles, September 3, 1861, *ORN,* 4:641.

7. Budd to Craven, August 22, 1861, *ORN,* 4:629; Craven to Welles, August 30, 1861, *ORN,* 4:645; Parker to Craven, September 4, 1861, *ORN,* 4:661. The slaves belonged to John Wilson and Dr. Frederick Wheelwright. On September 4, 1861, Parker informed Craven that Henry Young had reported the presence of a keg of powder and a sack of musket balls in a barn on the plantation of a Captain Cox three miles from Chapel Point, Maryland. "Young further says that Captain Cox's colored overseer told him he could show him a place where many arms were concealed."

8. Craven to Welles, August 30, 1861, *ORN,* 4:645; Welles to Cameron, August 31, 1861, *ORN,* 4:646.

9. Craven to Fox, September 11, 1861, *ORN,* 4:668; Welles to Craven, September 15, 1861, *ORN,* 4:675; Craven to Welles, September 16, 1861, *ORN,* 4:675–76. Welles merely assured Craven that if he were cut off, he would receive supplies by a land route. Given the force he had at present, Craven suggested that the army place batteries in positions where the rebels were likely to make a demonstration.

10. Haines to Craven, September 20, 1861, *ORN*, 4:679–80; Norton to Craven, September 23, 1861, *ORN*, 4:687; Gillis to Welles, enclosure, McCrea to Gillis, September 25, 1861, *ORN*, 4:688–89. While at Pope's Creek, Edward Haines took aboard two blacks who informed him that their owner, Henry Ferguson, a Maryland resident, had been engaged in carrying the mail and passengers from Maryland to Virginia.

11. Welles to Craven, October 14, 1861, *ORN*, 4:716; Craven to Welles, October 15, 1861, *ORN*, 4:718; Welles to McClellan, October 18, 1861, *ORN*, 4:726–27; Welles to Cameron, October 21, 1861, *ORN*, 4:730, enclosure, Harrell to Craven, October 30, 1861, *ORN*, 4:730–31; Harrell to Craven, October 30, 1861, *ORN*, 4:741; Lewis McKenzie to Welles, October 26, 1861, and enclosure, *ORN*, 4:736–37; Sears, *George B. McClellan*, 119–20. Stephen Sears notes that the general reacted to the blockade of the Potomac with "indifference" and assumed that his campaign against Richmond would outflank any rebel units along the river and force them to abandon their batteries or entrenchments. Cockpit Point, where the rebels located a battery, commanded Freestone Point on the north and Shipping Point on the south. The general sent infantry and cavalry to examine the countryside "to ascertain whether or not it is necessary to erect heavy batteries for protection of navigation."

12. Harrell to Craven, November 8, 1861, *ORN*, 4:748; "The Conduct of the War: Report of the Congressional Committee, Army of the Potomac: Causes of Its Inaction and Ill Success" (New York, 1863), 5–6, Samuel J. May Antislavery Collection, Cornell Library online; Street to Craven, November 12, 1861, *ORN*, 4:751–52.

13. Craven to Welles, October 23, 1861, *ORN*, 4:733; Dahlgren to Craven, October 23, 1861, *ORN*, 4:734; Welles to Craven, October 24, 1861, *ORN*, 4:734–35; Craven to Welles, October 31, 1861, *ORN*, 4:741; Craven to Welles, November 20, 1861, *ORN*, 4:754–55; Street to Wyman, December 11, 1861, *ORN*, 5:4–5. In early December, Captain Thomas Craven received his long-sought transfer from the Potomac Flotilla to the steam sloop *Brooklyn*. His tenure as commander of the Potomac Flotilla had been a discouraging one, marked by insufficient naval forces and the army's failure to send troops to support Union control of the river. Furthermore, many of Craven's aging vessels leaked badly, suffered with boilers and engines in need of repair, and frequently collided with one another in the river. As the weather turned cold, Potomac Flotilla crews often found themselves without pea jackets, shoes, and blankets. See Harrell to Craven, November 11, 1861, *ORN*, 4:750.

14. Du Pont to Sophie, November 4, 18, 1861, *SFDP Letters*, 1:210, 248. Rumor had it, Du Pont told his wife, that Confederate flag officer Josiah Tattnall, commander of the rebel vessels defending Port Royal, had gone back to Savannah after the battle of Bay Point "and told people to *make peace*, that the naval power could subjugate the country, by holding every point of coast, and that nothing could resist what he had witnessed on the 7th."

15. Gillis to Du Pont, January 2, 1862, *ORN*, 12:460–61; Wright to Drayton, January 2, 1862, *ORN*, 12:461; Drayton to Du Pont, January 3, 1862, *ORN*, 12:461; Du Pont to Sophie, January 4, 1862, *SFDP Letters*, 1:308; Du Pont to Charles Irene Du Pont, February 20, 1862, *SFDP Letters*, 1:339; Reed, *Combined Operations*, 46–50. These reports confirmed that since the attack on Port Royal in November, the Confederates had brought in reinforcements and beefed up their defenses at Savannah, at Charleston, on James Island, and in the Stono River. Under the lead-

ership of Robert E. Lee, the Confederacy had reorganized its defense of the coast, concentrating on strengthening the major ports and employing small, mobile units and the rail system to move forces quickly to threatened points.

16. Welles to Du Pont, February 28, 1862, *ORN*, 12:565–66; Du Pont to Welles, July 5, 1861, *ORN*, 12:195–96. For the composition of the expeditionary corps, see *ORA*, 6:237. From Fernandina, the rebels could load supplies onto cars of the Florida Railroad, which ran across the state to Cedar Keys.

17. Du Pont to Mrs. Du Pont, February 28, 1862, *SFDP Letters*, 1:344; Browning, *Success*, 67–68.

18. Du Pont to Welles, March 4, 1862, *ORN*, 12:573–74; Du Pont memorandum to Lardner, March 1, 1862, *ORN*, 12:572; Symonds, ed. *Charleston Blockade*, 121; Du Pont to Mrs. Du Pont, March 2, 1862, *SFDP Letters*, 1:348–49. On February 19, 1862, General Robert E. Lee ordered the guns removed from these Florida fortifications, but lack of transportation forced the army to leave some of them behind.

19. Du Pont to Lardner, March 1, 1862, *ORN*, 12:572; Du Pont to Drayton, March 2, 1862 *ORN*, 12:573; *ORA*, 6:240; Du Pont to Sophie, March 2, 1862, *SFDP Letters*, 1:349; Du Pont to Welles, March 4, 1862, in Du Pont, *Official Dispatches*, 112–13. The lighthouse keeper confirmed the abandonment of the fort and the return of Georgia troops from Cumberland Island, so, Du Pont told his wife, "there seems no doubt of all the contraband told us."

20. Du Pont to Mrs. Du Pont, March 4, 1862, *SFDP Letters*, 1:351; Du Pont to Welles, March 4, 1862, in Du Pont, *Official Dispatches*, 113–14; Symonds, ed., *Charleston Blockade*, 124–25, 128. In his journal entry on March 5, 1862, John Marchand explained that when the Union fleet entered Cumberland Sound as if to take Fernandina from the rear and cut off their retreat, the Confederates had fled to the mainland on the railroad, taking everything they could carry. He wrote, "The Confederates supposed the attack would be made directly from sea."

21. Du Pont to Welles, March 28, 1862, in Du Pont, *Official Dispatches*, 138, 139; Browning, *Success*, 72; Balch to Godon, March 9, 1862, *ORN*, 12:590–91; Balch to Godon, March 10, 1862, *ORN*, 12:591–92; Du Pont to Welles, March 19, 1862, enclosure, Godon to Du Pont, March 10, 1862, *ORN*, 12:606–8; Du Pont to Welles, March 21,1862, enclosure, Godon to Du Pont, March 16, 1862, *ORN*, 12:612–15. Godon told Du Pont that all the blacks had been removed from St. Simon's, "and at Doboy we met the only negro seen, who was old and alone on the place. He had been the father of thirteen children, but he informed me that every one had been sold as they reached 18 years of age, and, as he graphically expressed it, 'for pocket money for his master.'"

22. Du Pont to Welles, March 27, 1862, enclosure and subenclosure, John P. Gillis to Du Pont, March 25 and 26, 1862, *ORN*, 12:663–65.

23. Conroy to Parrott, February 13, 1862, *ORN*, 12:546.

24. Conroy to Parrott, February 15, 1862, *ORN*, 12:547; Parrott to Du Pont, February 23, 1862, *ORN*, 12:548–49. "Their respective crews were all foreigners and negroes," Conroy told Parrott, "and not having enough room in the boat to bring them off they were set ashore and allowed to retain their personal effects, except arms."

25. Braine to Glisson, January 5, 1862, *ORN*, 6:499; Wise, *Lifeline of the Confederacy,* appendix 6, 242–45.

26. Browning, *Success*, 105–6; Symonds, ed., *Charleston Blockade*, 139–40. For more on the effectiveness of the Union blockade, see McPherson, *Battle Cry of Freedom*, 382–83, and Surdam, *Northern Naval Superiority*, 53, 207.

27. Symonds, ed., *Charleston Blockade* 152–53. Marchand had command of the squadron off Charleston in Captain Lardner's absence. He explained that he had "sent the *Bienville* which, with *Huron* and *Restless*, will guard the entrance to the north and east of Rattlesnake Shoal; the *Pocahontas* to take a position 4000 yards from the battery on Sullivan's Island north and west of Rattlesnake Shoal and have a boat at night anchored half way between her and the battery; *Alabama* to guard the Main Ship, Pumpkin, and Lawford's channels to the south; *Augusta* to watch the southern edge of the Rattlesnake Shoal."

28. Marchand journal entries, April 30 and May 10, 1862, in Symonds, ed., *Charleston Blockade,* 155, 158. Ten days after returning to Port Royal, Marchand noted, "All the unemployed contrabands which came to the *Bienville* off Charleston and we brought down, were today sent to Hilton head, and I wrote to General Benham about the most intelligent of the party, from whom information might be obtained."

29. Bright diary entries, November 15 and 17, 1862, George A. Bright Papers, Huntington Library, San Marino, Calif.; notes of Captain Taylor, U.S. Navy, in regard to Charleston, S.C., and vicinity, November 17, 1862, *ORN,* 13:447–48; Du Pont to Welles, November 25, 1862, *ORN,* 13:448–49; Taylor to Du Pont, November 15, 1862, *ORN,* 13:449–50, and enclosures, Strong to Taylor, Gibson to Taylor, and Beers to Taylor, all November 15, 1862, *ORN,* 13:450–51.

30. Godon to Du Pont, November 21, 1862, *ORN,* 13:457; Bright diary entry, December 3, 1862, Bright Papers. In a journal entry, surgeon Bright referred back to two steamers escaping from Charleston and to information from contrabands about more blockade runners waiting to run out of Charleston. He wrote: "Dec 3—Some darkies came off Monday morning to the *Marblehead;* they report five steamers inside ready to run out, one Spanish, also two steamers ran out on the night of the 17th, and one in on the 18th, or thereabouts."

31. Parrott to Susan, May 11, 1863, E. G. Parrott Papers, South Caroliniana Library, Duke University; Parrot to Turner, May 12, 1863, *ORN,* 14:190. Although he knew nothing about the rams or the *Isaac Smith,* the informant did tell Parrott that a large steamer had recently run in to Charleston by the southern channel and that two steamers had run out the same night, but only one, a schooner, was ready to come out. With this fresh information, Parrott's blockade ships captured a few prizes. J. F. Green took the sloop *Secesh* on May 15, Charles Steedman captured a sloop leaving Charleston on May 16, and Master Cresy sailing in the *Courie* out of Port Royal took the sloop *Emeline* and schooner *Maria Bishop* out of Charleston bound for Nassau. See Du Pont to Welles, May 26, 1863, *ORN,* 14:196, 198, Cressy to Welles, May 22, 1863, *ORN,* 14:200.

32. General McClellan's report to Secretary of War Edwin Stanton, April 7, 1862, *ORA,* 11(1):7–8. The army initially received reports from deserters and from local inhabitants, contrabands, and persons of color about the Confederate positions and movements. See, for example, McClellan to Stanton, April 4, 1862, *ORA,* 11(3):66–67; Keyes to Marcy, April 5, 1862, *ORA,* 11(3):69–70 .

33. McClellan to Stanton, May 8, 1862, *ORA,* 11(3):151; Fishel, *Secret War for the Union,* 146–48, 150–51; Reed, *Combined Operations,* 133–36; Wert, *Sword of Lincoln,* 65–68; Browning, *From Cape Fear,* 8–49. After the war, McClellan blamed the Army of the Potomac's slow progress on the navy's unexpected lack of cooperation at Yorktown, poor roads, rain and mud, the strength of the rebel army in front of him, and the loss of McDowell's First Corps, which had been recalled from its

embarkation point at Alexandria to defend Washington. As late as May 8, 1862, as the army advanced up from Yorktown, McClellan candidly explained to Secretary Stanton, "we have absolutely no information in detail of the country in our front and are obliged to grope our way."

34. Goldsborough instructions to commanding officers of naval vessels in Hampton Roads, April 12, 1862, *ORN*, 7:228; Goldsborough to Welles, April 12, 1862, *ORN*, 7:219; Tattnall to Mallory, April 12, 1862, *ORN*, 7:223–34; Goldsborough to Welles, April 13, 1862, *ORN*, 7:230; Goldsborough to Welles, April 14, 1862, *ORN*, 7:233; Wool to Goldsborough, April 14, 1862, *ORN*, 7:234; Keeler to Anna, April 15, 1862, in Daly, ed., *Aboard the USS* Monitor, 80.

35. Missroon to McClellan, April 14, 1862, *ORN*, 7:235.

36. Cram to Goldsborough, April 27, 1862, *ORN*, 7:286.; Wool to Goldsborough, May 1, 1862, and Goldsborough's endorsement, May 1, 1862, *ORN*, 7:298–99; Hoogenboom, *Gustavus Vasa Fox*, 123–24. Assistant Navy Secretary Gustavus Vasa Fox reminded Lincoln that Goldsborough's "first duty was to take care of the *Merrimac.*" On April 27 Colonel T. J. Cram, General Wool's topographical engineer and aide-de-camp, had volunteered to send Goldsborough a contraband "who, with several others, has just arrived from Portsmouth navy yard. He is intelligent and can give you some information as to the talk of the *Merrimack's* intention to come out to-morrow."

37. McClellan to Goldsborough, May 4, 1862, and McClellan to Smith, May 4, 1862, *ORN*, 7:309; Tattnall to Mallory, *ORN*, 7:337–38; Stanton to McClellan, May 7, 1862, *ORA*, 11(3):148; Hoogenboom, *Gustavus Vasa Fox*, 125. For Lincoln's participation in the affair, see Symonds, *Lincoln and His Admirals*, 149–53. Late on the evening of May 7, Goldsborough came ashore and saw Lincoln, who told him it was urgent that the *Galena* or the *Monitor* be sent up the James River. Goldsborough hesitated, but Stanton appeared and insisted. Lincoln then mediated a compromise, giving Goldsborough the choice of commanders. Hoogenboom's May 8 date is incorrect. According to Symonds, it was May 7 when Lincoln asked Goldsborough why the navy had not silenced the rebel batteries at Sewell's Point. The admiral had no answer but said he could order a demonstration. That afternoon the president watched as the *Monitor* and five other Union vessels shelled a battery on the riprap island near Sewell's Point. The *Merrimac* appeared but then turned back.

38. McClellan to Fox, telegram, May 4, 1862, *ORN*, 7:309; Goldsborough to Rodgers, May 7, 1862, *ORN*, 7:327; abstract log of USS *Galena*, *ORN*, 7:706–7; Daly, ed., *Aboard the USS* Monitor, 120–23; Rodgers to Goldsborough, May 12, 1862, *ORN*, 7:345–46; Bearss, *River of Lost Opportunities*, 71–73; *Richmond Dispatch*, May 19, 1862; Civil War Richmond, www.mdgorma.com. When the squadron reached Jamestown Island on May 11, a cutter went ashore with two officers to reconnoiter. The men discovered two batteries and spiked four guns but found no white people. They brought off five contrabands but obtained no information.

39. Geer, May 15, 1862, in Marvel, ed., *Monitor Chronicles*, 72; W. S. Fort to Rodgers, May 16, 1862, *ORN*, 7:363; Rodgers report, May 16, 1862, *ORN*, 7:357–58.

40. Bearss, *River of Lost Opportunities*, 73; Anne Rodgers quoted Welles's letter in hers to John Rodgers dated May 20, 1862, Rodgers Family Papers, Library of Congress; McClellan to Goldsborough, telegram, May 16, 1862, *ORN*, 7:371; McClellan to Stanton, May 17, 1862, *ORN*, 7:373–74. Assistant Secretary Fox thought the *Monitor* should have led the attack on Drewry's Bluff. "They should

pile rocks upon the decks on *Monitor* at the farthest side from the elevated battery and give her a list, they could then reach the (Confederate) battery." McClellan's optimism stemmed in part from the fact that Union naval forces now controlled the York River up to White House and the James River all the way to City Point.

41. Bearss, *River of Lost Opportunities*, 79; Goldsborough to Welles, May 23, 1862, *ORN*, 7:416; Goldsborough to Smith, May 18, 1862, *ORN*, 7:387; Smith to Goldsborough, May 20, 1862, ORN, 7:404; Goldsborough to Welles, May 23, 1862, *ORN*, 7:416.

42. Smith to Goldsborough, May 20, 1862, *ORN*, 7:393–94; Keeler to Anna, May 22, 1862, in Daly, ed., *Aboard the USS* Monitor, 133–34; Goldsborough to Smith, May 22, 1862, *ORN*, 7:396–97.

43. Welles to Smith, May 27, 1862, ORN, 7:399.

44. Bearss, *River of Lost Opportunities*, 80; *Maratanza* log, *ORN*, 7:715; McClellan to Goldsborough, June 1, 1862, *ORN*, 7:444; Smith to Goldsborough, June 4, 1862, *ORN*, 7:440–42; enclosures, Stevens to Smith, May 30, 1862, and Beaumont to Smith, June 1, 1862, *ORN*, 7:442–43; Browning, *Success*, 55, 275–76. Smith wrote that he had not heard from McClellan or been informed of his movements or present position. On June 2 a man from the *Island Belle* who was familiar with Richmond and vicinity volunteered to take a dispatch in army signal cipher to the general's headquarters. The next day Smith sent the *Island Belle* up to find the man, but the commander, Acting Master Harris, "learned from some negroes that the messenger had been captured by rebel pickets a few miles from the river." The same blacks told Harris that the rebels were concentrated "in considerable force in the woods a short distance in the rear of Aiken's farm, numbering 30,000 men, with 100 pieces of artillery."

45. Bearss, *River of Lost Opportunities*, 82; Gillis to Goldsborough, June 4, 1862, *ORN*, 7:453; Goldsborough to Gillis, June 11, 1862, *ORN*, 7:474–75. On June 11 Goldsborough told Gillis to make up any crew deficiencies on his vessels by using contrabands, if possible.

46. Abstract log of *Wachusett, ORN*, 7:734; Bearss, *River of Lost Opportunities*, 83; Gillis to Goldsborough, June 7, 1862, *ORN*, 7:460.

47. Reed, *Combined Operations*, 176–77; Bearss, *River of Lost Opportunities*, 87–88; Sears, *George B. McClellan*, 205–6; Fishel, *Secret War for the Union*, 160–61. According to Sears, the contraband's report shattered McClellan's "fragile confidence." Fishel claims that Pinkerton's men were preoccupied with their move to Harrison's Landing.

48. Reed, *Combined Operations*, 185–87; Wilkes to Welles, telegram, August 5, 1862, 1 A.M., *ORN*, 7:629; Welles diary entry for August 25, 1862, in Niven, ed., *Diary of Gideon Welles*, 91–92; Sears, *George B. McClellan*, 239–42; Fishel, *Secret War for the Union*, 162; Wert, *Sword of Lincoln*, chap. 6; *ORA*, 11:373–75; Welles to Goldsborough and Welles to Lee, September 2, 1862, *ORN*, 7:695. Without reinforcements, McClellan held little hope for success; delays in resuming the offensive had allowed the Confederacy to reinforce Richmond's defenses.

49. Du Pont to Sophie, November 23, 1861, *SFDP Letters*, 1:236–37. *Fingal* had indeed run the blockade, arriving safely at Savannah with a cargo of arms; see F. W. Pickens to President Jefferson Davis, November 13, 1861, *ORN*, 12:828.

50. Du Pont to Welles, October 25, 1862, *SFDP Letters*, 2:266; Du Pont to Mrs. Du Pont, November 28, 1862, *SFDP Letters*, 2:294–95. When the contraband told Du Pont that he had waited on Commodore Tattnall and that he "was well but

seemed very old," Du Pont decided to test the man by asking him about a Mr. Lamar who had helped build the *Fingal*. "To see if the boy really knew about him, I asked him if there had been a death lately in Mr. Lamar's family. He said he did not know, that he saw him with a crepe on his hat."

51. Green to Worden, January 25, 1863, *ORN*, 13:536; Du Pont to Drayton, January 26, 1863, *ORN*, 13:536–37; Du Pont to Welles, January 28, 1863, *ORN*, 13:544.

52. Worden to Du Pont, January 27, 1863, *ORN*, 13:544–45; abstract log of USS *Montauk*, *ORN*, 13:547; Du Pont to Worden, January 28, 1863, *ORN*, 13:547; Worden to Du Pont, February 2, 1863, *ORN*, 13:626–28; Wm. Gibson to Du Pont, February 3, 1863, *ORN*, 13:629–30; Sheldon to Colonel Stager, telegram, February 2, 1863, *ORN*, 13:632.

53. Du Pont to Davis, January 4, 1863, *SFDP Letters*, 2:340; Reed, *Combined Operations*, 267, 274–76, 284–85.

54. Memorandum by Captain Drayton, USN, of information given by two contrabands from Thunderbolt battery, Georgia, February 18, 1863, *ORN*, 13:671–72. At the end of March 1863 the Thunderbolt battery boasted a total of fourteen guns. One of the contrabands told Drayton that early on February 7, 1863, the *Fingal* had followed a small steamer into the Skiddaway River. When the *Fingal's* commanding officer, Joseph Tattnall, heard that the *Montauk* had blocked the way, he took his ship back to Thunderbolt. Drayton explained, "They seem to think that the movement was made to satisfy the Savannah ladies, who insisted something must be done."

55. Holden, "First Cruise of the Monitor *Passaic*," 600; Browning, *Success*, 147–8; *Harper's Weekly*, March 28, 1863.

56. Welles to Rodgers, June 25, 1863, *ORN*, 14:284; Rodgers to Du Pont, June 17, 1863, *ORN*, 14:265–66; Browning, *Success*, 204–7; Loring, "The Monitor *Weehawken*," 111–20; Downes to Rodgers, June 18, 1863, *ORN*, 14:267, Barton to Du Pont and Gillmore, June 17, 1863, *ORN*, 14:269; Hunter, *A Year on a Monitor*, 86, 75–79; Rodgers to Anne, June 18, 1863, Rodgers to William Hodge, June 19, 1863, and Du Pont to Rodgers, June 21, 1863, Rodgers Family Papers; Hoogenboom, *Gustavus Vasa Fox*, 178. Hoogenboom argues that the success of the engagement restored Fox's faith in his monitors. President Lincoln and Congress also sent Rodgers a commendation and promoted him one grade. Privately, Rodgers confided to his wife, Anne, "The *Atlanta's* guns were wicked looking rifles, and I am not sorry we were not touched by them."

57. Case to Lee, March 12, 1863, *ORN*, 8:599; Case to Lee, March 11, 1863, *ORN*, 8:5 93. William Parker's February 23, 1863, report to Lee in the Lee Papers is quoted in Gould, *Diary of a Contraband*, 135. They did get a chart of batteries and obstructions on the Cape Fear River from a Mr. Savage; see D. L. Braine to Lee, January 7, 1863, *ORN*, 8:409.

58. Case to Lee, March 16, 1863, *ORN*, 8:613; Lee to Urann, March 16, 1863, *ORN*, 8:614. According to Wise, *Lifeline of the Confederacy*, 252, 256, eighteen blockade runners ran into Charleston in the first three months of 1863, and sixteen ran out.

59. Sands to Boggs, March 23, 1863, *ORN*, 8:624–25.

60. Boggs to Lee, May 14, 1863, *ORN*, 9:21–22; Browning, *From Cape Fear*, 285–86; Welles to Lee, April 28, 1863, *ORN*, 8:830–31. The rebels thought they could take Beaufort with the ironclad, Boggs warned Lee. "Should she succeed in

getting to that port, Fort Macon, having all barbette guns, would not hold out an hour against such a battery at short range."

61. Lee to Fox, March 29, 1863, in Fox, *Confidential Correspondence*, 253–54; Lee to Welles, May 28, 1863, *ORN*, 9:49. On May 28 Lee informed Welles that he had learned from Commander Ludlow Case that the rebels were occupying the west end of Smith's Island. He urged Welles to send General Foster more troops and artillery "to enable him to initiate the land part of the operations designed for getting possession of the entrances to Cape Fear River."

62. Breck to Parerr, May 1, 1864, *ORN*, 9:714–15; Civil War Soldiers and Sailors System, Sailor Search Black Sailors Project, www.itd.nps.gov/cwss/sailors. Furthermore, Wesley told Lieutenant Breck that both the *North Carolina* and the ironclad *Raleigh* could steam at only very slow speeds. Breck promptly enlisted Charles Wesley as a crewman. His navy enlistment records indicate he was twenty-one years of age, five feet five inches tall, born in Wilmington, North Carolina, and employed as a mason.

63. Sands to Lee, May 5, 1864, *ORN*, 9:729–30; Browning, *From Cape Fear*, 240–42. The enclosed map showed nine positions off New Inlet and seven to the other side of Frying Pan Shoals. Lee's response, if any, is not available, perhaps because the second engagement with the *Albemarle* followed Sands' report.

64. Parker to Lee, May 7, 1864, enclosure, Trathen to Parker, May 7, 1864, *ORN*, 10:19–20; Huse to Lee, May 8, 1864, *ORN*, 10:21–22; Balch to Parker, May 7, 1864, *ORN*, 10:20–21; Sands to Lee, May 8, 1864, enclosure, Porter to Sands, May 7, 1864, *ORN*, 10:22–24; extract from report of the Secretary of the Navy of the Confederate States, November 5, 1864, Hollins to Greenhow, report of inquiry in the case of the loss of CSS *Raleigh* in Cape Fear River, June 6, 1864, *ORN*, 10:24–25.

65. Lee to Butler, June 1, 1864, *ORN*, 10:130; statement of Archy Jenkins, *ORN*, 10:112–13. He also listed six other vessels: *Nansemond*, two guns; *Raleigh*, two guns; *Hampton*, two; *Beaufort*, one; *Torpedo*, two; and *Patrick Henry*. All were fitted with torpedoes.

66. Statement of John Loomis, May 30, 1864, enclosure to Lee to Welles, June 1, 1864, *ORN*, 10:111–12.

67. Lee to Welles, June 1, 1864, *ORN*, 10:113; Welles to Lee, June 4, 1864, *ORN*, 10:117; Lee to Welles, June 7, 1864, and enclosures, *ORN*, 10:129; Lee to Butler, June 1, 1864, *ORN*, 10:130; Grattan, *Under the Blue Pennant*, 106–7. General Butler had been pressuring Admiral Lee to sink obstructions in the river to prevent an attack by Confederate ships, but according to John Grattan, "The admiral was not in favor of the general's naval tactics." Lee clearly preferred to fight the rebels in the river with his own ships, but he acknowledged that the Confederates' torpedo boats presented a possible advantage to them. All this led to what some began to call "ram fever."

CHAPTER 5. CONTRIBUTING TO VICTORY

1. Craven to Welles, November 9, 1861, enclosure, Harrell to Craven, November 8, 1861, *ORN*, 4:748.

2. Craven to Dahlgren, September 19, 1861, *ORN*, 4:681–82; Craven to Fox, September 11, 1861, *ORN*, 4:668; Pattison to Craven, September 10, 1861, *ORN*, 4:66.

3. Vincent Colyer, "Report of the Services Rendered by the Freed People to

the United States Army in North Carolina" (New York, 1864), 10, Samuel J. May Antislavery Collection, Cornell Library online; Reid, *Freedom for Themselves*, 218. According to Reid, Colyer devoted much of his effort to assisting destitute white refugees. When Colyer resigned in July 1862, his successor James Means focused on black refugees near New Bern.

4. Sherman to William H. Nobles, U.S. Agent, December 3, 1861, *ORA*, 6:200–201; Grimsley, *Hard Hand of War*, 55–56.

5. Thomas to Sherman, November 27, 1861, *ORA*, 6:192; Sherman to Meigs, December 10, 1861, *ORA*, 6:202; Sherman to Thomas, December 14 and 15, 1861, *ORA*, 6:203–5; Scott to Wool, October 5, 1861, *ORA*, 6:175; Saxton to Sherman, November 9, 1861, *ORA*, 6: 186–87; *ORA*, 6:192.

6. Drayton to Du Pont, November 28, 1861, in Berlin et al., eds., *Freedom*, 1:118n.

7. Copp, *Reminiscences of the War of the Rebellion*, 7; Sherman to Adjutant General, January 15, 1862, *ORA*, 6:218. Yet ironically, the Union government's commitment to free labor and its insistence that contrabands work to support themselves undermined the efforts of newly freed African Americans to control their own time, labor, and wages—in other words, to experience true freedom. Forbes, *African American Women during the Civil War*, 21, 31.

8. Sherman to Adjutant General U.S.A., February 9, 1862, enclosure, General Order No. 9 by Brigadier General T. N. Sherman, signed by Captain L. H. Pelouze, February 6, 1862, *ORA*, 6:222–23. "The helpless condition of the blacks inhabiting the vast area in the occupation of the forces of this command calls for immediate action on the part of highly-favored and philanthropic people," Sherman wrote in General Order No. 9.

9. Burnside to Stanton, March 21, 1862, in Berlin et al., eds., *Freedom*, 1:80–81; American Freedman's Inquiry Commission Preliminary Report, 1863, sec. I, 4–8, in Samuel J. May Antislavery Collection, Cornell Library online. According to Superintendent Colyer's 1861 report, 7,500 contrabands resided in New Bern and vicinity, 1,000 at Roanoke Island, and another 1,500 at Washington, Hatteras, Carolina, and Beaufort. "In all 10,000, of whom 2,500 were men, 7,500 women and children." Major General John Dix testified that the refugees employed by the military as laborers in his department had fully earned their rations and wages, although he made an exception for rations given to dependent women and children on Craney Island. In June 1863 General Rufus Saxton testified that the 18,000 refugees under his care had been no expense to the government. "They have received a good many articles of clothing from charitable societies at the north; but the balance of credit, I think, is largely in favor of these negroes."

10. Browning, *From Cape Fear*, 150–52, 159–60; Murray to Lee, March 4, 1863, *ORN*, 8:587; Murray to Lee, March 13, 1863, ORN, 8:601. In his letter Murray mentioned that engineer Lay was already using "one of the small shops for work, which I entirely approve, some his contrivances being wonderfully ingenious, but he is at personal expense which I would like to have it in my power to meet."

11. Du Pont to Welles, May 1, 1863, *ORN*, 14:167, enclosure, John S. Cunningham, Fleet Paymaster, May 1, 1863, *ORN*, 14:170; Browning, *Success*, 259–60; Wegner, "Port Royal Working Parties."

12. Page, *Letters of a War Correspondent*, 129; Porter, *Campaigning with Grant*, 233; Butler to Major General Birney, August 6, 1864, *ORA*, 42(2):70. Butler called for 1,000 volunteers from Birney's Tenth Army Corps to labor on the canal and told

Birney they would be paid eight cents each extra hour and given a ration of one-half gill of whiskey. "A hospital had been established at City Point large enough to accommodate 6000 patients, and served a very useful purpose," Lieutenant Colonel Horace Porter, aide to General U. S. Grant, recalled. "The general manifested a deep interest in the hospital, frequently visited it, and constantly received verbal reports from the surgeons in charge as to the care and comfort of the wounded." According to war correspondent Charles Page, soldiers wounded in the fighting were "rapidly transported over smooth roads to City Point, and instantly placed on ship-board for Washington."

13. Blackett, ed., *Thomas Morris Chester*, 95–96.

14. Horatio Robinson to his mother, August 9, 1864, H. Robinson Papers, Duke University; J. Clitz to M. Smith, August 10, 1864, *ORN*, 10:346.

15. Porter, *Campaigning with Grant*, 273–75.

16. Blackett, ed., *Thomas Morris Chester*, 95–96; Porter, *Campaigning with Grant*, 273–75; Rufus Ingalls to General S. Williams, August 9, 1864, *ORA*, 42(2):95–96; Ingalls to Williams, August 10, 1864, *ORA*, 42:102; Grant to Halleck, August 11, 1864, *ORA*, 42(2):112; Special Orders No. 74, T. S. Bowers, August 15, 1864, *ORA*, 42(2):197; Grant to Butler, August 22, 1864, *ORA*, 42(2):411; Martin to Butler, September 1, 1864, and Palmer to Davis, September 1, 1864, *ORA*, 42(2):653–54; Ward, *Slaves' War*, 185; Miller and Smith, *Dictionary of Afro-American Slavery*, 107–9. For more on military laborers and slave families in contraband camps, especially in the Appalachian Mountains, see Dunaway, *African-American Family*, 204–10. Ward does not cite a source for the claim that one-fourth of all military laborers impressed in 1862 and 1863 died. The first official report of the explosion called it accidental. Ingalls's second report noted, "I have heard of no report of the ordnance department as to cause of explosion or loss of property." Black troops and laborers were in great demand at the time.

17. M. Smith to Lee, August 9, 1864, *ORN*, 10:345; A. C. Rhind to Smith, August 14, 1864, *ORN*, 10:348; Browning, *From Cape Fear*, 78; Grattan, *Under the Blue Pennant*, 127–28; Smith to Welles, August 13, 1864, *ORN*, 10:350–51; Flag Officer J. Mitchell, CSN, to S. R. Mallory, August 14, 1864, *ORN*, 10:352; Maxwell to Z. McDaniel, December 16, 1864, *ORA*, 42(1):954. The rebel ironclads *Virginia II*, *Richmond*, and *Fredericksburg* opened fire on the work party and pickets at Dutch Gap.

18. Berlin et al., eds., *Freedom*, 3:26–29. See also Berlin et al., eds., *Freedom*, vol. 1, doc. 107, and vol. 2, docs. 17, 30, 55–57, 59A and B, 64, 66, 76. For Dix, see *ORA*, 2:569; Berlin et al., eds., *Freedom*, vol. 2, doc. 11, n. 41. Well-intentioned white women from the North who came to assist in schools for the contrabands (in what has become known as the Port Royal experiment) felt that many of the newly freed women and even children on St. Helena Island worked willingly for wages. One of these white women, Laura Towne, wrote that the contrabands were "obliged to work. All who can are kept busy with the cotton, but there are some women and young girls unfit for the field, and these are made to do their share of housework and washing, so that they may draw pay like the others—or rations—for Government must support them all whether they work or not. . . . So far as I have seen, they are eager to get a chance to do housework or washing." As historian Ella Forbes has pointedly argued, Towne and other white women failed to see that by seizing and selling the cotton grown and picked by blacks on the Sea Islands, the government was taking advantage of their labor to support the philanthropic efforts

of whites in the Port Royal experiment. Not all Union officials welcomed the families of black laborers, some considering them "useless mouths." Forbes, *African American Women*, 21.

19. Reid, *Freedom for Themselves*, 14–15; Ringle, *Life in Mr. Lincoln's Navy*, 14–15; Glatthaar, *Forged in Battle*, 66–67, 170–71, 184–85. Union commanders at Beaufort, North Carolina, continued to use or abuse African Americans as laborers, and in November 1863 seventeen black men sent a petition to Major General B. F. Butler, calling his attention to the treatment of the black population in Beaufort. The petition stated that they were being impressed to work on public works without compensation and "that in Consequence of this system of fource labor they Have no means of paying Rents and otherwise Providing for their families." Robert Henry et al. to Butler, November 20, 1863, in Berlin et al., eds., *Free at Last*, 208–9.

20. Sterner, *In and Out of Harm's Way*, 3 6; Ringle, *Life in Mr. Lincoln's Navy*, 107–10; Forbes, *African American Women*, 51–52; Silber, *Daughters of the Union*, 215–16; Gillette, *U.S. Army Medical Department*, 182; Leander Chapin to Mrs. Amelia Chapin, March 18, 1863, Connecticut Historical Society; Schultz, *Women at the Front*, 55. In 1861 the Union Army Medical Department seemed reluctant to use female nurses. Many doctors thought women lacked the physical strength to care for wounded soldiers and preferred male hospital stewards, who received twice the pay of female nurses. As the war progressed and casualties grew, the Union Army employed contract nurses (civilians hired to provide nursing care) and contraband women as laundresses, nurses, and nursing attendants. The war gave employment to hundreds of African American women who served in newly constructed hospitals at Washington, Nashville, Louisville, and St. Louis. By the end of 1862 the Union Army had 15 general hospitals employing 40 stewards, 300 wardmasters, 6,051 male and female nurses, 3,053 laundresses, and 2,017 cooks. In her study of women at the front during the Civil War, Jane E. Schultz found that of the 20,208 women listed as Union hospital workers, 2,096 (10 percent) were African American. The largest proportion of these black women worked in hospitals as cooks (36 percent of all hospital cooks were black) and laundresses (14 percent were black). In addition, 778 contract nurses served during the war, 281 of them African American.

21. Du Pont to Mrs. Du Pont, January 16, 1863, *SFDP Letters*, 2:360, n. Du Pont wrote, "I have not laughed more since the war commenced when Dr. C. told me this in a most serious manner—of course I thought it was a joke but it is a literal truth. I suppose these women read somewhere what Miss Nightingale had and act accordingly."

22. Katherine Wormeley to mother, June 5, 1862, in "The Other Side of War," Sanitary Commission to the rescue, Home of the American Civil War Web site, www.civilwarhome.com/sanitarycommtorescue.htm; *United States Sanitary Commission*, 66, 69, 72, 79; Schultz, *Women at the Front*, 36, 118. The first Sanitary Commission hospital ship acquired during the 1862 campaign was the *Daniel Webster*. The shipboard hospital company was composed of surgeons, dressers, and nurses, some of them women; on May 1, 1862, the first patients arrived. For a list of paroled prisoners of war received on board the *Knickerbocker* at City Point, Virginia, on July 22, 1862, see National Archives record group 249, entry 107, box 1, file 5, in Pennsylvania in the Civil War, www.pa-roots.com/~pacw/pows/knickerbockerjuly22.html.

23. Marvel, ed., *Monitor Chronicles*, 207.

24. Hunter, *A Year on a Monitor*, 99, 42–43.

25. George Bright journal entry, December 19, 1862, George A. Bright Papers,

Huntington Library, San Marino, Calif. The James Island expedition to which Bright referred took place in June 1862 and involved moving General Horatio Wright's troops from Edisto Island on the *Bienville* and *Henry Andrew* to John's Island. From there, they marched twenty-five miles overland to the Stono River before crossing to James Island.

26. Boyer, *Naval Surgeon*, 43, 100–101.

27. Du Pont to Mrs. Du Pont, May 24, 1862, *SFDP Letters*, 2:70–71; Forbes, *African American Women*, 54, 57; "Harriet Tubman—From Slavery to Freedom," www.womenshistory.about.com/od/harriettubman/a/tubman_civilwar.htm.

28. Boyer, *Naval Surgeon*, 119.

29. Harrell to Craven, November 21, 1861, *ORN*, 4:756.

30. Boyer, *Naval Surgeon*, 96.

31. Bull, *Soldiering*, 188. Not all army officers valued their contraband cooks. For Colonel Charles Wainwright's comments about a new contraband cook who replaced a French cook hired by the West Point hotel for the summer, see Wainwright, *Diary of a Battle*, 209.

32. Forbes, *African American Women*, 56–57.

33. Boyer, *Naval Surgeon*, 48, 50, 68, 70.

34. Balch to Godon, March 11, 1862, enclosing report of Dr. Rhoades, *ORN*, 12:610–13.

35. Keeler to Anna, June 3–4, 1862, in Daly, ed., *Aboard the USS* Monitor, 146–47.

36. Hunter, *A Year on a Monitor*, 93.

37. Horace Henry Messenger to Susan, February 20, 1864, ms. 93413, box I, folder B, Civil War Manuscripts Project, Connecticut Historical Society; Norton, *Army Letters*, 223. An army correspondent covering the Peninsular Campaign described a transaction between slaves on the George W. Custis estate: "Upon the arrival of our cavalry the negroes at once quit their work and commenced a traffic with the troops. A large business was done in shad, thousands being caught by the slaves in the Pamunkey, and for a week while we lay there elegant fresh shad were our staple food." See Crouse, "The Army Correspondent," 630.

38. Marvel, ed., *Monitor Chronicles*, 93–94.

39. Hunter to Du Pont, March 13, 1863, Special Orders from Charles Halpine, Assistant Adjutant 10th Army Corps, March 13, 1863, *ORN*, 13:750–51.

40. Forbes, *African American Women*, 56; Du Pont to Mrs. Du Pont, July 9, 1862, *SFDP Letters*, 2:158.

41. Sneden, *Eye of the Storm*, 114.

42. Wainwright, *Diary of a Battle*, 274; Acken, ed., *Inside the Army of the Potomac*, 51, 75.

43. Keeler to Anna, April 7, 1864, in Daly, ed., *Aboard the USS* Florida, 158.

44. Lee, *Wartime Washington*, 306, 308–9, 357.

45. Du Pont to Sophie, May 29, 1862, *SFDP Letters*, 2:77.

46. Silber, *Daughters of the Union*, 215, 230–31. In contrast, northern black women endeavored to support the freed people by organizing relief societies.

47. Instructions from Rear Admiral Dahlgren, August 7, 1863, *ORN*, 14:429; Browning, *Success*, 233; Major Zeilin to Dahlgren, August 13, 1863, *ORN*, 14:439.

48. Ringle, *Life in Mr. Lincoln's Navy*, 142–44; "Civil War Prisons and Prisoners," www.civilwarhome.com/prisonsandprisoners.htm.

49. Blackett, ed., *Thomas Morris Chester*, 155–62; Ramold, *Slaves, Sailors, Citi-*

zens, 136. See also Speer, *Portals to Hell;* Sanders, *While in the Hands of the Enemy;* Denney, *Civil War Prisons & Escapes;* Casstevens, *Out of the Mouth of Hell.* Ramold gives the date as November 19, 1864, but Chester clearly states that the truce boat arrived on October 18 and the exchange took place shortly thereafter. Six of the exchanged Union sailors were African American. According to the list provided by Chester, the exchange included two black seamen, William H. Ellingworth and William A. Johnson of the USS *Southfield.*

50. Newlin, *An Account of the Escape of Six Federal Soldiers,* 34–55. The other escapees were L. B. Smith, W. Sutherland, W. C. Trippe, J. F. Wood, and R. G. Taylor. In his memoir of an escape from Danville, John J. Munnell of the 100th Pennsylvania Volunteers wrote, "We heard of many loyal people of Wilkes County, N.C.; the darkies told about them." His account was written in the early 1900s and transcribed and contributed to the 100th Pennsylvania's Web site by his great-great-great-grandson, Andrew Clark. See www.100thpenn.com/munnellescape.htm.

51. Varon, *Southern Lady,* 90–91, 131.

52. Foote, "Narrative of an Escape," 68.

53. Alonzo Jackson, in Berlin et al., eds., *Free at Last,* 156–59.

54. Ibid. Jackson claimed to have picked up two more escaped prisoners and taken them to North Island, and in February 1865 he brought another four to Georgetown, which was by then in Union possession.

55. Pennell to Dahlgren, December 5, 1864, *ORN,* 16:118–19; New Georgia Encyclopedia: Civil War Prisons, www.georgiaencyclopedia.org.

56. Ibid.; Brunswick and the Golden Isles of Georgia, www.bgivcvb.com/about_us/index. After the Civil War, African Americans from Hopeton, Elizafield, Grantly, and New Hope plantations settled into small communities nearby and continued to work for their former masters for pay. These communities were called Freedman Rest, Needwood, and Petersville (the last named after an old slave, Peter, who was the first to settle there).

57. Dahlgren to Welles, January 2, 1865, enclosure, Pennell to Dahlgren, December 22, 1864, *ORN,* 16:135–36.

58. Davenport to Lee, May 26, 1863, *ORN,* 9:44–45; Henry Phelon to Josie, May 28, 1863, Henry Phelon Papers, Southern Historical Society Collection, Wilson Library, University of North Carolina, Chapel Hill. Phelon then left but told Josie, "I saw several men around the house, but I kept my eyes . . . while on shore." Phelon's gunboat had remained to protect the men who were withdrawn on May 29 because, in Davenport's words, he found Wilkinson's Point "not suitable."

59. Phelon to Stephanie, June 21, 1863, Phelon Papers.

60. Phelon to Josephine, July 14, 1863, Phelon Papers; Phelon to Davenport, July 8, 1863, *ORN,* 9:77; Phelon to Davenport, July 12, 1863, *ORN,* 9:124. In his official report, Phelon explained that he had sent an armed boat crew up Spring Creek and captured the schooner *Henry Clay.* He sent another boat crew up Dumbargon Creek and seized a small schooner carrying turpentine.

61. Markle, *Spies and Spymasters,* 62.

62. Fishel, *Secret War for the Union,* 3–4, 54–55, 84, 117–18; 136–37; Rose, "The Civil War"; Pinkerton, *Spy of the Rebellion,* xx–xix, 360–61, 395–403; Welles quoted in Forbes, *African American Women,* 41; Varon, *Southern Lady,* 173. Forbes lists several other black women as spies, but all of them worked primarily for the Union Army. Mary Kelsey Peake, whose black husband spied for the Union, opened the first school sponsored by the American Missionary Association in late September

1861 in Hampton, Virginia. Pinkerton partly fictionalized his autobiography. Rose identifies nine blacks who made significant contributions to Union intelligence during the war.

63. Rodgers to Lee, September 21, 1862, *ORN*, 8:79–80.

64. Lee to Welles, October 24, 1862, *ORN*, 8:143.

65. Gillis to Lee, January 27, 1862, *ORN*, 8:480–81.

66. Parker to Lee, December 26, 1862, *ORN*, 8:321–22.

67. Lee to Welles, January 29, 1864, enclosure, "Conversation between Major General Butler and Henry Mosbey, table servant of Jefferson Davis, January 1864," January 25, 1864, *ORN*, 9:419–21; Butler to Stanton, January 25, 1864, *ORN*, 9:421.

68. Lee to Foster, September 26, 1862, *ORN*, 8:92; Lee to Scott, October 2, 1862, *ORN*, 8:103; Flusser to Lee, October 18, 1862, *ORN*, 8:158–59; Lee to Welles, November 14, 1862, enclosure, Davenport to Lee, November 10, 1862, *ORN*, 8:180–83.

69. "An Expedition Planned by a Freedman," in Colyer, *Report of Services Rendered*, pt. 2, www.rootsweb.ancestry.com/~ncusct/freemen2htm.

70. Dahlgren to Senior Officer off Georgetown, S.C., September 15, 1864, *ORN*, 15:679–80. The fugitives might have been three Union officers who "escaped from a train of cars, on the night of 28th ultimo, while on the way from the prison at Macon, Ga., to Charleston, S.C." See I. A. Pennell to Dahlgren, August 2, 1864, *ORN*, 15:615. Pennell informed Dahlgren that he had picked up three officers in a small canoe.

71. Flusser to Murray, March 21, 1863, *ORN*, 8:621–22.

72. Phillips to Welles, January 18, 1863, *ORN*, 8:449–50; Lee to Welles, January 21, 1863, *ORN*, 8:455.

73. Du Pont to Fox, October 23, 1862, *ORN*, 13:408–9; Steedman to Du Pont, October 27, 1862, *ORN*, 13:400–402; Browning, *Success*, 123–25. Browning blames Confederate pickets for giving the alarm and warning of the approach of Brannan's troops.

74. Reid, *Freedom for Themselves*, 216, 222; Berlin et al., eds., *Freedom*, 2:202–4.

CHAPTER 6. CONTRABAND PILOTS

1. "The Coast Survey in the Civil War 1861–1865," www.lib.noaa.gov/edocs/CW1.htm. In preparing for the Port Royal expedition in November 1861, Du Pont wrote that he and Davis "feel ourselves . . . leaning more and more on the Coast Survey & its marvelous results, no official or other declarations of that effect can convey a little of my estimate of their importance." Quoted in Weddle, *Lincoln's Tragic Admiral*, 128–29.

2. Welles to Dahlgren, April 25, 1861, *ORN*, 4:427; Dahlgren to Welles, April 25, 1861, *ORN*, 4:427; Dahlgren to Welles, April 27, 1861, *ORN*, 4:431; Dahlgren to Sproston, April 28, 1861, *ORN*, 4:436.

3. Sproston to Dahlgren, abstract log of *Mt. Vernon*, May 13–19, 1861, *ORN*, 4:470; Gillis to Welles, April 27, 1861, *ORN*, 4:433; Rhind to Du Pont, April 30, 1862, *ORN*, 12:790–91; Du Pont to Welles, May 2, 1862, *ORN*, 12:789; Du Pont to Mrs. Du Pont, May 1, 1862, *SFDP Letters*, 2:26–27. Du Pont did not mention the pilot to his wife. Some Union commanders credited their pilots for the success of their missions. In March 1862, for example, Commander S. W. Godon wrote that he

312 Notes to Pages 171–174

could not speak "too highly" of the service rendered by Mr. Godfrey, the pilot, during a reconnaissance of the inland passage from Brunswick to Darien, Georgia. See Du Pont to Welles, enclosing Godon's report of March 16, 1862, *ORN*, 12:613–15.

4. Goldsborough to Welles, telegram, June 30, 1862, *ORN*, 7:530–31; Welles to Goldsborough, telegram, July 1, 1862, *ORN*, 7:531; Rodgers to Goldsborough, July 1, 1862, *ORN*, 7:533–34.

5. Welles to Lieutenant Colonel Martin Burke, November 26, 1862, *ORN*, 8:235; Fox to Blunt, November 28, 1862, *ORN*, 8:237; Fox to Lee, December 9, 1862, *ORN*, 8:269. When Daniel Ammen of the ironclad *Patapsco* failed to find a pilot in Philadelphia, he turned to Commander Worden in New York, who located a pilot in that city.

6. Lee to Welles, March 19, 1863, *ORN*, 8:390–91; enclosure, Rhind to Lee, March 17, 1863, *ORN*, 8:391–92; enclosure, G. Peirce Crosby to Lee, March 17, 1863, *ORN*, 8:392–93; Ammen to Welles, February 2, 1863, *ORN*, 8:380; Lee to Welles, March 19, 1863, *ORN*, 8:391. On December 2 Lee also told Fox that a gunner on the *Marion*, Samuel Hines, was a "clever Wilmington and sounds pilot" who had worked for Murray on the coast survey. See *ORN*, 8:246.

7. Ramold, *Slaves, Sailors, Citizens*, 89.

8. Prentiss to Du Pont, July 2, 1862, *ORN*, 3:123; Du Pont to Turner, June 2, 1863, *ORN*, 14:228. Du Pont to Welles, June 10, 1863, *ORN*, 13:251; Aptheker, "The Negro in the Union Navy." Using Black Sailor Search, I found only William Ayler rated as pilot. At least five Confederates became Union Navy pilots by virtue of being captured or deserting: A. L. Drayton, Elias Lee, John J. Orrell, John H. Pucket, and Charles Tooker. These men were actually appointed pilots by the Union Navy to guide their ships on southern waterways. See Terry Foenander, "CS Personnel Who Were Appointed Union Navy Pilots," www.tfoenander.com.

9. Du Pont to Welles, April 29, 1862, enclosure, Le Roy to Du Pont, April 25, 1862, *ORN*, 12:677–79.

10. Prentiss to Goldsborough, December 24, 1861, *ORN*, 6:487; e-mails from Paul Branch to author, February 23, 2006; Paul Branch, "Armament of Fort Macon," www.crystalcoast.com/formacon/armament.htm; Cecelski, *Waterman's Song*, 272n3. "The black workers were used until August 1861 when the Confederacy took over all authority for the fort's defenses from the State," Branch explains. Branch says that between September 1861 and January 1862, Fort Macon received one 10-inch Columbiad, two 8-inch Columbiads, a 5.8-inch rifled Columbiad, and four 32-pounder smoothbores that were rifled by the Confederates. By the time of the siege, the fort had about fifty-four guns. Cecelski says that 175 slaves and free blacks had been employed to strengthen Fort Macon and its guns the previous year, and there is speculation that Union officials may have obtained information from some of those who had worked on the fort.

11. Trotter, *Ironclads and Columbiads*, 135–43; Cecelski, *Waterman's Song*, 155n4, citing Michael H. Goodman, "The Black Tar: Negro Seamen in the Union Navy 1861–1865 (PhD diss., University of Nottingham, 1973); Branch, *Siege of Fort Macon*; Parke to Burnside, March 31, 1862, *ORA*, 9:280; Parke to Burnside, enclosing report of Captain Wilson, May 9, 1862, *ORA*, 9:281–83; report no. 3 of Lieutenant Daniel W. Flagler, April 29, 1862, *ORA*, 9:287–88; e-mail from Branch to author, February 23, 2006. As historian David Cecelski points out in his study of maritime Beaufort, this required a skillful local pilot with intimate knowledge of the sound who could safely guide a forty-ton steamer on a flood tide without grounding

it and exposing it to Fort Macon's withering fire. Paul Branch argues that the federals used an eighty-ton stern wheeler, the *Old North State*, during the siege, but it "was said to draw too much water to get close to the banks to transport the artillery, etc. A battery of four 10-inch siege mortars were loaded onto a bark. The four 8-inch mortars came from New Bern by barge to Slocum Creek and then by land to Carolina City."

12. Lockwood to Goldsborough, April 27, 1862, *ORN*, 7:279–80; Parke to Captain Lewis Richmond, Assistant Adjutant General, May 9, 1862, *ORA*, 9:284; report of Colonel Moses J. White, C.S. Army, May 4, 1862, *ORA*, 9:293–94; Trotter, *Ironclads and Columbiads*, 144–47; Fort Macon, CWSAC Battle Summaries, HPS, www.cr.rips.gov/hps/abpp/battles/nc004/htm. White noted, "Had the fort been built and armed for defense from a land attack the siege might have lasted longer, but as neither was the case the enemy were able to complete their batteries, completely masked, in a shorter time than I had hoped."

13. T. W. Sherman to Du Pont, January 16, 1862, *ORN*, 12:486.

14. Statement of Isaac Tattnall, December 6, 1861, enclosure to Du Pont to Gillis, January 17, 1862, *ORN*, 12:487–88. "They did not, I learn, reach the short bend mentioned by pilots, around which vessels have to be swung by hawsers," Gillis told Du Pont. "The fort on Fig Island, near the city of Savannah, 1 mile above Fort Jackson (mentioned by the contraband Jim whom I sent you by *Alabama*), is not placed on the chart."

15. Gillis to Du Pont, January 9, 1862, enclosure, Gillmore and Rodgers's report of January 9, 1862, *ORN*, 12:468–70; Du Pont to Gillis, January 11, 1862, *ORN*, 12:470. Gillis stated that Fort Jackson was "a strong work, covered." Du Pont also received detailed reports of Confederate batteries on Cole's Island from four white men who emerged from Stono Inlet in a small sailboat; see Balch to Du Pont, January 10, 1862, *ORN*, 12:475–76.

16. Du Pont to Rodgers, January 17, 1862, *ORN*, 12:491–92; Rodgers to Du Pont, January 18, 1862, *ORN*, 12:492–93; Wilson to Pelouze, January 18, 1862, *ORN*, 12:493; Johnson, *Rear Admiral John Rodgers*, 182–84; Rodgers to Du Pont, January 28 and 29, 1862, *ORN*, 12:494–95.

17. T. W. Sherman to Du Pont, January 16, 1862, *ORN*, 12:485–86; Rodgers to Du Pont, February 4, 1862, *ORN*, 12:496–97; Sherman to Du Pont, February 7, 1862, *ORN*, 12:498; Rodgers to Du Pont, February 18, 1862, *ORN*, 12:501; Browning, *Success*, 60–66; McClellan to Sherman, February 14, 1862, *ORA*, 6:225; Du Pont to Mrs. Du Pont, February 28, 1862, *SFDP Letters*, 1:344n2. On February 14, 1862, four Confederate gunboats attacked the new battery on Jones Island in what Rodgers described as a "smart engagement," but the *Hale* and the *Western World*, assisted by Captain Gould's Third Rhode Island gunners, repulsed the rebel gunboats, which then returned to Savannah.

18. Du Pont to Law, May 31, 1862, *ORN*, 13:65; Hunter to Du Pont, June 1, 1862, *ORN*, 13:67, Du Pont to Hunter, June 1862, *ORN*, 13:68. The 177-ton screw steamer *Henry Andrew*, one of many acquired by the navy in 1861, had been operating on the St. John's River in Florida and had taken part in the action at Mosquito Inlet in March 1862.

19. Marchand to Du Pont, April 28, 1862, *ORN*, 12:784–85; statement made by a contraband regarding condition of defense of Charleston, S.C., *ORN*, 12:785–86; Mullany to Marchand, April 28, 1862, *ORN*, 12:787; Browning, *From Cape Fear*, 173; J. W. Livingston to Stringham, August 15, 1861, *ORN*, 6:85–86.

20. Woodhull to Charles Steedman, October 7, 1862, *ORN*, 13:367–70. A group of women asked to meet with Commander Woodhull at the wharf. Insisting that the men had fled to the swamps and that she had no control over the guerrillas or the partisans, a Mrs. Boyd begged him not to shell the town. He promised her that if the force in back of the town left, the *Hale* would not fire on the town. Mrs. Boyd replied that she had already sent such a message to the guerrilla commander.

21. McKeige to Du Pont, August 9, 1862, *ORN*, 13:245–46. The spelling of Batten Island varies; some sources call it Batton Island.

22. Woodhull to Du Pont, November 3, 1862, *ORN*, 13:427–28; Woodhull to Du Pont, November [7], 1862, *ORN*, 13:436–37.

23. Woodhull to Du Pont, November 24, 1862, *ORN*, 13:461–62; Du Pont to Saxton, November 26, 1862, *ORN*, 13:463; Saxton to Du Pont, November 28, 1862, *ORN*, 13:463–64; Buker, *Blockaders, Refugees, and Contrabands*, 177–78. On October 1, 1862, General John M. Brannan's 1,500 infantrymen arrived from Hilton Head on the *Boston, Ben De Ford, Cosmopolitan,* and *Neptune* to secure St. John's Bluff, where the rebels had located a battery to control the river. When Union soldiers landed at Mayport Mills and Mount Pleasant Creek, in the battery's rear, and Commander Charles Steedman's gunboats approached the bluff, Confederate troops under Lieutenant Colonel Charles F. Hopkins abandoned the position.

24. Lamson to Kate, October 22, 1863, in Lamson, *Lamson of the Gettysburg,* 141–42; Captain B. F. Sands to Lee, October 21, 1863, enclosure, Lamson to Lee, October 21, 1863, *ORN*, 9:248–50. Going abreast of the *Venus*, Lamson opened fire. As the ship began taking on water, the crew had no choice but to run it ashore. Men from the *Nansemond* then boarded the *Venus* and captured twenty-two officers and crew. The *Niphon,* commanded by Acting Master J. B. Breck, came along to assist, but neither ship was able to tow the *Venus* off the beach in the ebbing tide. Lamson then ordered the *Venus* set on fire. Praising both Lamson and Breck, Captain Sands wrote, "Give us a few such and we will put a stop to this nefarious British trade and make Wilmington a closed port."

25. F. S. Wells to Lee, January 4, 1864, *ORN*, 9:375.

26. C. B. Wilder to MacDiarmid, December 25, 1863, *ORN*, 9:380; Colonel J. Jourdan to Captain E. T. Parkinson, Assistant Adjutant General, December 26, 1863, *ORN*, 9:381; Jourdan to Edward Stone, December 27, 1863, *ORN*, 9:378. The 158th, commanded by Colonel James Jourdan, had been organized as a regiment in Brooklyn in August 1862 and was sent first to Virginia and then to New Bern and Beaufort.

27. Brown to Lamson, April 17, 1863, *ORN*, 8:735–36.

28. Brown to Welles, May 13, 1863, *ORN*, 8:736; G. S. Franklin to Wm. Maxwell Wood, April 21, 1863, *ORN*, 8:759; Lamson to Lee, April 22, 1863, enclosure, casualty report, *ORN*, 8:725; Black Sailor Search. During the naval engagement in the upper Nansemond in mid-April 1863, John W. Small, a pilot serving on the USS *Mt. Washington,* also suffered severe wounds. Although he is not listed as African American, two African American sailors on the *Stepping Stones* were slightly injured: Giles Scott, a twenty-seven-year-old North Carolina native who enlisted for one year in February 1863 as a first-class boy; and John Down, only sixteen years old, who had signed on in November 1862 as a third-class boy.

29. Du Pont to Budd, March 19, 1862, *ORN*, 12:646; Du Pont to Welles, March 24, 1862, *ORN*, 12:645–46; C. R. P. Rodgers to Du Pont, March 23, 1862, *ORN*, 12:647–48; Williamson to Du Pont, March 29, 1862, enclosure C, Captain D. B.

Bird to T. A. Harris, March 26, 1862, *ORN*, 12:649. Initially only two men were listed as prisoners, but Bird confirmed a third man.

30. Dilworth to Major Washington, April 4, 1862, *ORN*, 12:651; Wise, *Lifeline of the Confederacy*, 60. When the Union sailors attempted to land at Smyrna from the gunboats *Penguin* and *Henry Andrew*, Dilworth wrote, "our men fired into them. The enemy retreated to the opposite side of the river and abandoned their launches, five in number."

31. Ammen to Du Pont, May 31, 1862, *ORN*, 13:64–65; Ammen, *Old Navy and the New*, 363–64; Du Pont to Welles, June 11, 1862, *ORN*, 13:83–84, enclosure, Ammen to Du Pont, June 8 and 11, 1862, *ORN*, 13:90–91. Sproston had distinguished himself, Du Pont noted, "while in the command of one of the boats which destroyed the rebel privateer under the guns of the Pensacola navy yard in September, 1861, and his whole conduct during his war has been gallant and meritorious." Sproston graduated from the Naval Academy in 1846 and served on the *Powhatan* and then as the executive officer of the *Seneca*. Two destroyers were later named for him.

32. Webber to Nannie, February 19, 1865, Samuel G. Webber Papers, South Caroliniana Library.

33. Dahlgren to Sherman, January 24, 1865, *ORN*, 16:188; Dahlgren to Welles, January 31, 1865, *ORN*, 16:190–92; Chaplin to Dahlgren, January 28, 1865, *ORN*, 16:192–94.

34. Chaplin to Dahlgren, January 28, 1865, *ORN*, 16:192–94; report of Commander Balch of *Pawnee* to Dahlgren, January 27, 1865, *ORN*, 16:195–97; report of Rear Admiral Dahlgren, transmitting findings of the court of inquiry, February 10, 1865, enclosure, *ORN*, 16:197–200. The *Dai Ching* was one of five federal vessels (*Pawnee*, *Sonoma*, *Wissahickon*, and *McDonough*) menacing the flank of the rebel position. Admiral Dahlgren later described the *Dai Ching* as the least valuable of the light-draft gunboats, "her speed under steam being less than 5 knots, and her only heavy gun a 100-pounder."

35. Report of Flag Officer Du Pont, May 14, 1862, enclosures, Parrott to Du Pont, May 13, 1862, Nickels to Parrott, May 13, 1862, *ORN*, 12:821–25; Du Pont to Sophie, May 11, 1862, *SFDP Letters*, 2:50–51; Welles to Du Pont, July 15, 1862, *ORN*, 12:823; Du Pont to Welles, August 19, 1862, *ORN*, 12:825; Aptheker, "The Negro in the Union Navy," n. 78. The Robert Smalls Foundation has a Web site: www.robertsmalls.org. Other men involved in the *Planter* escape were John Smalls, A. Gridiron, A. Alston, A. Jackson, G. Turno, and J. Chisholm, along with two women identified only as Annie and Lavinia.

36. Du Pont to Sophie, May 11, 1862, *SFDP Letters*, 2:50–51; Du Pont to Rhind, June 14, 1862, *ORN*, 12:99; Aptheker, "The Negro in the Union Navy." The *Planter* was in naval service for just four months, after which it was turned over to the army's Quartermaster Department at Hilton Head.

CHAPTER 7. CONTRABAND SAILORS

1. Reidy, "Black Men in Blue"; Bennett, *Union Jacks*, 1–2, 283n9; Ramold, *Slaves, Sailors, Citizens*, 7–20, 22–24. Many recruits came from the South: 933 from North Carolina, 707 from South Carolina, 417 from Georgia, 255 from Florida, and 480 from the District of Columbia. A large number also enlisted in the North: 189 in Connecticut, 433 in New Jersey, 348 in Delaware, 159 in Rhode Island, 434 in Mas-

sachusetts, 29 in New Hampshire, and 75 in Maine. Ramold says African Americans accounted for 2.5 percent of the navy's enlisted ranks in 1861. Of the 7,600 enlisted men serving in the U.S. Navy when the Civil War began, only a few hundred listed themselves as black or mulatto. Reidy's article includes a table of aggregate percentages of black enlisted men serving on U.S. Navy vessels by calendar quarter. During the first quarter of 1862 the navy was 8 percent black; the high mark was 23 percent during the third and fourth quarters of 1864.

2. Reidy, "Black Men in Blue," 41, 150. Reidy's research suggests that contrabands "made a considerable majority of black sailors, and by extension, a significant segment of the navy's entire enlisted force during the Civil War."

3. www.bjmjr.com/union_navy/uss_vermont.htm; Ramold, *Slaves, Sailors, Citizens*, 55. Records of enlistments can be found in Records of the Bureau of Naval Personnel, vols. 7–44, record group 24, National Archives, Washington, D.C. The muster rolls of the armed ferryboat USS *Hunchback* also provide information about contrabands in its crew in 1864.

4. Browning, *From Cape Fear*, 203–4; Bennett, *Union Jacks*, 1–4; Samuel G. Webber to Nannie, July 15, 1862, Samuel G. Webber Papers, South Caroliniana Library. According to Robert Browning, black enlistments in the navy peaked in July and August 1863. As historian Michael Bennett has shown, most white American men who joined the Union Navy came from poor, working-class neighborhoods in eastern cities. Unlike army recruits, who came largely from rural areas, these men often possessed skills as butchers, bakers, firemen, machinists, blacksmiths, or carpenters; however, almost a third listed their occupation as "none," indicating that they were unemployed or went from job to job.

5. Ramold, *Slaves, Sailors, Citizens*, 18, 19; Bennett, *Union Jacks*, 6–8; Miller, *Biography of David Hunter*, 99–103; Browning, *From Cape Fear*, 202. The Union Navy also paid civilian agents to recruit sailors, and critical manpower shortages in 1864 prompted the navy to send the USS *Rhode Island* to Maine to recruit sailors. As the war went on, more and more men chose to become sailors rather than soldiers because the navy offered more comfortable, less dangerous service. There is also little doubt that the promise of prize money convinced many men to opt for navy rather than army service.

6. William Keeler, October 28, 1863, in Daly, ed., *Aboard the USS* Florida, 106–7.

7. Ramold, *Slaves, Sailors, Citizens*, 41; Reynolds to Dahlgren, May 15, 1865, in Berlin et al., eds., *Freedom*, 3:342.

8. "African American Sailors in the Union Navy from North Carolina," www .rootsweb.com/ncusct.htm. In addition, five U.S. Colored Troop regiments were formed in North Carolina during the Civil War. My search of black sailors with surnames beginning with the letters *G* and *H* from the North Carolina–U.S. Colored Troops Project found that only five men out of more than a hundred listed their occupation as mariner, boatman, or waterman. They came from all over North Carolina, but not surprisingly, many recruits listed New Bern or Wilmington as their home.

9. Ramold, *Slaves, Sailors, Citizens*, 43; Bennett, *Union Jacks*, 163–64, 170; Ringle, *Life in Mr. Lincoln's Navy*, 95. Ringle has a navy pay schedule for 1864 in which the highest-paid rating is first-class fireman, at $30 a month, and the lowest rating is boy, at $10 a month. Yeomen, cabin stewards, and commanding officers' cooks also received higher wages.

10. Conroy to Du Pont, November 5, 1862, *ORN*, 13:431; Russell to Conroy, November 5, 1862, *ORN*, 13:431–32; Du Pont to Conroy, November 10, 1862, *ORN*, 13:432; Du Pont to Welles, November 11, 1862, *ORN*, 13:431. Praising Conroy for his "discretion as well as determination," Du Pont told Welles that subject to the Navy Department's approval, he had made Conroy an acting ensign.

11. Gillis to Du Pont, January 2, 1862, *ORN*, 12:460–61.

12. Goldsborough to Rowan, February 16, 1862, *ORN*, 6:650; Geer to wife, May 20, 1862, in Marvel, ed., *Monitor Chronicles*, 79–80; Boyer, *Naval Surgeon*, 59, 61. Not all the refugees picked up by the *Monitor* were black. According to George Geer, when the *Monitor* prepared to fire an incendiary shell into City Point, "several Boats came out to us from the Dock and begged us to give them time to get their familys away, and all claimed to be Union men, but we know they all lide." Even though Goldsborough knew there was "not a Union man on shore," Geer explained, he gave the people time to move, "so they went at it, and all night long and this morning the Boats are passing with Furniture, Pigs, Chickens, Negros, and all other kind property." He also noted that eight contraband sailors had been sent to the *Galena* to replace crewmen wounded or killed at Drewry's Bluff.

13. Du Pont, General Order No. 11, May 15, 1862, *ORN*, 13:5.

14. Calvin Hutchinson, "Service on a Ferry-boat," 10–11, Calvin Hutchinson Papers, Huntington Library, San Marino, Calif.

15. Truxtun to Du Pont, September 6, 1862, *ORN*, 13:299–300.

16. S. C. Rowan to Welles, April 12, 1864, *ORN*, 15:397, enclosure, Rowan, April 11, 1864, *ORN*, 15: 397. According to Rowan, Moses Bryan also said that "detachments were sent to Richmond and Florida in February and March."

17. Scott to Lee, September 25, 1862, *ORN*, 8:87, enclosure, Braine to Scott, September 22, 1862, *ORN*, 8:88. Benjamin Berry was going to fit the *North Carolina* with an engine from the steamer *Uncle Ben;* Braine told Scott the ship would be ready "by the 10th of October, 1862." Lieutenant Braine, appointed a midshipman in the U.S. Navy in 1847, had served in the Mexican War and made the navy his career. His mother was Agnes Dean Hamilton, daughter of Alexander Hamilton.

18. Lee to Scott, October 5, 1862, *ORN*, 8:119–20; Lee to Welles, October 5, 1862, *ORN*, 8:118–19. Three of the seven contrabands on the *Monticello* enlisted in the Union Navy in September 1862. Identifying himself as a cook, Samuel Mince enlisted for three years on September 21 and was rated as a first-class boy. James Brown, age twenty-three and five feet five inches tall, enlisted the same day and was also rated as a first-class boy. Brown served in the Union Navy throughout the Civil War on the *Monticello, Valley City,* and *Commodore Morris.* The third man, Horace Smith, also signed up for a three-year enlistment; he was rated as a second-class boy. Smith told the navy that in civilian life he had been a house servant.

19. Gould, *Diary of a Contraband,* xix, 15, 105, 108, 109. William Gould IV used his great-grandfather's diaries in *Diary of a Contraband,* which includes biographical information about five of the other eight men. Joseph Hall later settled in Old Port Comfort, Virginia; George Price, who left to join the *Cambridge,* may have deserted, but he later represented New Hanover County in the state house of representatives and senate; Andrew Hall, Joseph's brother, settled in Cambridge, Massachusetts; and John Mackey and Charles Giles continued to correspond with Gould after the war.

20. Reidy, "Black Men in Blue," 4; Gould, *Diary of a Contraband,* 108; Ringle, *Life in Mr. Lincoln's Navy,* 64–65.

21. *Christian Recorder,* December 31, 1862 (item 59982), September 10, 1864 (item 61698), January 16, 1864 (item 59989), www.accessible.com. For more on African Americans and literacy during the war, see Williams, *Self-taught.*

22. Reidy, "Black Men in Blue," pt. 2, 5, 6; Bennett, *Union Jacks,* 164–65; Roswell Lamson to Flora, August 20, 1863, in Lamson, *Lamson of the Gettysburg,* 126. Bennett argues white sailors took pleasure in relegating hard manual labor to black sailors and derived a feeling of power from supervising black sailors at these menial tasks.

23. Hunter, *A Year on a Monitor,* 113. Only sixteen years old when he joined the navy in November 1862, Alvah Hunter kept a diary and later wrote of his experiences as a ship's boy on the *Nahant.*

24. Keeler to Anna, February 13, 25, 28, March 4, 1862, in Daly, ed., *Aboard the USS* Monitor, 12, 17, 19, 23.

25. Webber to Nannie, October 3, 1864, July 24, 1863, Webber Papers.

26. Keeler to Anna, March 5, 1862, in Daly, ed. *On Board the USS* Monitor, 24.

27. Reidy, "Black Men in Blue," pt. 2; Sherman Adams, draft of a letter dated December 12, 1863, Letter No. 2, Sherman W. Adams Papers, Connecticut Historical Society.

28. Lamson to Kate, June 11, 1863, in Lamson, *Lamson of the Gettysburg,* 112–13.

29. Webber to Nannie, February 21, 1864, March 12, 1865, Webber Papers.

30. Marvel, ed., *Monitor Chronicles,* 88; Steedman to wife, May 20, 1863, in Steedman, *Memoirs and Correspondence,* 361; Steedman to Du Pont, May 20, 1863, *ORN,* 13:777.

31. Calvin Hutchinson, "The Cruise of the USS *Pequot,*" HM41748, Hutchinson Papers.

32. Jordan, *Black Confederates and Afro-Yankees,* 143; Bennett, *Union Jacks,* 166–67, 176–77. The practice of segregating crews was more common in the Mississippi Squadron but was generally left to the commanding officer's discretion. Many Union Army soldiers echoed the sailors' low opinion of black navy enlisted men, yet others admired African Americans' willingness to serve and fight for their country. Among the latter was Reese B. Gwilliam, a corporal with the Twenty-second Connecticut Infantry. In a journal entry dated April 22, 1863, Gwilliam described disinterring bodies for reburial in Suffolk, Virginia. They found a body, he wrote, "sewed up in a sack; they uncovered it so as to see the face and found it was *only* a colored man (killed on a gunboat, also) then buried it again." Gwilliam noted, "It was only a nigger, And yet had doubtless done his duty and deserved more honored burial." Reese Gwilliam Journal, Connecticut Historical Society.

33. Geer to his wife, May 24, 1862, in Marvel, ed., *Monitor Chronicles,* 89–90; Boyer, *Naval Surgeon,* 102, 221; Ringle, *Life in Mr. Lincoln's Navy,* 104–6; Bennett, *Union Jacks,* 179–80.

34. Hunter, *A Year on a Monitor,* 40.

35. Ibid., 20; Marvel, ed., *Monitor Chronicles,* 177.

36. George Bright journal, George Bright Papers, Huntington Library, San Marino, Calif.

37. Boyer, *Naval Surgeon,* 49.

38. Ibid., 32–33.

39. Ibid., 317; Stephen C. Bartlett to sister, February 5 and 12, 1865, in Bartlett and Murray, eds., "The Letters of Stephen Caulker Bartlett," 73, 75; Webber to Nannie Sturdevant Webber, July 4, 1863, Webber Papers.

40. George Bright journal, Bright Papers.

41. Ibid.

42. Kendricksen, *Memoirs*, 209.

43. Reidy, "Black Men in Blue," pt. 2, 7–8.

44. Gould, *Diary of a Contraband*, 24; Johnson, *Rear Admiral John Rodgers*, 183–85; Scott to Lee, October 20, 1862, enclosure, Scott to Parker, October 6, 1862, Parker to Scott, October 6, 1862, *ORN*, 8:153–54; Parker to Scott, October 17, 1862, *ORN*, 8:154.

45. Gould, *Diary of a Contraband*, 24; Bunce to Scott, October 16, 1862, *ORN*, 8:154–55. In their reports of the expedition to Lee, the *Penobscot*'s skipper, F. M. Bunce, and the *Cambridge*'s, William Parker, expanded Gould's account. According to Parker, the expedition was organized in response to a proposal from Bunce to Scott to "go in at night and burn the rebel steamer *Kate*."

46. Gould, *Diary of a Contraband*, 114–15; Parker to Scott, November 17, 1862, *ORN*, 8:214–15. Parker listed the men taken prisoner as William Maies, Henry W. Wells, W. C. Odiorne, H. C. Reed, John Graham, Daniel Derocher, George Lily, William B. Frost, Hans DeBaor, Dick Haman, Thomas McGee, William Haley, and William Thomas.

47. Du Pont to Bacon, January 27, 1863, *ORN*, 13:528.; F. S. Conover to Welles, May 7, 1863, *ORN*, 13:563–65; Du Pont to Welles, February 1863, *ORN*, 13:556–57, enclosure, Bacon to Du Pont, January 30, 1863, *ORN*, 13:558–59.

48. Colonel Joseph A. Yates to Captain W. F. Nance, February 1, 1863, *ORN*, 13:567; Conover to Welles, May 7, 1863, *ORN*, 13:563–65; Major Brown to Captain Nance, February 1, 1862, *ORN*, 13:568–69. Major W. Brown of the Second South Carolina Volunteers commanded the battery that fired on the second gunboat to come up. John H. Gray of the battery at Grimball's also reported. One of the *Smith*'s crewmen injured in the attack was a white landsman, Richard Stout, who was "severely wounded and lost his right arm while returning rebel fire." Stout, born in 1836 in New York, was awarded the Medal of Honor for his brave actions that day in the Stono.

49. Bacon to Du Pont, February 15, 1863, *ORN*, 13:560.

50. Brigadier General Thomas Jordan to Lieutenant F. S. Conover, February 2, 1863, *ORN*, 13:561; Thomas Jordan, Chief of Staff, to Lieutenant F. S. Conover, USN, February 7, 1863, *ORN*, 13:562. General Jordan explained: "I have only to say that were the language of President Lincoln's proclamation of doubtful import, the meaning would be made clear by the fact that there are now at Hilton Head or that vicinity fugitive slaves who have been recently employed in armed expeditions against the people of Georgia and South Carolina."

51. Stellwagen to Du Pont, January 31, 1863, *ORN*, 13:579–80; Du Pont to Welles, February 3, 1865, report of attack of Confederate ironclads upon the federal blockading squadron of Charleston, S.C., January 31, 1863, *ORN*, 13:577–78; T. H. Eastman to Mrs. T. H. Eastman, February 3, 1863, *ORN*, 13:586; Browning, *Success*, 140; W. E. Le Roy to Du Pont, January 31, 1863, enclosure, Report of Casualties, *ORN*, 13:581–83; letter of James Tomb, January 30, 1863, *ORN*, 13:622–23; abstract log of USS *Keystone State*, *ORN*, 13:583–85. Although Eastman failed to mention it to his wife, he, not Le Roy, decided to keep on fighting. When Le Roy hauled down the colors, Eastman apparently threw down his sword and cried, "God D___ it. I will have nothing to do with it." Le Roy then asked him if he would take responsibility, and when Eastman agreed, they ran the flag back up and continued to fight.

52. Acting Assistant Surgeon C. H. Mason to Captain H. S. Stellwagen, January 31, 1863, *ORN*, 13:581; Du Pont to Welles, February 1863, *ORN*, 13:577–78; W. E. Le Roy to Du Pont, January 31, 1863, enclosure, Report of Casualties, *ORN*, 13:581–83; T. H. Eastman to Mrs. T. H. Eastman, February 3, 1863, *ORN*, 13:586. Eastman later told his wife that they had mustered 196 men the morning of the attack, had buried twenty-three, and would probably lose another three men.

53. Murray to Lee, December 30, 1862, *ORN*, 8:291; Manchester to Murray, December 16, 1862, *ORN*, 8:291–92; Browning, *From Cape Fear*, 87–88. In his report Manchester explained, "At daylight on the 13th got underway and, with much difficulty and labor, worked our way up to within 2 miles of Kinston, meeting with but slight opposition from the guerillas on shore, by whose fire one man (of the crew of the late *Ellis*) was seriously wounded."

54. Rodgers to Anne, January 19, 1862, in Johnson, *Rear Admiral John Rodgers*, 183–85; Rodgers to Du Pont, January 28 and 29, 1862, *ORN*, 12:494–95; Du Pont to Mrs. Du Pont, January 28, 1862, *SFDP Letters*, 2:320–21. "John Rodgers made remarkable reconnaissances at the risk of his life, is a gifted man in this way, and more to be relied upon than any man in the squadron," Du Pont told Sophie.

55. Acting Master's Mate George Drain to Lee, March 29, 1862, *ORN*, 8:585–86.

56. H. H. Savage to B. F. Sands, March 4, 1863, *ORN*, 8:584–85. Unfortunately, Jesse Smith is not listed in Black Sailor Search.

57. Drain to Lee, March 29, 1862, *ORN*, 8:585–86.

58. Lee to Cushing and Lamson, April 13, 1863, Lamson to Lee, April 12, 1863, *ORN*, 8:716–17. "Their field artillery, properly placed, is more than a match for our little gunboats in that situation," Lee warned Lamson, "where even their sharpshooters can drive our men from their guns." At midnight on April 13 the admiral did, however, telegraph an urgent request to Welles for some light-draft, rifle-screened boats from the Potomac. "The situation is critical," he wrote. See *ORN*, 8:720. Lee was concerned about reports that the rebels might cross the Nansemond above the Western Branch using pontoons, but he had few larger vessels to send upriver.

59. Lamson to Lee, April 22, 1863, *ORN*, 8:722–25.

60. Ibid. Black Sailor Search has no records for either Lody or Jackson on the *Mt. Washington*. Lamson also named Robert J. Jordan, Quartermaster Delon, and Robert Wood for special commendation. The *West End* also went aground but was towed free, and the *Minnesota* provided gun crews. The fiery young Lamson was determined to retaliate against the rebel battery, which, he told Lee, "if not taken, will cut off entirely our communications with the fleet below." Lamson offered to take 500 soldiers on board his ship, land them close to the upper end of the Confederate defenses, and attack the batteries and rifle pits. He planned to support the attack using his ship's guns and by landing four of his howitzers on shore. General Peck approved the plan, but the late arrival of Union troops forced Lamson to call off the attack. Lamson to Lee, April 18, 1863, *ORN*, 8:739.

61. Lamson to Lee, April 22, 1863, *ORN*, 8:722–25; Peirce Crosby to Lee, telegram, April 19, 1863, *ORN*, 8:742–43; Lamson's report to Lee, April 20, 1863, *ORN*, 8:746–47; Getty to Foster, May 12, 1863, *ORN*, 8:793; Lamson to Kate, April 14 and 24, 1863, in Lamson, *Lamson of the Gettysburg*, 96–97, 101–2. A detailed chronology of these actions is recounted by Master Harris of the USS *Stepping Stones* in a letter to Admiral Lee dated April 24, 1863, *ORN*, 8:759–62. When the *Stepping Stones* glanced off a pile and drifted on the ebb tide, General Getty wrote, "Lieu-

tenant Lamson with admirable presence of mind, reversed the paddle wheels and backed her aground. The men jumped off from both ends of the boat up to their waists in mud and water, and scrambled hastily ashore, and with a cheer dashed for the battery."

62. Gregory to Dahlgren, December 15, 1863, *ORN*, 15:153; Dahlgren to Welles, January 5, 1864, enclosure A, J. F. Green to Dahlgren, January 4, 1864, *ORN*, 15:156–57, enclosures D, E, and F, Gregory to Welles, January 4, 1864, and George Anderson to Welles, October 22, 1864, *ORN*, 15:159–60. Anderson did not make his report until October 1864. Gregory later learned that his son was uninjured.

63. Anderson to Welles, October 22, 1864, *ORN*, 15:159–60. The Confederates came from two companies of the Fifth and Twenty-first Georgia Cavalry under Captains H. K. Harrison and C. C. Bowen.

64. Dahlgren to Green, December 23, 1863, *ORN*, 15:155. The admiral micromanaged the expedition, instructing Green to bring his boats in at night; use grape and canister mostly in the howitzers; carry axes, spades, and picks in case they had to dig a breastwork; and not allow the men to straggle.

65. Ibid., 154; Dahlgren to Welles, January 5, 1864, enclosure A, report of J. F. Green, January 4, 1864, *ORN*, 15:156–57; enclosure B, report of J. H. Spotts; enclosure C, report of John C. Collins Jr.; enclosure D, report of Sam Gregory, *ORN*, 15:159–60. According to Master Collins, thirteen contrabands had appeared at 4 A.M. on December 30 in a boat coming out from shore. In the boat they "discovered 13 contrabands who had last night effected their escape from slavery, and including among them 4 females and 1 infant, all of whom are now on aboard this schooner well cared for. They imparted considerable information respecting this locality and the salt works now in progress which, if correct must prove of value." The contrabands reported the presence of the rebel schooner in the inlet and that the rebels had four companies of soldiers, principally cavalry, in the vicinity protecting local salt manufactures and patrolling the beach.

66. Dahlgren to Welles, January 5, 1864, *ORN*, 15:155–56; enclosure D, Gregory to Dahlgren, January 4, 1864, enclosure E, Gregory to Dahlgren, December 30, 1863, enclosure F, Gregory to Dahlgren, January 4, 1864, *ORN*, 15:159–60. In his January 4 letter, Gregory refers to one from Dahlgren dated January 3, but this is not in *ORN*.

67. George W. Reed, May 14, 1864, printed in *Christian Recorder*, May 21, 1864, Letter 121 in Redkey, ed., *Grand Army of Black Men*, 272; Parker to Welles, April 22, 1864, *ORN*, 5:411–12; Black Sailor Search for George Reed. Reed, who enlisted for one year, is on the *Commodore Read*'s muster roll as of March 31, 1864. In his letter to the *Christian Recorder*, Reed claimed to be a navy veteran. He wrote: "Sir, having been engaged in the naval service nearly six years, I have never before witnessed what I now see on board this ship. Our crew are principally colored, and a braver set of men never trod the deck of an American ship." Based on this information, Reed must have joined the navy before the beginning of the Civil War.

68. Terry Foenander, "Naval Skirmishes 2: The USS *Eureka* at Urbana, Virginia, April 21, 1864," www.tfoenander.com/eureka.htm. The crew list appeared in the *New York Daily Tribune*, April 27, 1863. Reed letter, May 14, 1864, in Redkey, ed., *Grand Army of Black Men*, 273; Parker to Welles, April 22, 1864, *ORN*, 5:411–12; Bay, "A Flotilla Cries 'Eureka.'" The *Eureka* had a crew of sixteen, including Treadwell Scott, a twenty-one-year-old African American born in Flushing, New

York. When he enlisted in 1863, Scott told the navy he had been a coachman and a cook.

69. Ammen, *Old Navy and the New*, 368.

70. Browning, *Success*, 281; Balch to Dahlgren, December 25, 1863, *ORN*, 15:189; Meade to Dahlgren, December 25, 1863, *ORN*, 15:190–91; Kidder to Meade, report of casualties, December 25, 1863, *ORN*, 15:191. For a report on Meade's expedition to bring off the guns, see Meade to Balch, December 28, 1863, *ORN*, 15:194–96. The Confederate reports are in *ORN*, 15:201ff.; www.itd.nps.gov/cwss/history/aa_medals.htm. William Carney served with the Fifty-fourth Massachusetts Infantry. African American sailors awarded the Medal of Honor included William Brown, Wilson Brown, John Lawson, James Mifflin, and Joachim Please. In his report Meade also noted, "The enemy's fire was very effective, and the vessel is badly cut up aloft (losing main topmast) and on deck, has several shot in the hull and one or two in the foremast."

71. Lee to Welles, January 4, 1863, *ORN*, 8:343–47, enclosures, Armstrong to Lee, January 3, 1863, *ORN*, 8:352, Bankhead to Lee, January 1, 1863, *ORN*, 8:347–49; Marvel, ed., *Monitor Chronicles*, 230; Butts, "Loss of the *Monitor*," 299; Clancy, *Ironclad*, 113–14. Bankhead's report enclosed a list of the missing, but the list is not included in *ORN*. "The USS *Monitor*," http://id.essortment.com/ussmonitor_rxuh.htm, has a list of the missing. Black Sailor Search provides no information about Robert H. Howard. George Geer lost his good friend and ship's cook Daniel Moore in the sinking; records do not indicate that Moore was black.

72. Boyer, *Naval Surgeon*, 109.

73. Dean to Virginia, September 27, 1864, Ashael Sumner Dean Civil War letters to his family, USS *Harvest Moon* Historical Society; Ramold, *Slaves, Sailors, Citizens*, 103–4. Naval surgeons assigned to larger ships often visited smaller vessels without doctors to diagnose and treat ill and injured sailors. In a letter to his wife dated August 19, 1864, surgeon Samuel G. Webber, serving on the *Nahant*, wrote that he had been asked to examine some sick men on the *John Adams*. "I was then asked by Capt. Green to go on aboard a tug and see a person said to have consumption. I then had to see five men on board another tug" (Webber Papers). Webber did not mention whether any of these men were contrabands.

74. Gray and Ropes, *War Letters*, 422.

75. Welles to Chase, January 17, 1862, *ORN*, 12:490; Freemon, *Gangrene and Glory*, 94.

76. William Maxwell Wood to Welles, August 2, 1862, *ORN*, 7:616–18, enclosure, J. C. Spear, *ORN*, 7:618; Ringle, *Life in Mr. Lincoln's Navy*, 114, 117–18; Browning, *Success*, 110–12. Surgeon Wood also recommended that the men be given a daily dose of quinine in wine or whiskey (to make it more palatable) to prevent malaria. At the time, the *Rhode Island* was stationed off Cape Hatien, Haiti; it also spent time off Mariguana Island in the Bahamas. Cases of scurvy cropped up in the army during the Peninsular Campaign; see Schumm, *Doctor in Blue*, 225. In July 1862 the Army of the Potomac had 20 percent of its men on the sick list.

77. Webber to Nannie, July 3, 1863, Webber Papers.

78. Daly, ed., *Aboard the USS* Monitor, 198.

79. Webber to Nannie, October 1, 1864, Webber Papers.

80. Stephen Chaulker Bartlett to his parents, March 17, 1865, in Bartlett and Murray, eds., "The Letters of Stephen Caulker Bartlett," 81–82.

81. Terry Reimer, "Smallpox and Vaccination in the Civil War," National Museum

of Civil War Medicine Web site, www.civilwarmed.org/articles.cfm; Ringle, *Life in Mr. Lincoln's Navy*, 117–18. Smallpox scabs from those infected with the disease were used to produce the vaccine. Reimer claims that authorities harvested scabs from children, black and white, "and in at least one instance a small group of African American children were kept vaccinated [*sic*] to provide usable material."

82. George Harlan to Margaret, December 13, 1861, George Harlan Papers, Huntington Library, San Marino, Calif.

83. Welles to Du Pont, January 3, 1862, *ORN*, 12:462; B. F. Sands to Lee, October 19, 1863, *ORN*, 9:247.

84. Lee to Welles, December 10, 1863, *ORN*, 9:346, enclosure A, Lee to Fleet Surgeon Wm. Maxwell Wood, USN, on USS *Minnesota*, December 9, 1863, enclosure B, Wood to Lee, December 9, 1863, *ORN*, 9:346; Ringle, *Life in Mr. Lincoln's Navy*, 117–18. Ringle does not identify the source of the *Commodore Barney* smallpox cases as individuals from contraband camps in the vicinity of the navy yard. Ramold, *Slaves, Sailors, Citizens,* does not discuss this incidence of smallpox.

85. Hutchinson, "Cruise of the USS *Pequot.*" The *Pequot's* quarantine is not listed in *ORN* vol. 15; nor is the ship listed as part of the South Atlantic Blockading Squadron on the March 15 or April 1, 1864, list. The *Pequot* is listed as being on station in New Inlet, North Carolina, in Lee's March 17, 1864, list; see *ORN*, 9:554.

86. Webber to Nannie, August 16, 1864, Webber Papers.

87. Ward, *Slaves' War,* 214, 223–25, 230–31. Ward recounts the experiences of many slaves who encountered Union and Confederate troops foraging for livestock and supplies but does not mention any who suffered from navy foraging parties.

CHAPTER 8. JOINT ARMY-NAVY OPERATIONS

1. For combined operations, see Browning, *Success* and *From Cape Fear;* Trotter, *Ironclads and Columbiads,* 239–46, chaps. 27–29; Reed, *Combined Operations,* 52–56, 356–58, chap. 11.

2. T. W. Higginson journal entry, January 21, 1863, in Looby, ed., *Complete Civil War Journal,* 91–92; Higginson, *Army Life in a Black Regiment,* 85.

3. Higginson, *Army Life in a Black Regiment,* 83.

4. Higginson, *Army Life in a Black Regiment,* chap. 3. Samuel P. Boyer, the *Fernandina's* surgeon, recorded the visit in his diary on January 24, 1863: "The suspected enemy proved to be the Army transport *Ben De Ford* with the 1st Regiment of South Carolina Volunteers on board. Col. Higginson and the surgeon paid us a visit" (Boyer, *Naval Surgeon,* 49). Higginson was told, "It proved impossible to dislodge those fellows from the banks, they had dug rifle pits, and swarmed like hornets, and when fairly silenced in one direction were sure to open on us from another."

5. Higginson journal, February 4, 1863, in Looby, ed., *Complete Civil War Journal,* 92–97; Higginson, *Army Life in a Black Regiment,* chap. 3; King, *Reminiscences of My Life in Camp,* 26–27. Susie Taylor King wrote that the *John Adams* "carried several guns and a good gunner, Edward Herron." The largest house in Woodstock was owned by a Mr. and Mrs. Alberti. The latter was introduced to Corporal Sutton, the expedition's pilot, whom she had once owned as a slave, prompting Colonel Higginson to write in his journal, "Ah, said she, after some reflection, we called him, 'Bob.'" The colonel recalled, "Oh dear, it was all very dreamlike and funny beyond description." After an expedition up the Edisto River, during which his men rescued

numerous slaves, Higginson noted in chapter 7 of his memoirs, *Army Life in a Black Regiment:* "Before the war, how great a thing seemed the rescue of even one man from slavery; and since the war has emancipated all; how little seems the liberation of two hundred! But no one knew then how the contest might end; and when I think of that morning sunlight, those emerald fields, those thronging numbers, the old women with them—prayers, and the little boys with them; living burdens, I know that the day was worth all it cost, and more."

6. Gooding, *On the Altar of Freedom,* xxvii, 26–27; Cornish, *Sable Arm,* 130–31; Smith, ed., *Black Soldiers in Blue,* introduction. By August 1863 the Union Army had fourteen black regiments in the field. Eventually, approximately 180,000 African Americans served in 163 units the Union Army.

7. Civil War in South Carolina, various losses, www.sciway3.net/dark/civilwar/losses.html; Rose, *Rehearsal for Reconstruction,* 246. W. C. Heyward submitted a claim in June 1863 for his lost property, including slaves, whom he listed by name. Heyward also claimed that Union troops had burned or destroyed a dwelling house, two barns, overseer's house, thrashing mill, grist mill, several sheds, hospital, five "negro" houses, 800 bushels of corn, and 10,000 bushels of rough rice. General Hunter also mentioned a raid by Colonel. Hawley into the interior of Florida that netted 188 head of cattle, mules, and horses belonging to a man who was a beef contractor to the Confederate Army.

8. Cornish, *Sable Arm,* 148–49; Boyer, *Naval Surgeon,* 130, Gooding, *On the Altar of Freedom,* 29–30.

9. Cornish, *Sable Arm,* 148–49 ; Higginson journal, July 7, 1863, in Looby, ed., *Complete Civil War Journal,* 157–58; Boyer, *Naval Surgeon,* 130–31; Rankin, *Diary of a Christian Soldier,* introduction; www.darien.net/aatrainhistory.html. According to the Darien Web site, all that was left after the fire was a portion of the Methodist church, two or three smaller buildings, and the walls of the two-story warehouse on the upper bluff. Shaw called the destruction of Darien "barbarous" and "distasteful," but not everyone agreed. In a biography of Rufus Kinsley, a white officer in the Second Louisiana Corps d'Afrique, David Rankin argues that Kinsley believed that the burning of Darien was "the fulfillment of God's will and would have been dumfounded by Shaw's characterization." Higginson wrote in his journal, "Montgomery has been a sore disappointment here."

10. Vincent Colyer, "Valuable Supplies Obtained," in *Report of the Services Rendered by the Freed People,* pt. 2, Eastern North Carolina Digital Library, http://digital.lib.ecu.edu.

11. Paludan, *A People's Contest,* 26. Historians Philip Paludan; Michael Fellman, *Inside War;* and Stephen Ash, *When the Yankees Came,* have argued that irregular warfare played a significant role and affected both Confederate and Union military policy. For more information on this scholarship, see Sutherland, ed., *Guerillas, Unionists and Violence;* Sutherland, "Guerilla Warfare"; Fellman, Gordon, and Sutherland, eds., *This Terrible War.*

12. Reid, *Freedom for Themselves,* 114; Lee to Welles, June 7, 1863, *ORN,* 9:59, enclosure, Gillis to Lee, June 6, 1863, *ORN,* 9:60–61; Calvin Hutchinson to Roxanna Hutchinson, June 6, 1863, HM1743, Calvin Hutchinson Papers, Huntington Library, San Marino, Calif.

13. Hutchinson to Roxanna, June 6, 1863, Hutchinson Papers.

14. Lieutenant Hooker to Street, telegram, n.d., *ORN,* 5:443, enclosure, Street to Parker, June 15, 1864, *ORN,* 5:443–44; Reid, *Freedom for Themselves,* 133. For

more on Draper, see Lause, "Turning the World Upside Down," 198–99. The regiment was attached to U.S. forces in Norfolk and Portsmouth, Virginia, until April of that year, when it was sent to guard prisoners at Point Lookout, Maryland, under the District of St. Mary's Department of Virginia and North Carolina.

15. Hooker to Parker, June 21, 1864, *ORN*, 5:447–48; Street to Parker, June 15, 1864, *ORN*, 5:443–44; Hooker to Parker, June 12, 1864, *ORN*, 5:444.

16. Hooker to Parker, June 21, 1864, *ORN*, 5:447–49.

17. Hooker to Parker, September 1, 1864, *ORN*, 5:451; Reid, *Freedom for Themselves*, 133–35; Lause, "Turning the World Upside Down," 199n26; Draper's report, June 22, 1864, *ORA*, 37(1):163–67; Eastman to Hooker, August 5, 1864, *ORN*, 5:451. This June 1864 raid was just one of several undertaken by Colonel Draper, with General Butler's permission, to provide for the families of his soldiers. Draper reported that this joint army-navy operation had also netted "about 600 contrabands, including 60 to 70 recruits for the army and navy, and a large number of plows, harrows, cultivators, wheat drills, corn-shellers, harness, carts, and carriages, etc. for the use of the contraband settlement on the Patuxent." Confederate rumors claimed that Draper's black troops had raped or attempted to rape "white ladies." According to Reid, an officer dismissed from the regiment later wrote that "some of the men committed *rape* & Col. Draper never endeavored to ferret out the person."

18. Wright to General T. W. Sherman, March 7, 1862, *ORA*, 6:239–40; Davis, *History of Early Jacksonville*, 160–61; Browning, *Success*, 70–71; Stevens to Du Pont, March 13, 1862, *ORN*, 12:599–600; Wright to Captain Louis H. Pelouze, Acting Assistant Adjutant General, March 10 and 13, 1862, *ORA*, 15:243; Wright to Pelouze, March 28, 1862, *ORA*, 6:256; Stevens to Du Pont, March 31, 1862, *ORN*, 12:686–87; Wright to Pelouze, March 31, 1862, *ORA*, 6:126–27; Du Pont to Captain J. L. Lardner, March 15, 1862, *ORN*, 12:603. "The one railroad out of town was taxed to its utmost capacity, carrying refugees to Lake City and other points in the interior of Florida" (Davis, *History of Early Jacksonville*, 160). Subsequently, on March 15, six companies of the Fourth New Hampshire Regiment came ashore and peacefully occupied the town, which was not defended by the disorganized and poorly equipped Confederate soldiers camped in nearby Baldwin.

19. Du Pont to Stevens, April 5, 1862, *ORN*, 12:715; "Major-General Hunter, U.S.A.," *Harper's Weekly*, March 14, 1863, 165; Hunter to Secretary of War Stanton, April 3, 1862, *ORA*, 6:263; Sherman to Hunter, March 31, 1862, *ORA*, 6:257. At this same time, Hunter asked the War Department to send him 50,000 muskets with 200 rounds per musket to arm "such loyal men as I can find in the country," as well as 50,000 pairs of scarlet pantaloons. He did not specify in this letter that he intended to arm loyal blacks and outfit them in red pants.

20. Du Pont to Drayton, April 5, 1862, *ORN*, 12:717; Stevens to Du Pont, April 10, 1862, *ORN*, 12:728; Stevens to Drayton, April 13, 1862, *ORN*, 12:739–40, Benham to Wright, April 2, 1862, *ORA*, 6:127–28. The lieutenant had decided to withdraw his naval forces to Mayport, Florida, to "prevent the destruction of property which belonged to Union people" in the probable event of hostilities between Union forces and the approaching Confederate troops.

21. Report of General Wright, April 13, 1862, *ORA*, 6:124–25; Wright to Bisbee, April 10, 1862, *ORA*, 6:130. The federal troops at Jacksonville were the Ninety-seventh Pennsylvania Regiment, six companies of the Fourth New Hampshire Regiment, and two sections of Hamilton's battery.

22. Davis, *History of Early Jacksonville,* 162–70; Ammen to Stevens, April 2, 1862, *ORN,* 12:695–96; Ammen to Du Pont, April 10, 1862, *ORN,* 12:712–13. Buker's *Blockaders, Refugees, and Contrabands* devotes only the last chapter to the east coast of Florida.

23. Stevens to Budd and Budd to Stevens, April 12, 1862, *ORN,* 12:738–39; Stevens to Drayton, April 3, 1862, *ORN,* 12:705; Stevens to Drayton, April 13, 1862, *ORN,* 12:739–40; report of Colonel W. S. Dilworth to Captain T. A. Washington, April 5, 1862, *ORA,* 6:131–32. In a letter to Elizabeth Gray written on May 21, 1864, John Chipman Gray referred to Judge Burritt as one of the leading men in Florida and wrote that Burritt "has at last taken the oath of allegiance. When that place was first occupied by our troops Judge Burritt's slaves got carried off by Col Montgomery; the Judge went to Washington and by some hocus pocus managed to get them back. He took them immediately up the St. John's, posted them off to Richmond, made some arrangement there, sold his slaves and invested the proceeds in land." See Gray and Ropes, *War Letters,* 339.

24. Stevens to Colonel W. G. M. Davis, April 15, 1862, *ORN,* 12:745–46.

25. Du Pont to Marchand, May 15, 1862, *ORN,* 13:5–6; Marchand journal, May 16, 1862, in Symonds, ed., *Charleston Blockade,* 164–66; Du Pont to Welles, May 14, 1862, *ORN,* 12:820–21; Browning, *Success,* 96–97. The fullest account is Miller, *Gullah Statesman.* When Marchand's gig pulled out of range of the enemy's shot, he rejoined Lieutenant Bankhead, and they completed the soundings in the Stono. At high water, they found only ten feet of water over the bar. With such low water and a heavy sea, Marchand decided, "much to my chagrin," that his gunboats could not cross the bar into the Stono. Although the determined commander hoped for calmer seas, the unfavorable weather continued for several days.

26. For this joint army-navy attack on the Stono, see Battle of Secessionville, Civil War @ Charleston Web site, www.awod.com; Foote, *Civil War,* 1:473; Reed, *Combined Operations,* 267–68; Browning, *Success,* 103–5; Brennan, *Secessionville.* Assistant Navy Secretary Gustavus Fox refused to consider any future joint attacks against Charleston. He insisted that before mounting a direct attack on the city, Du Pont wait for completion of the new Passaic-class monitors. According to Hoogenboom, *Gustavus Vasa Fox,* 166, Union officials exaggerated Charleston's importance, and "no one exaggerated its importance more than Fox." When the South Atlantic Blockading Squadron finally attacked Charleston in April 1863, Du Pont did not follow Marchand's scheme of approaching the city by way of the Stono River.

27. Drayton to Du Pont, June 17, 1862, *ORN,* 13:104–5; Du Pont to Department, June 16, 1862, enclosure, Truxtun to Du Pont, June 13, 1862, *ORN,* 13:95–97; Marchand journal, June 15, 1862, in Symonds, ed., *Charleston Blockade,* 208–10.

28. Report of Du Pont to Navy Department, June 16, 1862, enclosure, Truxtun to Du Pont, June 13, 1862, *ORN,* 13:95–97; Reed, *Combined Operations,* 268.

29. Report of Major R. J. Jeffords, Sixth Battalion, South Carolina Cavalry, June 14, 1862, *ORA,* 8:38.

30. Report of Du Pont to Navy Department, June 16, 1862, enclosure, Truxtun to Du Pont, June 13, 1862, *ORN,* 13:95–97.

31. Ibid.

32. Gillis to Guert Gansevoort, September 27, 1863, *ORN,* 9:205; Lee to Welles, September 30, 1863, *ORN,* 9:206; Lee to Foster, October 3, 1863, *ORN,* 9:226. The expedition also included detachments from Colonel Spear's Eleventh Cavalry and Captain Poor's First New York Mounted Rifles, along with two sections of artillery

from the Eighth New York Battery and one from Battery E, First Pennsylvania Light Artillery. See Report of General Foster to General Halleck, October 10, 1863, *ORN*, 9:209–10. On September 18 Captain Beall took a party of twenty-five irregulars in boats from Mathews County, Virginia, on a raid across the bay. They first captured the schooner *Alliance*, David Ireland master, which was loaded with sutler's goods. Beall's men, armed with revolvers, then boarded the *J. J. Houseman* and seized it. That same night they took the *Samuel Pearsall* and the *Alexandria*.

33. Lee to Welles, October 10, 1863, enclosure B from Gillis, October 8, 1863, *ORN*, 9:207–8; Foster to Halleck, October 10, 1863, *ORN*, 9:209–10. Foster wrote that General Wistar "speaks in high terms of praise of the marching discipline, cheerfulness, and obedience of the Fourth Regiment U.S. Colored Troops."

34. Lee to Welles, October 10, 1863, enclosure B from Gillis, October 8, 1863, *ORN*, 9:207–8; Brigadier General Henry Lockwood, USA, to Lieutenant Colonel W. H. Chesebrough, Assistant Adjutant General, November 16, 1863, *ORN*, 9:307.

35. Lucy Chase to Anna Lowell, November 29, 1863, in Swint, ed., *Dear Ones at Home*, 98–99.

36. Babcock to Lee, January 24, 1864, *ORN*, 9:414; "The Mother's Prayer, October 7, 1865, *Christian Recorder*, item 72698.

37. "Mother's Prayer."

38. George W. Reed letter, May 21, 1864, *Christian Recorder*, Letter 121 in Redkey, ed., *Grand Army of Black Men*, 272–73.

CHAPTER 9. THE FINAL MONTHS

1. Glatthaar, *March to the Sea*, 56, 63–64.

2. Hartwell and Racine, eds., *Fiery Trail*, 54; Ward, *Slaves' War*, pt. 9. For the reaction of Confederate women and slaves to Sherman's hard war policy in the Carolinas, see Campbell, *When Sherman Marched North*.

3. Dahlgren to Scott, December 31, 1864, *ORN*, 16:154; Dahlgren to Welles, January 4, 1865, *ORN*, 16:156–58. At the end of December 1864 Admiral Dahlgren had twenty-seven vessels, including seven monitors (*Patapsco, Montauk, Nahant, Leheigh, Catskill, Nantucket,* and *Passaic*), off Charleston. Four vessels of the squadron were on station in the Stono River, two at North Edisto, two at St. Helena, and three in the Savannah River. Others were on blockade duty in Wassaw, Ossabaw, St. Catherine's, Sapelo, Doboy, St. Simon's, St. John's, and St. Andrew's sounds; at Fernandina; and a large number at Port Royal.

4. Dahlgren to Welles, January 4, 1865, *ORN*, 16:156–58; Symonds, *Lincoln and His Admirals*, 349–50. Symonds points out that Sherman thought Charleston "wrecked."

5. Pearson, *Letters from Port Royal*, 293–96.

6. Ibid.

7. Ibid.

8. William Waring, chaplain, 102nd USCT, Beaufort, S.C., February 15, 1865, Letter 30 in Redkey, ed., *Grand Army of Black Men*, 75.

9. Berlin et al., eds., *Freedom*, 3:112; Sherman, *Memoirs*, 127, 250–52, 247–48; *New Georgia Encyclopedia*, s.v. "Black Troops in Civil War Georgia"; Mohr, "Before Sherman," 331–52. Although perfectly willing to employ African Americans as laborers, General William T. Sherman initially refused to allow blacks to enlist. In fact, he issued Field Order No. 16, forbidding the recruitment of blacks already work-

328 NOTES TO PAGES 252–255

ing for the army. When the northern public learned of Sherman's attitude toward black soldiers and the possible abuse of former slaves by white soldiers, Secretary of War Edwin Stanton met with the general and black leaders in early January 1865 in Savannah to discuss the issue. The result was Sherman's Order No. 15, granting black refugees the right to land on Sea Island plantations and those rice plantations between the St. John's River and Charleston.

10. Campbell, *When Sherman Marched North,* 17. A report in the January 19, 1865, *New York Herald,* for example, quoted the Richmond papers, which claimed that "the negroes continue nightly to flee from that city in gangs, in apprehension of being conscripted into the rebel army" (item 10933, www.accessible.com).

11. Dahlgren to Welles, January 16, 1865, *ORN,* 16:171–75; S. P. Quakenbush to Welles, January 16, 1865, *ORN,* 16:175. Ironically, in November 1863 the ironclad had tested a large obstruction-clearing explosive device designed by Swedish inventor John Ericsson.

12. Webber to Nannie, January 16, 1865, Samuel G. Webber Papers, South Caroliniana Library; S. P. Quakenbush to Welles, January 16, 1865, *ORN,* 16:175–76; W. T. Sampson to S. P. Quakenbush, January 16, 1865, *ORN,* 16:177–78; Dahlgren to Welles, January 29, 1865, *ORN,* 16:179, enclosures B and C. Black Sailor Search did not yield any other African Americans serving on the *Patapsco.* Alexander Davis, a twenty-one-year-old, five-foot-five-inch black waiter from North Carolina, had enlisted in the navy in July 1864, was rated a landsman, and worked as a wardroom steward on the *Patapsco.* Twenty-two-year-old landsman Henry Williams, a waiter born in Baltimore, had enlisted at Philadelphia in July 1864. Two of the *Patapsco*'s African American cooks, Edward A. Davis and Samuel Macra, were also killed. Two first-class boys died in the explosion and sinking of the ship: Eugene Cone, a seventeen-year-old North Carolinian, and Seth Brinkley. Cone, who listed his occupation as tobacconist, enlisted in New York in August 1864; Brinkley, age eighteen, was a waiter who also joined in New York in 1864 for a three-year enlistment.

13. Balch to Dahlgren, February 1, 1865, *ORN,* 16:213–14. The employment of black servants in Confederate homes, hospitals, and headquarters as spies was not uncommon. See Rose, "The Civil War"; Browning, *Success,* 343.

14. Dahlgren to Welles, February 6, 1865, *ORN,* 16:219–20; Sherman, *Memoirs,* vol. 2, pt. 6; Sherman to Dahlgren, February 7, 1865, *ORN,* 16:220; Winslow to Lieutenant Commander J. Stillwell, USS *Ottawa,* February 9, 1865, *ORN,* 1:224. According to Sherman, he arranged "with Admiral Dahlgren and General Foster to watch our progress inland by all the means possible, and to provide for us points of security along the coast, as, at Bull's Bay, Georgetown, and the mouth of the Cape Fear River." In his memoirs, Sherman recalled that he had reached the South Carolina railroad early that day, "in the midst of a rain-storm." He quickly sent out details of men to "burn the tie and twist the bars," the same "Sherman's neckties" tactic he had employed in Atlanta. Sherman also told Dahlgren, "The country thereabouts was very poor but the inhabitants mostly remained at home. Indeed, they knew not where to go."

15. Sheffield to W. H. Dana, February 9, 1865, *ORN,* 16:225.

16. McPherson, *Battle Cry of Freedom,* 827–30; Sherman, *Memoirs,* 278. General Sherman was awakened during the night by the bright light of flames on the wall of the house where he was sleeping. He sent a staffer to inquire whether the provost marshal was doing his duty, and when the man returned, he reported that "the block of buildings directly opposite the burning cotton of that morning was on fire, and that it was spreading."

17. Grattan, *Under the Blue Pennant,* 162–63; Symonds, *Lincoln and His Admirals,* 349–51. As Symonds explains, Grant supported a renewed attack on Wilmington but was determined to have a new command team and insisted that Butler be replaced.

18. Braine to Porter, January 18, 1865, *ORN,* 11:479–80; Trotter, *Ironclads and Columbiads,* 388–89; Calvin Hutchinson to William Hill, January 14, 1865, Calvin Hutchinson Papers, Huntington Library, San Marino, Calif. Braine said that Paymaster Hutchinson "took careful notes of the action, for which I am indebted." Porter related some of the planning for the attack on Fort Fisher in his *Incidents and Anecdotes of the Civil War,* 268–69.

19. Braine to Porter, January 18, 1865, *ORN,* 11:479–80; Trotter, *Ironclads and Columbiads,* 395–99; Anthony Smalley to Braine, January 16, 1865, *ORN,* 11:481; Calvin Hutchinson, "The Cruise of the *Pequot,*" Hutchinson Papers. James Conors and William Cox were killed in the attack; William Brown, George Hagan, and John Riley were wounded.

20. Temple to Porter, January 20, 1865, *ORN,* 11:487–88.

21. Temple to Welles, March 31, 1865, *ORN,* 11:488; Ramold, *Slaves, Sailors, Citizens,* 131; Porter to Welles, January 28, 1865, *ORN,* 11:453–54; Port Columbus Civil War Naval Museum Web site, www.portcolumbus.org. A Pennsylvanian, landsman George W. McWilliams, was among those in the *Pontoosuc*'s crew awarded the Medal of Honor. He suffered severe wounds during the assault on Fort Fisher. For more on Dees, see Hanna, *African American Recipients of the Medal of Honor.*

22. Parker to Lanman, enclosure, Robert H. Cross, gunner, to Lanman, January 16, 1865, *ORN,* 11:502–3.

23. Ibid.

24. Ibid.; Lanman to Porter, January 19, 1865, *ORN,* 11:503–4. Parker also singled out Assistant Surgeon William Longshaw Jr. for conspicuous bravery; Longshaw was "always near the front with instruments and tourniquets, and was bending over the wounded and dying man when he was shot in the head and instantly killed." Listed in the *Minnesota*'s muster roll for January 1, 1865, as "Negro," "mulatto," or "colored" were James Ackimer, twenty-three, Negro; William Bobie, twenty-one, mulatto; James Campson, twenty-two, mariner, Negro; John H. Connor, twenty-one, Negro; Jacob Conway, twenty-seven, Negro; William Davison, thirty-six, seaman, Negro; William H. Francis, thirty-two, Negro; William Fukler, twenty-nine, landsman, colored; George Gordon, twenty-six, colored; Samuel Elliot, twenty-four, landsman, Negro; Hamilton Green, twenty-three, landsman, Negro; John E. Groomis, forty-three, steward, Negro; Charles H. Hicks, thirty, mariner, mulatto; William A. Jackson, seventeen, first-class boy, Negro; Moses Jeferson, twenty-one, Negro; William Johnson, nineteen, waiter, Negro; Rufus King, twenty-two, Negro; Robert Lee, nineteen, landsman, Negro; Charles McFarland, twenty-one, landsman, Negro; James Monroe, twenty-two, landsman, Negro; Henry Newton, twenty-seven, second-class fireman, Negro; Thomas Ockerme, eighteen, landsman, Negro; Anthony A. Portlock, twenty-five, landsman, Negro; Reuben R. Randale, eighteen, landsman, Negro; Henry Ray, twenty, landsman, colored; Charles Robertson, twenty-seven, wardroom cook, Negro; Joseph Samuel, twenty-two, landsman, mulatto; Isaac Smith, nineteen, landsman, Negro; J. C. Stokes, twenty-one, landsman, Negro; Anthony Wiggins, twenty-three, landsman, Negro; George Williams, twenty-six, landsman, Negro; John Williams, twenty-four, seaman, mulatto; Charles W. Wilson, twenty-two, landsman,

Negro; Joseph H. Wolff, twenty, landsman, mulatto; Zephaniah Wood, thirty-three, landsman, Negro; and William Woods, twenty-seven, landsman, Negro. See www.tfoenander.com/minnesota.htm.

25. Porter to Welles, January 28, 1865, *ORN*, 11:452–56; Porter to Welles, February 6, 1865, *ORN*, 12:8; Porter to Macomb, February 6, 1865, *ORN*, 12:8; Porter to Grant, February 11, 1865, *ORN*, 12:15; Trotter, *Ironclads and Columbiads*, 400–402.

26. Porter to Welles, February 24, 1865, enclosure, Febiger to Macomb, February 19, 1865, *ORN*, 12:50–51.

27. Macomb to Porter, February 20, 1865, *ORN*, 12:44; Harrison, "Conscription in the Confederacy," 17–18.

28. Porter, General Order No. 88, January 19, 1865, *ORN*, 11:615; Porter to Dahlgren, January 19, 1865, *ORN*, 11:615.; Schofield to Porter, February 12, 1865, *ORN*, 12:27; Porter to Schofield, February 16, 1865, *ORN*, 12:30–31; Porter, *Incidents and Anecdotes*, 275–76. Although Porter's ships had sealed up the entrances to Wilmington, he had trouble getting gunboats over the bar. Nonetheless, the admiral intended to move on Wilmington as soon as mines could be removed. They accomplished this by towing a mock monitor to within a short distance of the rebel batteries, which fired on the monitor, exploding some of the mines.

29. Hutchinson, "Cruise of the *Pequot*"; Braine to Porter, February 17, 1865, *ORN*, 12:31; Porter to Welles, February 19, 1865, *ORN*, 12:33–34.

30. Grattan, *Under the Blue Pennant*, 185–86; Porter to Welles, February 19, 1865, *ORN*, 12: 33–34. Porter also sent Assistant Navy Secretary Gustavus Fox the news: "We took Fort Anderson this morning, that is the gunboats whipped the Rebels clear out by sunset and they left afterwards taking their artillery with them, leaving nothing but twelve large guns which they could not carry off. The Army claims the victory! Of course owing to their *strategic* movements when they were twelve miles away." Porter to Fox, February 19, 1865, in Fox, *Confidential Correspondence*, 200–201. The letter is erroneously dated 1864.

31. Porter to Welles, February 22, 1865, *ORN*, 12:45; Porter, *Incidents and Anecdotes*, 277–78; Sterrett to editor, March 11, 1864, printed in *Christian Recorder*, April 1, 1865, item 71380, www.accessible.com; Grattan, *Under the Blue Pennant*, 190; Temple to Bailey, February 21, 1865, *ORN*, 12:34–35. That night the rebels attempted to counter by sending some 200 floating torpedoes downriver. According to Temple, commanding the USS *Pontoosuc*, "Last night after a half days fighting, the rebs sent down about 50 torpedoes, but although 'Old Bogey' took no notice of them, they kept the rest of us pretty lively so long as the ebb tide ran."

32. Stanly to Ridgeley, February 19, 1865, *ORN*, 16:239–40; Belknap to Dahlgren, February 19, 1865, *ORN*, 16:258–59. "During the mid and morning watches heavy fires broke out in the city, and heavy explosions were heard now and then in the direction of the town, as well as on James Island," Belknap wrote.

33. Sydney Byram to Napoleon Broughton, February 18, 1865, and Broughton to Dahlgren, February 18, 1865, *ORN*, 16:252–53.

34. Dahlgren to Welles, February 18, 1865, *ORN*, 16:250.

35. Ashael Sumner Dean, Civil War letters to his family, USS *Harvest Moon* Historical Society; "Delaware's Own: Saga of the 144th Regiment, New York Volunteer Infantry," *Walton Reporter*, August 1958, www.dcnyhistory.org/Saga144th.pdf. In 1958 the flag was at the state archives in Albany, New York, along with the colors of the regiment.

36. F. M. Montell, USS *Potomska*, to Dahlgren, February 20, 1865, *ORN*, 16:260.

37. Dahlgren to Creighton, February 22, 1865, *ORN*, 16:261–62; Dahlgren to Gilmore, February 22, 1865, *ORN*, 16:261.

38. Creighton to Stellwagen, February 24, 1865, *ORN*, 16:268. Creighton also wrote to Dahlgren on February 24 that he was in possession of Fort White.

39. Noyes to Dahlgren, February 25, 1865, *ORN*, 16:277; Dahlgren to Welles, February 26, 1865, *ORN*, 16:272.

40. Dean to his wife, February 25, 26, 27, 1865, Ashael Sumner Dean Civil War letters to his family, USS *Harvest Moon* Historical Society.

41. Ibid. In May 1862 Commander George Prentiss had taken the *Albatross* and *Norwich* into Winyah Bay, skirted a brig set on fire by the rebels, and steamed along the wharves of Georgetown. Prentiss refused to land, however, and the two federal vessels went back downriver. In August 1862 the Union Navy returned; Commander George Balch made a reconnaissance up the Black River past Georgetown, but once again the navy made no effort to capture the city. The squadron kept at least one blockader off Georgetown for the remainder of the war, and for a time, it protected a contraband colony at North Island.

42. Webber to Nannie, February 28?, 1865, Samuel G. Webber Papers, South Caroliniana Library; Berlin et al., eds., *Freedom*, 1:70; Manning, *What This Cruel War Was Over*, 189, Ward, *Slaves' War*, 242–44.

43. Browning, *From Cape Fear*, 79–80; Mallory to Mitchell, January 16, 1865, *ORN*, 11:797–98. Secretary Mallory wrote, "I regard an attack upon the enemy and the obstructions of the river at City Point, to cut off Grant's supplies, as a movement of the first importance to the country and one which should be accomplished if possible." Grant and Union Army commanders doubted that the navy had sufficient forces to stop any such Confederate attack. The senior officer in the James River, Commander William Parker, merely suggested that the army reinforce the batteries commanding Trent's Reach with heavy guns to sink more vessels near the obstructions.

44. Parker to Porter, January 31, 1865, *ORN*, 11:656; Grant to Parker, January 24, 1865; Grant to Welles, January 24, 1865, 6 P.M.; Grant, special orders to gunboat commanders, *ORN*, 11:635–36; Parker to Gibbon, January 23, 1865, *ORN*, 11:634; Fox to Grant, January 24, 1865, *ORN*, 11:637; Welles to Captain J. M. Berrien, telegram, January 24, 1865, *ORN*, 11:638.

45. Porter to Parker, January 26, 1865, *ORN*, 11:644; G. Watson Sumner to Parker, January 24, 1865, enclosure, Jno. Latson to Sumner, January 24, 1865, *ORN*, 11:647; Schneider and Singer, eds., *Blueprint for Change; Tilley, Lewis Howard Latimer*. Porter pointedly wrote, "I should be very much disappointed if any vessel of your division budges an inch downstream owing to any rebel ram." The *Massasoit*, which took station astern of the monitor, opened fire on the batteries at Howlett house but was hit several times by rebel guns at the Crow's Nest battery and suffered five wounded.

46. Browning, *From Cape Fear*, 81–82; R. Chandler to G. Young, March 2, 1865, *ORN*, 12:59. During the month of January, General Sherman wrote to his old friend Porter, "I shall account it a happy day if I stand once more on your deck." *ORN*, 11:612.

47. Porter to Welles, March 29, 1865, enclosure, Acting Master H. Walton Grinnell to G. W. Young, March 12, 1865, *ORN*, 12:90–91.

48. Hartwell and Racine, eds., *Fiery Trail,* 178–79.

49. Ibid., 810–11nn1, 2; William S. Craig to wife, April 3, 1865, William S. Craig Civil War letters, Ohio State University ehistory Web site, http://ehistory.osu.edu/uscw/library/letters/index.cfm, and *ORA,* 47(2): 803, 186n5; Young to Porter, March 10, 1865, enclosure, Newman to Young, March 9, 1865, *ORN,* 12:62–63; Young to Porter, March 16, 1865, *ORN,* 12:70–71; Browning, *From Cape Fear,* 388n60; Trotter, *Ironclads and Columbiads,* 390. General Sherman authorized General Howard to send the refugees, including a Mrs. Feaster and her "two beautiful daughters," to Wilmington. For Howard's and Rufus Saxton's reaction to the arrival of Sherman's troops on the coast and the situation on the Sea Islands and Savannah, see McFeely, *Yankee Stepfather,* 54–57.

50. Dahlgren to Welles, March 1, 1865, *ORN,* 16:282–83; log of *Harvest Moon, ORN,* 16:283; logbook of the USS *Harvest Moon,* a summary of events based on the ship's logbooks and personal journal of Acting Lieutenant Commander Joshua D. Warren and Admiral Dahlgren's journal, http://www.riverboatdaues.com/aboutboats/log.html. The *Harvest Moon*'s Web site has the proceedings of the court of inquiry held April 27, 1865, on board the USS *Mingoe* and lists the black crewmen rated landsmen as of March 1, 1865, as Archie Davis, John Francis, Samuel Frazier, John Gaddson, Windsor Hamilton, John Holland, James Hughs, Albert Johnson, George Knox, Amos Lewis, Pomfy Pious, Joseph Piott, Moses Richardson, Paris Rutledge, William Skipper, Benjamin Small, and William William(s). Although at first reported missing and supposedly drowned, at 10:30 A.M. they found Hazzard's body by dragging in the ship's hold. In his journal, Dahlgren noted on March 3, "Act. Ensign D. B. Arey took the body of John Hazzard on shore & gave it a respectible [*sic*] burial."

51. For example, the *Jonquil* detonated a mine in the Ashley River on March 6, 1865. The *Massachusetts* struck another mine coming out of Charleston Harbor on March 19, but it failed to explode. The Coast Survey steamer *Bibb,* returning to Charleston on March 17 after making surveys on the bar, hit a sunken mine that exploded under the port bow. "The shock was very severe" and threw up an enormous column of water, Charles Boutelle reported. Boutelle to Dahlgren, March 18, 1865, *ORN,* 16:295–96.

52. George U. Morris to Captain H. S. Stellwagen, March 9, 1865, *ORN,* 16:288.

53. Eastman to Parker, March 18, 1865, *ORN,* 5:535–36; Parker to Welles, April 29, 1865, *ORN,* 5:537; Aptheker, "The Negro in the Union Navy," 8n68. Black Sailors Search did not yield an Aaron Anderson.

54. Newton to Dahlgren, March 22, 1865, *ORN,* 16:297–98; Hanson to Dahlgren, May 10, 1865, *ORN,* 16:298.

55. Stellwagen to Dahlgren, March 27, 1865, *ORN,* 16:300–30.

56. Dahlgren to Welles, March 28, 1865, *ORN,* 16:301; Ward, *Slaves' War,* 280–82, chap. 31. In *Rehearsal for Reconstruction,* Willie Lee Rose discusses the failure of the Port Royal experiment and the beginning of Reconstruction.

57. Telegram from Robert E. Lee, in Petersburg, to Jefferson Davis, in Richmond, April 2, 1865, in Long and Long, eds., *Civil War Day by Day,* 663, 664; Breese to Ronckendorff, April 3, 1865, *ORN,* 12:97; *Richmond Whig,* April 4, 1865; T. S. Bowers, Acting Adjutant General, to Stanton, April 3, 1865, *New York Herald,* April 4, 1865, Civil War Richmond Web site, www.mdgorman.com.

58. Porter to Welles, April 5, 1865, *ORN,* 12:101; Porter, *Incidents and Anec-*

dotes, 295; Ward, *Slaves' War,* 244–45; John B. Howard, "An Order in Relation to Contrabands," *New York Herald,* April 13, 1865, Civil War Richmond Web site, www.mdgorman.com. This Web site has many personal memories of the fall of Richmond and other articles about the evacuation and occupation.

59. E. T. Nichols to Porter, April 4, 1865, *ORN,* 12:100–101. "I had hoped, after watching and waiting for eleven months in the James River, that I should have been at the front when the move was made, and am much disappointed not to be able to move up with you," Nichols wrote.

60. Welles to Parker, April 5, 1865, *ORN,* 5:543; Colonel Sewall to Lieutenant Colonel J. H. Taylor, April 5, 1865, *ORN,* 5:541–42; Parker to Hooker, April 5, 1865, *ORN,* 5:543.

61. Parker to Eastman, April 5, 1865, *ORN,* 5:543; Parker to Hooker, April 6, 1865, *ORN,* 5:544; Hooker to Parker, April 6, 1865, *ORN,* 5:544; Parker to Hooker, April 6, 1865, *ORN,* 5:544.

62. Hooker to Parker, April 7, 1865, *ORN,* 5:545–46.

63. Hooker to Parker, April 13, 1865, *ORN,* 5:546; Parker to Welles, April 15, 1865, *ORN,* 5:551; Parker to Welles, April 26, 1865, *ORN,* 5:552.

64. Parker to Welles, June 7, 1865, *ORN,* 5:574; Parker to Welles, July 31, 1865, *ORN,* 5:577.

65. Parker, general order to the officers and men of the Potomac Flotilla, July 31, 1865, *ORN,* 5:578.

SELECT BIBLIOGRAPHY

MANUSCRIPT COLLECTIONS

Adams, Sherman W. Papers. Connecticut Historical Society, Hartford.

Bright, George Adams. Collection. Henry E. Huntington Library, San Marino, Calif.

Craven, Thomas T., Letters. Naval Historical Center, Washington, D.C.

Crossman, Norris. Diary. South Carolina Historical Society, Charleston.

Dahlgren, John Adolphus. Papers. Naval Historical Foundation, Manuscript Division, Library of Congress.

Drayton, Percival. Papers. Pennsylvania Historical Society, Philadelphia.

Fox, Gustavus Vasa. Papers. New York Historical Society, New York, N.Y..

Glazier, James. Collection. Henry E. Huntington Library, San Marino, Calif.

Goldsborough, Louis. Papers. Duke University, Durham, N.C.

Gwilliam, Reese. Journal. Connecticut Historical Society.

Harlan, George. Papers. Henry E. Huntington Library, San Marino, Calif.

Head, John. War Diary. South Carolina Historical Society, Charleston.

Higginson, Thomas W., Papers, Houghton Library, Harvard University, Cambridge, Mass.

Himrod, James. Papers. South Caroliniana Library, University of South Carolina, Columbia.

Holmgren, Virginia. Research Papers. South Carolina Historical Society, Charleston.

Hutchinson, Calvin G., Papers. Henry E. Huntington Library, San Marino, Calif.

Jewett, Levi. Papers. Connecticut Historical Society, Hartford.

Lee Family Papers. Princeton University Library, Princeton, N.J.

Lee, Samuel Phillips. Papers. Naval Historical Foundation, Manuscript Division, Library of Congress.

May (Samuel J.) Antislavery Collection. Cornell University Library, Ithaca, N.Y.

National Archives and Records Administration. Record groups 19, 45. Washington, D.C.

Parker, William J., Papers. Pennsylvania Historical Society, Philadelphia.

Parrott, Enoch G., Papers. Duke University, Durham, N.C.

Petit, H., Papers. South Caroliniana Library, University of South Carolina, Columbia.

Phelon, Henry, Papers. Southern Historical Society Collection. Wilson Library, University of North Carolina, Chapel Hill.

Porter, David Dixon. Papers. Henry E. Huntington Library, San Marino, Calif.

Read, Will. Papers. Duke University, Durham, N.C.

Robinson, Horatio. Papers. Duke University, Durham, N.C.

Rodgers Family Papers. Naval Historical Foundation, Manuscript Division, Library of Congress.

Rodgers Family Papers. Pennsylvania Historical Society, Philadelphia.

Rouse, Charles. Diary. Connecticut Historical Society, Hartford.

Southern Historical Collection. Wilson Library, University of North Carolina—Chapel Hill.

Stevens, Thomas Holdup. Papers. Duke University, Durham, N.C.

U.S. Navy Collection. Manuscript Division, New York Public Library.

Webber, Samuel G., Papers. South Caroliniana Library, University of South Carolina.

Welles, Gideon. Papers. Henry E. Huntington Library, San Marino, Calif.

Wilder, C. B. Testimony before the American Freedman's Inquiry Commission, May 9, 1863. O-28–1863, Letters Received, series 12, record group 94. Adjutant General's Office, National Archives.

BOOKS

Acken, J. Gregory, ed. *Inside the Army of the Potomac: The Civil War Experience of Captain Francis Adams Donaldson*. Mechanicsburg, Pa.: Stackpole, 1998.

Ammen, Daniel. *The Navy and the Civil War*. Vol. 2, *The Atlantic Coast*. New York: C. Scribner's & Sons, 1885.

———. *The Old Navy and the New*. New York: Lippincott & Crowell, 1891.

Ash, Stephen. *When the Yankees Came: Conflict and Chaos in the Occupied South*. Chapel Hill: University of North Carolina Press, 1999.

Ball, Edward. *Slaves in the Family*. New York: Ballantine Books, 1998.

Beale, Howard, ed. *Diary of Gideon Welles*. Boston: Houghton Mifflin, 1911.

Bearss, Ed. *River of Lost Opportunities: The Civil War on the James River, 1861–1862*. Lynchburg, Va.: H. E. Howard, 1995.

Bennett, Michael J. *Union Jacks: Yankee Sailors in the Civil War*. Chapel Hill: University of North Carolina Press, 2004.

Berlin, Ira, et al., eds. *Free at Last: A Documentary History of Slavery, Freedom, and the Civil War*. New York: New Press, 1992.

———. *Freedom: A Documentary History of Emancipation*. Vol. 1, *The Destruction of Slavery*. Vol. 2, *The Wartime Genesis of Free Labor, the Upper South*. Vol. 3, *The Wartime Genesis of Free Labor, the Lower South*. Cambridge: Cambridge University Press, 1993.

Blackett, R. J. M., ed. *Thomas Morris Chester, Black Civil War Correspondent*. New York: Da Capo Paperback, 1989.

Blassingame, John W., ed. *Slave Testimony: Autobiographies Published in Periodicals and Books, 1828–1878*. Baton Rouge: Louisiana State University Press, 1977.

Bolster, W. Jeffrey. *Black Jacks: African American Seamen in the Age of Sail*. Cambridge, Mass.: Harvard University Press, 1997.

Boyer, Dr. Samuel P. *Naval Surgeon, Blockading the South 1862–1866*. Bloomington: Indiana University Press, 1963.

Branch, Paul, Jr. *The Siege of Fort Macon*. Published by the author, 1997.

Brennan, Patrick. *Secessionville: Assault on Charleston.* Campbell, Calif.: Savas Publishing Company, 1996.

Brewer, James H. *The Confederate Negro: Virginia's Craftsmen and Military Laborers, 1861–1865.* Chapel Hill, N.C.: Duke University Press, 1969.

Browning, Robert. *From Cape Fear to Cape Charles: The North Atlantic Blockading Squadron during the Civil War.* Tuscaloosa: University of Alabama Press, 1993.

———. *Success Was All That Was Expected.* Washington, D.C.: Brassey's, 2002.

Buker, George E. *Blockaders, Refugees, and Contrabands.* Tuscaloosa: University of Alabama Press, 1993.

Bull, Rice C. *Soldiering: The Civil War Diary of Rice C. Bull.* Edited by K. Jack Bauer. Novato, Calif.: Presidio, 1995.

Butler, Benjamin F. *Autobiography and Personal Reminiscences of Major General Benjamin F. Butler.* Boston: A. M. Thayer, 1892.

Campbell, Jacqueline Glass. *When Sherman Marched North from the Sea: Resistance on the Confederate Home Front.* Chapel Hill: University of North Carolina Press, 2003.

Canney, Donald L. *The Old Steam Navy.* Annapolis, Md.: U.S. Naval Institute Press, 1990.

Casstevens, Frances H. *Out of the Mouth of Hell: Civil War Prisons and Escape.* Jefferson, N.C.: McFarland, 2005.

Cecelski, David. *The Waterman's Song: Slavery and Freedom in Maritime North Carolina.* Chapel Hill: University of North Carolina Press, 2001.

Clancy, Paul. *Ironclad: The Epic Battle, Calamitous Loss, and Historic Recovery of the USS* Monitor. New York: McGraw Hill, 2005.

Click, Patricia. *Time Full of Trial: The Roanoke Island Freedmen's Colony, 1862–1867.* Chapel Hill: University of North Carolina Press, 2001.

Copp, Col. Elbridge J. *Reminiscences of the War of the Rebellion, 1861–1865.* Nashua, N.H.: Telegraph Publishing Company, 1911.

Cornish, Dudley. *The Sable Arm: Black Troops in the Union Army, 1861–1865.* Lawrence: University Press of Kansas, 1987.

Cornish, Dudley, and Virginia Laas. *Lincoln's Lee: The Life of Samuel Phillips Lee.* Lawrence: University Press of Kansas, 1986.

Dahlgren, Madeline. *Memoirs of John A. Dahlgren Rear Admiral United States Navy.* Boston: J. R. Osgood, 1882.

Daly, Robert W., ed. *Aboard the USS* Florida: *Letters of Paymaster William Frederick Keeler, U.S. Navy to His Wife Anna.* Annapolis, Md.: U.S. Naval Institute Press, 1968.

———. *Aboard the USS* Monitor: *The Letters of Acting Paymaster William Frederick Keeler, U.S.* Annapolis, Md.: U.S. Naval Institute Press, 1964.

Davis, Thomas P. *The History of Early Jacksonville.* 1911. Reprint, Gainesville: University of Florida Press, 1969.

Denney, Robert E. *Civil War Prisons & Escapes: A Day-by-Day Chronicle.* New York: Sterling Publishing, 1995.

Donald, David H. *Lincoln.* New York: Simon & Schuster, 1995.

Dowdey, Clifford. *Lee.* Boston: Little Brown, 1965.

Drayton, Percival. *Naval Letters from Captain Percival Drayton, 1861–1865.* New York: New York Public Library, 1906.

Dunaway, Wilma A. *The African-American Family in Slavery and Emancipation.* New York: Cambridge University Press, 2003.

Du Pont, H. A. *Rear-Admiral Samuel Francis Du Pont United States Navy.* New York: National Americana Society, 1926.

Du Pont, Samuel F. *Official Dispatches and Letters of Rear Admiral Du Pont U.S. Navy 1861–1863.* Wilmington, Del.: Ferris Bros., 1883.

Durham, Roger S. *High Seas and Yankee Gunboats: A Blockade Running Adventure from the Diary of James Dickson.* Columbia: University of South Carolina Press, 2005.

Eaton, John. *Grant, Lincoln, and the Freedmen.* New York: Longmans, Green, 1907.

Feis, William B. *Grant's Secret Service: The Intelligence War from Belmont to Appomattox.* Lincoln: University of Nebraska Press, 2004.

Fellman, Michael. *Inside War: The Guerilla Conflict in Missouri during the American Civil War.* Oxford: Oxford University Press, 1989.

Fellman, Michael, Leslie Gordon, and Daniel Sutherland, eds. *This Terrible War: The Civil War and Its Aftermath.* New York: Longman, 2007.

Fishel, Edwin. *The Secret War for the Union: The Untold Story of Military Intelligence in the Civil War.* Boston: Houghton Mifflin, 1996.

Fladeland, Betty. *Men and Brothers: Anglo-American Antislavery Cooperation.* Urbana: University of Illinois Press, 1972.

Foner, Eric. *Forever Free: The Story of Emancipation and Reconstruction.* New York: Alfred A. Knopf, 2005.

Foote, Shelby. *The Civil War: A Narrative.* 3 vols. New York: Vintage Books, 1986.

Forbes, Ella. *African American Women during the Civil War.* New York: Garland Publishing, 1998.

Fox, Gustavus. *Confidential Correspondence of Gustavus Vasa Fox 1821–1883.* 2 vols. New York: Devine, 1918.

Freemon, Frank R. *Gangrene and Glory: Medical Care during the American Civil War.* Urbana: University of Illinois Press, 2001.

Gallagher, Gary W. *The Confederate War.* Boston: Harvard University Press, 1997.

Gara, Larry. *The Liberty Line: The Legend of the Underground Railroad.* Lexington: University Press of Kentucky, 1967.

Gerteis, Louis S. *From Contraband to Freedman: Federal Policy toward Southern Blacks, 1861–1865.* Westport, Conn.: Greenwood Press, 1973.

Gillette, Mary C. *The U.S. Army Medical Department, 1818–1865.* Washington, D.C.: Center for Military History, 1995.

Glatthaar, Joseph T. *Forged in Battle: The Civil War Alliance of Black Soldiers and White Officers.* New York: Free Press, 1990.

———. *The March to the Sea and Beyond: Sherman's Troops in the Savannah and Carolinas Campaign.* New York: New York University Press, 1985.

Gooding, Cpl. James Henry. *On the Altar of Freedom: A Black Soldier's Civil War Letters from the Front.* Edited by Virginia Adams. Amherst: University of Massachusetts Press, 1991.

Goodwin, Doris Kearns. *Team of Rivals: The Political Genius of Abraham Lincoln.* New York: Simon & Schuster, 2005.

Gould, William B. *Diary of a Contraband: The Civil War Passage of a Black Sailor.* Stanford, Calif.: Stanford University Press, 2002.

Grattan, John W. *Under the Blue Pennant or Notes of a Naval Officer.* Edited by Robert J. Schneller Jr. New York: John Wiley & Sons, 1999.

Gray, John C., and John Ropes. *War Letters 1862–1865 of John Chipman Gray and John Codman Ropes.* New York: Houghton Mifflin, 1927.

Grimsley, Mark. *The Hard Hand of War: Union Military Policy towards Civilians.* Cambridge: Cambridge University Press, 1995.

Guelzo, Allen C. *Lincoln's Emancipation Proclamation: The End of Slavery in America.* New York: Simon & Schuster, 2006.

Hanna, Charles W. *African American Recipients of the Medal of Honor: A Biographical Dictionary, Civil War through Vietnam War.* Jefferson City, N.C.: McFarland, 2002.

Hartwell, Richard, and Philip Racine, eds. *The Fiery Trail: A Union Officer's Account of Sherman's Last Campaigns.* Knoxville: University of Tennessee Press, 1986.

Hawks, Esther Hill. *Woman Doctor's Civil War.* Columbia: University of South Carolina Press, 1989.

Hayes, John, ed., *Samuel Francis Du Pont: A Selection of His Civil War Letters.* 2 vols. Ithaca, N.Y.: Cornell University Press, 1969.

Hesseltine, William B., ed. *Civil War Prisons.* Kent, Ohio: Kent State University Press, 1972.

Higginson, Thomas, W. *Army Life in a Black Regiment.* Boston: Fields & Osgood, 1870.

Holmes, Bishop Nathaniel H. *Voyage of a Paper Canoe: A Geographical Journey of 2,500 Miles from Quebec to the Gulf of Mexico during the Years 1874–5.* Mechanicsburg, Pa.: Stackpole Books, 2001.

Hoogenboom, Ari. *Gustavus Vasa Fox of the Union Navy: A Biography.* Baltimore: Johns Hopkins University Press, 2008.

Hunter, Alvah. *A Year on a Monitor and the Destruction of Fort Sumter.* Columbia: University of South Carolina Press, 1987.

Hutchins, Frank W. *Virginia: The Old Dominion.* Whitefish, Mont.: Kessinger Publishing, 2004.

Johnson, John. *The Defense of Charleston Harbor Including Fort Sumter and the Adjacent Islands, 1863–1865.* Charleston, S.C.: Walker, Evans & Cogswell, 1890.

Johnson, Robert. *Rear Admiral John Rodgers, 1812–1882.* Annapolis, Md.: U.S. Naval Institute Press, 1967.

Johnston, Terry A., Jr., ed. *Him on the One Side and Me on the Other: The Civil War Letters of Alexander Campbell, 79th New York Infantry Regiment and James Campbell, 1st South Carolina Battalion.* Columbia: University of South Carolina Press, 1999.

Jordan, Ervin L., Jr. *Black Confederates and Afro-Yankees in Civil War Virginia.* Charlottesville: University of Virginia Press, 1995.

Kane, Harriet T. *Spies for the Blue and Gray.* Garden City, N.Y.: Doubleday, 1954.

Kendricksen, Paul. *Memoirs of Paul Henry Kendricksen.* Boston: privately printed, 1910.

King, Susie Taylor. *Reminiscences of My Life in Camp.* Boston: published by the author, 1902.

Korn, Jerry. *Pursuit to Appomattox.* Alexandria, Va.: Time-Life Books, 1987.

Lamson, Roswell. *Lamson of the Gettysburg: The Civil War Letters of Lieutenant Roswell Lamson, U.S. Navy.* Edited by James M. McPherson and Patricia McPherson. New York: Oxford University Press, 1977.

Lancaster, Robert Alexander. *Historic Virginia Homes and Churches.* Philadelphia: Lippincott, 1915.

Langley, Harold D. *Social Reform in the U.S. Navy, 1797–1862.* Urbana: University of Illinois Press, 1962.

Lee, Elizabeth Blair. *Wartime Washington: The War Letters of Elizabeth Blair Lee.* Edited by Dudley Cornish and Virginia Laas. Urbana: University of Illinois Press, 1991.

Lewis, Charles L. *David Glasgow Farragut.* North Stratford, N.H.: Ayer, 1980.

Litwack, Leon F. *Been in the Storm So Long: The Aftermath of Slavery.* New York: Alfred A. Knopf, 1979.

Long, E. B., and Barbara Long, eds. *The Civil War Day by Day: An Almanac, 1861–1865.* New York: Da Capo, 1971.

Looby, Christopher, ed. *The Complete Civil War Journal and Selected Letters of Thomas Wentworth Higginson.* Chicago: University of Chicago Press, 2000.

Lusk, William Thompson. *War Letters of William Thompson Lusk.* New York: privately printed, 1911.

Manning, Chandra. *What This Cruel War Was Over: Soldiers, Slavery and the Civil War.* New York: Alfred A. Knopf, 2007.

Markle, Donald E. *Spies and Spymasters of the Civil War.* New York: Hippocrene Books, 1994.

Marvel, William, ed. *The Monitor Chronicles: One Sailor's Account.* New York: Simon & Schuster, 2000.

McCarthy, B. Eugene, and Thomas Doughton, eds. *From Bondage to Belonging: The Worcester Slave Narratives.* Amherst: University of Massachusetts Press, 2008.

McFeely, William S. *Yankee Stepfather: General O. O. Howard and the Freedmen.* New York: W. W. Norton, 1994.

McPherson, James. *Battle Cry of Freedom: The Civil War Era.* New York: Oxford University Press, 1988.

Merrill, James M. *Du Pont: The Making of an Admiral: A Biography of Samuel Francis Du Pont.* New York: Dodd, Mead, 1986.

Miller, Edward A., Jr. *The Biography of David Hunter, Lincoln's Abolitionist General.* Columbia: University of South Carolina Press, 1997.

————. *Gullah Statesman: Robert Smalls from Slavery to Congress, 1839–1915.* Columbia: University of South Carolina Press, 1995.

Miller, Randall, and John D. Smith. *Dictionary of Afro-American Slavery.* Westport, Conn.: Greenwood Press, 1997.

Mitchell, Lt. Col. Joseph P. *The Badge of Gallantry.* New York: Macmillan, 1968.

Mohr, Clarence L. *On the Threshold of Freedom: Masters and Slaves in Civil War Georgia.* Baton Rouge: Louisiana State University Press, 2001.

Moore, Frank, and Edward Everett, eds. *The Rebellion Record: A Diary of American Events.* 1862. Reprint, Whitefish, Mont.: Kessinger Publishing, 2006.

Nevins, Allan. *The War for the Union: The Organized War to Victory 1864–1865.* New York: Charles Scribner's Sons, 1971.

The New Georgia Encyclopedia. Athens: University of Georgia Press. Online.

Newlin, H. W. *An Account of the Escape of Six Federal Soldiers from Prison at Danville, Va.* Cincinnati: Western Methodist Book Concern, 1887.

Niven, John, ed. *The Diary of Gideon Welles.* New York: Oxford University Press, 1973.

Norton, Oliver W. *O. W. Norton Army Letters 1861–1865.* Privately printed by the author, 1903.

Pacheco, Josephine. *The Pearl.* Chapel Hill: University of North Carolina Press, 2005.

Page, Charles A. *Letters of a War Correspondent.* Boston: L. C. Page, 1899.

Paludan, Philip. *A People's Contest.* New York: Harper & Row, 1988.

Paullin, Charles Oscar. *History of Naval Administration, 1775–1911*. Annapolis, Md.: U.S. Naval Institute Press, 1968.

Pearson, Elizabeth, ed. *Letters from Port Royal, 1862–1868*. New York: Arno Press, 1969.

Penningroth, Dylan C. *The Claims of Kinfolk: African American Property and Community in the Nineteenth Century South*. Chapel Hill: University of North Carolina Press, 2003.

Pinkerton, Allan. *The Spy of the Rebellion*. Lincoln: University of Nebraska Press, 1989.

Porter, Adm. David Dixon. *Incidents and Anecdotes of the Civil War*. New York: D. Appleton, 1885.

Porter, Gen. Horace. *Campaigning with Grant*. Secaucus, N.J.: Blue and Grey Press, 1984.

Quarles, Benjamin. *The Negro in the Civil War*. Boston: Little Brown, 1953.

Racine, Philip N., ed. *"Unspoiled Heart": The Journals of Charles Mattocks of the 17th Maine*. Knoxville: University of Tennessee Press, 1994.

Ramold, Steven. *Slaves, Sailors, Citizens: African-Americans in the Union Navy*. De Kalb: Northern Illinois University, 2002.

Rankin, David C. *Diary of a Christian Soldier*. Cambridge: Cambridge University Press, 2004.

Rawick, George P. *The American Slave: A Composite Autobiography*. Vol. 3, pt. 3. Westport, Conn.: Greenwood Press, 1972.

Redkey, Edwin S., ed. *A Grand Army of Black Men: Letters from African American Soldiers in the Union Army, 1861–1865*. Cambridge: Cambridge University Press, 1992.

Reed, Rowena. *Combined Operations in the Civil War*. Annapolis, Md.: U.S. Naval Institute Press, 1978.

Reid, Richard M. *Freedom for Themselves: North Carolina's Black Soldiers in the Civil War Era*. Chapel Hill: University of North Carolina Press, 2008.

Ringle, Dennis J. *Life in Mr. Lincoln's Navy*. Annapolis, Md.: U.S. Naval Institute Press, 1998.

Roberts, William H. *Now for the Contest: Coastal and Oceanic Naval Operations in the Civil War*. Lincoln: University of Nebraska Press, 2006.

———. *USS Ironsides in the Civil War*. Annapolis, Md.: U.S. Naval Institute Press, 1999.

Rose, Willie Lee. *Rehearsal for Reconstruction: The Port Royal Experiment*. New York: Oxford University Press, 1964.

Roske, Ralph, and Charles Van Doren. *Lincoln's Commando: The Biography of Commander W. B. Cushing, U.S.N.* New York: Harper Brothers, 1957.

Rowland, Leslie S., Ira Berlin, and Joseph P. Reidy, eds. *Freedom's Soldiers: A Documentary History*. Cambridge: Cambridge University Press, 1998.

Rush, Richard, et al. *Official Records of the Union and Confederate Navies in the War of the Rebellion*. 31 vols. series 1. Washington, D.C.: Government Printing Office, 1894–1914.

Sanders, Charles W. *While in the Hands of the Enemy: Military Prisons of the Civil War*. Baton Rouge: Louisiana State University Press, 2005.

Scharf, J. Thomas. *History of Confederate States Navy*. Albany, N.Y.: Joseph McDonough, 1894.

Schneider, Janet, and Bayla Singer, eds. *Blueprint for Change: The Life and Times of Lewis H. Latimer*. Queens, N.Y.: Queens Borough Public Library, 1995.

Schneller, Robert J., Jr. *Farragut: America's First Admiral*. Dulles, Va.: Potomac Books, 2003.

———. *A Quest for Glory: A Biography of Rear Admiral John A. Dahlgren.* Annapolis, Md.: U.S. Naval Institute Press, 1996.

Schultz, Jane E. *Women at the Front: Hospital Workers in Civil War America.* Chapel Hill: University of North Carolina Press, 2004.

Schumm, Henry. *Doctor in Blue.* New York: George Adams, 1951.

Scott, R. N., et al., eds. *The War of the Rebellion: A Compilation of the Official Records of the Union and Confederate Armies.* 70 vols. Washington, D.C.: Government Printing Office, 1880–1901.

Sears, Stephen. *George B. McClellan: The Young Napoleon.* New York: Ticknor & Fields, 1988.

Sherman, Gen. William T. *Memoirs of General William T. Sherman.* 2 vols. New York: D. Appleton, 1875.

Silber, Nina. *Daughters of the Union.* Cambridge, Mass.: Harvard University Press, 2005.

Silverstone, Paul H. *Warships of the Civil War Navies.* Annapolis, Md.: U.S. Naval Institute Press, 1989.

Smith, John D., ed. *Black Soldiers in Blue.* Chapel Hill: University of North Carolina Press, 2004.

Sneden, Robert Knox. *Eye of the Storm: A Civil War Odyssey.* Edited by Charles F. Bryan Jr. and Nelson D. Lankford. New York: Free Press, 2000.

Speer, Lonnie. *Portals to Hell: Military Prisons of the Civil War.* Mechanicsburg, Pa.: Stackpole Books, 1997.

Steedman, Charles. *Memoirs and Correspondence of Charles Steedman Rear Admiral, United States Navy, with His Autobiography and Private Journals, 1811–1890.* Cambridge: Riverside Press, 1912.

Sterner, Capt. Doris M. *In and Out of Harm's Way: A History of the Navy Nurse Corps.* Seattle: Peanut Butter Publishing, 1996.

Still, William. *Iron Afloat: The Story of the Confederate Ironclads.* Columbia: University of South Carolina Press, 1989.

Surdam, David G. *Northern Naval Superiority and the Economics of the American Civil War.* Columbia: University of South Carolina Press, 2001.

Sutherland, Daniel E., ed. *Guerillas, Unionists and Violence on the Confederate Home Front.* Fayetteville: University of Arkansas Press, 1999.

Swint, Henry L., ed. *Dear Ones at Home: Letters from Contraband Camps.* Nashville, Tenn.: Vanderbilt University Press, 1966.

Symonds, Craig, L. *Lincoln and His Admirals: Abraham Lincoln, the U.S. Navy, and the Civil War.* New York: Oxford University Press, 2008.

———, ed. *Charleston Blockade: The Journals of John B. Marchand, U.S. Navy 1861–1862.* Newport, R.I.: Naval War College Press, 1976.

Thompson, Robert Means. *Confidential Correspondence of Gustavus Vasa Fox, Assistant Secretary of the Navy 1981–1865.* New York: Books for Libraries Press, 1972.

Tilley, Glenette. *Lewis Howard Latimer.* Englewood Cliffs, N.J.: Silver Burdett Press, 1991.

Time-Life Books, ed. *The Blockade: Runners and Raiders.* Alexandria, Va.: Time-Life Books, 1983.

Trotter William R. *Ironclads and Columbiads: The Civil War in North Carolina, the Coast.* Winston Salem, N.C.: John F. Blair, 1989.

The United States Sanitary Commission. Boston: Little, Brown, 1863.

Valle, James E. *Rocks and Shoals: Order and Discipline in the Old Navy 1800–1861.* Annapolis, Md.: U.S. Naval Institute Press, 1980.

Valuska, David. *The African American in the Union Navy, 1861–1865.* New York: Garland, 1993.

Varon, Elizabeth R. *Southern Lady, Yankee Spy: The True Story of Elizabeth Van Lew, a Union Agent in the Heart of the Confederacy.* New York: Oxford University Press, 2005.

Vorenberg, Michael. *Final Freedom: The Civil War, the Abolition of Slavery, and the Thirteenth Amendment.* New York: Cambridge University Press, 2001.

Wainwright, Col. Charles. *Diary of a Battle: Personal Journals of Col. Charles S. Wainwright.* Edited by Allan Nevins. New York: Da Capo Press, 1998.

Ward, Andrew. *The Slaves' War: The Civil War in the Words of Former Slaves.* Boston: Houghton Mifflin, 2008.

Weddle, Kevin J. *Lincoln's Tragic Admiral: The Life of Samuel Francis Du Pont.* Charlottesville: University of Virginia Press, 2005.

Wert, Jeffrey D. *Sword of Lincoln: The Army of the Potomac.* New York: Simon & Schuster, 2005.

West, Richard. *Mr. Lincoln's Navy.* New York: Longmans Green, 1957.

Williams, Heather A. *Self-taught: African American Education in Slavery and Freedom.* Chapel Hill: University of North Carolina Press, 2005.

Wise, Stephen R. *Gate of Hell: Campaign for Charleston Harbor, 1863.* Columbia: University of South Carolina Press, 1994.

———. *Lifeline of the Confederacy: Blockade Running during the Civil War.* Columbia: University of South Carolina Press, 1988.

Wood, Peter. *Black Majority: Negroes in Colonial South Carolina from 1670 through the Stono Rebellion.* New York: W. W. Norton, 1974.

Woodson, Carter G. *A Century of Negro Migration.* 1918. Reprint, Dover, N.H.: Dover Publications, 2003.

ARTICLES AND CHAPTERS

Abbot, John C. "The Navy in the North Carolina Sounds." *Harper's New Monthly Magazine,* April 1886.

Aptheker, Herb. "The Negro in the Union Navy." *Journal of Negro History* 32, no. 2 (April 1947).

Bartlett, Russell, Jr., and Paul Murray, eds. "The Letters of Stephen Caulker Bartlett Aboard USS *Lenapee,* January to August 1865." *North Carolina Historical Review* 33 (January 1956).

Bay, William B., Jr. "A Flotilla Cries 'Eureka.'" *Naval History Magazine,* June 1998.

Bennett, Michael. "Frictions: Shipboard Relations between White and Contraband Sailors." *Civil War History,* June 2001.

Butts, Frank B. "The Loss of the *Monitor.*" *Century Magazine,* 1885.

Crouse, L. L. "The Army Correspondent." *Harper's New Monthly Magazine,* October 1863.

Dhalle, Kathy. "The Battle of Honey Hill." *Bits of Blue and Gray,* February 2002.

Foote, Morris C. "Narrative of an Escape from a Rebel Prison Camp." *American Heritage Magazine* 11, no. 4 (June 1961).

Harrison, Lowell. "Conscription in the Confederacy." *Civil War Times Illustrated* 9 (July 1970).

Hayes, John D. "The Battle of Port Royal, S.C., from the Journal of Sanford Barnes." *New York Historical Quarterly* 45 (October 1961).

Henig, Gerald. "Admiral Samuel F. Du Pont, the Navy Department, and the Attack on Charleston, April 1863." *Naval War College Review,* February 1979.

Holden, Edgar. "First Cruise of the Monitor *Passaic.*" *Harper's New Monthly Magazine,* October 1863.

James, Elizabeth. "Letter from Miss E. James." *American Missionary* 8 (February 1864).

King, Lisa Y. "They Called Us Bluejackets": The Transformation of Self-Emancipated Slaves from Contrabands of War to Fighting Sailors in the South Atlantic Blockading Squadron during the Civil War." *International Journal of Naval History* 1, no. 1 (April 2002).

Laas, Virginia. "'Sleepless Sentinels': The North Atlantic Blockading Squadron, 1862–1864." *Civil War History* 31 (March 1985).

Lause, Mark. "Turning the World Upside Down: A Portrait of Labor and Military Leader Alonzo Granville Draper." *Labor History* 44, no. 2 (May 2003).

Loring, B. W. "The Monitor *Weehawken* in the Rebellion." *U.S. Naval Institute Proceedings* 12 (1886).

Melton, Maurice. "Casualties of War: Two Georgia Coast Pilots and the Capture of the U.S.S. *Water Witch.*" *Journal of South Georgia History* 16 (fall 2004).

Mohr, Clarence. "Before Sherman: Georgia Blacks and the Union War." *Journal of Southern History,* August 1979.

Packard, Kent, ed. "Jottings by the Way: A Sailor's Log, 1862–1864." *Pennsylvania Magazine of History and Biography* 71 (April 1947).

Pierce, Edward. "The Contrabands at Fortress Monroe." *Atlantic Monthly,* November 1861.

———. "The Freedmen at Port Royal," *Atlantic Monthly,* September 1863.

Reid, Dr. Richard. "Raising the African Brigade: Early Black Recruitment in Civil War North Carolina." *North Carolina Historical Review* 70 (1993).

Reidy, Joseph P. "Black Men in Blue during the Civil War," pts. 1 and 2. *NARA Prologue* 33, no. 3 (fall 2001).

Rose, P. K. "The Civil War: Black Americans' Contributions to Union Intelligence." *Studies in Intelligence,* winter 1998–1999. www.cia.gov/publications/dispatches/dispatch.html.

Schafer, Daniel L. "Freedom Was as Close as the River." In *The African American Heritage of Florida.* Edited by Jane L. Landers and David R. Colburn. Gainesville: University of Florida Press, 1995.

Sprout, James G. "Blueprint for Radical Reconstruction." *Journal of Southern History* 22 (February 1957).

Sutherland, Daniel E. "Guerilla Warfare, Democracy, and the Fate of the Confederacy." *Journal of Southern History,* May 2007.

Wartman, Michelle. "Contraband, Runaways, Freedmen: New Definitions of Reconstruction Created by the Civil War." *International Social Science Review,* fall–winter 2001.

Wegner, Dana. "Port Royal Working Parties." *Civil War Times Illustrated* 15, no. 8 (December 1976).

———. "The Union Navy, 1861–1865." In *In Peace and War.* Edited by Kenneth Hagan. Westport, Conn.: Greenwood Press, 1984.

Westwood, Howard C. "Benjamin Butler's Naval Brigade." *Civil War History* 34, no. 3. (1988).

———. "Generals David Hunter and Rufus Saxton and Black Soldiers." *South Carolina Historical Magazine* 86 (July 1985).

INDEX

Abbot, John C., 50
abolition, 12
Abromson, Laura, 288n17
Adams, Charles, 198
Adams, Sherman, 200
advertisements: for enlistment in the
    Union Navy, 190–91
African American children: smallpox
    vaccines and, 323n81
African Americans: aid to Union
    prisoners of war, 153–58;
    conscription by the Confederacy,
    261, 288n16; demographics
    in 1861, 1; in the District of
    Columbia, 60–61; issue of equal
    rights and, 14; in the Port Royal
    area, 64–65; recruitment and,
    286n38; Sherman's "March to the
    Sea" and, 59–60, 251–52, 271;
    smallpox vaccines and, 323n81; in
    spying and intelligence gathering,
    159–67, 310n62. *See also* black
    pilots; black sailors; black
    soldiers; contrabands; contraband
    sailors
African American women: early
    escapes to Union forces, 33–34;
    as nurses and hospital workers,
    308n20; as spies, 161–62, 310n62.
    See also contraband women
A. Houghton (hospital ship), 143
Aiken, William, 293n16

Aiken's Landing, 95
Aiken's plantation, 95, 293n16
Alabama (USS), 195–96, 301n27
Albatross (USS), 77, 173, 331n41
alcohol consumption, 203–4
Alert, 183, 215
Alexandria, 327n32
Allen (bark), 217
Alliance, 327n32
Allison, 212–13
Almy, John J., 42–43
Almy, Thomas, 119
Alston, A., 315n35
Altamaha River, 93, 108, 158
ambushes, 213–14
Amelia Island, 107
Amelia River, 107
American Freedman's Inquiry
    Commission, 18, 55, 64
Ammen, Daniel: on contrabands
    at Port Royal, 293n12; Edisto
    area contraband colonies and,
    68, 69, 70, 71; expedition up
    Port Royal Sound and, 46; the
    George Huston affair and, 184;
    Jacksonville expedition and,
    240–41; pilots and, 312n5
Anacostia (USS), 31, 236, 287n3
Anderson, Aaron, 273
Anderson, George, 216, 217
Anderson, Nelson, 172
Anderson, Robert, 288n17

leaves, 299n13; determining the loyalty of Maryland residents and, 101–2; informants and, 99–104; Mathias Point and, 103–5; Foxhall Parker's farewell to, 279; ships of, 298n2

Potomac River, 31–32

Potomska (USS), 76, 108, 230, 264, 265, 297n60

Powhatan (USS), 32, 170, 315n31

POWs. *See* prisoners of war

Prentiss, George, 77–78, 81, 173–74, 331n41

Price, George, 317n19

prisoner exchanges, 153–54

prisoners of war, 153–58

prisons, 153

prize money, 110

Proteus, 291n46

Pucket, John H., 312n8

Putnam, 277

Quakenbush, Stephen Platt, 253

Quaker City, 212

Quamer, Samuel, 55

Quantico Creek, 104

quinine, 322n76

Raleigh (CSS), 127, 128–29, 305n62, 305n65

"ram fever," 305n67

Ramold, Steven, 192, 193, 221–22

rams, 260–61

Rankin, David, 324n9

ranks, 193–94

Ransom, Lewis, 8

Rappahannock River, 16, 32, 52, 219

ratings: in the Union Navy, 142, 193–94, 195

Rattlesnake (Confederate ram), 124–25

Rattlesnake Shoal, 301n27

Rebel (Confederate side-wheeler), 196

recruiters, 316n5

Red Rover (hospital ship), 143

Reed, George, 218–19, 248, 321n67

Reed, Harry, 109, 110

Reed, H. C., 319n46

Reefer (sloop), 8

refugeeing, 292n58, 295n44

refugees: early escapes to Union forces, 33; following Sherman's "March to the Sea," 59–60, 251–52, 271; Samuel Lee on the disposal of, 286n43; Peninsular campaign and, 52–54. *See also* contrabands; runaway slaves

Reid, Richard, 75

Reidy, Joseph, 190, 197, 207

Reimer, Terry, 323n81

Release (screw steamer), 33

Reliance, 9, 32, 40

Relief (screw steamer), 138

Remittance (schooner), 102

rendezvous, 189, 191

Rescue (steamer), 104

Resolute (screw steamer), 287n1; attack on the Herring Creek depot, 100; contrabands and, 35, 40; Mattox Creek expedition, 273; in the Potomac Flotilla, 32, 298n2; reconnaissance missions, 9

Restless (bark), 109, 110, 193–94, 301n27

reward money, 164

Reynolds, William, 49, 192

Rhind, Alexander, 71, 72, 170, 171

Rhoades, Archibald C., 148–49

Rhode Island (USS), 200, 206, 221, 223, 316n5

Richards, John P., 102

Richmond (CSS), 130, 163, 268, 307n17

Richmond, Virginia, 275–76

Richmond Whig, 275

Riley (Union captain), 247–48

Ringgold, W. H., 161

Ripley, Roswell, 44

river pilots. *See* black pilots; pilots

Wilson Small, 16
Wingate (refugee), 87
Winnissimet, 55, 235, 236
Winona, 254, 264
Winslow, W. H., 254
Winyah Bay, 77, 81, 88
Wissahickon, 123, 124
Withers Island, 39
Wood, Robert, 320n60
Wood, William Maxwell, 222, 225–26,
    322n76
Woodhull, Maxwell, 54, 178–80,
    314n20
Woodstock, 323n5
Woodward, E. T., 260
Woodworth, Selim, 19
Wool, John E., 115, 116–17
Worden, John, 123–25
Wright, Horatio, 86, 108, 239, 240,
    241

Wright, Mrs. J. G., 196
Wright's River, 177
Wyandank, 273

Yadkin (CSS), 128
Yankee (side-wheel tug), 54, 100, 102,
    103, 277, 298n2
Yates, Eliza, 247
Yates, Joseph, 210
Yellow Bluffs, 241
York River, 303n40
Yorktown, 115
Yorktown, Virginia, 117
Young, Henry, 40–41, 103, 298n7

Zeek's Island, 112
Zeilin, Jacob, 153
Zouave (gunboat), 165